The Origins of
Academic Geography
in the United States

The Origins of
Academic Geography
in the United States

edited by

Brian W. Blouet

with the assistance of Teresa L. Stitcher

1981
ARCHON BOOKS

© 1981 The Shoe String Press, Inc.

First published 1981 as an Archon Book,
an imprint of The Shoe String Press, Inc.,
Hamden, Connecticut 06514

Library of Congress Cataloging in Publication Data
Main entry under title:

The Origins of academic geography in the United States.

Papers from a conference held at the University of Nebraska—Lincoln,
April 26-27, 1979.
Includes bibliographies.
1. Geography—United States—History—Congresses.
I. Blouet, Brian W., 1936-   .   II. Stitcher, Teresa L.
G96.074   917.3   81-8091
ISBN 0-208-01881-6   AACR2

199121

Contents

Study in Professionalization

The Scholars

W. M. Davis and American Geography (1880—1934)
Environment and Inheritance: Nathaniel Southgate Shaler and the American Frontier
William Morris Davis—The Course of Development of His Concept of Geography
Rollin Salisbury and the Establishment of Geography at the University of Chicago
Carl O. Sauer

The Schools

The Midwest as a Hearth Area in American Academic Geography
Geographers and Their Mentors: A Genealogical View of American Academic Geography
Berkeley Geography, 1923-33

The Ideas

Geographia Generalis and the Earliest Development of

Preface

The papers in this volume are drawn from among those originally delivered at a conference entitled "The Origins of Academic Geography in the United States," held at the University of Nebraska, Lincoln on 26—27 April 1979 under the auspices of the Department of Geography and the International Geographical Union, Commission on the History of Geographical Thought.

One of the themes which emerges from the papers is the strength of the indigenous tradition of American geography. In the past, we have been aware of some of the important influences and ideas which did enter United States geography from overseas. Several papers in the present volume, however, highlight the "Americanness" of American geography. Rather than the subject being launched in East Coast institutions and diffusing across the country, there is evidence of the widespread offering of physical geography courses in land grant and state universities in the late nineteenth century long before the formal organization of departments. Over and over again substantial scholars in the discipline are found to have their roots in the Midwest, particularly in the state of Wisconsin. For example, Emory Johnson, one of the earliest recipients of a doctoral degree in geography, was born in Wisconsin in 1864. When he went to the university at Madison, Wisconsin, he enrolled in Frederick Jackson Turner's seminar in American history and, according to Johnson's autobiography, it was under the influence of Turner that he developed his interest in "the policy of the Federal Government regarding the improvement of the coastal and Great Lakes harbors, the canalization of rivers, and the construction of canals." Of course, as Preston James tells us in the concluding chapter of this volume, Emory Johnson went on to be a leading figure in transportation geography and a member of the Panama Canal commission in the early years of the twentieth century. It is particularly interesting that Johnson should have been influenced early in his academic career by Turner, a scholar who stressed the distinctive nature of American historical experience.

The need for a conference usually emerges when a group of scholars begin to exchange ideas in relation to an expanding research focus. They feel the need to take stock and to formulate questions which remain to be addressed. In fact, if all the questions have been answered, there is little point in a conference. A good gathering asks questions and identifies gaps in existing knowledge—which, of course, means that coverage in any book emerging from a symposium is unlikely to achieve complete coverage. There are gaps in this volume. Some important early academic figures are not treated at length. There is little on the origins of geographical journals and, surprisingly, not one paper is concerned with the foundation, growth, and influence of the numerous national, regional, and local geographical societies. When the call for papers went out, it was suggested that studies of the "sociology of societies" would be welcome. The call was unanswered but here, surely, is a rich field for investigation.

Research on societies could follow a number of courses, but a good starting point would be to examine the initial role of the organization. A society is an interest group. Superficially it may appear that if the term geography appears in the title of a society, then geography is what the interest group wishes to promote. This is a naive view. If we were to encounter a society with a council of seventeen which included three members with banking and shipping interests and seven members who were publishers, editors, or authors, we would no doubt conclude that we were dealing with an organization with strong publishing and merchant interests. In fact, the illustration is drawn from the American Geographical Society in 1852, the year after its foundation. The majority of the editors and publishers were associated with Horace Greeley, the advocate of westward expansion. For example, Charles Dana was a promoter of the idea of a railroad to the Pacific. However, it is wrong to see the American Geographical Society as purely a front for commercial interests. Motivations were complex. Another council member, A. I. Cotheal, was a substantial banker but he helped found the American Geological Society, the American Ethnological Society, and the American Geographical Society.

Overall, commercial considerations were important in establishing geographical societies and sometimes the link is explicit. The Geographical Society of Baltimore was founded in 1902 for "the promotion and diffusion of geographical knowledge, more particularly of that which is of commercial importance to Baltimore." There is a need for studies which examine the changing pattern of membership in societies and, in particular, the background of persons holding controlling positions in the affairs of geographical societies.

No paper in the book attempts to place the development of academic geography in a broad social, political, and economic context. What forces created the conditions in the late nineteenth century which allowed a series of disciplines, including geography, anthropology, and sociology, to become established as new areas of specialization in universities? As a commentator pointed out, however, geography was not simply one of a group of new subjects which benefitted from a phase of university expansion; it was a remarkably successful discipline that expanded more rapidly than most and not only in America. In Germany, France, and Britain, the subject made an impressive imprint upon university teaching. It is difficult to believe that success was not related to widespread national interests in territorial expansion, commercial competition, and strategic questions.

There is no room in a preface to discuss every paper contained in a book. But Malcolm Lewis's paper on Amerindian antecedents of American geography raises a particularly interesting point. If, as Lewis suggests, American Indians had developed in some form many of the geographical concepts subsequently generated independently by Euro-Americans, can we ask to what degree humans are genetically programmed to organize knowledge about the earth's surface in common ways? Are many geographical concepts cross-cultural in the sense that all humans have the capability to generate them as a part of their inherited mental equipment, in rather the same way as migratory geese are born with a sense of space that allows them to navigate vast distances by instinct rather than by instruments?

The conference from which this book came owes a debt to many scholars. The program committee consisted of John Allen, Martyn Bowden, Anne Buttimer, Gary Dunbar, Ralph Ehrenberg, Walter Freeman, William Koelsch, Geoffrey Martin, Dean Rugg, and David Stoddart. In addition, Robert Block, Roger Bruhn, Robert Campbell, Wes Dow, Herbert Eder, Leslie Hewes, George Kish, Duane Knos, Clyde Kohn, Max Larsen, Gordon Lewthwaite, Fred Lukermann, Cotton Mather, James McDonald, Richard Morrill, Philippe Pinchemel, Robert Sack, and William Thomas chaired sessions, contributed to televised discussion groups, or otherwise made valuable contributions.

The National Science Foundation provided a grant to cover most of the conference expenses and the Research Council of the University of Nebraska—Lincoln provided additional support. Without this generous financial assistance, the conference would not have existed in the form which it did. And we all owe a debt to my wife, Olwyn, who suggested casually one Sunday morning that a conference on the history of American geography might be an idea worth thinking about.

Brian W. Blouet
University of Nebraska—Lincoln

Continuity and Change

Marvin W. Mikesell

A conference on the origins of American academic geography invites speculation on its subsequent development. Speculation is the proper label for these remarks, which are less disciplined than the more sharply defined contributions to this volume. To say that I have tried to see a forest rather than trees would imply self-confidence that I do not possess. It would be more appropriate to say that I have tried to find evidence of intellectual "climate." The trials and errors, novelties and relics, and above all the mixture of persistence and restlessness that are evident in the record of American geography call for a wide range of both specific and general inquiry.

Continuity

Studies of the history of geography usually stress change. Yet continuity is an equally detectable theme. Geographers have been united by their commitment to discover the logic of location and distribution. New and old have to do with methods employed in this effort rather than the effort itself, which has been if not a unique preoccupation certainly a common obsession. Terms that reflect this obsession (area, region, hinterland, frontier) are diagnostic of our lore. The same can be said for a corresponding set of terms (land, resources, habitat, site) that reflect an equally persistent interest in environments. In spite of frequent predictions that the discipline is coming apart, that it is too disparate to survive in competition with more tidy enterprises, geography continues to be practiced and professed without manifest disunity. Although many geographers believe that they are working on the periphery of the field and some even publish their findings in the journals of other fields, cases of permanent emigration are rare. .

1

Origins of Academic Geography

The continuity of American geography has also been enhanced, ironically perhaps, by its inherent pluralism. Although a more singular conception of the discipline can be found in the statements of the occupants of the first university chairs, by the time the first departments were established geographers were devoted to both topical and regional studies, and sought understanding of both natural and cultural landscapes. Therefore, the numerous subfields that were encouraged by centrifugal forces could be seen as a welcome rather than a divisive progression. The persistence of a common commitment to the why of where permitted geography to grow like a cell without rupture or independent development. The mutations that have occurred have affected the entire organism more often than they have fostered the creation of new organisms. Although revolution has been claimed (and hoped for), the history of geography, like the history of most subcultures of academia, has displayed the evidence of continuity within change that is the essence of evolution.

Change

The fact that the changes evident in the record of American geography can be described as variations on a common theme does not mean that such changes have been insignificant, automatic, or devoid of drama. To be sure, some members of our profession acquire an intellectual orientation early in their careers and often even in graduate school that permits them to function henceforth without concern for disturbing innovations. However, most academics show a keen appreciation of change, and worry about its effect on their currency and status. Between the Young Turks and Old Pashas of any period is a troubled middle-aged group that is neither secure in its position of real or imagined leadership, nor ready to surrender it to impatient aspirants.

Yet even when an academic fashion can be resisted, aspects of a new style may ultimately prevail. As textbooks change, teachers, however reluctantly, must also change. And as editorial policies change, a corresponding, if belated, change will also be evident in the behavior of authors. Change is part of the experience of all academic geographers. If I take my own twenty- year career as a sample, at its beginning the teaching of introductory courses was keyed to the climatic classification of Wladimir Köppen, urban geography was only beginning to emerge as an important commitment, competence in statistics or mathematics was seldom encountered (or expected), and opportunity was knocking for

2

foreign-area specialists. A decade later these characterizations were no longer valid and a "new geography" proclaimed in the early 1960s was well established. At present, consensus seems to be lacking and the pluralism that has always been evident in the discipline is a governing nonparadigm.

The procession of old, new, and newer new, which has been so conspicuous during the past two decades, can be seen in the lore of earlier decades. In the 1900s the first generation of American geographers sought to create a new discipline that could serve as a bridge between the physical sciences, especially geology, and the social and biological sciences. In the 1920s geographers experienced the trials and errors of what a later generation condemned as "environmentalism." In the 1930s such generalization was set aside in favor of a cautious empiricism that is perhaps best exemplified by unit-area mapping and a series of articles on the delimitation of agricultural regions. The decade of the 1940s included devotion to the effort of winning the war, which for some prominent geographers meant service in OSS, and an effort to reestablish training programs in an atmosphere of rapidly increasing enrollments after the war. In the 1950s geographers produced a new generation of textbooks and cultivated an elaborate series of topical and regional subfields. Indeed, by the end of this decade specialization was so advanced that "geography" and "geographer" were usually preceded by a qualifying adjective. It was in this atmosphere of rapid growth and proliferation of subfields that the various methods and aspirations known collectively as the "new geography" propelled the discipline toward an era of deductive thinking, model building, and quantification.

These admittedly subjective remarks beg the question of other perceptions. They also beg a more important question: the reasons for change. If one disregards invidious thinking—progress versus stagnation, lab coats versus muddy boots, and so on—several propositions can be offered about the forces, circumstances, and attitudes that have made change a fact of life for American geographers.

From Physical Science to Social Science

The most important trend in the history of American academic geography has been a migration from physical science toward social science. Many of the founders of the discipline in this country were trained as geologists, and the physical geography that evolved under their leadership was a prominent feature of geographical education and research until the 1920s. Much of the subsequent evolution of the discipline can be interpreted as a movement away from this initial orientation. The physical-scientific foundation of the discipline can also be invoked as an explanation of the environmentalism that characterized the first phase of deductive thinking and generalization among human geographers. The initial orientation of American geography also provides an explanation of the international distinctiveness of American geography.

In Germany geography evolved out of eighteenth-century cosmography, and can be regarded as a parent of disciplines rather than an offspring. Geography's antecedents in France can be traced to interests aroused by that country's commitments abroad and to an evolution from history. In Britain the first scholars to identify themselves with geography were conscious of the contribution they might make in the clarification of Britain's role in the world and the management of its empire. Only in America can one speak of geography as an offshoot from geology, and of the subsequent history of the discipline as a progression from physical to social science. The fact that the several fields of physical geography continue to be cultivated and that some geographers can still be regarded as physical scientists is not a denial of this trend. It merely indicates that migration has been sustained by majority "votes" rather than unanimity.

Thesis and Antithesis

In geography as in most academic disciplines, periods of confident generalization are often followed by periods of skeptical empiricism. The creative tension between the general and the particular is, of course, a permanent feature of our lore. Yet at times deduction and law seeking seem to prevail, whereas debunking or the search for exceptions to announced rules may be characteristic of other times. Environmentalism belongs to the generalizing or law-seeking spirit of the geographical profession. The cautious inductive spirit that followed was an understandable and perhaps necessary phase of antithesis, which gave way in time to a new era of thesis making.

Needless to say, not all geographers hear the same drummer or march under the same banner. Nevertheless, movement toward or away from general propositions constitutes one of the persistent forces of change in our discipline. In principle all geographers should accept the premise that case studies should be expanded (or at least be compared), and generalizations should be challenged by specific exceptions. In practice theory and empiricism may represent opposing or alternating professional styles. If deductive thought acts as a trigger to generate inductive criticism and empiricism acts similarly (though perhaps more gradually) as a stimulus to generalization, then the Hegelian progression of thesis and antithesis deserves serious consideration as a force producing change in our discipline. The analogy of the pendulum, swinging back and forth but not going anywhere, is misleading. Most generalizations in geography are works of temporary synthesis and the act of constructing, dismantling, and reconstructing them is an innovative occupation.

The progression of thesis and antithesis also helps to explain that perennial intellectual game, the making and unmaking of dichotomies. If dichotomies are theses, then the phase of antithesis is represented by continua. Dichotomies offered for the edification of the geographical profession in recent decades have ranged from all-inclusive proclamations about scholarly style (idiographic versus nomothetic) to generalizations derived from empirical studies (nodal versus uniform regions), or designed to orient such studies (site versus situation). Since geography is an open rather than a closed system (to use another dichotomy), it has also been influenced by distinctions of interdisciplinary (versus intra-disciplinary) character; e.g., structuralism versus functionalism. Nor have geographers been able or willing to avoid the radical versus conservative dichotomy. Scholars skeptical of or provoked by "black and white" distinctions seldom offer alternative dichotomies; it is the idea of the continuum that they embrace—"shadings of gray."

Research Progression

Each of the major geographical literatures displays a pattern of semicontrolled evolution. For example, the literature devoted to hazards research shows a topical progression from floods to other natural hazards (drought, hurricanes, earthquakes, and so on), and then to hazards of man-made origin. There is also evidence of a progression from an initial interest in the delimitation of hazard-prone areas to later studies of how hazards are perceived, damage reduction strategies, and possible optimum adjustments. Although it could not have been predicted that research would evolve in this way, the evolution that has occurred is understandable and perhaps inevitable. Similar patterns can be found in other cumulative literatures, most notably in the large literature devoted to urban geography.

Progress, by definition, is only implicit in additive literatures, which require some organizing principle (e.g., scale conversion, cross-cultural comparison) to pass from disparity through redundancy to synthesis and common growth.

The progression of research, or at least the rationale of its initiation, often reflects real or perceived imperfections of prior efforts. It is rare that an author fails to make a claim of originality; yet most contributions to the literature of geography represent qualifications or elaborations of previous claims. What was previously thought to be simple is in fact complex. What was once believed to be complex can be explained by a newly discovered principle. A postulated correlation neglects the possibility of other correlations. An alleged universal model fails to explain what can be observed in some specific area. The methodology designed to explain a particular phenomenon or association of phenomena can also be applied to something else. And, of course, what may be true at present in "our world" may not be true in a "second," "third," or "fourth" world, or even in "our world" in some prior period of time.

Importation

No one has attempted to assess whether American geographers have a favorable or unfavorable "balance of payments." However, we can say with confidence that the discipline has been enriched and stimulated by imports from other countries and other scholarly professions. Mention has already been made of the early use of the Köppen climatic classification as an organizing theme in undergraduate education. The concept of bioclimatic zones, derived from Siegfried Passarge's *Landschaftsgürtel*, also made an early entry into American textbooks and classrooms. The idea that geographers should devote themselves to studies of the development of cultural landscapes, which had substantial support in the 1930s, was an additional German import. And when Richard Hartshorne published "The Nature of Geography" in 1939, a generation of American geographers was obliged to take account of his formidable review of German geographical thought and especially the thought of Alfred Hettner.

Moreover, the "new geography" of the 1960s, which seemed in so many ways to be a manifestation of the restlessness of younger American geographers, drew its initial inspiration from German location theorists (Alfred Weber, August Lösch, Walter Christaller), the studies of the diffusion of innovations undertaken by Torsten Hägerstrand in Sweden, and even the early nineteenth-century speculations of a gentleman-farmer of Mecklenburg.

A good case can also be made for the influence of ideas imported from France. The philosophical position of possibilism, in spite of its vagueness, was embraced as an alternative to determinism, and in so doing Americans, like their French colleagues, were following the lead of Paul Vidal de la Blache. The precocious work of Jean Brunhes also helped Americans during the groping phase of their effort to profess a comprehensive human geography. In time many American geographers and especially cultural geographers drew stronger support from Max. Sorre.

Mention of the economists Weber and Lösch in reference to location theory introduces the equally important issue of borrowing from other disciplines. Even if attention is restricted to major influences—imported concepts or methods that have had decisive influence—it is difficult to know where to begin. Perhaps it is sufficient here to suggest that a comprehensive history of American geography, should it ever be written, will have to take account of the influence in every field of the discipline of scholars who had or have little or no awareness of the relevance of their thought to geographers. In so far as human geography is concerned this comment applies especially to the "Big Three" of social science: Karl Marx, Talcott Parsons, and Max Weber.

At the risk of overselling a proposition that requires no feat of salesmanship, one can point to Carl Sauer's work on agricultural origins, which is usually regarded as his most original and provocative contribution. The philosophical foundation of this work was derived from the conception of stages in the evolution of livelihood presented by the German geographer Eduard Hahn, the delimitation of major centers of plant domestication made by the Russian geneticist N. I. Vavilov, the catalogue of the cultivated plants of the Malay peninsula published by the British botanist I. H. Burkill, and the theories of animal domestication offered by Hahn and the German zoologist Max Hilzheimer. This combination of influences, showing a range of both disciplines and nationalities, has been characteristic of much seminal work in geography.

Leadership and Schools

If it is correct to suggest that the role of importation from other countries and other disciplines has been relatively neglected in studies of the history of American geography, the same can not be said of leadership and schools. Indeed, the tendency to personalize and institutionalize academic history is so strong that this entry in our list of forces producing change can be taken for granted. Much of the early history of American geography concerns the leadership of William Morris Davis at Harvard University and Rollin D. Salisbury at the University of Chicago. The story of environmentalism concerns the leadership of Ellen Semple, Ellsworth Huntington, and Griffith Taylor. The development of American cultural geography, initially conceived as an alternative to environmentalism, has often been described in reference to Carl Sauer and his "Berkeley school." The constellation of interests, methods, and aspirations that was characteristic of the "new geography" of the 1960s reflected the pioneer efforts of Harold McCarthy at the University of Iowa, William Garrison at the University of Washington, and William Warntz at the American Geographical Society.

The issue of individual or institutional leadership becomes interesting only after automatic assertions of this character have been made. For example, since Sauer's work was so strongly influenced by prior efforts, how can one distinguish between his influence and that of his many acknowledged predecessors? Was the "school" he founded and led for more than thirty years a school of cultural geography, as is often supposed, or one of biogeography, historical geography, Latin American geography, or indeed of geography without a qualifying adjective? How can so many schools be *a* school? Again, did the interest in environmental perception, which became pervasive in the late 1960s, have a singular or multiple origin, and if the latter how can one unravel complementary influences?

Questions of this character could be posed indefinitely. The ease with which they can be asked and the difficulty we encounter in supplying convincing answers demonstrates that the history of academic disciplines is both a drama, with leading and supporting actors, and also an expression of cultural or, more properly, subcultural evolution that can not be reduced to individuals and schools. Not all students are permanent disciples and not all disciples are former students. In addition to scholars to whom such labels can be attached, much can be learned from the work of bastards of doubtful paternity and mavericks who display evidence of mutation as well as heredity.

Reform Movements

Periodically, someone decides that the venerable discipline of geography needs to be reformed. A professional commitment is condemned as a deviation or dismissed as an irrelevancy. New tools are perfected and their power proclaimed. Imports are championed. Geographical findings or aspirations are placed in a new context, or forced into a new mold. Programmatic statements intended as directives to less enlightened colleagues often are laments that others are not doing what a particular author has done or hopes to do. "Come on in, the water is fine" would be a fair characterization of this class of statement.

Yet most programmatic statements have another message. They represent attempts to tidy up an untidy discipline, and hence are protests against the pluralism of geography. Occasionally such statements ring true, and the sprawling enterprise of geography seems to achieve a new focus as the study of "human ecology," "landscape morphology," "areal differentiation," or "spatial organization." Reforms intended to sharpen the focus of geography may provoke counterreformations inspired by faith in the virtue of diversity. Regardless of their rationale or fate, reform movements have played and doubtless will continue to play a key role in the evolution of American geography. Even if eventually discarded, the new geography of any period is likely to be replaced by a newer, rather than an older, geography. That some scholars may have the inclination or the security to resist such pressures is beside the point. Bandwagons do exist, and progress usually represents movement from an acknowledged prior position as well as movement toward an anticipated new position.

Episodes

In addition to the major trends that constitute chapters in the history of American geography it is possible to identify temporary enthusiasms or episodes. For example, during the 1920s much energy was devoted to attempts to explain the reasons for dispersed and concentrated patterns of rural settlement. A decade later, interest centered on the delimitation of agricultural regions. Immediately after the Second World War several geographers exhibited interest in climatic classification. In the late 1950s a spate of articles appeared on the character of central business districts. Urban geographers at this time were also concerned about a presumed distinction between basic and nonbasic economic activities and the functional classification of cities. The distinction between uniform and nodal regions attracted attention immediately before and after the war, and the central place studies of the 1960s superseded an earlier venture known as areal functional organization.

The distinction between episodes and trends is, of course, difficult to make and impossible to predict. Nevertheless, any history of the discipline that fails to take account of temporary enthusiasms neglects much if not most of our collective action. It is not surprising that episodes have been overlooked. Several years ago I tried to treat the fate of sequent occupance as an example of temporary enthusiasm. I found it easy to explain the initial popularity of this concept, but I could only speculate on the reasons for its eventual abandonment. Perhaps sequent occupance, like the basic/nonbasic ratio and areal functional organization, succumbed from a combination of boredom and intervening opportunities. If so, the episodes of our history may be manifestations not only of the fickleness of human nature, but also of mental fatigue.

Environmental Influences

One can accept the premise that geography does not have an objective existence independent of the inquirer (i.e., geography is what geographers have done, are doing, and will do), and still assert that the discipline must be influenced by what is "out there." It would be difficult to deny that American geographers have been influenced by the American environment. In so far as we see ourselves as interpreters of a world as well as of an American scene, we have also been influenced by that much larger environment. It is not surprising that the preoccupation of the profession with land use and agricultural areas occurred during a period when a substantial part of the American population was still rural. The later prominence of urban interests undoubtedly reflects the growing prominence in the United States of urban environments. Nor is it surprising that foreign-area commitments were most popular during the post–World War II decade when the nation as a whole was committed to the notion that it had global responsibility. The relative decline of foreign-area studies after the Vietnam war seems to reflect a contrary spirit of neo-isolationism.

This line of reasoning could be extended far beyond the American scene. For example, central place theory, regardless of its presumed universality, is a more appealing conceptual framework in regions that have a full range of settlement types (hamlets, villages, towns, cities) than it would be where a settlement hierarchy is not evident (New Guinea), or is "distorted" by a primate city (Venezuela). Similarly, interest in the geography of languages is more likely to be pursued in Switzerland than in Nebraska. The issue here is not only that geography can influence geographers, but also that geographical change may encourage changes in the practice of geography. For example, it can not be denied that national concern about environmental deterioration in the early 1970s had an impact on geographers. Without this external stimulus a reassertion of our status as "earth scientists" might not have occurred, or at best would have occurred with less sense of urgency and public responsibility.

The proposition that geographers can be influenced by environment permits other speculation. For example, Sauer's playful (or not so playful) claim that geographers in the Midwest adopted a functional and nonhistorical attitude because of the peculiarities of that environment invites thoughts about the peculiarities of the environment of northwestern Mexico, which served for many years as a training ground for members of the "Berkeley school." Similarly, the cultural ecology that became evident in the 1960s is best understood in reference to field studies undertaken in New Guinea. Contrary propositions can also be entertained. It is difficult, for example, to imagine Australian geographers developing a major research program from an initial interest in the hazard of floods. And it is hard to imagine rural geography in the Ruhr. Yet urban studies have flourished in the improbable setting of Iowa, and the University of Chicago has a world-renowned Oriental Institute. Such "anomalies" do not prevent us from speculating (as unembarrassed possibilists) about environmental influences.

Cultural Influences

It is difficult to find a label for the complicated problem of how a community of scholars can be influenced by economic, social, and political issues that transcend its boundaries and may even seem irrevelant to its values. To speak of the influence of American culture on a species of the subculture of academia is to raise the appropriate question. How can it be answered? Perhaps the best approach is to take account of the changing experience of persons who elect to become geographers.

The first generation of American geographers grew up in a country that was still strongly influenced by the mores of small towns. Most of the students now attracted to geography are products not only of an urban but increasingly of a suburban environment. The early preoccupaton of American geographers with nature and land use was an easy commitment for persons raised in small towns. Crops could be seen and identified on the way to or from school. The woodlot and creek and the wildlife found there were objects of early curiosity and increasingly sophisticated observation. Moreover, the values of the small town, close to the rural world but not of it, permitted a dedicaton to rural studies that would have been less likely for persons who were in fact farmers. For a farm boy, higher education usually meant escape from rural life. For a boy from a small town, higher education could mean escape from small-town life into a profession devoted to disciplined study of familiar surroundings.

This caricature is useful as a point of departure for speculation on how the geographical profession has been changed and is changing as a consequence of the suburban, middle-class origin of most of its current members. The suburban world permits no easy awareness of nature, and farms are at best the dimly perceived source of food found in plastic containers after a short walk from a parking lot. The world of suburbia is a world of lawns and ornamental vegetation, a place of departure and arrival for commuters, a world in which land use has to do mainly with houses, streets, and shopping centers. From this perspective the rural world, if seen at all, is something indistinct beyond an interstate highway. Relatively undisturbed natural landscapes, if they are ever encountered, have meaning mainly as places for recreation.

Since geography is seldom elected in the freshman year and many professional geographers have degrees in other disciplines, a related issue concerns the changing pattern of professional recruitment. The small-town boy mentioned above probably elected geography after a previous commitment to botany, geology, or some other natural science. His suburban counterpart is likely to come to geography from sociology, psychology, or some other behavioral science. Our suburbanite will have a keener awareness of technology and be more personally influenced by automation than his or her small-town predecessor. He or she will also be more apt to appreciate the advantages of space-age technology in the solution of scientific problems. This sophistication or potential sophistication will be offset by a corresponding ignorance not only of foreign areas, which has always been true of our recruits, but also of rural America, inner-city America, and what is left of nature in America.

Thanks to Mark Twain and Norman Rockwell, we have no difficulty imagining the world that spawned the first generation of American geographers. The dichotomy of small-town boys and suburban boys and girls is at best a playful response to a problem that demands serious effort. When that effort is made we can be sure that much will be said about the impact on American geography of the Depression and TVA, of World War II and the founding of the United Nations, and of the Cold War and the Peace Corps. For more recent years, account will have to be taken of the response of our profession to the social movements of the 1960s and the ecology movement of the early 1970s. Consideration of current influences brings us across the thin line that separates history from prediction.

What Next?

It is safe to predict that most of the forces, circumstances, and attitudes that have encouraged change in the character of American geography will continue. The movement toward social science is sure to persist. A continued interplay of thesis and antithesis can also be taken for granted, as can the perennial game of dichotomy making and unmaking. Importations, more likely from other disciplines than from other countries, can also be assumed. Since any agreement about the nature of the discipline is likely to be temporary, reform movements designed to overcome seeming disparity are bound to appear and reappear, as will countless "episodes."

It may also be safe to predict that innovation will continue to be regarded as a virtue. Much of the development that has already taken place in American geography is a consequence of the attempt of individual scholars to stake a claim for themselves, to be or at least to seem to be different from their rivals. The fact that most academics see virtue in innovation means that there is reward for innovation. The Young Turks of our future will only seem to be held back by aging Pashas, and the complaints uttered by either group will have an unconvincing quality because they will be denials of mortality. In the future as in the past any consensus that may be achieved will be but an interlude in a permanent condition of restless striving.

Our best hope for more specific prediction may come from appreciation of the changing character of the American and world environment. Geographic research responsive to trends now evident in the United States will have to include studies of population redistribution and the dispersal of industry, inner-city blight and prospects for renewal, the impact of higher energy costs and shortages on a wide range of economic activities, highway-oriented landscapes, and the conflict between preservationist and utilitarian views in environmental planning. It is also possible that geographers will need to give serious thought to alternatives to the present settlement pattern of the country and the optimum size of our cities. The greatest opportunity for the geographical profession may come from appreciation of the inefficiency, and indeed the obsolescence, of many features of our built environment.

The global or at least international thinking that has always been evident among American geographers may encourage a new political geography capable of throwing our professional light on OPEC and other new geopolitical blocs as well as multinational corporations. A global geography of capital flows, immigration, and perhaps even social conflict is well within the reach of our collective imagination.

The nature of American geography is also sure to be affected by curtailment of opportunities for academic employment. The response to this situation thus far has been to look outward, to search for unconventional or at least less familiar applications of geographical findings and skills. The fact that "applied geography" has such great promise does not mask its current pretentiousness and ambiguity. The notion of two geographies, one basic and one applied, suffers from our inability to offer a clear definition of either of these qualifying terms. Most if not all of geography has potential relevance to public policy; even a house type buff may be called upon to serve as a witness for historic preservation. And any enterprise devoted to understanding the logic of location can be useful to business leaders who must make location decisions. Nevertheless, meetings devoted to applied geography in recent years have adjourned in the spirit of impotent activism that was characteristic of the teach-ins of the 1960s. The inherent frustration of applied geography is that experience in this case really is the best teacher. Assertions that geographers have something useful to say ignore the more immediate issue of what they need to hear. That message when it is offered may not come from business leaders, bureaucrats, or professors. It may come from persons with bachelor's degrees in geography, or perhaps only a course or two in geography, who have found ingenious ways to use their geographical skills. It may also come from the professional schools to which we are already sending some of our best graduating seniors.

Meanwhile, geographers fortunate enough to have secure teaching positions will worry about what they should do. The best response to this concern could be a decision to do what they have been doing, but with a keener appreciation of context and a greater willingness to be influenced by environment. A discipline that combines the insights of natural and social science, encourages awareness of a multiplicity of explanations, and is blessed with unrivaled appreciation of the logic of location and the importance of scale has much to offer to persons who are unable or unwilling to become geographers. "Geography for nongeographers" is perhaps the only motto we need in a time of limited growth for the academic part of our profession. It is also possible that a policy of "back to basics" will better serve the cause of nonacademic geography than programs that are self-consciously "applied."

Afterword

The history of American geography is best described, I think, as a gradual, cumulative venture. Stagnation has never been evident in spite of the complaints of some reformers. Continuity has always been evident in spite of occasional claims of revolution. If human geography were an exact science governed by a Kuhnian scenario, it would not exhibit so much evidence or nonparadigmatic behavior.

To see the history of geography as evolution is not to endorse nihilism or anarchy. This view invites responsible speculation on why some species evolve more rapidly than others, when and where mutation can occur, and the influence of surrounding environments. Although a golden age may never have existed and hard times can be anticipated, geography exhibits too much vitality to be on any list of endangered species. The major current challenge for academic geographers is to see a new era of limited growth as a time of still unlimited opportunity.

Preacademic Origins

Amerindian Antecedents
of American Academic Geography

G. Malcolm Lewis

Academic geography has a long and complex prehistory. Yet surprisingly, historiographers of geography have tended to reconstruct its descent as essentially unilinear, differentiated through time only by fluctuations in the rate of development and occasional aberrations. They have paid remarkably little attention to ideas about the spatial organization of land, man and man-land relationship outside the Graeco-Roman, Judeo-Christian and, to far lesser extents, Moslem and Chinese traditions. Yet the records of exploration and the literature of cultural anthropology are replete with accounts of the ways in which members of other cultures cognize(d), spatially structure(d), and communicate(d) ideas about these aspects of their worlds. A systematic study of the spatial structuring of environmental information, if drawn from a representative sample of past and present societies at different levels of cultural achievement, might well reveal similar sequences of development and in so doing throw light on the hypothesis that the ethnogenesis of these ideas presages their ontogenesis. Such a study would also help to establish the stage at which the development of geography as a discipline ceased to be primarily concerned with recording and communicating data organized according to indigenous principles developed in the normal course of ethnogenesis, and began to be concerned with the organization and analysis of data according to operations derived through reflection, reason, or instruction—i.e., the stage at which geography might be said to have ceased to be a customary art and became an investigatory science. These are hypotheses which might be tested by someone in time for a report at a conference on the universal history of geography, for which the seventy-fifth anniversary of the International Geographical Union in 1997 might provide an appropriate, occasion. Meanwhile, on the seventy-fifth anniversary of the Association of American Geographers, when a national perspective is more appropriate, a less ambitious objective will be essayed: to indicate by example ways in which the objectives and methods of geographers in North America during the past three-quarters of a century were anticipated by Amerindians during the Post Contact period.[1] The evidence will be drawn mainly from maps (pictographs containing spatially arranged environmental information), the earliest of which predate the founding of the association by almost four centuries. The emphasis on cartographic evidence, though regrettable, is inevitable in dealing with past preliterate societies, the oral communications from which were incapable of conveying the relatively complex concepts of spatial and environmental relationships, at least during the earliest (and, for this purpose, most interesting) periods of contact with the Caucasians.

Description of the Earth as a Site

In the retrospective section of a monograph written on the eve of the recent revolution within American geography, Edward Ackerman observed that the methods and objectives of modern geographical inquiry could be arranged according to a sixfold hierarchy of steps. The first of these, which was already essentially complete and with which geographers had not been seriously involved for a century or more, had involved the "accurate determination of the shape and extent of the physical matrix" of the earth.[2] For Caucasians this had been essential for several reasons: establishing the limits of land holdings, administrative areas, and political units; sea and air navigation; preparing for intercontinential ballistic warfare, etc. Among the Amerindians none of these requirements had ever existed. Land ownership (as distinct from a sense of territory) was alien to low-density, mainly migratory populations; coastal dwellers rarely had cause to venture beyond the sight of land; and warfare required quite different skills. Movement via land, inland waterways, or coastal waters necessitated a detailed knowledge of landscape features and environmental conditions rather than a Euclidian sense of absolute distance and cardinal direction. Distance was almost always expressed in units of travel time and, even when lost, most Amerindians would seem to have oriented themselves by means of terrestrial rather than astronomical clues. The representations on maps of lakes, sea coasts, and drainage networks affords incontrovertible evidence of this, though the causes of the deviations from orthomorphism vary. For example, in 1767 two intelligent Chipewyan Indians presented the factor at Churchill Fort with a map of what is now the north central part of mainland Canada.[3] The area was then virtually unknown to the Hudson's Bay Company servants, and the map provided the basis for planning Samuel Hearne's third and ultimately successful attempt to reach the lower Coppermine River. Hearne later described one of the the two Indians as the "most ... sensible Indian I had ever met with ... of universal knowledge and generally respected,"[4] yet the more than three thousand miles of complex coastline, incorporating four major peninsulas and a right-angle change in dominant direction at what was later to be named the Fury and Hecla Strait, was represented on the Chipewyans' map as essentially a straight line. In contrast, Inuit representations of the northwest coast of Hudson Bay were characterized by much detail and gross exaggeration of certain features.[5] To the Chipewyans, the coastline was just beyond the edge of their world and not a feature of significance, merely meriting the most schematic representation possible. Conversely to the Inuits, it was the boundary between two important worlds, certain stretches of which were more imageable than others, because they either were strategically more important or possessed distinctive scenic properties. Chipewyan and Inuit representations of the coastline were both characterized by inconsistencies of scale attributable either to different rates of travel (a function of littoral conditions), or to varying degrees of imageability (and hence memorability) of the different sections. Simplification of the commonplace, exaggeration of the distinctive, and disregard for both true scale and cardinal direction were, and still are, characteristics of Amerindian and Inuit maps. They reflect techniques and purposes closer to those of pre-Hellenic cartography in the Near East or pre-Renaissance cartography in Europe than to the western tradition of scientific cartography. As such they parallel the precursors of Ackerman's Stage One. We will call this "Ackerman's Stage Zero". Given this conclusion, it may seem pointless to seek for parallels between Amerindian methods and objectives and later stages in the Ackerman hierarchy. Surprisingly, however, they do exist and the absence of a parallel to Stage One would seem to reflect a lack of necessity rather than of abiltiy.

Identification of the Specific Phenomenal Content of Earth Space

According to Ackerman, the "second step is to identify the specific phenomenal content of earth space: quantity, qualities, degree." In the modern tradition of geography, field survey and remote sensing are the recognized methods of observation. In North America techniques for large-scale field surveying were formulated by a group of geographers at the University of Chicago between 1910 and 1920, and further developed in the Midwest during the next two decades. Thereafter, attention was switched to remote sensing and questionnaire surveys, with geographers contributing to the development of both.

Amerindians rarely collected information quite so systematically as twentieth-century geographers, but one notable example closely follows the single-phenomenon mapping characteristic of some large-scale ecological and behavioral research. In 1838 a Cree Indian suggested to the Hudson's Bay Company's factor at Fort Rupert that Charlton Island, some forty miles to the north in James Bay and approximately one hundred square miles in extent, would make a good beaver preserve, even though it was then without beaver.[6] In the winter of 1838-39 two Crees were sent to map the island. They produced "in pencil, on a sheet of Cartridge paper [given to] them for the purpose ... a very satisfactory chart [which had been] laid down by them daily as they proceeded. The sixty one Lakes laid down by them, they consider eligible and desirable in every respect for Beaver to inhabit but they say there are many other smaller Lakes they did not note, but which nevertheless if Beaver were numerous on the Island they would with their customary sagacity render inhabitable by their dams...."[7] In the spring of 1839 several mature beaver were shipped to the island and the chart plots "old George's start," where "Father George ... a lusty and rather amorously disposed" male had been released with his mate.[8] A later map included thirty-one additional lakes which had been recorded by the Indians in the course of a second survey during the winter of 1839–40. For the purpose of future reference these were indexed A-Z and 1-66.[9] The back of the map recorded that in the winter of 1839-40 there was one occupied lodge on lake F (very close to "old George's start"), where young were seen in the spring, and that in the following winter there were lodges with pairs of beaver on lakes A, B, and C, with a single beaver on lake E and with either one or a pair of beaver on lake D. During the next four winters Indians were sent from Fort Rupert to record the proliferation and diffusion of occupied lodges. The survey of 1844-45 recorded by index letter or number thirty-six lakes which it had not been possible to visit, and the locations of thrity-five occupied lodges with young, one occupied lodge without young, and one lodge about the occupance of which there was some doubt.[10] This is perhaps a unique case of Amerindians practicing field survey in the modern professional sense, and the method may possibly have been determined in advance by the factor at Fort Rupert. However, there are many examples of Indians having compiled from memory maps which identify and record selected categories from the phenomenal content of earth space. Ishi, the last Yahi Indian, who lived for a while on the campus of the University of California at Berkeley, drew a map in or about 1914 of the east bank tributaries of the upper Sacramento, on which he located and named five "rich villages," fourteen other "villages," and eleven "places". The classification was doubtless subjective but it was clearly intended to indicate a hierarchy.[11] Some Amerindian maps employed techniques which were not formally introduced into western cartography until the nineteenth century. In 1602, in the course of an inquiry into the discoveries made during Oñate's expedition to New Mexico, the investigator questioned an Indian named Miguel, who had been captured somewhere in the Pecos valley and brought back to Mexico City by the expedition. He was asked "by signs to mark with a pen and ink on a sheet of paper ... the pueblos of his land. Miguel proceeded to mark on paper circles resembling the letter "O", some larger than others; [adding that] in the settlements where he was born and raised and where the Spaniards seized him, there were many people, emphasizing their numbers by gestures."[12] The contemporary copy of the map depicts the pueblos by circles of various sizes and carries a "key" consisting of four circles, within which are the names of four important Mexican settlements: Mexico City, Zacatecas, Sombrerete, and Guadalajara. The interrogation of Miguel took place in Mexico City and it is reasonable to suppose that he had been taken through the other three settlements en route from New Mexico. Evidently he communicated to the investigators the sizes of the populations in the New Mexican pueblos in relation to his impressions of the populations of settlements known to them. This is not an isolated use of the techniques. It is employed on contemparary copies of at least four different maps drawn by Chickasaw Indians during the early eighteenth century. One of these, originally on skin, was prepared by a war chief in 1737 to convey to the French the "number of their [i.e. the Chickasaws'] friends and also their enemies."[13] The contemporary copy is remarkably stylized and topologically structured. Villages and nations are represented by circles, colored according to whether they were friend or foe and proportional in size to the number of men (presumably warriors). The circular nodes are linked by straight paths, differentiated according to whether they connect the Chickasaws to their friends, lead toward (but do not link with) their enemies, or link their enemies. The map covers a vast territory, from the English in their South Atlantic seaboard colonies to the Arkansas Indians west of the lower Mississippi, and from the French in their colonies on the eastern Gulf Coast to the Iroquois south of Lake Ontario. A map of the upper Arkansas, Platte and upper Missouri basins drawn by an Oto

Indian in 1825 distinguished between Caucasian frontier settlements (rectangles), Indian villages (circles), and camps or councils (the tepee symbol).[14] The symbols each enclose or are surrounded by dots, the number of which varies in such a way to suggest the use of the dot distribution technique. In this case there is no confirmatory key, but it is reasonable to suppose that the technique would be employed and interpreted instinctively since Indians and Inuits throughout the continent conveyed fairly precise numerical values pictographically. For example, in 1696 the Comte de Frontenac's army, in the course of pursuing the Iroquois, "found a Tree . . . on which the Indians had, in their Manner, painted the French Army, and had laid by it two Bundles of cut Rushes. This was a Defiance in the Indian Manner . . . to tell them by the Number of Rushes, that fourteen hundered thirty four Men would meet them."[15]

Identification of Generic Relations: Categorization, Classification and Differentiation

The third step in the hierarchy recognized by Ackerman "is the identification of generic relations: categorization, classification, differentiation" with the "objective of . . . reducing to comprehensible scope the nearly infinite observations which may be made concerning the distribution of earth phenomena." Ackerman cites as examples the classification of phenomena into types and their spatial aggregation into special purpose (topical) regions. Indians of the eighteenth and early nineteenth centuries classified the macro vegetation of northern North America into barren lands, woods, and grasslands, and represented on maps boundaries between these three types.[16] This was not a level of mental activity to be included within "Ackerman's Stage Zero". The diversity and spatial distribution of vegetation types within each of the major systems and the spatial transitions (rather than boundaries) between the three involved categorizations, classification, and differentiation of a far higher order. It is not known at what stage in Indian prehistory these abilities emerged, or whether they were ever possessed by more than a small minority, but it is interesting to note that it was not until 1858 that James G. Cooper produced a map with comparable divisions[17] and that contemporary geographers of the eminence of J. Kenneth Hare, J. Ross Mackay, and A. William Küchler have made significant contributions to this type of mapping within the past quarter of a century.

Identification of Genetic Relations and the Determination of the Dynamic Aspects of Space

Ackerman's fourth step "is the identification of genetic relations [in which the geographer] ... seeks determination of the dynamic aspects of space content ... a phase of study which geography shares with other disciplines [but in which the focus] ... is uniquely centered on distributional problems." The Amerindian's comprehension of space and environments had a temporal dimension stretching back only through orally transmitted and pictographically recorded history. The genesis of phenomena and distributions within the lithosphere, hydrosphere, biosphere, and atmosphere were at best matters for speculation, but historical changes were sometimes comprehended in spatial contexts. In 1761 a Micmac chief in northern New Brunswick "made almost a circle with his forefinger and thumb, and pointing at the end of his forefinger, said there was Quebec, the middle joint of his finger was Montreal, the joint next to the hand was New York the joint of the thumb next [to] this was Halifax, the interval betwixt his finger and thumb was Pookmoosh, so that the Indians would soon be surrounded, which he signified by closing his finger and thumb."[18] Boston had been an English settlement for 131 years and New York for 93, but Halifax had been settled by the English only 12 years before and both Quebec and Montreal had been captured by the British from the French within the previous 2 years. Appreciation of temporal changes and spatial distributions on this grand scale must have been associated in the mind of the chief with the recent withdrawal of French military protection and the deportation by the British of Acadians from the agricultural valleys just a short distance to the south of him.

In 1837 at a council meeting convened in Washington, D.C., between delegations of Indians from the upper Mississippi and middle Missouri valleys, an Iowa chief presented a boldly executed map of virtually the whole of the Mississippi and Missouri drainage systems above St. Louis. It was presented as part of his evidence in a claim that his people, who since 1813 had been living on the Missouri, deserved a share of the price which had been paid to Sauk and Fox Indians on the Mississippi for a significant part of what is now the state of Iowa. The map shows by means of a network of dotted lines connecting irregular circles "the route of my forefathers ... it is the land we have always claimed from old times we have the history we have always owned this land it was ours it bears our name."[19] A redrafted and engraved version of a similar map drawn in or just before 1848 by another Iowa Indian "with a black-lead-pencil, on a large sheet of white paper, furnished at the mission house" near the Missouri River in what is now northeastern Kansas confirms in essence that of a decade before.[20] It plots in sequence "the places where the Iowas had lived during the sixteen migrations" which preceded their residence near the mission.

Certain birch-bark scrolls of the Southern Ojibway Indians show the spatial diffusion of the Mide religion.[21] Oral tradition claims that it was first brought to Indians on the Atlantic coast. Historical sources record that it had reached the Sault Ste. Marie by the mid-seventeenth century, and that after 1780 it spread into what is now northern Minnesota. The diffusion route is represented linearly on the scrolls in a manner not unlike that on European strip (route) maps of the seventeenth and eighteenth centuries, but unlike these the scrolls do not represent distance according to scale. Each terminates at Leech Lake in north central Minnesota, from where the diffusion route can be traced back with certainty as far as Sault Ste. Marie and with reasonable certainty as far as Montreal. These pictographic representations of the diffusion of a religious tradition over a distance of more than one thousand miles during considerably more than three hundred years are perhaps the most impressive examples of Indian representations of dynamic aspects of space content.

Determination of Covariation Among Earth Features

Ackerman's fifth step "is the determination of covariation among earth features ... an important and complex step in ascertaining space relations." Because of their dependence on scant resources, the Amerindians knew how to associate concealed resources and potential hazards with their visible manifestations, and how to plan their spatial activities in relation to the spatial and seasonal distribution of both. However, cartographic evidence of these strategies is relatively rare. On a number of Amerindian maps the representation as boundaries of the transitions between the barren grounds and woods and between the woods and grasslands of the northern interior of the continent were, as I have demonstrated elsewhere, cartographic expressions of their association of each of these vegetation systems with quite different modes of life and travel. These associations are not, however, explicit in the maps themselves and can only be established by reference to supporting evidence.

Indeed, relatively few maps present clear evidence of the association and covariation of phenomena. A somewhat diagrammatic sketch map by an Oglala Sioux, drawn to show the locations of the camps of Indians participating in the Blacks Hills Peace Talk of 1876, distinguishes very clearly by symbols between the sites supporting deciduous trees (cottonwoods), and those which were treeless—i.e., the classic associations of the northwestern Plains of pines with escarpments and buttes, grasses with the benchlands, and cottonwoods with the valley floors.[22] A map drawn by a York Fort Indian in 1809 of the area between the Nelson and lower Churchill Rivers depicts a ridge transverse between the two, "the same ridge as Limestone Rapid Nelson River and Big Fall Churchill River. "[23] This clearly associates major falls on river systems which are approximately one hundred miles apart with a common geological feature, the boundary between the Ordovician limestone and the Pre-Cambrian schists beneath. A map drawn by a Blackfoot chief in 1802 of the dry prairies of what are now southeast Alberta and northeast Montana shows the main routes across this harsh region, from the shelter of the woods to the north to that of the front ranges of the Rocky Mountains to the south.[24] The routes are divided according to days marches and several of the campsite are shown to occur at or in close proximity to berries, poplar, pines, or unspecified types of trees. Access to these resources for food, fuel, and shelter was always desirable and occasionally vital in the course of the approximately twenty days normally taken to cross this inhospitable region.

Integration of Data on Site, Phenomena, and Process to Reveal the Full Pattern of Space Relations

Ackerman's sixth and final step "is the integration of data on site, phenomena, and process so as to reveal the full pattern of space relations." It uses the "concepts of the region and the compage," involves both "the analysis and synthesis of earth-space content," and aims at the comprehension of reality. Evidence that Amerindians were capable of distinguishing between various parts of their world in a manner akin to this is to be found in contemporary records of their oral statements rather than on their maps.

John Lederer based "A General and Brief Account of the North American Continent," in part at least, on information obtained from Indians in the course of his explorations of the Piedmont in North Carolina and the Piedmont and Blue Ridge in Virginia.[25] Lederer's use of Indian names to describe what we now recognize as physiographic regions with distinctive landscape characteristics extending far beyond the limits of his own observations suggests that his informants recognized regions which physiographers of the late nineteenth and early twentieth centuries would have had little cause to dispute. The inner and outer coastal plains were together known as Ahkynt and according to Indian tradition as well as stratigraphical evidence were "supposed some ages past to have lain under the sea." The Ahkynt terminated inland at "the falls of the great rivers" or, as we would say, "at the fall line." Beyond were the highlands or Ahkontshuck, known to us as the Piedmont. These in turn terminated at a "great ridge of mountains," known to the Indians as Paemotinck, perhaps embracing the whole of the Appalachian sequence from the Blue Ridge, across the Ridge and Valley Province to the Cumberland Plateau but probably referring to the Blue Ridge only. The Paemotinck consisted of barren rocks and was "deserted of all living creatures but bears," but it was said to "shoot out to the eastward great promontories of rich land, known by the high and spreading trees which they bear: these promontories, because lower than the main ridge" were called by the Indians Tanx-Paemotinck (alias Aquatt). These were surely the outliers and spurs of the Blue Ridge which interrupt the inner Piedmont in the Carolinas and northeast Georgia. Whether any of this information was conveyed to Lederer in map form we do not know, but at the Monakin village by the falls on the James River an old Indian did describe to him "with a staffe two paths on the ground; one pointing to the Mahocks, and the other to the Nahyssaus."

One of the finest recorded examples of an Indian's ability to comprehend and express the full pattern of space relations over a large area is contained in a Crow chief's description of his tribe's territory during the early nineteenth century.[26] His description stresses climate, water, fodder, game, and shelter, and distinguishes between the various parts of the western Great Plains and adjacent mountains in terms of these resources. "Crow country" was essentially the valley bottoms, benchlands, plateaus, and isolated mountains drained by the Yellowstone River and its tributaries. According to the chief, it was "a good country ... exactly in the right place" within which one "fared well." Beyond "Crow country" conditions deteriorated in every direction. To the south, "on the great barren plains," the water was warm and bad and fevers were prevalent. To the north the winters were long and cold, and the absence of grass for much of the year precluded the keeping of horses. To the west, on the Columbia River, the natives were poor, dirty, paddled around in canoes, and had bad teeth from living on fish. To the east the Indians admittedly lived well, but were confined to villages and had to drink the muddy waters of the Missouri River—water which even the Crows' dogs would not drink. Somewhat nearer, at the confluence of the Missouri and Yellowstone, conditions in summer were almost as good as in the "Crow country" but there was neither grass or saltweed for horses in winter. In contrast, "Crow country" had a good mix of closely juxtaposed environments, "many mountains and sunny plains, all kinds of climates and good things for every season." In the summer the several groups of mountains afforded fresh water, cool air, good grass for the horses, and plenty of elk, deer, and antelope with skins fit for dressing. In the autumn the plains were an abundant source of buffalo and beaver. In the winter the wooded bottoms of the incised valleys provided shelter, cottonwood bark or saltweed for the horses, and buffalo meat for the members of the tribe.

This example of regionalization by an Indian embraced an area of well over a hundred thousand square miles, and is a remarkable forerunner of the more deterministic and idiosyncratic type of geography with a monocultural perspective which characterized some of the teaching and writing by American geographers in the years before and immediately after the incorporation of the Association of American Geographers.

Modelling and the Behavioral Tradition

Much of Ackerman's monograph and most of his presidential address to the Association of American Geographers of five years later were concerned with suggesting new concepts, procedures, and objectives for geographical research.[27] In retrospect they can be seen as major contributions to the then seminal movement within American geography, but Ackerman drew most of his suggestions from developments which were already underway in other sciences. Both works contain numerous references to post-1950 publications by nongeographers, but for two of his suggested developments Indians provide far earlier, albeit cruder and quite unrelated, antecedents. Ackerman's plea for studies of distributions in the abstract clearly anticipated the emergence of model building within geography. Likewise, his recommendation that the heavy commitment to studies within economic constraints should be supplemented by other approaches, together with his advice to seek a common front with the behavioral sciences, heralded the study of behavioral patterns by geographers.

Modelling had been practiced by Indians from a relatively early date. In 1607 the Indians of Virginia entertained John Smith "with strange conjurations."[28] A fire was encircled with meal. In turn this was encircled by two further circles of corn, after which sticks were placed between the middle and outer circles. They imagined the world to be like a trencher (a flat, wooden, and usually circular plate), of which they occupied the center. The fire symbolized themselves, the inner circle the limits of their territory, the middle circle the coast of their land mass, and the outer circle the edge of the world. The sticks between the middle and outer circles symbolized Smith's country. In 1762 an itinerant preacher of the Delaware nation used as a visual aid a kind of map which he claimed to have drawn under th direction of the Great Spirit.[29] It was a fifteen-inch square of deerskin, on which was drawn or painted an eight-inch inner square, two adjacent corners of which were left open. The inner square represented the heavenly region intended by the Great Spirit as the home for all Indians in their future life. The surrounding area had been intended as their home in this life. When oriented correctly, the right-hand edge of the skin was the edge of the Great Salt Water Lake (Atlantic Ocean), across which the white men had come. The open lower right corner of the inner square had once been the Indians' corridor from this world to the next, but it had been closed by the white men. That at the upper right had been opened up by the Great Spirit as an alternative corridor, but the approach was both dangerous and difficult to pass through. This visual aid was used in urging the Delawares to forswear the ways of the whites, but the preacher must rank as one of North America's earliest commercial cartographers as he recommended its use as a mnemonic and traded copies either for one buck skin or two doe skins each. As a visual aid it was clearly effective, and is further evidence of the ability of Indians to develop and comprehend simple concentric models of the kind developed by von Thünen for rural land use, or Burgess for urban growth and structure.

The introduction of network analysis into transport geography in the late 1950s and early 1960s might have come earlier if geographers had had less ready access to accurate cartographic representations of complex contemporary networks, and had been more familiar with the topological representations of routeways which were a characteristic of Amerindian maps. That drawn by a Chickasaw chief in 1737 and already referred to is a good example, but a somewhat earlier one dating from between 1720 and 1725 shows the linkages between the nations in the hinterland of the British colonies of South Carolina and Virginia in a purely topological manner and without reference to any topographical features.[30]

The behavioral approach which has recently gained strength within geography has necessitated, among other things, monitoring the spatial behavioral activities of individuals in connection with various kinds of activity. It is doubtful if Amerindians ever had cause to record spatial patterns of human activity at the scale of the dwelling or the settlement, but for larger areas they did so relatively frequently. It was natural extension of their pictographic methods for conveying messages and recording events. Examples occur from throughout the continent. At their simplest, they were representations of specific journeys. Of these a fairly early example is that drawn by a young Indian on his arrival in northern Virginia in 1707 at the end of a devious journey through the Southern Appalachians from what is now southeastern Alabama.[31] Among the drawings made just before her death in 1829 by the last of the Beothucks of Newfoundland is a map which plots in great detail the spatial behavior of both the Indians and whites some eighteen years before, when Captain Buchan had led forty-two marines to Red Indian Lake near the center of the island.[32] It records in remarkable detail Buchan's base camp, his outward and return routes, the killing of two marines by the Beothucks, their retreat after the killing, their camps, etc. Three maps incised on birch bark by a Passamaquoddy chief near Eastport, Maine, in or before 1887, each reconstructed the spatial activities of pairs of Indians on hunting activities.[33] They are of a kind frequently left as messages by Indians for other members of the tribe. One which was found in 1842 by a British officer on the divide between the Ottawa River and Lake Huron was "Forwarded to the United Service Institution [London] in the hope that it may shew young officers how small an effort is needed to acquire that most useful art, Military Sketching, since even Savages can make an intelligible plan."[34] In 1825 an Otto Indian at Council Bluff sketched the route of an expedition against the Arapahos which had terminated in a battle to the south of the upper Arkansas, probably not far from the Spanish settlement at Taos.[35] The map also showed General Atkinson's route of earlier that year up the Missouri from Council Bluff, and the locations of numerous tribes and villages along the upper Missouri before and during the several councils which preceded the various treaties negotiated by him. This map, covering more than three hundred thousand square miles, is an excellent example of the vast areas which some Indians could comprehend.

Retrospect

This chapter has considered similarities between the methods and objectives of geographical inquiry among Amerindians and twentieth-century professional geographers. Obviously the methods and objectives of the former had no influence on those of the latter, but to a surprising extent the one did anticipate the other. The following allegory explains the relationship. Imagine a great opera house in the late eighteenth century, on the occasion of the first night of a new work by a virtually unknown composer. The aristocratic audience arrives late and people greet one another during the performance of a simply scored overture. Having been ignored by most it has been forgotten by the rest when, after an embarrassingly long delay, the curtain rises on the first act. The opera is a great success and becomes part of the standard repertoire but without the overture, the score of which had been overlooked for almost two hundred years until it was quite recently rediscovered by a musicologist. Already fairly familiar with the opera he quickly recognized what the first night audience had failed to appreciate, that the overture anticipates most of the themes in the first act, a few of those in the second, but apparently none of those in the difficult and admittedly problematical third. The musicologist may of course be proved wrong by others who have not yet had time to examine the score of the overture; especially, perhaps, in his opinion that it contains no clues to the third act.

Acknowledgements

The research upon which this chapter is based was supported by financial assistance received at various times from the Newberry Library, the British Academy, the Social Science Research Council (U.K.), and the University of Sheffield Research Fund.

Notes

1. Pre Contact evidence, particularly that which has survived in petroglyphic form, is difficult both to date and to interpret, but there is no reason to suspect that the geographical skills and perspectives of Amerindians changed immediately on contact with Caucasians.
2. Edward A. Ackerman, *Geography as a Fundamental Research Discipline,* University of Chicago Department of Geography Research Paper no. 53 (Chicago: Department of Geography, The University of Chicago, 1958), pp. 4-5.
3. [An untitled manuscript map of the coastline and interior features between Churchill and the lower Coppermine River with an attached key entitled] "An Explanation of a Draught brought by two Northern Indian Leaders Calld Meatonabee and Idot ly azee ..," ca. 1767, Hudson's Bay Company Archives, Winnepeg (hereafter HBCA), G.2/27.
4. Samuel Hearne, *A Journey from Prince of Wales Fort, in Hudson's Bay to*

the Northern Ocean, ed. Richard Glover (Toronto: Macmillan, 1958), pp. 35-36.

5. [A manuscript map of the coast and rivers north of Churchill to beyond Chesterfield Inlet] "Drawn by Nak hek til lok an Iskemo 40 years of age 8th July 1809...," HBCA, E 3/4, fol. 16r; "Chart of North West Coast of Hudsons Bay by an Esquimaux Indian," *Edinburgh Philosophical Journal* 1820/21, p.4, plate 5; "Map of West Shore of Hudson Bay and vicinity by Powon, Churchill, Oct. [1894]," Tyrrell Papers, Thomas Fisher Rare Book Library, University of Toronto.

6. "Rupert House Journals 1838-39," HBCA, B.186/a/58, p. 33, 20 April 1839.

7. Ibid., entry for 16 April 1839; "Survey of Charlton as laid down by Kennewap and Canc-chi-chenis themselves in pencil whilst at Charlton, February and March 1839...," HBCA, G.1/65.

8. Ibid., entry for 13 April 1839.

9. "Sketch Simpson's Beaver preserve Charlton Island as originally laid down by the Indians. 1838/39. Red Ink additions thereto by them 1839/40," dated 1842, HBCA, G.1/68.

10. "Ruperts River District—Copy of Official Correspondence Outfit 1844," HBCA, B.186/b/49, fols. 25r. and v. and 26 r., with untitled map of Charlton Island similar to that dated 1842 but with additions.

11. The original has not survived, but a contemporary copy of Ishi's map of ca. 1914 of the east bank tributaries of the upper Sacramento River appears in Alfred L. Kroeber, "Handbook of the Indians of California," *Bulletin of the Bureau of American Ethnology* 78 (1925): 344, fig. 32.

12. Contemporary transcript of the map and record of the interrogation in Archivo General des Indias, Patronato, Estante l, Cajón 1, Legajo 22, ramo 4, Seville. Translation in George P. Hammond and Agapito Rey, "Don Juan de Oñate ..." *Coronado Cuarto Centennial Publications, 1540-1940,* vol. 6 (Albuquerque: University of New Mexico Press, 1953), 2: 871-77.

13. Alexander de Batz, "Nations Friendly and Hostile to the Chickasaws" with map, Mobile, 7 September 1737, Ministry of the Colonies, Paris, C.13, V.22, General Correspondence of Louisiana, p. 67, translation published in Dunbar Rowland and A. G. Sanders, eds., *Mississippi Provincial Archives 1729-40* (Jackson: Mississippi Department of Archives and History, 1927), 1: 355-56.

14. Gero-Schunu-wy-ka-ie, "This Map was sketched by an Otto Indian Called ... 12 August 1825," National Archives, Washington, D.C., RG75, Map 931.

15. Cadwallader Colden, *The History of the Five Nations* (1727; reprint ed., Ithaca: Cornell University Press, 1958), p. 169.

16. G. Malcolm Lewis, "The Recognition and Delimination of the Northern Interior Grasslands during the Eighteenth Century," in *Images of the Plains,* ed. Brian W. Blouet and Merlin P. Lawson (Lincoln: University of Nebraska Press, 1975), pp. 34-36.

17. James G. Cooper, "On the Distribution of the Forests and Trees of North America, with Notes on the Physical Geography," in *Annual Report of the Board of Regents of the Smithsonian Institution for the Year 1858* (Washington, D.C.: Smithsonian Institution, 1859), pp. 245-80, map on p. 267.

18. Gamaliel Smethurst, *A Narrative of An Extraordinary Escape out of the Hands of the Indians in the Gulph of St. Lawrence ....* (London: printed for the author, 1774), p. 14.

33

19. [Untitled manuscript] map, RG75, Map 821; "Journal of proceedings of a council held in the city of Washington, D.C. with a delegation of Chiefs and braves ... Oct. 7, 1837 at 10 Oclock A.M.," Microcopy T-494, Roll no. 3, National Archives, Washington, D.C.

20. "Map of the Country formerly occupied by the Ioway Tribe of Indians from a map made be Waw-Non-Que-Skoon-A, an Ioway Brave," in Henry R. Schoolcraft, *Information Respecting the History Condition and Prospects of the Indian Tribes of the United States* (Philadelphia: Lippincott Grambo, 1853), Vol. 3, plate 30, with explanation on pp. 256-59.

21. Selwyn Dewdney, *The Sacred Scrolls of the Southern Ojibway* (Toronto: University of Toronto Press, 1975), pp. 57-80.

22. A photographic copy of an untitled topographical sketch by Amos Bad Heart Bull of the setting of the Black Hills Conference of 1876, drawn between 1891 and 1913 and interred in 1947 with the body of Amos Bad Hear Bull, in Amos Bad Heart Bull and Helen Blish, *A Pictographic History of the Oglala Sioux* (Lincoln: University of Nebraska Press, 1967) p. 287.

23. [Transcript by Peter Fidler of a map of the area between the Nelson and Churchill Rivers endorsed] "This sketch Drawn by a YF Indian when I passed Owl River 29th July, 1809," HBCA, E.3/3, fol. 65v.

24. [Transcript by Peter Fidler of a map of the area between the upper South Saskatchewan and Missouri Rivers endorsed] "Drawn by Ki oo cus—or the Little Bear, a Blackfoot Chief 1802," HBCA, E.3/2, fol. 206v and 207r.

25. John Lederer, *The discoveries of ... collected and translated out of Latine ... by Sir William Talbot Baronet* (London: Samuel Heyrick, 1672).

26. [Arapooish in a statement made to Robert Campbell and reported by James H. Bradley in] "My Country," *Contributions to the Historical Society of Montana* 9 (1923) 306-7.

27. Edward A. Ackerman, "Where is a research frontier?," *Annals of the Association of American Geographers* 53, no. 4 (1963): 429-40.

28. Captain John Smith, in Samuel Purchas, *Hakluytus Posthumus or Purchas His Pilgrimes* (London: printed by William Stansby for Henry Fetherston, 1625), the fourth part, pp. 1708-9.

29. John Heckewelder, "An account of the history, manners, and customs of the Indian natives ...," *Transactions of the Historical and Literary Committee of the American Philosophical Society* 1 (1819): 286-90.

30. Indian Cacique, "This Map describing the Scituation of the Several Nations of Indians to the NW of South Carolina was coppyed from a Draught drawn & painted on Deer Skin by an Indian Cacique ...," ca. 1720, British Museum Manuscript Department, London, Sloane 4723.

31. [Contemporary manuscript copy of a map showing the journey made in 1707 by Lamhatty, an Apalachee, from the eastern Gulf Coast through the Southern Appalachians to Northern Virginia], Virginia Historical Society, Ludwell Papers, vol. 4, no. 13, Richmond; reproduced in David I. Bushnell, Jr., "The Account of Lamhatty," *American Anthropologist,* n. 5. 10(1908); between 570 and 571.

32. Shannadithet, "Captain Buchan's visit to the Red Indians in 1810-11 when the two marines were killed," manuscript ca. 1829, Newfoundland Museum, St. Johns. Redrafted version published in James P. Howley, *The Beothucks*

or Red Indians. The Aboriginal Inhabitants of Newfoundland (Cambridge: Cambridge University Press, 1915), sketch 1.

33. Sapiel Selmo [three maps incised on birch bark, probably collected by Garrick Mallery in 1887], Department of anthropology, National Museum of Natural History, Washington, D.C. Redrafted versions published in Garrick Mallery, "Picture writing of the American Indians," in *10th Annual Report of the Bureau of American Ethnology 1888-9* (Washington, D.C.: Smithsonian Institution, 1893), figs. 456-58.

34. [Untitled birch bark accompanied by the following explanation] "Map drawn by Indians on Birch-Bark and attached to a tree to show their route to others following them, found by Capt. Bainbrigge R1. Engineers at the 'ridge' between the Ottawa and Lake Huron. May 1841," British Library Map Room, London, Royal United Services Institution (Misc.), Folio 3. Reproduced in Ralph T. Coe, comp., *Sacred Circles; Two Thousand Years of North American Indian Art* (Kansas City, Mo.: Nelson Gallery of Art—Atkins Museum of Fine Arts, 1977), p. 236.

35. Gero-Schunu-wy-ka-ie, "The Map was sketched by an Otto Indian . . . he was a member of the war party traced hereon," National Archives, Washington, D.C., R.G. 75, Map. 931.

The Role of Geographers and Geography in the Federal Government 1774-1905

Herman R. Friis

In the National Archives in Washington, D.C., is a treasure trove comprising an official record of the role of geographers and geography in the federal government since 1774. This is a considerable volume, and a significant record of that role of which surprisingly few geographers are aware. Academic training in geography as a recognized discipline in an established university or college department in the United States apparently was not formalized until the last decade of the nineteenth century.

In this review therefore, geography, often in close association with cartography and surveying and mapping, and indeed practices with other earth sciences, has been described; and its professional proponents have been identified and their works noted to the extent that the individuals have been employed by the federal government. It is important to note that throughout the period discussed, "geographer" often has been applied to or used interchangeably with "cartographer," "topographer," and "geologist"; and "geography" with "cartography," "topography," and "geology." Indeed, this close association exists even to this day and for understandable reason.

Gen. George Washington's knowledge of terrain, gained through his years of practical experience in surveying and mapping and exploration, gave him keen appreciation of the significance of geographic and cartographic information in achieving successful operations (Cappon 1971, 1976; De Vorsey 1972; Friis 1958, 1967a; Harley 1976, 1978). He had in his library a copy of Roger Stevenson's *Military Instructions for Officers Detached in the Field*, printed in Philadelphia in 1775 (Harley 1978, chapter 1; Stevenson 1775). You will recall that Washington was attending a meeting of the Continental Congress there in June of that year when he was unanimously elected (15 June) general and commander in chief of all the forces raised, or to be raised, by the United Colonies (Continental Congress 1774–89). It is possible that Stevenson's references to the importance of having a geographer for reconnaissance work in the army were responsible for Washington's early and frequent requests to the Congress for authority to establish a Geographers' Department was still carried in his pocket. On 26 January 1777, he again requested that Congress authorize him to establish a central mapping corps because "the want of accurate Maps of the Country which has hitherto been the Scene of War, has been of great disadvantage to me ..." (Fitzpatrick 1907).

More than two years had elapsed since Washington entered upon his duties before Congress authorized him to employ and attach to his staff personnel qualified to make maps and describe terrain. On 25 July 1777, the Continental Congress resolved

> ... that George Washington be empowered to appoint Mr. Robert Erskine, or any other person that he may think proper, geographer and surveyor of the roads, to take sketches of the country, the seat of war, and to have the procuring, governing, and paying of the guides employed under him .... [Continental Congress 1907, 8:580]

In this resolution is perhaps the first official authorization by the federal government of a geographic agency, the Geographers' Department, which included a geographer-surveyor and assistants on Washington's headquarters staff. Robert Erskine accepted the position and on 27 July entered upon his duties as geographer and surveyor general to the Continental Army (Cappon 1971; Guthorn 1966; Harley, chapter 1; Heusser 1966; Hindle 1956). Upon Erskine's death in 1780, Simeon DeWitt, a much respected member of the staff, was named successor on 15 December 1780 (Burnham 1930; Guthorn 1966; Heusser 1966; Ristow 1961, 1968). During the existence of the department through 1783 more than 130 maps were compiled, nearly all from field reconnaissance, as for example Map No. 105 of the Morristown locale in New Jersey (Heusser 1966). Many were used and annotated by General Washington (Heusser 1966; L. Martin 1932).

Washington was aware of the need for attaching a geographer-surveyor to his Southern Army. On 11 July 1781, after considerable negotiations, he obtained the services of Thomas Hutchins, a former British officer of considerable skills, for the post (Brown 1959; Cappon 1971; Continental Congress, 1775–89, index; Guthorn 1966; Harley 1976; Hicks 1932; Hutchins 1778; Marshall 1973; Ristow 1968). Among the maps in the

Continental Congress Papers is a copy made by Hutchins of the so-called "Western Country" in 1781 (Continental Congress Item 48, p.249). With the termination of hostilities in 1783 and the nearly complete dissolution of the army, all but several of the geographer-surveyors attached to the Geographers' Department returned to civilian life (Friis 1965, 1967a; Guthorn 1966; Hindle 1956, pp. 243, 319, 332).

One of the first acts of the Congress following the Treaty of Peace in 1783 was to establish a system of surveying and mapping, and to provide for the orderly disposal of the large public domain. The General Land Office, created by the Ordinance of 1785, initiated the land surveys and the preparation of land plats and related terrain descriptions westward from the Ohio River where it crosses the Ohio-Pennsylvania boundary (Conover 1923; Ford 1910; Pattison 1957, 1959; Treat 1910). Thomas Hutchins, geographer of the army in 1784, was appointed geographer of the United States to administer the General Land Office.

William Tatham, a rather eccentric geographer-cartographer, explorer, and confidante of prominent American philosophers, scientists, and government officials, notably Thomas Jefferson, in 1789 was appointed by Gov. Beverley Randolph of Virginia to organize and supervise a geographical department at the capitol building in Richmond (Herndon 1969, pp. 346-98; Williams 1921, pp. 154-79). Perhaps the first state geographical department, its establishment was made possible in response to a request from Secretary of War Henry Knox, who was interested in the compilation of a map of and related intelligence pertaining to the western frontier of Virginia.

Tatham also was commissioned to compile from field survey and archival sources a large-scale county map of Virginia and the contiguous area of Maryland. In conjunction with the projection of this map, he compiled and published "A Topographical Analysis of the Commonwealth of Virginia, 1790-1791." Tatham was employed from time to time by the War Department and the State Department in the compilation and drafting of maps and a variety of engineering drawings. During the War of 1812, for example, he was employed by the State Department to prepare a map of the northeastern bounday area astride the St. Johns River, which became evidence submitted by the United States during the arbitrations with Great Britain concerning the boundary.

During the last several years of his life he lived in Richmond, Virginia. On 22 February 1819, the inhabitants of the city gathered on the grounds of the capitol building to honor George Washington's birthday. The first of several guns sounded in deafening salute. Before the smoke of the first salvo had cleared and as the second resounded across the square, a figure sprang into the path of fire and was blown to bits. William Tatham was no more! What happened to his archival collection and library of books which contemporary obituaries describe as occupying several rooms of his home? During the later years of his life he tried valiantly, but unsuccessfully, on numerous occasions to sell it to the federal government as the nucleus of a national library. The War Department was interested, especially for the Topographical Bureau at that moment being created, but the Congress failed to approve funds for the purchase (Herndon 1969, pp. 346–98; Morrison 1917, 1922).

It is of interest to note that in the United States Military Academy at West Point in April 1818, a Department of Geography, History, and Ethics was organized and instruction was initiated by Rev. Cave Jones, the chaplain, who was appointed professor in charge (Cullum 1891; Depuy 1951; Friis 1967a; Heitman 1903).

In August 1818, a Topographical Bureau was added to the Engineer Department of the army in Washington, D.C. Capt. John James Abert, a topographical engineer officer, was appointed in 1829 to succeed Isaac Roberdeau as chief. He remained in charge until his death in 1863 (Beers 1942; Friis 1967a; Dupuy 1951; Heitman 1903). From these beginnings there evolved a centralized office of the federal government responsible for topographical, geographical, and cartographical activities performed by a corps of professionally trained topographical engineers. Many of their field notes, maps, illustrations, and reports are excellent examples of professional geographical observation and interpretation. It is of interest to point out that Abert was elected a member of the Council of the American Geographical and Statistical Society for 1859–60 (Wright 1952, p. 399).

Throughout the 1830s, Lieutenant Colonel Abert actively urged the formation of a Corps of Topographical Engineers. After much persuasion and with ample proof of the competencies of his associates in the Topographical Bureau, he was successful. On 7 July 1838 the secretary of war appointed him colonel in charge of the corps (Beers 1942; Friis 1967a). He was given a rather generous opportunity to develop the program in which he recognized geographical training. He expressed himself at some length on this subject in a communication to the secretary of war in the spring of 1839 (Abert 1839).

In the late 1830s David H. Burr, topographer in the Post Office, was appointed "Geographer to the House of Representatives of the United States." His most important contribution was an "Atlas Exhibiting the Post Offices, Railroads, Canals, and the Physical and Political Divisions of the United States. . ." published in Washington in 1839.

One of the most important topographical surveys and detailed descriptions of an extensive landscape during the 1830s and 1840s was that made by the French-born topographer-geographer, Joseph Nicolas Nicollet (Bray 1969; Gallaher 1945; Jackson 1970; Quetelet 1844; Winchell 1891). It comprised much of the Missouri River basin. He was ably assisted in these surveys, in map compilation, and in the preparation of the reports by Lt. John Charles Frémont. A significant product of these surveys were two large maps of the region. One, on a scale of 1:1,200,000 (roughly twenty miles to one inch), was published with Nicollet's lengthy report which is filled with a wealth of information about the physical and cultural features of the landscape (Nicollet 1843a, 1843b).

Frémont was one of the most noteworthy and knowledgeable topographic engineers of the 1840s. His passion for geographical observation and topographical mapping played a large role in opening the American west to settlement (Dupuy 1951; Goetzmann 1966; Gudde 1958; Jackson and Spence 1970). He pioneered the surveying, mapping, and description of the Oregon Trail and defined and described with surprising clarity and accuracy the primary physiographic regions and gross morphology of western United State (Crampton 1956; Frémont 1845a, 1845b, 1845c; Jackson and Spence 1970, volumes 1-3; Nevins 1955).

Matthew Fontaine Maury was appointed officer-in-charge of the navy's Depot of Charts and Instruments in 1842 (Friis 1960, 1970, 1972; Williams 1963; Wright 1952). During his nearly twenty years of this charge, he became one of the federal government's most proficient and expressive geographers. His works, including *The Physical Geography of the Sea* ... (first published in 1855) and *Wind and Current Charts* of the world, gained for him international recognition (Leighly 1963; Maury 1844, 1851, 1854, 1855).

He abstracted the large fund of observations recorded in diaries, journals, and logbooks that had lain dormant in the navy and in private hands. According to plan, he systematically plotted this information in map form as wind and current charts, sailing charts, and whale charts. He was responsible for the compilation of many nautical charts based primarily on the results of extensive hydrographic surveys made during explorations of the Arctic, Pacific, and Atlantic Oceans, most of which were authorized on the basis of his recommendations. He prepared, read, and published many scientific papers of a geographical nature, and authored geographies and atlases (Brown 1944; Williams 1963). He was one of this country's foremost crusaders for scientific geographical exploration, thematic mapping, and geographical analysis during the nineteenth century. It was Maury who, in the late 1850s, urged international cooperation in scientific exploration and investigation of Antarctica, one hundred years before the International Geophysical Year activities on that vast continent (1956-58).

Maury was a member and an officer of the American Geographical and Statistical Society of New York, and a contributor to its *Bulletin*. Dr. John K. Wright recognized Maury's contributions to science when he said that indeed Maury

> touched upon most of the larger geographical problems and developments that were of special interest to the Society during its early years.... [Wright 1952, p. 24]

In February 1854, two years after the founding of the society, Maury was invited to give its first "Annual Address," which was published in its *Bulletin* (1, no. 3 [1854]: 1–31). He was elected vice-president of the society for 1855, 1856, and 1858 (Wright 1952, p. 33).

In 1853 Congress authorized the secretary of war to undertake a systematic survey along four east-west routes from the Mississippi River to the Pacific Ocean, to determine the best and most practicable route for a railroad. A fifth route was run in California (Albright 1921; Goetzmann 1966; W. Jackson 1952; Lewis 1962; Meisel 1926; Wheat 1957–63; Wright 1952). In order to achieve the prescribed goals, the secretary of war wisely established an Office of Explorations and Surveys which became in effect a kind of detached office of the Corps of Topographical Engineers. Civilian scientists—geologists, topographers, botanists, biologists, anthropologists, archeologists, artists, cartographers, meteorologists, and physical geographers especially—were appointed to positions with each of the topographical engineer units in charge of specific assigned segments of the route to be surveyed (Brendel 1880; Brown 1930; Emmons 1897; McVaugh 1956; Taft 1951).

One of the most important accomplishments of these surveys was the compilation and publication of a reasonably accurate two-sheet landform map of the United States west of the Mississippi River, on a scale of 1:3,000,000 (roughly fifty miles to one inch).

The twelve volumes of published reports, maps, diagrams, tables, and numerous black-and-white and color plates (such as the landscape view of "Sheyenne") covered a wide variety of scientific subjects, including specially landscape description. They constitute a primary source of information about the American west at midcentury (Albright 1921; Meinig 1955; Meisel 1926; War 1854–55, 1859–60; Webb 1931).

Johann G. Kohl, a professional employee of the U.S. Coast Survey and an articulate exponent of geography in government, gave a rather lengthy public lecture in 1856 at the Smithsonian Institution in Washington on the meaning of geography and maps (Kohl 1857). In his introduction, he noted that

> It cannot be denied that there has from the beginning been something that was called *geography*; but it has been a plant of very tardy growth. So far as it was not a part of astronomy it was at best always considered as a handmaid to other sciences, and had never that noble independence of which it is susceptible. Even yet, geography is far from the culminating point. But we predict for it better days ... geography, rightly understood, is not to be considered merely as the humble assistant and follower of the sciences but as the guide or governor of them all. [Kohl 1857].

As had William Tatham half century earlier, Kohl strongly advocated the need of a central "chartographical library" for the federal government. This suggestion bore fruit in the 1890s as the Map Division of the Library of Congress. We should note that in Daniel Coit Gilman's address of 31 January, 1871 given before the American Geographical and Statistical Society in New York, covering the advances in geographical work in the United States during the decade 1861–71, he observed that the records of these numerous government activities were tucked away in the offices in Washington where

> the extreme difficulty of ascertaining what there is ... is only surpassed by the difficulty of knowing how to get at it .... [Wright 1952, p. 86]

He further enunciated the need for the government to authorize the creation of a

> bureau of maps, charts, and geographical memoirs where "all these vast accumulations" could be "stored, classified and rendered accessible, like the books in the Library of Congress." [Wright 1952, p. 86]

Gilman of Yale and Arnold Guyot of Princeton were the two leading college professors of geography during this period of the nineteenth century. Gilman's speech is further evidence of the need so clearly demonstrated earlier by Tatham, Abert, Kohl, Maury, and others. In

1934 such a centralization of the archives of the federal government was achieved with the creation of the National Archives in Washington, D. C.

Lorin Blodget, pioneer American meteorologist, was responsible for compiling from statistics in the Office of the Surgeon General of the War Department a set of "Isothermal and Hyetal Charts for the Mean of the Seasons and the Year," and with it a report on "The Principal Features of the Distribution of Heat and Rain in the United States," both of which were published by the War Department in 1856 (Blodget 1856). A number of these maps appear to have been included in his *Climatology of the United States . . .*, published in 1857 (Blodget 1857). This is one example of many government publications during the 1830s through the 1860s authored by physical scientists (geographers) during a period of tenure with a federal agency (Friis 1974).

Immediately following the Civil War, the federal government launched a major program of topographical, geological, and geographical surveys of the United States west of the Mississippi River (Bartlett 1962; Emmons 1897; Friis 1958; Jackson 1952; Schmeckebier 1904; Stegner 1954). Two of these surveys, one by John Wesley Powell and one by Ferdinant V. Hayden, were administered by the Interior Department. Two others, one by Clarence King and one by George M. Wheeler, were administered by the War Department. Interestingly, three of these surveys have "Geographical" in their official title. All four did indeed produce geographical publications of fundamental importance, especially to historical geographers and historians.

Lieutenant Wheeler's survey was titled "U.S. Geographical Surveys West of the Hundredth Meridian." In addition to surveying and mapping for topography compiled on matching sheets, many of the published or printed sheets were overprinted in gradient tints denoting the kind of land use. One of the published volumes of scientific results includes a chapter on "geographical results."

In 1879 Congress, with the recommendation of the National Academy of Sciences, dissolved these four surveys and in their place authorized the creation of the "U.S. Geological and Geographical Survey," in the Department of the Interior (Bartlett 1962). Subsequently "Geographical" was deleted from the title. In its second year John Wesley Powell, geologist, geographer, ethnologist, and explorer (who in 1879 had published his classic study of the arid lands of the United States [Hewes 1975; Powell 1879]), was appointed director of the survey. Under his leadership, it included emphasis on geographical research on and studies of natural resources.

Francois E. Matthes, geologist, geographer, and topographer, was assigned in the 1890s to survey and map the area in the Grand Canyon identified on his planetable drawing and quadrangle compilation as the "Bright Angel Sheet" at a scale of 1:45,000 with contour interval at fifty feet. Matthes was elected a founding member of the Association of American Geographers.

Shortly after his appointment as director, Powell selected the exceptionally well-qualified Henry Gannett, topographer of the Hayden surveys, to be "Chief Geographer of the U.S. Geological Survey," a position he held until his death in 1914 (Bartlett 1962; Brown 1932; Darton 1917; North 1914). During his nearly thirty-five years as "Geographer," Gannett

> supervised [and authored] the compilation of gazetteers, compiled geographical materials for general and contour maps, analyzed river profiles, compiled publications on boundaries and areas of our States and Territories, and was responsible on detail to the Bureau of the Census as Geographer for work on the 1880, 1890 and 1900 census publications .... [Darton 1917, p. 69]

One of his many maps compiled for the censuses shows the "Yield of Hay and Forage per acre in the United States, 1900." In 1891 Gannett published in the *Journal of the American Geographical Society* a map showing the physiographic regions of the United States (p. 23). Between 1897 and 1899 he contributed the "Map Notices" to the *Journal.*

Collaborating with Gannett from time to time in the survey were several geographers, among them Richard U. Goode and E. M. Douglas. Gannett was a founding member of the Association of American Geographers (1904).

The status and value of geography were frequently discussed in the reports of the commissioner of education. In his report for 1888–89, for example, is the following statement: "the value of geography is questionable, since it is so ephemeral as information ... " However, in the 1892–93 report we learn that

> the report of the Committee of Ten on secondary studies has indicated that the study of geography in the schools is the center of all scientific instruction ... the link as it were which connects all branches of science ...

In 1890 President Benjamin Harrison by executive order created the United States Board of Geographical Names. This board included appointed members, most of whom were in federal agencies. Through the years to date, many members have been geographers and members of the

Association of American Geographers (Burrill 1945, pp. 647–48).

At the annual meeting of the American Association for the Advancement of Science held in St. Louis on 26 December 1903, Prof. William Morris Davis, as vice-president and retiring chairman of Section E (geology and geography), presented a paper on "Geography in the United States" that has achieved historic significance (Davis 1904). Near the end of his paper, Davis emphasized that "from such a union [an American geographers' union] I am sure that geography would gain strength" (Davis 1904, p. 185). During 1904 Davis and other earth scientists discussed the subject, and in Washington perfected plans for a formal organizational meeting of interested qualified scientists in Philadelphia at the 29 December 1904 sessions of the American Association for the Advancement of Science.

Davis presided at the Philadelphia meeting of the new organization (AAG), and read a short prologue titled "The Opportunity for the Association of American Geographers, " in which he prophesied that by a cooperative effort on the part of the members in so associating themselves,

> We shall have taken an important step in the development of geographical science for it cannot be doubted that students on the different sides of our subject have as a rule lived too far apart .... [Davis 1905, p. 86]

Membership in the new organization was limited by election to persons who had done creditable original work in some branch of geography, the scope of which subject as then understood included a wide variety of disciplines in the earth sciences. Significantly, of the forty–nine professional geographers who qualified for and accepted founding membership in the association, fourteen, or nearly a third, held positions of responsibility in the federal government and had professional qualifications. These members were as follows (Association of American Geographers Council Minute Books, pp. 11–12):

Cleveland Abbe, Jr.: geological aid, U.S. Geological Survey.
Oscar P. Austin: chief, Bureau of Statistics, Department of Commerce.
Alfred H. Brook: geologist in charge. Division of Alaskan Mineral Resources, U.S. Geological Survey.
Marius R. Campbell: geologist, U.S. Geological Survey.
Nelson H. Darton: geologist, U.S. Geological Survey.
Henry Gannett: geographer, U.S.Geological Survey.

R. A. Harris: Coast and Geodetic Survey.
George W. Littlehales: U.S. Navy Hydrographic Office.
Françcois E. Matthes: topographer, U.S. Geological Survey.
G. Hart Merriam: chief, U.S. Biological Survey.
W. W. Rockhill: director, Bureau of American Republics.
Leonhard Stegneger: curator, Division of Reptiles and Batrachians, Smithsonian Institution.
Bailey Willis: geologist, U.S. Geological Survey.

We conclude our brief history with this list of founding members of the Association of American Geographers who in 1904–5 were employed by the federal government in responsible positions and with creditable original work as an indication that the persons discussed earlier in this paper and their creditable original work could well have qualified them to election to membership in the association, and therefore that they can be identified as geographers. This paper perforce covers only a selection of representative examples. There is much more to this history, deserving of recognition, than we have presented here!

Published Finding Aids to Relevant Records in the National Archives

The following finding aids published by the National Archives include references to records of particular research value to the study of the role of geography and geographers in the federal government prior to 1905. The entries with an asterisk before them are out of print, but may be available in reference libraries. Available in the Central Search Room of the National Archives are various inventories, lists, and other finding aids, and detailed identification and accession inventories.

Guides
    1974. *Guide to the National Archives of the United States.* 884 pp.
    1976. *Index: Journals of the Continental Congress, 1774–1789.* 429 pp.

Preliminary Inventories (arranged by number)
    17. *Adjutant General's Office.* 1949. 149 pp. (RG94)
    23. *United States Senate.* 1950. 284 pp. (RG46)
    38. *Climatological and Hydrological Records of the Weather Bureau.* 1952. 76 pp. (RG27)
  *81. *Cartographic Records of the Office of the Secretary of the Interior.* 1955. 11 pp. (RG48)

103. *Cartographic Records of the Bureau of the Census.* 1958. 108 pp. (RG29)
*105. *Coast and Geodetic Survey.* 1958. 83 pp. (RG23)
*113. *United States House of Representatives, 1789–1946.* 1959. 2 vols. (RG233)
144. *War Department Collection of Revolutionary War Records.* 1970. 29 pp. (RG93)
155. *Office of the Chief Signal Officer.* 1963. 26 pp. (RG111)
185. *United States Military Academy.* 1976. 116 pp. (RG404)

References Cited

The following published or printed references have been useful in the preparation of this paper. There is, of course, a large number of other relevant publications.

Abert, John James. 1839."Communication from John James Abert to the Secretary of War, Spring 1839." In *Letters Issued, Topographical Bureau*, 4: 510–15. Record Group 77 in the National Archives, Washington, D.C. Also Microfilm No. 66, Reel 10–35–5.

Albright, George L. 1921. *Official Explorations for Pacific Railroads.* Berkeley: University of California Press.

Alden, Roland H. 1943. "Early Naturalists in the Far West." *California Academy of Sciences* 20:1–59.

Anonymous. 1820. "William Tatham." *Annual Biography and Obituary for the Year 1820* 4:149-59.

Association of American Geographers Archives 1904–70. In the *American Anthropological Archives of the Smithsonian Institution, Washington, D.C., Council Minute Books, 29 December 1904, pp. 11–12.*

Bartlett, Richard A. 1962. *Great Surveys of the American West.* Norman: University of Oklahoma Press.

Beers, Henry P. 1935. *The Western Military Frontier, 1815–1846.* Philadelphia: published privately.
1942. "A History of the U.S. Topographical Engineers, 1813–1863." *The Military Engineer* 34:287–91, 348–52.

Blodget, Lorin. 1857. *Climatology of the United States, and of the Temperate Latitude of the North American Continent with Isothermal and Rain Charts for Each Season, the Extreme Months, and the Year* ... Philadelphia: J. B. Lippincott and Co.

Bray, Martha C. 1969. "Joseph Nicolas Nicollet, Geographer." In

Frenchmen and French Ways in the Mississippi Valley, edited by John Francis McDermott, pp. 29–55. Urbana: University of Illinois Press.

Brendel, Frederick. 1880. "Historical Sketch of the Science of Botany in North America, 1840–1858." *American Naturalist* 14:25–58.

Brown, Lloyd A. 1959. *Early Maps of the Ohio Valley: A Selection of Maps, Plans, and Views Made by Indians and Colonials from 1763 to 1783.* Pittsburgh: University of Pittsburgh Press.

Brown, Ralph M. 1930. "Trans-montane Routes in Colorado." *Economic Geography* 4:412–24.

1948. *Historical Geography of the United States.* New York: Harcourt, Brace.

Brown, Ralph M. 1930. ". . . Bibliography of Commander Matthew Fontaine Maury, Including a Biographical Sketch." *Virginia Polytechnic Institute* 17, no. 12:1–46.

Brown, Robert M. 1932. "Gannett, Henry (Aug. 24, 1846–Nov. 5, 1914) Geographer . . . . "*Dictionary of American Biography,* 4:123–24.

Burnham, Guy H. 1930. "De Witt, Simeon (Dec. 25, 1756–Dec. 3, 1834)." *Dictionary of American Biography,* 5:274–75.

Burrill, Meredith F. 1945. "Reorganization of the United States Board on Geographical Names." *The Geographical Review* 35, no 4:647–52.

Camp, Charles L. 1953. *Henry R. Wagner's "The Plains and Rockies: A Bibliography of Original Narratives of Travel Adventure, 1800–1860."* Columbus, Ohio: Long's College Book Co.

Cappon, Lester J. 1971. "Geographers and Map-makers, British and American, from about 1750 to 1789." *Proceedings of the American Antiquarian Society* 81:243–71.

1976. *Atlas of Early American History: The Revolutionary Era, 1760–1790.* Princeton: Princeton University Press.

Conover, Milton. 1923. *The General Land Office: Its History, Activities, and Organization.* Baltimore: The Johns Hopkins Press.

Continental Congress, 1774–89. Papers of the Continental and Confederation Congresses and the Constitutional Convention Record Group 360 are in the National Archives, Washington, D.C. They have been microfilmed as Microfilm Publication M247 in 204 rolls. A subject, name, and place index has been compiled, from which a readout is available from the National Archives for $8.60. These records are a primary source of information about the history of official mapping and geography in the Revolutionary Army during the period 1774-83, and for the beginnings of the United States 1783-89.

1907. *Journals of the Continental Congress, 1774-1789.* 8:580. Washington, D.C.: United States Government Printing Office.

Crampton, Gregory, and Griffin, Gloria G. 1956. "The San Buenaventura,

Mythical River of the West." *Pacific Historical Review* 25:163–71.

Cullum, George W. 1891. *Biographical Register of the Officers and Graduates of the U.S. Military Academy ... 1802 to 1890.* 3 vols. Boston: Houghton, Mifflin & Co.

Darton, N. H. 1917. "Memoir of Henry Gannett" *Annals of the Association of American Geographers* 7:68–70.

Davis, William Morris. 1904. "Geography in the United States." *Science, N. S.* 19:120–32, 178–186.

1905. "The Opportunity for the Association of American Geographers." *Bulletin of the American Geographical Society* 37:84–86.

De Vorsey, Louis, Jr. 1972. "A Background to the Surveying and Mapping at the Time of the American Revolution: An Essay on the State of the Art." In "Introduction to the American Revolution, 1775–1783," in *An atlas of eighteenth-century maps and charts...*, compiled by W. Bart Greenwood. Washington, D.C.: Naval History Division, Department of the Navy.

Dryer, Charles R. 1924. "A Century of Geographic Education in the United States." *Association of American Geographers, Annals* 14: 117–49.

Dupree, Hunter A. 1947. *Science in the Federal Government.* Cambridge: Harvard University Press.

Dupuy, Richard E. 1951. *Men of West Point: The First 150 Years of the United States Military Academy.* New York: Sloane.

Ehrenberg, Ralph E. 1968. "Cartographic Records of the Red River Region in the National Archives." *Red River Valley Historian* 2: 5–7.

Emmons, Samuel F. 1897. "The Geology of Government Exploration." *Science, n.s.* 5:1–5, 42–51, 105–6.

Fitzpatrick, John C. 1907. *The Writings of George Washington* 7:63–68. Washington, D.C.: Government Printing Office.

Flint, Timothy. 1828. *A Condensed Geography and History of the Western States, or the Mississippi Valley.* 2 vols. Cincinnati: E. H. Flint.

Ford, Amelia C. 1910. "... Colonial Precedents for Our National Land System as It Existed in 1800 ...." *University of Wisconsin Bulletin*, no. 352:323–477.

Freeman, Douglas S. 1948–54. *George Washington. A Biography*, 5:524. New York: Scribner.

Frémont, John C. 1845a. *Report of the Exploring Expedition to the Rocky Mountains in the Year 1843 and to Oregon and North California in the Years 1843–44.* Washington, D.C.: Blair & Rives.

———. 1845b. "*A Report of the Exploring Expedition to Oregon and North California in the Years 1843–44, by Brevet Capt. J. C. Fré*mont."

In *House Executive Doc.* 166, Serial 467, pp. 103–583. U.S., 28th Cong., 2d sess.

―――. *1845c.* *"Topographical Map of the Road from Missouri to Oregon ... In VII Sections ... From the Field Notes and Journal of Captain John C. Fre*mont . . . ." Scale ten miles to one inch. Dimensions of each sheet 15½ by 24½ inches. Printed map on paper. Records of the Office of Chief of Engineers, Map U.S. 155, NA.

1854. *The Exploring Expedition to the Rocky Mountains, Oregon and California: To Which is Added a Description of the Physical Geography of California.* Buffalo: Miller, Orton and Mulligan.

Friis, Herman R. 1958. "Highlights in the First Hundred Years of Surveying and Mapping and Geographical Exploration of the United States by the Federal Government, 1775–1880." *Surveying and Mapping Quarterly Journal* 18, no. 2:186–206.

―――. *1960. "Matthew Fontaine Maury, Captain, U.S. Navy, American Pioneer in Polar Research and Progenitor of the International Geophysical Year Program in the Antarctica, 1840–1860." U.S. Antarctic Projects Officer, Bulletin* 1, no. 6:23–29.

―――. *1965. "A Brief Review of the Development and Status of Geographical and Cartographical Activities of the United States Government: 1776–1818." In Imago Mundi: A Review of Early Cartography*, edited by C. Koeman, pp. 68–80. Amsterdam: N. Israel.

―――. *1967a. "Highlights of the Geographical and Cartographical Contributions of Graduates of the U.S. Military Academy with a Specialization as Topographical Engineers prior to 1860." Proceedings of the Eighth Meeting of the New York-New Jersey Division of the Association of American Geographers at West point*, 1:10–29.

―――. *1967b "The Image of the American West at Midcentury (1840–1860): A Product of Scientific Geographical Exploration by the United States Government." In The Frontier Re-examined*, edited by John Francis McDermott, pp. 49–63. Urbana: University of Illinois Press.

―――. *1970a. "The Documents and Reports of the United States Congress: A Primary Source of Information on Travel in the West, 1783–1861." In Travelers on the Western Frontier*, edited by John Francis McDermott, pp. 112–67. Urbana: University of Illinois Press.

―――. *1970b. "A Brief History of Matthew Fontaine Maury's Large Role in the Interests of the United States in the Arctic, Especially the Northwest Passage prior to 1861." In Etudes d'Histoire Maritime Presentees au XIIIe Congres International des Sciences Historiques par la Commission Internationale d'Histoire Maritime a l'Occasion de son*

XIIIe Colloque, Moscou, 16-23 Aout 1970, pp. 147–79. Paris: École Pratique des Hautes Études.

———. 1972. *"The Beginnings of Topo-hydrographic Activities of the United States Navy Department in Exploration of the Arctic Prior to 1870 as Reflected in the Official Records in the National Archives in Washington, D.C."* Proceedings of the Royal Society of Edinburgh, Section B (Biology) 73:35–43.

———. 1974. *"Statistical Cartography in the United States prior to 1870 and the Role of Joseph C. G. Kennedy and U.S. Census Office."* The American Cartographer 1, no. 2:131–57.

———. 1975. *"The Role of the United States Topographical Engineers in Compiling a Cartographic Image of the Plains Region."* In Images of the Plains: the Role of Human Nature in Settlement, edited by Brian W. Blouet and Merlin P. Lawson, pp. 59–74. Lincoln: University of Nebraska Press.

Gallaher, Ruth A. 1945. "J. N. Nicollet, Map Maker." *Palimpset* 26: 289–302.

Goetzmann, William H. 1966. *Exploration and Empire: The Explorer and Scientist in the Winning of the American West.* New York: Alfred A. Knopf.

Guthorn, Peter J. 1966. *American Maps and Map Makers of the Revolution.* Monmouth Beach, N.J.: Philip Freneau Press.

Hall, James. 1838. *Notes on the Western States; Containing Descriptive Sketches of their Soil, Climate, Resources, and Scenery.* Philadelphia: H. Hall.

Harley, J. Brian. 1976. "George Washington, Map Maker" *Geographical Magazine* 48:588-94.

———. 1978. *"The Contemporary Mapping of the American Revolutionary War."* In Mapping the American Revolutionary War, by J. Brian Harley, pp. 1–44. Chicago: University of Chicago Press. See pp. 19–20.

Heitman, Francis B. 1903. *Historical Register and Dictionary of the United States Army.* 2 vols. Washington, D.C.: Government Printing Office.

Herndon, G. Melvin. 1969. *William Tatham and the Culture of Tobacco*, pp. 346–98. Coral Gables, Fla.: University of Miami Press.

Heusser, Albert H. 1966. *George Washinton's Map Maker: A Biography of Robert Erskine . . . .* New Brunswick, N.J.: Rutgers University Press.

Hewes, Leslie. 1975. *"The Great Plains; One Hundred Years after Major John Wesley Powell."* In Images of the Prairies: The Role of Human Nature in Settlement, edited by Brian W. Blouet and Merlin P.

Lawson, pp. 203–214. Lincoln: University of Nebraska Press.

Hicks, Frederick C. 1932. "Hutchins, Thomas (1730–Apr. 28, 1789)." *Dictionary of American Biography*, 9:435–36.

Hindle, Brooke. 1956. *The Pursuit of Science in Revolutionary America, 1735–1789.* Chapel Hill, N.C.: University of North Carolina Press.

Hutchins, Thomas. 1778. *A Topographical Description of Virginia, Pennsylvania, Maryland, and North Carolina ... London.* Reprint. Edited by Frederick Charles Hicks. Cleveland: Burrows Brothers Co., 1904.

Jackson, Donald D., ed. 1962. *Letters of the Lewis and Clark Expedition with Related Documents, 1783–1854.* Urbana: University of Illinois Press.

Jackson, Donald D., and Spence, Mary Lee, eds. 1970. *The Expeditions of John Charles Frémont.* 3 vols. Vol. 1, *Travels from 1838 to 1844, with a portfolio of maps.* Urbana: University of Illinois Press.

Jackson, William T. 1952. *Wagon Roads West: A Study of Federal Road Surveys and Construction in the Trans-Mississippi West, 1846–1896.* Berkeley: University of California Press.

Leighly, John B. 1963. *The Physical Geography of the Sea and Its Meteorology, by Matthew Fontaine Maury.* Edited by John B. Leighly. Cambridge: Harvard University Press. See especially Leighly's introduction, pp. i–xxx.

Lewis, G. Malcolm. 1962, "Changing Emphases in the Description of the Natural Environment of the American Great Plains Area." *Transactions and Papers of the Institute of British Geographers* 30:75–90.

Marshall, Douglas W. 1973. "The British Engineers in America: 1755–1783." *Journal of the Society for Army Historical Research* 51:155–63.

Martin, Edwin T. 1952. *Thomas Jefferson: Scientist.* Lincoln: Nebraska State Historical Society.

Martin, Lawrence, ed. 1932. *The George Washington Atlas.* Washington, D.C.: U.S. George Washington Bicentennial Commission.

Maury, Matthew Fontaine. 1844. "Remarks on the Gulf Stream and Currents of the Sea." *American Journal of Science and Arts* 47:161–81.

_____. *1851. Explanations and Sailing Directions to Accompany the Wind and Current Charts....* New York: C. Alexander.

_____. *1854. "Progress of Geographical Science." American Geographical and Statistical Society* 1, no. 3:1–31.

_____. *1855. The Physical Geography of the Sea.* New York; Harper.

McVaugh, Rogers. 1956. *Edward Palmer, Plant Explorer of the American West.* Norman: University of Oklahoma Press.

Meinig, Donald W. 1955. "Isaac Stevens: Practical Geographer of the Early Northwest." *Geographical Review* 45:542–58.

———. 1965. *"The Mormon Culture Region: Strategies and Patterns in the Geography of the American West."* Association of American Geographers, Annals 55:191–220.

Meisel, M. 1926. *A Bibliography of American Natural History: The Pioneer Century, 1769–1865* 3 vols. New York: Premier Publishing Co.

Morrison, A. J. 1917. "Notes on the Career of William Tatham." *Virginia Magazine of History and Biography* 25:198–199.

———. 1922. *"Colonel Tatham and Other Engineers." William and Mary Quarterly*, 2d ser. 2:81–84.

Nevins, Allan. 1955. *Frémont: Pathmaker of the West.* New York: Longmans, Green.

Nicollet, Joseph N. 1843a. "Report Intended to Illustrate a Map of the Hydrographical Basin of the Upper Mississippi River, Made by I. [sic] N. Nicollet, while in Employ under the Bureau of the Corps of Topographical Engineers." In *Senate Doc.* 237, Serial 380, pp. 1–237. U.S., 26th Cong. 2d sess.

———. 1843b. *"Exhibited His Original Map of the Northwestern Territory of the United States, Made from Personal Observations,and Read an Account of His Geographical Exploration of the Sources of the Mississippi ₍sic₎."* Proceedings of the American Philosophical Society 3:140–42.

North, S. N. D. 1914. "Henry Gannett." *The National Geographic Magazine* 26:609–13.

Pattison, William D. 1957. *Beginnings of the American Rectangular Land Survey System, 1784–1800.* Chicago: University of Chicago Press.

———. 1959. *"The Survey of the Seven Ranges." Ohio Historical Quarterly* 68:115–40.

Powell, John Wesley. 1879. *Report on the Lands of the Arid Regions of the United States, with a More Detailed Account of the Land of Utah.* U.S. Geographical and Geological Survey of the Rocky Mountain Region. 2d ed. Washington, D.C.: Government Printing Office.

Preuss, Charles. 1958. *Exploring with Frémont.* Edited and translated by Erwin G. Gudde and Elizabeth K. Gudde. Norman: University of Oklahoma Press.

Quetelet, A. 1844. "Joseph Nicolas Nicollet, 1786–1843." *Academie Royale des Sciences, Des Lettres ... Belgique, Annuaries* 10:343–52.

Ristow, Walter W. 1968. " Simeon De Witt, Pioneer American

Cartographer. In *Kartengeschichte und Kartenbearbeitung* ... Bad Godesburg: Kirschbaum Verlag.

———. 1971. *"Maps of the American Revolution: A Preliminary Survey."* Quarterly Journal of the Library of Congress 28:196–215.

———. 1961. *A Survey of the Roads of the United States of America, 1789, by Christopher Colles.* Edited by Walter W. Ristow. Cambridge: Harvard University Press.

Schmeckebier, Lawrence F. 1904."Catalogue and Index of the Hayden, King, Powell and Wheeler Surveys." *U.S. Geological Survey Bulletin*, no. 222:1–208.

Smith, J. Russell. 1952. "American Geography: 1900–1924." *The Professional Geographer*, n.s. 4:4–7.

Stegner, Wallace. 1954. *Beyond the Hundredth Meridian: John Wesley Powell and the Second Opening of the West.* Boston: Houghton Mifflin Co.

Stevenson, Roger. 1775. *Military Instructions for Officers Detached in the Field: Containing a Scheme for Forming a Corps of Partisan* .... Philadelphia: R. Aitken.

Surface, Thomas G. 1909. "Thomas Jefferson: A Pioneer Student of America's Geography." *American Geographical Society Bulletin* 41:743–50.

Taft, Robert. 1951. "The Pictorial Record of the Old West: XIV. Illustrators of the Pacific Survey Reports." *Kansas Historical Quarterly* 19:353–80.

Treat, Payson J. 1910. *The National Land System, 1785–1820.* New York: E. B. Treat & Company.

Vernor, Coolie. 1959. "Mr. Jefferson Makes a Map." *Imago Mundi* ... 14:96–108.

War, secretary of. 1854–55. "Reports of Explorations and Surveys, to Ascertain the Most Practicable and Economical Route for a Railroad from the Mississippi River to the Pacific Ocean. Made under the Secretary of War, in 1854–55...." In *Senate Doc. 78*, vols. 1–11, Serials 758–68. U.S., 33rd Cong., 2d sess.

———. 1859–60."Reports of Explorations and Surveys." In *House Executive Doc.56*, vol. 12, pts. 1 and 2, Serials 1054 and 1055. U.S., 36th Cong., 1st sess.

Webb, Walter P. 1931. *The Great Plains.* Boston: Ginn and Company.

Wheat, Carl I. 1957–63. *Mapping the Transmississippi West, 1540–1861.* 5 vols. San Francisco: Institute of Historical Cartography.

Winchell, N. H. 1891. "Joseph Nicolas Nicollet, 1786–1846." *American Geologist* 8:343–52.

Williams, Frances L. 1963. *Matthew Fontaine Maury, Scientist of the Sea.* New Brunswick, N.J.: Rutgers University Press.

Williams, Samuel C. 1921. "William Tatham, Wataugan," *Tennessee Historical Magazine* 7, no. 3:154–79.

Wright, John K. 1952. *Geography in the Making; the American Geographical Society, 1851–1951.* New York: American Geographical Society.

Working the West: Public Land Policy, Exploration, and the Preacademic Evolution of American Geography

John L. Allen

From the first European settlement of the Atlantic seaboard to the official closing of the frontier in 1890, the cardinal problem in American history might well have been that of land and natural resource exploitation. Because of its pivotal character and because it predated the establishment of academic geography in the United States, the land problem shaped not only the utilitarian American responses to the fertile repository of hope that was the landscape itself, but also gave form to the ways in which that landscape was interpreted and analyzed by those who were the antecedents of academic geographers. As might be expected, the strongest bonds between the land problem and geography as an incipient discipline existed in the exploitation, settlement, and land policy of the American West.

In all the long story of the love affair between Americans and the reality and illusions of their land, no chapter is more meaningful or revealing than that which deals with the West. The West was symbol: for it, as for the New World itself at an earlier time, there existed only maps of blank spaces that had to be filled; also, as the entire continent had once been, the West was a fecund garden of expectation simply because it was such an attractive locale for illusion.[1] And if the responses to the New World landscape from Columbus on can be categorized into the four great classes—belief in limitless natural resources and concomitant unending wealth, hunger for the possession of land in ever-increasing amounts, curiosity about the workings of nature, and the romantic sense of mingled enchantment and awe[2]—which were so central to the land problem, then nowhere were those responses more clearly elicited than in the West.

There were, of course, a number of different Wests in the American mind, depending upon the spatial and temporal location of those who held images and acted upon them. But for the Puritan of 1633 and the Okie of 1933, and for all who came between, the operative spirit was the same—to move westward—and it was this spirit, generated by and, simultaneously, generating the great American responses to the land, which led Americans ever West. Thus the nation grew, westering, discovering its land as it went and thereby creating a decisive American anachronism: the land began to flourish prior to its "scientific" exploration, indeed, partly because it had not yet been discovered.[3]

By the beginning of the early national period, Americans had practiced more than a century and a half of this synchronous geographical expansion and geographical discovery, a time during which there existed no formal frameworks, governmental or academic, for channeling either the responses to the land or the expectation that a nation would grow as it was settled and its people discovered the land they had to work with. The responses and the expectation did not diminish during the first century of national existence. But with the very early emergence of a national government as responsive to the land as were its people, came the development of frameworks or mechanisms which could condition the responses to the land and influence the synchronous growth and discovery. Most of these mechanisms can be identified with public land policy, and they rapidly became something uniquely and distinctively American. It shall be the purpose of this essay to limn some key elements of this Americanization of land policy during the Republic's first century and, concurrently, to shed some light on the preacademic evolution of American geography.

Thomas Jefferson and the Garden of the World

If one great American anachronism was settlement before discovery, then surely equally anachronous was the mapping and sale of land before it had been surveyed, explored, or otherwise "scientifically" known; the second anachronism was to have effects as far-reaching as the first. Prior mapping and sale of land was carried out for good reason, since colonial experience had shown that the nature of society was conditioned heavily by land policy.[4] Recognizing this fact as early as 1784, Thomas Jefferson, chairman of a congressional committee to investigate the land problem, devised the first formal land legislation. Like all Americans, Jefferson responded to the American landscape in the four traditional ways although, for him, the elements of land hunger and scientific curiosity were always paramount. Jefferson's land hunger was not personal but vicarious, a wish to see American farmers—whom he considered "the chosen people of God ... a people which preserve a republic in vigor"[5]—continue to have all the land required for expansion. It was this philosophy which guided Jefferson's drafting of the document that, with revisions, became the Ordinance of 1784, a plan for developing the new territories west of the Alleghenies, territories viewed by Jefferson as the Garden of the World.

Jefferson's plans for the western lands, like the congressional debates that accompanied them, were exercises in metaphysics. They had little to do with the actual geographical facts of the landscape, being more products of Jefferson's geometric imagination and passion for tidiness. Jefferson's plan called for the rectangular definition of ten new states between the ridgeline of the mountains and the Mississippi, each of them comprising two degrees of latitude and with eastern and western boundaries consisting of lines of longitude which passed through the mouth of the Great Kanawha River and the lowest point of the falls of the Ohio.[6] To satisfy his passion for classical names and to forestall the a priori assumption of title by the original states through the designation of a host of "New Virginias," Jefferson provided his checkerboard pattern with synthetic names like Polyptamia and Metropotamia. This scheme of Jefferson's was incorporated in the Land Ordinance of 1784 and, in a version considerably modified as a consequence of James Monroe's experience in the Old Northwest and George Washington's recognition of the difficulties of surveying large divisions, became a part of the Northwest Ordinance of 1787.

Given that Jefferson's imaginatively named rectangles did not become the states west of the Alleghenies, it may seem profitless to point to his draft of 1784 as a meaningful piece of work within the broader context of public land policy. Yet if Jefferson's schema of statemaking by the imposition of vast quadrangles on the unknown landscape was scrapped, the tidy geometry of Jefferson's eighteenth-century French rationalism was not. For in a companion piece of draft legislation, designed to establish a land office for the United States, Jefferson combined his neat geometry with another of his pet ideas, the simplification of all units of measurement into a decimal system. His proposal was based on square units of ten miles on a side. Although the Ordinance of 1785 replaced the 100-square-mile unit with one based on the six-mile side that became the traditional township, Jefferson's concept of square divisions of land, oriented to the cardinal directions, was retained and became the basis for the American rectangular survey. Over three-quarters of the land area of the continental United States is visibly patterned according to this arrangement and is thus "one of the largest monuments to a priorism in all human history." The pattern on our landscape is a clear relic of

Jefferson's response to the land, and of the need he perceived for its mapping and sale prior to scientific exploration or settlement. As the American historian Daniel Boorstin has pointed out, "it is one of the first examples of the peculiar importance of packaging in America."[7]

The creation of a vast and extensive public domain caused a large practical problem in that the system as envisaged by Jefferson supposed survey prior to settlement, while settlers continued to function according to the by-now traditional American process of pouring into open land without regard to legal formalities. Partly in recognition of the need to resolve this issue and partly by way of satisfying his landscape response of scientific curiosity, Jefferson insured that the Ordinance of 1785 provided for the continued appointment of Thomas Hutchins, "Geographer of the United States."[8] Hutchins's reponsibility was the surveying of the first seven "ranges" of public lands in the West, perhaps the first legitimate linking of land policy with what passed for formal geography in the preacademic period.

As the role of Jefferson in the government grew even more important, there were additional similar associations. When he became president in 1801 Jefferson was well prepared to set in motion a chain of explorations that were quite clearly grounded on the two landscape responses that were always foremost with him—land hunger and scientific curiosity. Mingled with these was a third traditional American response, that of romantic enchantment with the unknown lands of the West. The three responses together evoked in Jefferson the Arcadian vision of the Garden of the World, with wonders discovered through scientific inquiry and with an abundance of fertile land which, when managed by effective public policy, could sustain a good and happy society.

The role of Jefferson as the sponsor of the Lewis and Clark Expedition is well known, as is the landmark geographic content of his specific instructions to Lewis which laid down the approach to scientific exploration in the public interest that became the standard for nineteenth-century topographers.[9] Throughout his participation in the planning and implementation of the expedition, Jefferson was influenced by the responses of land hunger, scientific curiosity, and belief in the Garden. What is often forgotten in the many investigations of the great captains and their epic trek is the fact that they were not the only explorers sent westward by Jefferson, nor were they alone in receiving from the president the guidance conditioned by his responses to the American landscape. Wishing to gain knowledge of those areas south of the territory which he had directed Lewis and Clark to traverse, Jefferson sent out parties to explore the country. The first of these expeditions, led by gentleman scientists George Hunter of Philadelphia and William

60

Dunbar of Natchez, was intended as an investigation of the Red River but ended up as a survey of the Ozark plateau.[10] The second, led by Army Capt. Thomas Sparks, traveled over six hundred miles up the Red River before being intercepted by Spanish soldiers sent out from Santa Fe.[11] Jefferson may even have been peripherally involved in the expedition of Zebulon Montgomery Pike into the central Rockies during the same period.[12] These explorations, along with the transcontinental journey of Lewis and Clark to the Pacific and back via the Missouri and Columbia systems, were prophetic of the government's continuing interest in the broadest considerations of the potential of the West, and of the tendency of public policy to prevent the country as a whole from looking at the West narrowly in terms of special interests.[13] And finally, the tasks of Lewis and Clark, of Pike and Hunter and Dunbar, were those of professional geographers. They were the forerunners of the topographical engineers who would take the next great steps in shaping the character of early academic geography in the United States.

Thomas Hart Benton and the Passage to India

For thirty years Thomas Hart Benton, Senator from Missouri, was a guiding force in the formulation of public land policy, exploration in the West, and the westward expansionist movement in general. Most often thought of as the spokesman of "Manifest Destiny," Benton's actual role was deeper than that of an effective orator in behalf of grandiose designs.[14] Throughout his congressional career he championed the cause of the small farmer on the western frontier, successfully arguing for the pricing of land according to actual quality; against the fixing of minimum prices for western lands; and, most significantly, for the protection of settlers who had cultivated public domain prior to legal formalities.[15] It was this latter defense, culminating in the Pre-emption Act of 1841,that secured Benton's fame as a defender of the yeoman. Additionally, his triumph in the passage of the 1841 legislation was clear indication of his perception of the realities of the American frontier process.The Pre-emption Act was the logical necessity that followed from the land legislation initiated by Jefferson in 1784; settlement before discovery was the American way, and Benton's view of the process and the yeoman empire it would create was remarkably like Jefferson's of forty years earlier.

Common understanding of the realities of the American settlement process was not the only link between Jefferson and Benton. Benton himself regarded with mystical reverence an 1824 meeting with the former president, viewing it as a virtual laying-on of hands in which the mantle of western expansionist philosophy was passed from Jefferson to the new senator.[16] Through his own speeches and writings Benton made it clear that he shared Jefferson's landscape response of land hunger, and this response certainly motivated a great deal of Benton's effort in helping to shape a land policy to benefit those who were making the West American. Benton made even more of a case for his role as heir to another of Jefferson's landscape responses, that of romanticism. Even more than Jefferson, Benton viewed the West with wonder and awe and he favored the creation of land policies concomitant with that view. More than just the living heart of the agrarian republic, the West was the passage to India and if it were vital that lands be secured for small settlers for the purpose of protecting the Republic, it was even more vital that these lands serve as the channel through which the wealth of Asia might flow.

Benton's exuberent conception of the passage to India meshed nicely with his interest in the use of public land policy to further republican interests. In 1840–41 he was one of the leaders in the passage of a Senate bill to grant a section of free land to every settler who would take up the land in Oregon, on the grounds that the Lewis and Clark Expedition had proven the logical terminus of the American route to the Orient's wealth to be the mouth of the Columbia River.[17] This bill failed to pass the House and did not become law, but it was the foundation for the Oregon Donation Act of 1850,[18] a piece of legislation which, in the minds of some later legislators, might have represented an experiment which warranted the extension of the doctrine of the homestead. In 1842, a year after the ultimately unsuccessful attempt to induce Oregon settlement, Benton won passage of the bill which authorized John Charles Frémont, his son-in-law, to map the trail to Oregon as far as the South Pass. And in 1849, following Frémont's major explorations along the Oregon Trail and elsewhere in the West (most of these travels at least partly directed by Benton's ambitions for the West), the Missouri senator introduced a bill which would have appropriated monies from public land sales for the development of a transcontinental railway, Benton's final conceptualization of a passage to India. Like his early efforts at land donation, this attempt to initiate a subsidy for a railway was initially fruitless; but Benton's early work and his grandiloquent support of "the grand idea of Columbus. . . An American road to India" were not only prophetic but instrumental in the eventual passage of the acts which subsidized with federal money the Pacific railroad of the 1860's.[19]

Throughout his long career as the imaginative developer of land policies for the West, Benton acted as a shaper of the development of American geography as well. In his sponsorship of John C. Frémont, in particular, Benton served as a catalyst for a sequence of events relating directly to the evolution of geography, as an academic discipline, out of geography, as a science contrived to fulfill national purpose. A few years before the advent of Benton and Frémont as forces in Western affairs, the Army had formally created a Corps of Topographical Engineers, an agency with its origins in George Washington's appointment in 1777 of Robert Erskine as the "first geographer and surveyor in the Continental Army."[20] This lineage of military geographers, which ended with the disintegration of the agency during the Civil War, was responsible for most of the effective exploration of the West from 1840 to 1860.

The most famous of the topographical engineers, even in his own time, was John C. Frémont; yet Frémont himself paid little real attention to his official army role and his mentor, Benton, actively disparaged it. Westward expansion, according to Benton, was "the act of the people going forward without government aid or countenance" and the explorations of his son-in-law, although outwardly the "conception of the government," were "in fact, conceived without its knowlege, and executed upon solicited orders, of which the design was unknown"[21] to anyone but, presumably, Benton and some of his close associates. Frémont did, of course, receive official orders for his explorations, but these were at some variance with the "design" of his private orders from Benton which were related to the aggrandizement of the western interests favored by the powerful senator. Yet, in spite of the curious nature of Frémont's dual derivation of authority from both public and private sectors, his first two expeditions were remarkably successful from the standpoint of Col. J. J. Abert, his commanding officer, and Benton, his "real" commander.

In the summer of 1842, Frémont mapped the Platte River route as far as the South Pass. In the years 1843–44, he carried out a much wider reconnaisance of virtually the entire region west of the Rockies and south of the Snake-Columbia system. During these explorations, his genuine talents for topographical engineering and accumulation of scientific data were not obscured by the semipolitical nature of his private charge. The reports of his expeditions, much publicized by Benton and augmented by the literary romanticism of his wife and amaneunsis, Benton's daughter Jessie, were nevertheless masterpieces of intricate and detailed observation of the western landscape. Such reports were exactly what Frémont's official commander wanted (Abert expressed "great personal pleasure as well as official satisfaction" with them)[22] and if the reports were also colored by Frémont's own boundless ambition and the spirit of manifest destiny of his unofficial commandant, it did not appear to matter.

Frémont's career as a member of the Corps of Topographical Engineers was significant for the evolution of geography as a science in that he became an archetypal figure within the corps and was consciously imitated by his colleagues—in terms of both his excellent scientific approach to data collection, and his willingness to ally himself with private interests. Throughout the period from the completion of Frémont's second expedition in 1844 to the beginning of the Civil War, the corps maintained a tradition which was Humboldtean in its geographic approach, and curiously dualistic in its position as a federal creation closely associated with distinctive regional factions. The romanticism of Benton and Frémont also became a part of the corps; comprehension and appreciation of the facts of the western landscape became more important than analysis of its character. Tremendous volumes of data, collections of specimens, tables of mathematical computations, hundreds of maps and charts, plates of animals and birds and plants, were the products of the corps. Together they presented a picture of the West that was comprehensive, and was the solid factual basis upon which and from which the great hypotheses of American geographic science in the 1870s would be built.

John Wesley Powell and the Arid West

By the time of Benton and Frémont, the synchronous nature of settlement and discovery in the United States had begun to show signs of deterioration, and with the massive surveys that followed Frémont's first efforts, the trend toward scientific exploration prior to effective economic utilization of the lands of the West slowly emerged. The romanticism and land hunger of men like Jefferson and Benton had, it is true, culminated in the Homestead Act of 1862, but that landmark legislation, particularly as it encountered the more arid lands in which previous customs were less feasible, marked the beginning of a new set of discovery and settlement procedures. In the years following the Civil War, as a new wave of settlers began to push into the West after the railways that had resulted, at least partly, from Benton's determination regarding the passage to India, a new system of government exploration related to land policy took form. In 1867, the Department of the Interior created its Geographical and Geological Survey of the Territories. At first the survey continued to provide "scientific" foundation for the mythic hope that the Homestead Act was operable in the West; emanating from the early work of the survey's first director, Ferdinand V. Hayden, came such land legislation as the Timber Culture Act (1873) and the Desert Land Act (1877), based on Hayden's "firm conviction" that increasing rainfall somehow came from settlement of the country. It is significant that, although the assumptions of Hayden and his colleagues were erroneous, the resulting legislation was evidence of the use of scientific exploration to design land policy well in advance of the arrival of major numbers of new settlers in a region.[23]

In the same year that the survey was founded, a little-known professor of natural history from Illinois Wesleyan College commenced the series of western travels in which the explorer's experience would be put to practical use in the promotion of efficient and socially utilitarian western development. From the efforts, in the field and in government bureaus, of John Wesley Powell would emerge a record of scientific achievement, ideas, and concepts that would eventually change the character of land policy, the face of the western landscape, and the nature of American geography as a science.[24] Like Jefferson and Benton earlier, Powell knew the West—but where their knowledge had been secondhand, his was based on experience; and where their visions of the future of the West had been colored by personal fantasies, his was developed out of scientific certainty.

Powell's first major expedition, the 1869 descent of the Colorado River, gave him stature as the greatest American explorer-hero since Frémont. This expedition, largely privately financed, traveled from the Green River in Wyoming all the way to the last set of rapids on the Colorado below the Grand Canyon. On the strength of the scientific potential in the area, as Powell had described it, the federal government appropriated funds for a "Geographical and Topographical Survey of the Colorado River of the West." Powell was appointed director of this survey and directed to make an additional Colorado River journey in 1871-72. On that trip, Powell spent a great deal of his time away from the actual expedition, exploring the plateau lands adjacent to the river and trying to make some sense out of the geographical maze of canyons and mesas and towers.

Out of this expedition and subsequent ones as the Powell Survey continued until 1879, major geographical and geological works were produced.[25] In these Powell concentrated on earth-forming processes and, being a confirmed uniformitarian, translated the processes as he saw them operating into the forces that shaped the mass of canyonlands. With the same Humboldtean sense of detail possessed by Frémont but with a more analytic mind, Powell devised a series of basic definitions which formed the foundation for a great deal of the geographical work of men like William Morris Davis; concepts such as the base level of erosion and definitions like antecedent valley, consequent valley, and transverse valley are just a few of the many precise terms applied by Powell to landforms which, to other explorers, were merely picturesque.[26] As the Powell survey continued, other scientists joined the efforts and, adopting

Powell's attention to process and uniformitarianism, men like Gilbert and Dutton had, by the end of the 1870s, established the nucleus of ideas and concepts around which the soon-to-emerge academic geography would initially coalesce.

As American geography was to benefit from the methods of analysis applied by Powell, so would American land policy be modified by his western experiences. In addition to his central interest in the landform processes that had shaped the West, Powell was concerned about the relationship between the western environment and the future of American settlement in the region. Beginning in 1873 with his first official report on the canyonlands[27] and continuing throughout the decade to culminate in his *Report on the Lands of the Arid Regions* (1878), Powell stressed the differences between the western environment and the eastern one upon which much American land policy had been based, and continued to press for land policies and classification systems more rationally developed for the West. Powell was asking much of the American public and the federal government, for his new land policies required nothing less than the abandonment of the Jeffersonian Garden theme and yielding of the ultimate faith in Benton's manifest destiny. Moreover, Powell required that the standard American rectangular system be abandoned in favor of a more rational division based upon topographic features, a system less arbitrary than that of dividing the land along the lines of Jefferson's tidy geometry.

As might be expected, Powell's report on the arid lands and his recommendations for revisions in land policy were not well received by westerners, particularly those with the dominant vested interests. Indeed, much of Powell's prescience in the report of 1878 seems even more so in the light of the virulent attacks directed against him by those interests. Partially because of the congressional dominance of factions under the control of land speculators, cattle combines, railroad promoters, and other boosters, Powell's rational programs were doomed to initial failure. In later years, with the passage of such land legislation as the Newlands Reclamation Act (1902), the Tennessee Valley Authority (1933), and the Taylor Grazing Act (1934), Powell would be vindicated.[28]

For us he needs no vindication. His work was the first of the land problem literature to focus on basic regional problems with precision and clarity, and to suggest solutions based on a fundamental sense of organization of scientific data. As such, it was a milestone in the development of American geography and marked the end of a transition that had begun with Jefferson's scientific curiosity and the resultant expeditions of Lewis and Clark and their contemporaries, and had carried through Benton's quest for the passage to India and the universalist attempts at data collection by Frëmont. Powell's work represents, as well, the beginning of the end of the relationship between land policy and the evolution of academic geography. It is somehow appropriate that Powell's efforts at the establishment of geographic rationality as a basis for land division would be finished with his resignation as director of the U.S. Geological Survey at the same time as a young University of Wisconsin historian would deliver, to the American Historical Association, a paper calling to the attention of that august body the fact that the frontier of American settlement had been closed. The work of the nineteenth-century geographers was over and the land policies which fostered much of their work were no longer relevant. But in a few short years their impressions on twentieth-century geographical thought would become highly visible.

Notes

1. D. J. Boorstin, *The Americans: The National Experience* (New York: Random House, 1965), p. 223.
2. H. M. Jones, *The Age of Energy: Varieties of the American Experience 1865-1915* (New York: Viking Press, 1970), p. 303.
3. Boorstin, *The Americans*, pp. 223–24.
4. R. M. Robbins, *Our Landed Heritage: The Public Domain 1776-1970*, (Lincoln: University of Nebraska Press, 1976), p. 7.
5. T. Jefferson, *Notes on the state of Virginia* (New York: Harper Torchbook edition, 1964)c pp. 157–58.
6. P. L. Ford, ed., *The Writings of Thomas Jefferson*, vol. 3, 1781-89 (New York: G. P. Putnam's Sons, 1894), pp. 407–11.
7. Boorstin, *The Americans*, p. 245.
8. W. H. Goetzmann, *Army Exploration in the American West 1793-1863* (New Haven: Yale University Press, 1959), p. 6.
9. D. Jackson, *Letters of the Lewis and Clark Expedition with Related Documents* (Urbana: University of Illinois Press, 1962), pp. 61–66.
10. T. Jefferson, *Message . . . Communicating Discoveries Made in Exploring the Missouri, Red River and Washita . . .* (Washington, D.C.: gov't. publ., 1806).
11. T. Freeman and P. Custis, *An Account of the Red River in Louisiana...* (Washingon, D.C.: gov't. publ., 1807).
12. D. Jackson, ed., *The Journals of Zebulon Montgomery Pike*, 2 vols. (Norman: University of Oklahoma Press, 1966).
13. W. H. Goetzmann, *Exploration and Empire: The Explorer and the Scientist in the Winning of the American West* (New York: A. Knopf, 1966), p.53.
14. Ibid., p. 125.
15. Robbins, *Our Landed Heritage*, pp. 39–42, 45–46, 74, 87–89, 93–94.
16. T. H. Benton, *Thirty Years' View*, 2 vols. (New York: Walker & Son, 1854),

I:14. See also H. N. Smith, *Virgin Land: The American West in Symbol and Myth* (Cambridge, Mass.: Harvard University Press, 1950), chapter 2.

17. Cf. "Oregon Territory," *The Family Magazine*, 1840, pp. 493–94.
18. *Congressional Globe*, 31st Cong., 1st Sess., 1, 841.
19. *Congressional Globe*, 30th Cong., 2nd Sess., 1, 473.
20. R. P. Thian, *Legislative History of the General Staff of the United States from 1775 to 1901* (Washington, D.C.: Government Printing Office, 1901), p. 488.
21. T. H. Benton, *Thirty Years' View, I:468–69, 478.*
22. Cited in Goetzmann, *Army Exploration*, p. 67.
23. Robbins, *Our Landed Heritage*, pp. 218–20.
24. See W. Stegner, *Beyond the Hundreth Meridian* (Boston: Houghton Mifflin Co., 1954). Also W. M. Davis, "John Wesley Powell, 1834–1902," in National Academy of Science *Biographical Memoirs*, vol.8 (Washington, D.C.: National Academy of Science, 1903), pp. 11–86.
25. Goetzmann, *Exploration and Empire*, p. 563.
26. J. W. Powell, *Exploration of the Colorado River of the West and Its Tributaries* (Washington, D.C.: Government Printing Office, 1875), p. 160.
27. J. W. Powell, *Report of Explorations in 1873 ...* (Washington, D.C.: Government Printing Office, 1874).
28. Robbins, *Our Landed Heritage*, pp. 330–33, 418–19, 421–22.

The Profession

Credentialism and Careerism in American Geography, 1890-1915

Gary S. Dunbar

Mark Twain's "Gilded Age" could also be called "The Guilded Age," because that was the period when the burgeoning American middle class concerned itself as never before with careers and credentials—in a word, with professionalization. The professionalization or institutionalization of geography—the emergence of the academic field of geography—seems to have occurred at roughly the same time in Europe and North America but in different ways and for different reasons, and these differences can still be seen today in the styles of geography practiced in the various European and North American countries.

The professionalization of American society in the post–Civil War era is seen as a natural concomitant of the urbanization and industrialization of the period. The American University, as the institution which conferred the most desirable credentials, began a meteoric rise which can be measured by the growth in numbers of students and faculty members (See Appendix A). The German-style doctorate became the highest credential for an aspiring academic, and semiautonomous departments grew up within the universities to provide for specialization in teaching and research. Previously the small size, unspecialized nature, and rigid classical curricula of the old-time colleges had mitigated against specialization or professionalization, and much of the serious work in science was produced in state and federal bureaus. Especially noteworthy was the concentration of scientists in Washington, D.C. Agencies such as the U.S. Geological Survey, the Coast and Geodetic Survey, and Army Engineers were producing much of the geographical work in the United States in the nineteenth century, but they could not confer degrees, and their eminence was fast eroding by the beginning of the new century. In the field of geography, the period was marked by the death or eclipse of such Washington geographers as John Wesley Powell and W J McGee, the diversion of the National Geographic Society toward popular goals, and the avowed anti-Washington bias of the new Association of American Geographers. Some of the older universities, such as Harvard and Yale, were revitalized to provide leadership in the professionalizing era, and new institutions were created with the express purpose of improving graduate instruction and research. These new universities included Johns Hopkins, Chicago, Clark, and Stanford, and the first two were able to leap immediately into the forefront. The private universities were usually larger and stronger than the state institutions, but the state universities of the upper Mid West—Michigan, Wisconsin, and Minnesota—as well as California were demanding a share of the limelight.[1]

Today we are so accustomed to think in terms of university departments that we take the organizational pattern for granted and think it must be of ancient origin, but this sort of compartmentalization only emerged in the late nineteenth century with the growth in numbers of specialists and graduate students. The confusion of nomenclature was well illustrated by the first catalogue of Cornell University (for the academic year 1868–69), in which it was stated that the courses in physical geography and climatology were taught by the Reverend William D. Wilson, professor of moral and intellectual philosophy and registrar. Wilson was a professor in the School of Philosophy, which was part of the College of Literature and Philosophy, but he taught physical geography and climatology in the School of Physical Geography, which was one of four schools of the College (or Department) of Natural History.[2] Although physical geography in the 1870s was taught by Charles Hartt, professor of geology, but the real beginnings of the teaching of geography at Cornell date from 1892, when Ralph Tarr, who completed his master's degree under Shaler and Davis at Harvard, was hired to teach physical geography and glacial geology. During the next two decades the Department of Geology at Cornell was a rather loose federation of subdepartments, which each bore the name of "Department." Tarr headed (and was for some time the sole member of) the Department of Dynamic Geology and Physical Geography, later called simply the Department of Physical Geography. Tarr repeatedly urged the president of the university to strengthen the Department of Geology and bring its sections, including geography, closer together. In the "Annual Report of the Department of Physical Geography for the Year 1906–1907" Tarr said:

I am by no means content with the present status of my department except as a temporary expedient to meet the unusual conditions that have arisen. . . . In the first place, I hope to see developed at Cornell a

Department of Geography....My second hope is to see a closer affiliation between this department and the department of Geology; indeed, it is my belief that Geography and Geology should be at least cooperative, or, better still, under a single general management, either with a head professor or else run by cooperation of all the professors. At present, there is no real cooperation....[3]

When Tarr was in Europe for the academic year 1909–10, he left his department in the care of a young instructor, O. D. von Engeln. Tarr planned to study the organization of European departments of geography and propose something similar for Cornell. His notion of creating a School of Geology and Geography was rejected by the president, and when Tarr died suddenly in 1912, von Engeln was again put in charge of the (sub) department of physical geography. In May 1914 the Cornell Board of Trustees finally merged all the subdepartments into a single Department of Geology with Professor Heinrich Ries as head.

Resolved, that the various sub-departments of Geology (Dynamic Geology, Paleontology and Stratigraphic Geology, Mineralogy and Petrography, Physical Geography, and Economic Geology) be consolidated in a single department under one head and that the Committee or Conference of Professors which has hitherto administered the affairs of the Geological Department be, and it is hereby, dissolved.[4]

Thenceforth, physical geography was referred to as a section or branch of the Department of Geology. Von Engeln remained the sole geographer in the department for most of the rest of his long career (he retired in 1949), and not since 1914 has the name geography been used in the title of a department at Cornell.

The first separate Department of Geography in a major university in the United States was created at the University of California in 1898, when the distinguished but aged scientist George Davidson was named professor of geography and placed in charge of the Department of Geography in the newly organized College of Commerce. Davidson's fifty-year career with the United States Coast and Geodetic Survey had ended somewhat abruptly in 1895. He had served as a member of the Board of Regents of the University of California in 1877–84 and had been an honorary professor of geodesy and astronomy since 1870. It is not clear why a Department of Geography was created in 1898, but the precedent of European commercial schools was cited, and it is possible that the model of the Univeristy of Pennsylvania's Wharton School, where the teaching of geography was initiated in 1893, was in the minds of those who created Berkeley's College of Commerce. In keeping with the stated intention of the organizers of the new college to stimulate Pacific trade, Davidson offered a two-semester course on "The Currents and Climatology of the Pacific Ocean," a very general course which ranged far beyond physical geography and far beyond the Pacific borderlands. A second member was added to the Department of Geography in 1901 when Lincoln Hutchinson was appointed instructor in commercial geography, but of greater importance was the appointment of Ruliff Holway as assistant professor of geography in 1904. Holway, a former chemist who was converted by Davis in a Harvard summer session, took over the Department of Geography at Berkeley after Davidson's retirement and managed its affairs until his own retirement in 1923, when he was succeeded by Carl Sauer. Although there was no provision for Ph.D. work in the pre-Sauer era, several M.A.'s were given in that period, the first of them in 1908.[5]

"Our professional geographers are all self-made men," said William Morris Davis in 1895.[6] Most of the "fathers" of American academic geography, such as Davis, Shaler, Brigham, Tarr, and Salisbury, did not have doctorates because the degree was not necessary in achieving their goals, but their successors had to get Ph.D.'s in order to climb the academic ladder. The situation was quite different from that in France, where the first university geographers all had doctorates (in history), and their students became the first holders of doctorates in geography. The American doctorate, however, was modeled after the German doctorate, a degree which did not take much time or depth of research to acquire, at least in the period around the turn of the century. The German-style Ph.D. was given first by Yale in 1861, and Cornell, Harvard, and Johns Hopkins followed in the 1870s. At the beginning of the twentieth century the number of doctorates awarded annually in the United States was about 350, which was 1 percent of the number granted each year in the 1970s.[7]

In this matter of the "paper chase," the case of Albert Perry Brigham is expecially interesting. Brigham had been a Baptist minister in upstate New York for several years before he encountered William Morris Davis and his students in their summer excursions near Utica. In the Harvard summer school in 1889 Brigham began a lifelong friendship with Richard E. Dodge, whom Shaler had diverted from the study of law. In the summer of 1890 Dodge was employed by Shaler as a U.S.G.S. assistant in northwestern Connecticut, and Brigham joined him there. In 1891 Brigham was appointed instructor in natural history at his alma mater, Colgate University, but the appointment was not to take effect until 1

August 1892, after Brigham had completed a master's degree at Harvard. He had tried for an appointment at the Univeristy of Chicago in 1891, but William Rainey Harper was after bigger fish at the time. After he began teaching at Colgate in 1892, Brigham sounded out Shaler on the possibility of working for a Ph.D. degree in geology at Harvard in absentia. Shaler replied:

> I fear that it is likely to prove under the regulations impossible to effect the arrangement. . . . It is desirable in order to give a better chance of success that you should propose at least two summers of work and a share of the term time for two years.[8]

These conditions were apparently not satisfactory to Brigham, although for several years he helped with local arrangements for the Harvard two-week summer field class in the Utica region. In 1893 he sought a professorship in geology at Cornell university, with help from his friend Charles Evans Hughes, a law professor there. According to Hughes,

> I was very glad of the opportunity to present his name. But I fear nothing will come of it. Candidates are as plenty as blackberries in summer and the fact that Brigham has so recently come from active work as a pastor will be in his way.[9]

Through another friend, Benjamin Terry, dean at the University of Chicago, Brigham proposed to T. C. Chamberlin that he spend the academic year 1898–99 at Chicago in pursuit of a Ph.D. degree in geology. Chamberlin replied favorably on 4 June 1898.

> It occurred to me that you might like to come as professor *pro tempore* and give us a course in physiography during the spring quarter [1899], and that this might offset all dues to the University.[10]

Brigham was granted a one-year leave from Colgate, beginning in January 1899, but his son Charles died at that time, and so he cancelled his plan of going to Chicago. Apparently Brigham had no more thoughts of getting a doctorate, and he stayed on at Colgate until his retirement in 1926.

It is interesting to note that Brigham's student Frederick V. Emerson (B.A., Colgate, 1898) became the first person to earn a Ph.D. degree in an American department of geography (Chicago, 1907). (But several doctorates were awarded in geography in American universities before

1907. See Apprendix B.) Emerson had been unsuccessful in his attempts to get a fellowship in Chicago's Department of Geology in 1899 and 1900, but he did get a fellowship in geography in 1905, after spending two years at Cornell and Harvard studying physical geography under Tarr and Davis. Although his background was in geology and physical geography, Emerson chose to work with J. Paul Goode at Chicago, perhaps partly because he did not care much for Salisbury ("the most angular man I ever touched"). Emerson's teaching career (1906–13 at the University of Missouri, 1913–19 at Louisiana State University) was spent in departments of geology, and he seems not to have played a rôle in the furtherance of geography in those institutions.[11]

The first separate department of geography to offer a Ph.D. degree in the subject was established at the University of Chicago in 1903. I shall say rather little about this development, because it is being covered more fully by Prof. William Pattison. I should merely like to record my impression that a major reason for the formation of the department seemed to be the desire to raise Rollin Salisbury to the rank and salary of a head professor (i.e., department head). He had been a professor since his arrival at Chicago in 1892, and in 1899 he assumed the additional duties of dean of the Ogden School of Science, but his salary of $3,500 (1903) was still far below that of T. C. Chamberlin and the other head professors. When Chamberlin took up a one-year Carnegie Institution grant in 1903, he arranged for Salisbury to get $500 for assuming the temporary headship of the Department of Geology, in addition to the $500 which he would get as head of the new Department of Geography. Salisbury's base salary of $3,500 would continue to come from the Department of Geology, and it would be augmented by $500 each year as head of geography until it reached $5,000. J. Paul Goode, the new assistant professor of geography, was to receive $2,000, one-third of which would come from the Extension Department, one-sixth from a supplementary fund, and only $1,000 would be charged initially to the Department of Geography. I mention these details because they show how the Department of Geography was founded on a shoestring, and how its origin depended more on the career strategies of an individual than on the intrinsic value of the field of geography.[12]

Undeniably William Morris Davis was the leading figure in this nascent period of academic geography. After surviving a shaky start at Harvard, when he was warned by President Eliot that he was unlikely to receive tenure (Eliot himself had left Harvard in 1858 when he failed to get a chair), Davis was made professor of physical geography in 1890 and began to dominate the young field. Although there was never a separate department of geography at Harvard, the Department of Geology and

Geography was so named by the mid-1890s. At first Davis was the sole geographer in the department, but the older geologists such as Josiah Whitney and Nathaniel Shaler were certainly sympathetic toward the development of geography. When Whitney died in 1896, his endowed chair, the Sturgis-Hooper professorship of geology, became vacant. Davis nominated I. C. Russell for the Sturgis-Hooper chair in 1898, but it went instead to Davis himself the next year. Davis tried in vain to convince Eliot that the word "geography" should be added to the title of the chair.

> I regret to lose the designation of "professor of physical geography", not only for personal reasons, but even more so because of the effect that the change of my title may have on the relation of Harvard to the educational development of geographical subjects. It has been a distinct advantage to be able to say that Harvard regarded physical geography as so important that a professorship was devoted to it: but now those among the more conservative school teachers who consider my work too geological will be able to say that to all appearances the authorities at Harvard agree with them. In view of these considerations, I venture to ask the Corporation to consider whether it would be possible for me to retain my former professorial title along with the new one.[13]

Eliot resisted the title change, and he also urged Davis to curtail his teaching of elementary courses. He asked Davis to devote less time to the writing of elementary textbooks and manuals. Eliot even discouraged Davis from taking a summer position at Berkeley working with elementary teachers of geography in 1904, but Davis wanted to continue such activities, partly for the money but mostly because they represented a fertile mission field for geography. Although Davis was reluctant to cut down his teaching duties, his acceptance of the Sturgis-Hooper chair enabled the department to retain and promote Robert Ward, who had been an instructor since 1894. Ward's duties expanded in the area of physical geography, especially climatology, and Davis hoped that the human side of geography would be cared for by the young anthropologist Roland Dixon. Douglas Johnson taught physical geography in the department from 1906 to 1912, and when Davis retired somewhat prematurely in the latter year, Wallace Atwood was brought in from Chicago to teach in that area.[14]

William Morris Davis delineated five classes of "professional geographers" in 1895: topographers, cartographers, explorers, teachers, and writers on geographical subjects. None could get adequate university training in geography, as compared with specialists in other fields, and so

Davis urged the vigorous promotion of geography at all levels in order that it might be strengthened in the universities. A concomitant interest of Davis was in the establishment of a "society of mature geographical experts," analogous to the Geological Society of America. These "experts" could be drawn from "at least four classes of geographical associates": schoolteachers; weather observers; other government workers, such as geologists and statisticians; and the members of the existing geographical societies.[15] These societies had begun as local laymen's educational societies (to use J. K. Wright's terminology), but in the 1890s two of them were expanding in areal and professional importance: the American Geographical Society and the National Geographic Society (see appendix C). Davis had been fairly active in the latter organization since its inception in 1888—or as active as a Cambridge man could be in that Washington-based society—but in 1904, when he despaired of diverting the National Geographic Society to his purposes, he resigned from the executive board and immediately founded the Association of American Geographers. Almost single-handedly Davis shaped this "society of mature geographical experts."[16]

In this early era when a university department might consist of only one person, the number of geographers at Yale University was truly remarkable. There was no department of geography at Yale, but the subject became a prominent part of the offerings of the Department of Geology. Daniel Coit Gilman had taught geography at Yale from 1863 to 1872, but its real development began in 1900, when Herbert Gregory was appointed instructor in physical geography. In 1902, when President A. T. Hadley urged him not to leave Yale for M.I.T., Gregory seized the opportunity to strengthen the teaching of geography and also his own position. In a letter to Hadley on 28 May 1902, Gregory urged the president to

> develop Physiography by increasing the courses; so as to fit teachers for secondary schools and colleges and to meet the demands of the national and state surveys for trained physiographers.... The part which I wish to take in the proposed scheme is: teach half of the elementary geology; teach physiography to graduates and under-graduates; train teachers; make the department directly useful to the schools of Connecticut; secure positions for graduates.

Gregory asked that "a young man be selected to teach Elementary Physical Geography and to assist with the Commercial Geography" beginning in 1903, and he further asked for his own promotion to a full professorship by March 1904 "so as to have better standing before the country and thus be better able to secure positions for graduates."[17] Hadley received the letter with great enthusiasm, and the Yale Geology Department began to add geographers: some of them to become well known, such as Isaiah Bowman, Ellsworth Huntington, and Angelo Heilprin; and others who were never to achieve prominence, such as George Surface, Theodore Harding Boggs, Avard Longley Bishop, and Loomis Havemeyer. Although Gregory can be given a major share of credit for the development of geography at Yale, he remained essentially a geologist and turned over much of the responsibility for the guidance of the geography program to Isaiah Bowman. Geography went into decline after 1915 when Bowman left for the American Geographical Society, Huntington left after failing to get a full professorship (only to reappear a few years later as a research associate), and Gregory divided his time after 1919 between New Haven and the Bishop Museum in Honolulu.[18]

In the period covered by this essay, 1890–1915, several people emerged who might be regarded at near-geographers or crypto-geographers. This was a time when university structures were changing and new disciplines were taking shape, and many opportunists had the option of joining any one of several promising bandwagons. After a brief flirtation with geography, they found their careers in another field. I should like to give as examples three men—William Z. Ripley, Emory Johnson, and Lindley Miller Keasbey. After completing his dissertation on the financial history of seventeenth-century Virginia at Columbia University in 1893, Ripley taught simultaneously at Columbia and M.I.T. until 1901, when he went to Harvard as professor of political economy. As a lecturer in "anthropo-geography" at Columbia, he imagined himself to be a pioneer in establishing the "new" geography. In a paper published in 1895 he said:

the Faculty of Political Science at Columbia College were the first to institute a regular and separate course of lectures upon this subject [i.e., the new or modern geography—the study of the influence of the physical environment upon people], distinct from those in descriptive and physical geography which belong to the departments of natural science. The tendency to broaden the scope of economics, and the new interest in sociology, have together made a distinct place for the new geography.[19]

After brief excursions into geography and anthropology, Ripley concentrated on economics after his appointment at Harvard. He declined an invitation to join the Association of American Geographers in 1905.

When the Wharton School of Finance of the University of Pennsylvania expanded its two-year course to four years in 1894, a young economist, Emory Johnson, volunteered to teach geography, initially without pay, and for the next nine years about one-third of his teaching was devoted to geography. His student, J. Russell Smith, eventually took over the teaching of geography, and Johnson concentrated on his specialties of commerce and transportation after 1903. Although he was a charter member of the Association of American Geographers and attended the first two annual meetings, Johnson was not very active in the organization, and he resigned in 1914. It is interesting to note that William Morris Davis, who arrogated to himself the power to make such distinctions, considered the Pennsylvania enonomic geographers to be economists rather than true geographers. It seems that Johnson and most of his students had committed the grievous error of trying to enter the field of geography without first muddying their boots in the manner of the geologists. Of Johnson's chief protege, Davis said in 1913:

> J. Russell Smith is an *economist*, rather than a geographer; he joins our Association to represent the economic side; hence I shd hesitate, as a member of the committee on *Geography* of the Am. Phil. Soc. to suggest him as a speaker or member; That shd come from Economists, as I see it.[20]

Lindley Keasbey, who is known today chiefly as the mentor of Walter Prescott Webb, took a Ph.D. degree in political science at Columbia in 1890 and then a second doctorate at the University of Strassburg in 1892. His dissertations concerned the diplomatic history of the Nicaragua Canal scheme. From 1894 to 1905 Keasbey was a professor of political science at Bryn Mawr College, where he taught courses in economic geography as well as sociology, commerce, and political science. As a recent biographer of Webb has said,

> Social scientists of Keasbey's generation were virtually free to make their own systems and their own methodology as they saw fit. For most of them, the broader problems were resolved or alleviated by the emergence of virtually independent disciplines—especially sociology, political science, and economics, with geography bringing up a rather uncertain rear.

Keasbey left Bryn Mawr in 1905 for the University of Texas, where he was professor of political science until 1910, when he became professor and head of the new Department of Institutional History. This department was created for the express purpose of easing Keasbey out of political science. At Texas Keasbey taught geography under such rubrics as "Economic Geography and Demography," "Commercial Geography," "The Geography of Eastern Civilization," and "The Geography of Western Civilization." These courses were rather strongly environmentalistic, and they left an indelible impression on an undergraduate student named Walter Prescott Webb. Although Keasbey was a popular professor and was even nominated for the presidency of the University of Texas in 1915, he was fired for his antiwar acivities in 1917 and never again held a regular academic position. The Department of Institutional History subsequently reemerged as the Department of Anthropology, and there was no department of geography in the University of Texas until 1949. Incidentally, Keasbey was proposed for membership in the Association of American Geographers by Ellen Churchill Semple in 1905, but the nomination died for lack of support from William Morris Davis, who wielded supreme power in the organization.[21]

Epilogue

Careers and credentials were availaible in geography in the United States by 1915 that were nonexistent in 1890. There was still only one department of geography that was prepared to turn out Ph.D.'s with some regularity. The 1920s would see the establishment of the Clark Graduate School of Geography and the separation of geography from geology in many influential univeristies, such as Michigan and Wisconsin. Despite hopeful beginnings, geography did not return to a position of prominence in some of the prestigious private universities, such as Harvard, Yale, Cornell, and Pennsylvania, chiefly because of the failure to retain or replace certain key individuals. The American Geographical Society was doing more to aid professional geography than were the other laymen's educational societies. Indeed, the A.G.S. helped the Association of American Geographers find its legs in this nascent period. The A.A.G., although perilously small, was improving and was no longer Davis's private fiefdom by 1915. Geography had definitely emerged as an academic discipline, but it was to suffer in comparison with most of its sister disciplines in terms of numerical strength, quality of leadership, and possession of a unified philosophy or methodology.

Appendix A

Instructors and Students at Selected American Universities, 1890–1915

Institution	1890[a] I.	1890[a] S.	1895[b] I.	1895[b] S.	1900[c] I.	1900[c] S.	1905[d] I.	1905[d] S.	1910[e] I.	1910[e] S.	1915[f] I.	1915[f] S.
Clark University	30	50	13	50	...	...	12	63	15	103	27	127
Colgate University	15	137	20	151	32	350	30	265	47	482	44	496
Columbia University	191	1,620	258	1,805	339	2,208	551	4,833	628	5,887	920	14,098
Cornell University	96	1,306	155	1,801	284	2,543	435	3,423	578	4,859	700	6,496
Harvard University	217	2,079	330	3,292	442	4,067	552	5,393	612	5,109	803	4,366
Johns Hopkins University	58	381	83	522	126	650	158	715	200	710	240	1,374
University of California	110	655	225	1,800	301	2,525	283	3,400	386	3,450	434	7,526
University of Chicago[g]	...	...	148	900	235	2,959	361	4,580	319	5,629	274	7,301
University of Michigan	79	2,100	165	2,950	197	3,192	292	4,000	425	5,223	460	6,258
University of Minnesota	104	904	139	2,100	245	3,200	290	3,900	352	5,066	496	8,972
University of Pennsylvania	163	1,222	275	2,300	264	2,641	316	2,692	500	4,800	560	6,332
University of Texas	15	294	43	890	83	800	110	1,348	88	2,573	288	2,617
University of Wisconsin	64	725	93	1,294	125	1,923	277	3,151	395	4,500	651	6,765
Yale University	143	1,477	206	2,375	275	2,700	330	2,995	400	3,276	457	3,272

[a] The World Almanac 1890 (New York: The Press Publishing Company, 1890), pp. 142–43, "Principal Universities and Colleges of the United States . . . condition at the close of 1889."

[b] The World Almanac and Encyclopedia 1895 (New York: The Press Publishing Company, 1895), pp. 279–83, "Principal Universities and Colleges of the United States . . . condition at the close of 1894."

[c] The World Almanac and Encyclopedia 1900 (New York: The Press Publishing Company, 1900), pp. 295–300, "Principal Universities and Colleges of the United States . . . condition at the close of 1899."

[d] The World Almanac and Encyclopedia 1905 (New York: The Press Publishing Company, 1905), pp. 303–8, "Principal Universities and Colleges of the United States . . . condition at the close of 1904."

[e] The World Almanac and Encyclopedia 1910 (New York: The Press Publishing Company, 1910), pp. 471–76, "Principal Universities and Colleges of the United States . . . condition at the close of 1909."

[f] The World Almanac and Encyclopedia 1915 (New York: The Press Publishing Company, 1915), pp. 628–34, "Principal Universities and Colleges of the United States . . . condition at the close of 1914."

[g] The University of Chicago opened in 1892.

The figures from *The World Almanac* can be compared with those given in *Minerva: Jahrbuch der Universitäten der Welt* (Strassburg: Karl J. Trübner, 1891/92–   ). The two sources are not perfectly comparable, but it is profitable to read *Minerva* because this provides additional data. For example, *Minerva* gave the following figures for the academic year 1909–10 in volume 20 (1910–11):

Clark University	25	Instructors; 99 fellows, scholars, and students; 11 undergraduates; and 12 students in Saturday courses
Colgate University	545	students (of whom 361 were in the college, 50 in the theological seminary, and 134 in the academy [secondary school])
Columbia University	6,529	students, including 1,971 in summer school
Cornell University	4,224	students
Harvard University	4,046	students
Johns Hopkins University	752	students
University of California	5,341	students, including 819 in vacation courses
University of Chicago	6,007	students
University of Michigan	5,383	students, including 1,224 in summer school
University of Minnesota	c. 5,000	students
University of Pennsylvania	5,033	students
University of Texas	2,594	students
University of Wisconsin	c. 4,500	students (*Minerva*, vol. 21)
Yale University	3,297	students

Appendix B

Dissertations in Geography in American Universities through 1915

The following list was taken from [Derwent Whittlesey, editor] "Dissertations in Geography Accepted by Universities in the United States for the Degree of Ph.D. as of May, 1935," *Annals of the Association of American Geographers* 25, no. 4 (December 1935): 211–37.

Emory R. Johnson, "Inland Waterways: Their Relation to Transportation," University of Pennsylvania, 1893.

Cleveland Abbe, Jr., "A General Report on the Physiography of Maryland," Johns Hopkins University, 1898.

O. L. Fassig, "Types of March Weather in the U. S., with Special Reference to the Middle U. S.," Johns Hopkins University, 1899.

J. A. Bonsteel, "The Soils of St. Mary's County, Maryland: Showing the Relationships of the Geology to the Soils," Johns Hopkins University, 1901.

John Paul Goode, "The Influence of Physiographic Factors upon the Occupations and Economic Development in the United States," University of Pennsylvania, 1901.

Joseph Russell Smith, "The Organization of Ocean Commerce," University of Pennsylvania, 1903.

George D. Hubbard, "Gold and Silver Mining as a Geographic Factor in the Development of the United States," Cornell University, 1905.

James Walter Goldthwait, "The Abandoned Shore Lines of Eastern Wisconsin," Harvard University, 1906.

Walter Sheldon Tower, "A Regional and Economic Geography of Pennsylvania," University of Pennsylvania, 1906.

Frederick V. Emerson, "A Geographic Interpretation of New York City," University of Chicago, 1907.

George Thomas Surface, "Regional and Economic Geography of Virginia," University of Pennsylvania, 1907.

Isaiah Bowman, "The Geography of the Central Andes," Yale University, 1909.

Ellsworth Huntington, "Changes of Climate in Recent Geological Time," Yale University, 1909.

John Lyon Rich, "Studies in the Physiography of Semi-arid Regions," Cornell University, 1911.

Charles Franklin Brooks, "The Snowfall of the Eastern United States," Harvard University, 1914.

Wellington D. Jones, "Studies in the Geography of Northern Patagonia," University of Chicago, 1914.

Almon E. Parkins, "The Historical Geography of Detroit," University of Chicago, 1914.

Stephen S. Visher, "The Geography of South Dakota," University of Chicago, 1914.

Carl O. Sauer, "The Geography of the Ozark Highland of Missouri," University of Chicago, 1915.

This list was admittedly arbitrary and incomplete, especially for the early years before there were departments of geography. The list was actually begun by Albert Perry Brigham, but he died in 1932 before the project was completed. Of special interest is the meticulous list of Cornell M.A. and Ph.D. theses drawn up by O. D. von Engeln and transmitted to Brigham on 6 November 1931 (Colgate Archives, Brigham Papers, Box "Letters Jan 1930–December 1931"). Von Engeln listed two early dissertations in physiography (Charles Foote, 1877; and Thomas Watson, 1897), but they were omitted in publication. Also omitted were the Alaskan glacial studies of O. D. von Engeln (1911) and Lawrence Martin (1913).

Although Frederick Emerson's dissertation (1907) was the first to be completed in a separate department of geography, there were several earlier dissertations presented in other universities, notably the University of Pennsylvania, by people who went on to make a name for themselves in geography. Of greater significance, I think, is the fact that the next Chicago dissertation was not completed until 1914, after which the department produced a regular flow of dissertations. In my opinion, the most important of the early dissertations—at least in the period before 1909—were the Pennsylvania dissertations of Goode, Smith and Tower. I would not include Johnson's dissertation (1893) because he was not a geographer in the way the others were.

Appendix C

Geographical Societies of the Late Nineteenth and Early Twentieth Centuries

1. American Geographical Society of New York, 1851–
2. Geographical Society of the Pacific, San Francisco, founded in 1881, defunct by 1918
3. National Geographic Society, Washington, D.C., 1888–
4. Geographical Society of Philadelphia, 1891–
5. Geographical Society of California, San Francisco, founded in 1891, defunct by 1908
6. Geographic Society of Chicago, 1898–
7. Geographical Society of Baltimore, founded 1902, defunct by 1912
8. Association of American Geographers, 1904–
9. Southern Geographic Society, Nashville, founded in 1914 (on the model of the Geographic Society of Chicago), but apparently had only a brief existence

These societies were all what J. K. Wright would call laymen's educational or research societies, with the exception of the Association of

American Geographers, which is a professional research society. See Wright's paper, "The Field of the Geographical Society," *Geography in the Twentieth Century*, ed. Griffith Taylor, 3rd ed. (New York: Philosophical Library, 1957), pp. 543–65.

The Association of American Geographers can be compared with the professsional societies in ancillary disciplines:

American Historical Association, 1884–
American Economic Association, 1885–
Geological Society of America, 1888–
American Anthropological Association, 1902–
American Political Science Association, 1903–
American Sociological Association, 1905–

Gary S. Dunbar

Notes

1. There is a large literature on professionalization and the rise of universities in nineteenth-century America. Among the most useful books I saw were Robert H. Wiebe, *The Search for Order, 1877–1920* (New York: Hill and Wang, 1967); Burton J. Bledstein, *The Culture of Professionalism: The Middle Class and The Development of Higher Education in America* (New York: W. W. Norton & Co., Inc., 1976); and Laurence R. Veysey, *The Emergence of the American University* (Chicago: University of Chicago Press, 1965). For Harvard, the bellwether of American universities, see also Robert A. McCaughey, "The Transformation of American Academic Life: Harvard University 1821–1892," *Perspectives in American History* 8 (1974): 239–332. The preeminence and subsequent decline of the scientific establishment in Washington in the late nineteenth century is described by J. Kirkpatrick Flack, *Desideratum in Washington: The Intellectual Community in the Capital City 1870–1900* (Cambridge, Mass.: Schenkman Publishing Company, Inc., 1975).
2. *Catalogue of the Officers and Students of the Cornell University, for the Academic Year 1868-9 . . .* (Ithaca: Steam Power Press Print., 1869).
3. Cornell University Libraries, Olin Library, Department of Manuscripts and University Archives, Ralph S. Tarr Collection, Box 2, carbon copy of "Annual Report of the Department of Physical Geography for the Year 1906–1907."
4. Ibid., von Engeln Papers, Box 1, carbon copy of J. G. Schurman to H. Ries, 4 May 1914.
5. G. S. Dunbar, "George Davidson, 1825–1911," in *Geographers: Biobibliographical Studies*, ed. T. W. Freeman and Philippe Pinchemel (London: Mansell, 1978), 2: 33–37 (based on George Davidson Collection in the Bancroft Library, University of California, Berkeley); "The Establishment of the College of Commerce," *University Chronicle* (University of California, Berkeley) 1, no. 6 (December 1898): 552–68.
6. W. M. Davis, "The Need of Geography in the University," *Educational Review* 10 (June 1895): 22.
7. *Comprehensive Dissertation Index, 1861–1972*, (Ann Arbor, Mich.: Xerox University Microfilms, 1973), vol. 16, *Geography and Geology*, p. ix.
8. Colgate University Archives, papers of Albert Perry Brigham, Box 1, N. S. Shaler to Brigham, 13 December 1892.
9. Ibid., C. E. Hughes to B. Terry, 28 January 1893.
10. Ibid., Box 2, T. C. Chamberlin to Brigham, 4 June 1898.
11. Ibid., F. V. Emerson to Brigham, 18 September 1899; Box 3, Emerson to Brigham, 21 May 1900; Box 7, Emerson to Brigham, 1 January 1906.
12. University of Chicago, Joseph Regenstein Library, Department of Special collections, Papers of Thomas Chrowder Chamberlin, Letterbook 16, copy of T. C. Chamberlin to W. R. Harper, 14 January 1903; Presidents' Papers 1889–1925, Box 16, Folder 9 (Geography), R. D. Salisbury to T. W. Goodspeed, 18 February 1904.
13. Harvard University Archives, Charles W. Eliot Papers, Box 106, Folder 68, W. M. Davis to C. W. Eliot, 2 April 1899. By permission of the Harvard University Archives.

14. Ibid., Davis to Eliot, 10 May 1899; Box 209 (Davis Folder), Davis to Eliot, 6 and 13 October 1903.
15. Davis, "The Need of Geography," pp. 33–37.
16. National Geographic Society Records, Board of Managers, vol. 5, p. 68 (Davis resigned from the board 4 November 1904, just a month before the inaugural meeting of the A. A. G.). In 1902 Davis had declined to serve as associate editor of the *National Geographic Magazine* because he "couldn't approve general policy of popularizing at expense of science." See W J McGee to Davis (with note added by Davis) 29 May 1902 in McGee Folder (299), Davis Papers, Harvard University, Houghton Library.
17. Yale University Library, Herbert E. Gregory Papers, copy of H. E. Gregory to A. T. Hadley, 28 May 1902.
18. Ibid., Folders 2 and 3, [anonymous, but presumably written by Gregory] "History of the Geological Department at Yale University" (Folder 2, 1802–1907; Folder 3, 1907–15).
19. "William Zebina Ripley," in *Dictionary of American Biography*, supplement 3 (1941–1945), ed. Edward T. James (New York: Charles Scribner's Sons, 1973), pp. 632-33; William Z. Ripley, "Geography As a Sociological Study," *Political Science Quarterly* 10, no. 4 (December 1895): 642.
20. Emory R. Johnson, *Life of a University Professor; An Autobiography* (Philadelphia: Printed by Ruttle, Shaw and Wetherill, Inc., 1943), pp. 26, 66; University of Pennsylvania, University Archives, Minutes of the Trustees, Microfilm, Box 5, vol. 13, p. 124; Geographical Society of Philadelphia, box labeled "Very Old Correspondence," W. M. Davis to Henry Bryant, 6 January 1913.
21. Mazie E. Mathews, "On the Hither Edge of Free Land: Lindley Miller Keasbey and the Evolution of the Frontier Thesis" (Master's thesis, Southwest Texas State University, 1973); Ronnie Dugger, *Our Invaded Universities: Form, Reform and New Starts* (New York: W. W. Norton & Co., Inc., 1974), pp.19–21; Gregory M. Tobin, *The Making of a History: Walter Prescott Webb and The Great Plains* (Austin: University of Texas Press, 1976), pp.40–45 (quotation on p. 43).

The New England Meteorological Society, 1884-96: A Study in Professionalism

William A. Koelsch

"One of the brightest gems in the New England weather is the dazzling uncertainty of it."

Mark Twain, "Speech on the Weather"

The concept of professionalization has emerged in recent years as one of the most powerful notions in the historiography of the American university and its disciplines.[1] This concept has led scholars to reexamine the processes by which lore becomes "science," its practitioners claim identity and receive recognition as "scientists," and their activities become systematized, nurtured, routinized, and institutionalized in a social system which guarantees continuation and extension of their newly achieved and ascribed status.

Professionalization embraces at least four separable subprocesses which, taken together, form the social and intellectual matrix of organized scholarship. First is the definition and delimitation of the new science, including the setting of disciplinary goals and boundaries. Second, formal standards of membership are established in the new discipline, including consensual standards of what constitutes valid research and training. Third is the emergence of a community of like-minded scholars with regular linkages to one another. Finally, one sees the creation or new modelling of academic and associated institutions within which scientists can gain support for their research.[2]

The New England Meteorological Society, which rose, flourished, and died within a dozen years in the late nineteenth century in the Boston area, provides us with an indicator institution illuminating the transformation of laymen's science into professional science. At the same time, it illustrates the fragility of attempts to institutionalize the research ethos in the America of the 1880s and 1890s, and the role of chance and personality in the early evolution of the academic disciplines.[3]

The New England Meteorological Society was established in June 1884 at a gathering of nine "gentlemen" (as the first president describes them) who met to advance the study of weather and climate in New England. The basis of such study would be weather records made by local observers, a lay activity indulged in by scientifically minded amateurs in America since colonial times. In order to meet late nineteenth-century standards of scientific data collection, however, the new society initially hoped to promote greater accuracy and uniformity of observations, increase the number of observations made and improve their distribution across the region, publish the data so gathered, and meet periodically to discuss problems of atmospheric phenomena.[4]

Membership in the society was open to "all persons who feel an interest in the observational study of meteorology and desire to encourage its further development," whether or not they chose to make observations themselves. In the beginning, then, the New England Meteorological Society appeared to be what John K. Wright has called a regional laymen's society, building on the popular interest in "natural history" which was so marked a characteristic of late nineteenth-century America.[5]

Yet the group included, and was to dominated by, a small number of ambitious young scientists, most notably William Morris Davis. As one founder argued, "it is advisable to set before ourselves definite objects of study, in order to prevent *mere aimless recording* of 'weather' phenomena" (emphasis mine). Such phenomena were to be recorded not for "the gratification of a temporary curiosity," but in the interest of a "higher utility," the advancement of science.[6]

This simple statement contained the kernel of professional purpose. There was a "hidden agenda" to be dealt with: the advancement in status for a new science and, indirectly, for those who would commit themselves to its practice. As its twelve-year history would show, this element became more explicit as, in part through the work of the society, its key members gained self-conscious identification with the process of meteorological research and, to some degree, with university-based teaching.

Members, elected after application, paid dues of three dollars per year to support the work of the society. The actual conduct of affairs, however, was in the hands of an annually elected council of five (later six) members. The council included a president, a secretary, a treasurer, and other councillors, one of whom was chosen by his fellows to be director. The first council consisted of W. H. Niles (forty-six years old), an old-fashioned M. I. T. "natural historian," for the largely ceremonial post of president; William Morris Davis (thirty-four), then in his seventh year at the rank of instructor in geology at Harvard, secretary; Desmond Fitzgerald (thirty-eight), a civil engineer in charge of the Brookline water works, treasurer; his counterpart at Providence, E. B. Weston (thirty-four), and Prof. Winslow Upton (thirty), a Brown astronomer and former assistant in the Harvard College Observatory, as councillors. Professor Upton was named director of observations and editor. The council was enlarged two years later to include Abbott Lawrence Rotch (twenty-six), director of the Blue Hill Meteorological Observatory, founded by him in 1884 and affiliated with Harvard the following year.

A close examination of the organizational structure of the society during its twelve-year history gives us the first important clue to the professionalizing forces at work. Although at the first meeting 60 new members were elected in addition to the 9 founders, and although the membership appears through much of the society's existence to have ranged between 90 and 110, only 9 men appear to have served on the council in any capacity whatever. Of these, 4 were civil engineers, and 5 were university-connected researchers.

Of the two groups, the academics both served longer terms and held the more important offices. Niles was president thoughout the society's existence. Davis was either secretary or director/editor for the whole twelve-year period. Upton served either as director or as secretary for the first eight years, and remained on the council for the last four. Rotch was on the council continuously after his initial election in 1886, and served breifly as treasurer. In 1892, Davis's graduate assistant, Robert DeCourcy Ward (twenty-five years old) was elected treasurer and councillor. By contrast, only one of the four civil engineers serving on the council ever held any other office: Fitzgerald, who served as treasurer for the first five years only.

Thus the structure of the society at its beginning might be described as two-tiered: a laymen's society at the bottom and, incipiently, a professional one at the top. Within the professional group, academically based scientists were to be more significant than civil engineers. As time passed, the professional component was enlarged by membership of atmospheric scientists from outside New England, including Signal Service personnel, though none of these ever held office, probably in part because elections were held at the lightly attended annual meeting rather than by mail ballot. In its last years, when it had become entirely professionalized, the society was clearly a Harvard oligarchy run by Davis, his friends, and his junior associates.[7]

Since the originally announced purpose of the society was to improve and extend atmospheric observations in the region, the first council moved swiftly to appoint a director and to begin the organization and collection of temperature and precipitation data. A circular of instructions to observers was prepared, three new rain gauges were designed and licensed for manufacture by a Boston firm, and self-registering maximum and minimum thermometers were endorsed and made available for purchase.

Under Upton's editorship, the first monthly *Bulletin* appeared in November 1884. It contained observations made by forty-five observers, including the handful of former Signal Corps observers now instructed to report to the society. The *Bulletin* also contained a general summary of weather for the month, and a map prepared by Davis showing each station and its precipitaion amounts and temperature ranges, a feature which he continued to draft until September 1886, when the task of compiling the data was turned over to the Signal Corps. The number of observers passed the 100 mark the following March, and reached 140 by February 1886. In the next two and a half years, the number of observations published and generalized ran between 135 and 155 per month, though the total number of observers reporting at some time in a given year (and thus within the society's purview) was higher.[8]

The observers, who might or might not also be members, represented the most purely lay element within the society's network. At the beginning it was intended that they be drawn from all sorts and conditions of folk: "School teachers, lighthouse keepers, and many others," including children. Observers were provided with copies of the *Bulletin*, technical instructional materials, testing services for their instruments, and occasionally instruments donated by members themselves or organizations. New Yorkers living east of the Hudson were encouraged to report observations, and regular efforts were made to secure more observations from the sparsely covered northern reaches of New England. The Appalachian Mountain Club, in which both Davis and Niles were active, sponsored observations and provided equipment in high-altitude areas.[9]

The maintenance of this voluntary weather service, however, became increasingly burdensome to the managers of the society. For one thing, since the society's work transcended state boundaries, there was no financial support forthcoming from any New England state legislature, although the society's counterparts in other states were receiving such state aid. The army's Signal Service, then in charge of weather observations in the United States, provided no cash for expense of publications, though it did provide a franking privilege and detailed an enlisted man to Cambridge to serve as editorial assistant and the actual compiler of the weather data. Membership fees were not enough to cover the cost of the *Bulletin*, and special contributions had to be sought at various times to keep the operation going. In 1888, however, the problem of publication expense was solved when the Harvard College Astronomical Observatory agreed to publish the *Bulletin* in cooperation with the society, in a new, enlarged format which could then be corrected and reprinted in permanent form as a part of the *Annals* of the observatory.

The Signal Service, whose range and support had been cut back in the late 1880s because of developing hostility to government science, gave up its weather function entirely in 1891. Once a new civilian Weather Bureau had been instituted in the Department of Agriculture with a competent academic scientist, Prof. Mark Harrington of the University of Michigan, as chief, there seemed little reason for a private society to pour intellectual and financial resources into the maintenance of a routine data-gathering system. Not long after the change of administrative arrangements for the national weather service, the council proposed and, in April 1892 the society ratified, a transfer of the society's weather service to the new Weather Bureau, which reconstituted it as the New England Weather Service, and superseded the society's *Bulletin* with one of its own. The larger number of those persons actively involved in some phase of the work of the society, the observers, were now transferred to the New England Weather Service.[10]

What of the "higher utility," the advancement of science? During its twelve-year life span the professional activities of the society were, in fact, impressive. Thirty-six regular meetings were held—three each year, normally in October, January, and April—from October 1884 through April 1896. Almost all of them were held at the M. I. T. building in Boston, academic base of President Niles; a few were held in the home cities of other members of the council, and the meeting of April 1889 was held in Worcester, for no discernable reason.

Typically, three papers would be read at each meeting, with Davis most often giving one of them. The programs were somewhat heterogeneous in topic, but a few sessions were thematically organized, such as the one of April 1890 on climatic change, and the memorial meeting of October 1894 on the work of the recently deceased government meteorological theorist William H. Ferrel. In addition to the formal papers, there was frequently general discussion of a topic or demonstrations of new materials (books, maps, and instruments), often of foreign origin. In January 1889, the society sponsored a well-attended loan exhibition of meteorological apparatus, photographs, and charts at the centrally located M. I. T. Physical Laboratory in Boston's Back Bay.[11]

The meetings served as a primary agent of professional socialization for those in New England who thought of themselves as in some sense meteorologists, or at least "friends of meteorological science." That the number of participants was not large, however, is hinted at from time to time. Although attendance figures are hard to come by, we know that in October 1893, at a time when the society claimed ninety-one members, only sixteen persons attended the annual meeting. And when in 1896 the society was finally disbanded, one of the stated reasons was lack of attendance at meetings. Still, they did provide a place where Boston-area environmental scientists of various sorts might become aware of new ideas and current meteorological research, to have a forum for and gain criticism of their own research, and to confirm their identities as part of a community of specialized scholars.

The publications of the society were important agents of professionalization, providing linkages with meteorologists who could not attend its meetings, as well as advancing the development of a consensual standard of what constituted valid research in the new field. As J. M. Ziman has ponted out, a specialized journal is not only a stimulus to further investigation but "implies a degree of sociability among those who subscribe to it;" that is, the specialized journal is "the hallmark of a new discipline ... an act of solidarity and sodality."[12] The society's initial publication was a simple monthly *Bulletin* which, in addition to providing the raw data of temperature and rainfall and other weather elements, carried some information about the professional activities of the society.

For more specialized, problem-oriented investigations, those representing "definite objects of study" in contrast to "the mere aimless recording of 'weather' phenomena," the Harvard College Observatory offered a respected outlet in its *Annals*. Two classic studies initiated by Davis and completed by his student Ward, investigations of the thunderstorms and of the sea breezes of New England, were so placed, as were other specialized studies by society members.[13] Both these major studies were carried on with special networks of volunteer observers, but the scientific involvement of the observatory staff and of the Harvard students whom Davis was attracting to meteorology through his advanced courses and research projects was critical to their success.

The first American scientific journal in this field had been started at the University of Michigan by Mark Harrington in 1884, the year of the society's founding. Very early the *American Meteorological Journal* became an outlet for reports of the society's activities, its announcements, papers given at its meetings, and the research of its members and its scholar-councillors, expecially Davis, Rotch, and Upton. With only 200 paid suscriptions by 1886, however,(50 of them subsidized by the Signal Service), the *Journal* was in precarious financial state. Several attempts were made by Harrington and Cleveland Abbe of the Signal Service to find a firmer institutional base for the journal, either at Johns Hopkins, Harvard, or a proposed National Meteorological Society.

Rotch became associate editor and co-financial backer of the *Journal* in September 1886. In May 1892, it was transferred to Davis's Boston publisher, Ginn and Company, to be edited by Ward as part of his assistantship responsibilities at Harvard. Although a proprietary venture, with its deficits now assumed by Ward and Rotch, in its last years the *Journal* was virtually the society's publication. Most copies appear to have been either distributed to members as partial return for their dues, or sent out to groups of prospective members. Costs of the latter venture were subsidized by Harvard through Davis's Laboratory of Physical Geography.[14]

The various statements of purpose of the society, examined comparatively, are illuminating commentaries on the efforts of Davis and his associates to legislate the goals of the emerging discipline of meteorological science.[15] In 1884 the founders of the society, in pursuit of its chartered purpose "to promote the study of atmospheric phenomena in New England," had urged membership on "all persons who feel an interest in the observational study of meteorology." In a circular issued in 1886, the council affirmed that "the fundamental work of the Society is the collection of systematic records of climatic elements, such as temperature, rainfall, and the tide, made by trustworthy observers with accurate instruments."

Yet by 1888, about the time arrangements had been made to publish cooperatively with the observatory, Davis was retrospectively assessing the motives for founding the society as twofold: "the advance of the *science* of meteorology, and the promotion of *popular* interest in its study" (emphasis mine). His statement is worth noting for two reasons. It is the first time the society made this kind of scientific/popular distinction explicit. And it is also clear from the context that both purposes were served primarily by the holding of three meetings a year "at which papers upon meteorological topics of general interest are presented." Davis also shifted the focus of recruitment, urging membership on "all friends of the science of meteorology," rather than "all persons" interested in making weather observations.

In 1892, at a time when Davis was still on record as proclaiming that "*one of the chief objects* of our Society is to gather and preserve meteorological records for New England," (emphasis mine), the council finalized arrangements to turn over its weather service to the federal government. Davis and Upton defended the decision to discard the function of most popular interest and utility by claiming that "a sufficient reason for the continued organization of the Society still remains in its meetings and investigations," which would "in no way diminish from the activity shown in the past eight years." A statement made in a circular sent to members, observers, and correspondents is more startling: "The work of carrying on special investigations ... with the holding of meetings, will become the chief work of the Society, *as was intended at its organization*" (emphasis mine).

The point is not that Davis and his associates were deliberately concealing something in 1884 which they could not reveal until 1892. It is simply that the processes associated with the ideal of the academic specialist had come finally to shape the thinking of the small group who ran the society to the extent that they could no longer conceive of a layman's scientific society or even a two-tiered compromise. What they sought to bring into existence in 1892 was a society run by professionals for the scientific, educational, and careerist purposes of professionals. In its last four years of life, then, this onetime regional laymen's society had purged its lay element and become a national professional society of sorts. Members were affiliated with it not primarily on the basis of locality, but because of their identification with scientific and professional meteorology and their desire to be linked with each other through professional meetings and a respected specialized journal. Why, then, should the society have declined over the next four years to the point of dissolution in 1896?

The key to the rise and decline of the society, as to that of meteorology at Harvard, lay in the changing career strategies of American academic geography's greatest entrepreneur, William Morris Davis.[16] Davis had no formal academic training in meteorology,and had backed into it originally almost accidentally. He had been a student of geology and mining engineering at Harvard under Nathaniel S. Shaler, Raphael Pumpelly, and Josiah Dwight Whitney, taking the S. B. degree in the School of Mining in 1869 and the degree of mining engineer the following year. Davis had wanted a career in science, but few American scientists then enjoyed a secure institutional base. So he took his first job in Argentina, as assistant to Benjamin A. Gould, American director of the Argentine National Observatory in Cordoba.

One of Gould's responsibilities was to set up a weather bureau and system of meteorological stations. As part of his duties at Cordoba, then, Davis worked in practical, observational meteorology as well as astronomy. Evidently having fallen out with Gould, Davis returned to his Philadelphia home in 1873 and spent the next two years in his father's coal business. Shaler, as director of the Geological Survey of Kentucky, found a place for him in 1875 in a summer field camp, and repeated the experience the following year. That fall Davis returned to Harvard as assistant in Shaler's burgeoning elementary geology course, and spent the next two years existing on such crumbs as he could get from Shaler's patronage.

Shaler presided over a geology department which, thanks to the new elective system at Harvard, was expanding in numbers and range as the university grew. So in 1878 Davis was appointed instructor in geology and given his own course, "Natural History 1," a general course in physical geography and meteorology. By his own account, Davis was untrained in this new field and an inexperienced and unskilled teacher; indeed, in 1882 President Eliot warned him that he had little future at Harvard. But he did have a great talent for organization, both of scientific data and of institutions, and he had had some experience in the organizational and observational side of meteorology in Argentina.

As a geologist Davis was naturally in competition with his mentor Shaler, yet in the 1880s he clearly could not compete with Shaler in teaching ability or institutional standing. What more natural impulse could he have had than to take the edge of an opportunity in which there was no competition at Harvard, and devote much of his considerable intellectual energies and organizational power to it, at least until he had made a name for himself?

In founding the New England Meteorological Society and especially in shaping its direction, in the process gaining the cooperation of other Harvard and Boston area agencies in the support of professional meteorological research and teaching, Davis was able materially to advance his own ambitions toward a full-time academic career in science. He published some forty articles and numerous notes on meteorology between 1884 and 1894, most of them either in the *American Meteorological Journal* or the *Annals of the Harvard College Observatory*. His students, too, found these an outlet; several articles in the *Journal* and other periodicals carry the legend "Publications of the Laboratory of Physical Geography, Harvard University," and others are clearly those of Davis's students as well.

By 1892, Davis had built at Harvard what can only be called an empire for scientific meteorology. Like any successful entrepreneur of the period, he had started in business in a small way, successfully shaped a group of institutions to a considerable degree to his own satisfaction, and maximized his own dividends (seen in scholarly terms). The admiring term "Harvard School of Meteorology" bestowed by his fellow scientists is evidence that Davis had succeeded in establishing a teaching and research program which both set and met consensual standards for the new discipline. Whatever the term "professional meteorologist" may have meant, clearly Harvard was capable of producing them at the highest contemporary standard.[17]

In the meantime, Davis had managed to run the society so as to cut its losses where possible, by getting the Signal Service and later the Weather Bureau to take over much of the routine work of data collection and administration, and by persuading the Observatory to fund another of the society's losing operations, the *Bulletin*. The observatory affiliation also meant that the cost of publication of his major meteorological research studies was borne by others. His student Ward was made assistant in meteorology in 1892, capable both of doing Davis's dog work in teaching and research projects, as Davis had done for Shaler years before, and of editing the *American Meteorological Journal*, indeed even of funding its deficits.

Davis himself had gone up the ladder to assistant professor of physical geography in 1885 and was given advanced, research-oriented courses; he had been promoted to professor of physical geography in 1890. Shaler was teaching less and spending more time on administrative work, especially after becoming dean of the Lawrence Scientific School in 1891. The geology program at Harvard was expanding and prospering; graduate students in physical geography were beginning to arrive at the university. It would appear that meteorology, still considered an important part of physical geography, might continue to have bright prospects at Harvard and that the society might become a beneficiary of an expanded graduate program.

During its four years as a purely professional organization, the New England Meteorological Society continued to hold its three stated meetings per year. In this final period, too, the council directed the society's efforts toward improving the understanding of weather phenomena in the public schools. At the twenty-eighth meeting (21 October 1893), the council was given power to act on behalf on meteorology at the school level. A committee consisting of Davis, Upton, and Ward proposed to develop a set of practical exercises along the lines recommended by the Committee of Ten, conference on Geography, in which Davis had been a leader. In 1894–95, Davis and Ward gave lectures to teachers in Cambridge and Hingham. Ward offered Harvard's first summer course in meteorology the following summer for the same purpose. And as late as December 1895, Ward was still going out afternoons to give society-sponsored lectures to teachers in a number of eastern Massachusetts localities, and working up a series of practical exercises in meteorology to serve as samples for teachers.[18]

Davis's meteorological work culminated in his classic text, *Elementary Meteorology*, in 1894. By that time Davis had everything in meteorology a professor could want, except a leading idea. Synoptic and observational meteorology had little appeal for him, and his attempts to apply theoretical-deductive methods, his "long suit," had resulted in no breakthrough in this area. Such a breakthrough, when it came, was in Davis's geology in the late 1880s, when he began to develop his famous "geographical cycle" and publish papers in that field. Davis had found his métier, and meteorology, for him, had served its professional purpose.

In 1895 he turned over all of his remaining meteorological work to Ward, now instructor in meteorology, in order to pursue his geomorphological interests, giving Ward the same opportunity for a scientific career that Shaler had provided Davis himself twenty years before. Ward, lacking in mathematical skills and uninterested in advanced meteorological research, had his title changed to instructor in climatology in 1896. Under his chaperonage, the field Davis had cultivated so vigorously at Harvard began a long period of intellectual decline there.

Ward had struggled for four years with the *American Meteorological Journal*, but was as unable as his predecessors to put it on a sound financial basis. Abbe's resignation from the Board of Associate Editors in August 1895, in part a reflection of growing tensions between Weather Bureau and university-based meteorologists, precipitated another lengthy review of the status of the magazine. By October the remaining editors had decided that, in Rotch's words, "there are not 500 persons in the U.S. who are willing to pay $3 for a journal of scientific meteorology, be it popular or otherwise." A proposal from Chief Willis Moore that the Weather Bureau take over the *Journal* as an organ of the now federally controlled State Weather Services (to be brought together with private meteorologists under a proposed new American Meteorological Society) was coldly rejected. The Board of Associate Editors (which included Davis, Harrington, and Rotch) finally determined that the *Journal* should be closed out after the completion of volume 12, in April 1896.[19]

The decision on the *Journal* then posed the question, as President Niles put it, "as to whether it is advisable to continue the organization of the Society," given that its weather service function had been transferred to the New England Weather Service and its support function for the *Journal* was ending. In a letter calling a meeting of the council to discuss the question of "whether there is still left an occasion for the existence and maintenance of the New England Meteorological Society," Niles offered two suggestions. One of these, probably his own, was that it become "more like a club for the benefit of those who attend its meetings." This, of course, would have been a reversion to the regional laymen's society of 1884, and was not likely to be satisfactory to Rotch, Upton, and Davis. The other, possibly stemming from Ward, was that it focus on the more practical questions of applied meteorology and climatology.[20]

On 29 February 1896, the council met in special session to consider the fate of the society. Rejecting the two suggestions offered by Niles, the council agreed to recommend dissolution of the society at the end of the *Journal's* current year, the members to act on that recommendation at the regular April meeting. At that meeting, held 25 April, ballots returned by absentees totalled thirty-two for dissolution and only seven for continuance. The members there gathered then voted to dissolve the society, expend its remaining funds "for some meteorological purpose," transfer remaining reports of its investigations to the Harvard Astronomical Observatory for disposal, and send out notices of its dissolution to scientific journals. It then adjourned sine die.[21]

Secretary Davis's final statement of purpose, which incorporated Niles's formulation of the problem, is quite different in tone from the determination to make the New England Meteorological Society into a purely professional organization announced so triumphantly four years before. Davis wrote:

> Since the system of meteorological observations in New England and the publication of a monthly *Bulletin* were transferred to the New England Weather Service several years ago, the chief service of the Society, apart from its meetings, has been in the assistance it gave to the *American Meteorological Journal*, by subscribing for it to all regular members. Now that the *Journal* is to be discontinued, *by reason of insufficient support*, the meetings of the Society, *attended by only a few of its small number of members*, seem a hardly sufficient object to warrant the continuance of the organization [emphasis mine].

The dream of a simon-pure professionalism had faded. Nothing was said here about the conduct of special investigations; the statement is almost apologetic about having given up the weather service; the real problem is that there was insufficient support for a specialized disciplinary journal and for scholarly meetings in the field. Closed, for lack of interest. Or, as Davis described it more gently in 1932, the society had been "a promising *young* organization that failed to reach *maturity*"[22] (emphasis mine).

The characteristically Davisian language and the judgment are both significant. Maturity in this context, for Davis, meant evolution from a society with a strong lay component into an elite group of researchers on the order of the original Association of American Geographers, which he called forth ten years later on a strict membership basis, specifying a prior record of publication which in effect met his own model of what constituted "valid" scientific research.

Yet neither Davis's statement of 1892, nor the one forty years later, suggest more than a partial explanation. Neither considers the personal dynamic in the equation—Davis himself. President Niles's letter to the council, couched in restrained language, nevertheless goes straight to the issue. "It must be borne in mind," he wrote, "that some of the members who have been the main supporters of the work of the Society in the past have, in the course of events, become occupied principally in other departments of science, and cannot in the future do what they have formerly done."

The characterization applies most clearly to Davis, whose career strategy had worked to establish him as chairman of a thriving department of geology and recognized exponent of a major theoretical construct in his chosen field. Although his standing in meteorology had been sufficient to make him a leading candidate to head the new civilian Weather Bureau in 1891, and although he built on his decade of meteorological research in some of his later work on the erosional cycle, by 1895 Davis had made a conscious decision to turn his energies away from meteorological research and institution-building.

Davis had little use for observational meteorology, or for the manipulation of meteorological data to work out climatic patterns. Unable to equal Ferrel and others in meteorological theory, and always the entrepreneur, he in effect cut his losses and transferred his investments to more profitable areas. One then might go on to speculate, if one wishes, that could Davis have rejuvenated American meteorology in the theoretical fashion he did geomorphology, the early history of American academic geography might have responded to a very different climate.[23]

The inside cover of Ward's final issue of the *American Meteorological Journal* carries an advertisement for Horsford's Acid Phosphate, a remedy for headaches, dyspepsia, morning sickness, nervous prostration, and the ill effects of tobacco. This all-purpose painkiller had been developed by Eben Norton Horsford, a member of the society and formerly Harvard's Rumford Professor on the Application of Science to the Useful Arts. A full generation before, Horsford had left academia to manage his Rumford Chemical Works, after concluding that there was no place at Harvard University or in the America of his time for the devotee of "pure research."[24] A third of a century later the advertisement stood as an ironic comment on the premature attempt on the part of William Morris Davis and his friends to create a purely professional meteorological society in a land where everybody could observe and speculate about the weather, but which still lacked the research facilities, university base, and professional support to sustain an effort to institutionalize the study in the interest of academic science.

101

Notes

1. Consult Magali Sarfatti Larson, *The Rise of Professionalism: A Sociological Analysis* (Berkeley: University of California Press, 1977), references and bibliography; Burton J. Bledstein, *The Culture of Professionalism: The Middle Class and the Development of Higher Education in America* (New York: W. W. Norton, 1976), references; and Daniel J. Kevles, *The Physicists: The History of a Scientific Community in America* (New York: Alfred A. Knopf, 1978), essay on sources for germane references to professionalism, to the disciplines, and to higher education in this period.

2. My categories are modified from Regna Darnell, "The Professionalization of American Anthropology: A Case Study in the Sociology of Knowledge," *Social Science Information* 10, no. 2(1971): 83–103; idem, "Part Three: Professionalization of Anthropology," in *Readings in the History of Anthropology,* ed. Regna Darnell (New York: Harper and Row, 1974), pp. 169–70.

3. On the latter point, see Howard S. Miller, *Dollars for Research: Science and its Patrons in Nineteenth Century America* (Seattle: University of Washington Press, 1970): and Lawrence R. Veysey, *The Emergence of the American University* (Chicago: University of Chicago Press, 1965).

4. "New England Meteorological Society," *American Meteorological Journal* 1, no. 8 (1884): 300–301; *Bulletin of the New England Meteorological Society* 1, no. 1 (1884): 1–20.

5. John K. Wright, "The Field of the Geographical Society," in *Geography in the Twentieth Century: A Study of Growth, Fields, Techniques, Aims and Trends*, ed. Griffith Taylor (New York: Philosophical Library, 1951), pp. 543–65; idem, *Geography in the Making: The American Geographical Society, 1851–1951* (New York: American Geographical Society, 1952); and item, *Human Nature in Geography: Fourteen Papers, 1925–1965* (Cambridge, Mass.: Harvard University Press, 1966).

6. "Current Notes," *American Meteorological Journal* 1,no. 4 (1884): 116; Winslow Upton, "Weather Observers in New England," abstracted in *American Meteorological Journal* 1, no. 4 (1884): 302.

7. Material on membership, officers, and terms compiled from reports of the society's meetings in *American Meteorological Journal*, 1884–96; *Bulletin of the New England Meteorological Society*, 1884–92; U.S. Department of Agriculture, Weather Bureau, *Bulletin of the New England Weather Service*, 1892–96; and scattered biographical sources.

8. Number of observers is indicated in each monthly issue of the *Bulletin.* Activities of the society may be traced most easily through its *Bulletin* and through the *American Meteorological Journal,* as well as in Rotch's correspondence, 1884–96, found in Blue Hill Meteorological Observatory, Office Files, 1884–1937, Harvard University Archives (hereafter "BHMO, Office Files").

9. *Appalachia* 5, nos. 1–2 (1887–89): 71, 83, and 143; 7, no. 1 (1893): 80–81; William Morris Davis, "Mountain Meteorology," *Appalachia* 4, nos. 3–4 (1886): 225–44 and 327–50.

10. William Morris Davis, introduction to "Observations of the New England Meteorological Society in the Year 1891," *Annals of the Astronomical Observatory of Harvard College* 31, pt. 2 (1892): 161–62; *Bulletin of the New*

England Weather Service 1, no. 1 (1892): 1. For the history of the nation's weather service and its political vicissitudes in this period, see Donald R. Whitnah, *A History of the United States Weather Bureau* (Urbana: University of Illinois Press, 1961), chapters 1–6; and A. Hunter Dupree, *Science in the Federal Government: A History of Policies and Activities to 1940* (Cambridge, Mass.: Belknap Press of Harvard University Press, 1957), chapters 9, 11, and references.

11. Meetings reported and papers often published in *American Meteorolojgical Journal*; see also "The Exhibition of the New England Meteorological Society," *Journal* 5, no. 10 (1888): 440–46; Rotch to Abbe, 16 January 1889, Cleveland Abbe Papers, U.S. Library of Congress; Davis to Abbe, 4 October 1891, Cleveland Abbe Collection, Milton Eisenhower Library, Johns Hopkins University; Abbe to Davis 18 October 1891, William Morris Davis Papers, Houghton Library, Harvard University; "Announcement of 36th Regular Meeting of the N.E.M.S., Saturday, January 19, 1895," Thomas Corwin Mendenhall Papers, Niels Bohr Library, American Institute of Physics.

12. J. M. Ziman, *Public Knowledge: An Essay Concerning the Social Dimension of Science* (Cambridge: University Press, 1968), p. 105.

13. "Investigations of the New England Meteorological Society" *Annals of the Astronomical Observatory of Harvard College* 21, pt. 2 (1889): 107–273; ibid., 31, pt. 1 (1890): 1–156.

14. *American Meteorological Journal* 3, no. 5 (1886): 197, and 8, no. 12 (1892):578–79; Abbe to Ginn and Co., Boston, 10 June 1882, Abbe Collection; Rotch to Abbe, 15 October 1888, Abbe Papers, U.S. Library of Congress; Abbe to Davis, 24 December 1890, 5 January 1891, Davis Papers; Davis to Eliot, 10 June 1893, Ward to Eliot, 25 October 1893, Charles W. Eliot Papers, Harvard University Archives; Abbe to Gilman, 7 August 1886, 20 January 1892, Daniel Coit Gilman Papers, Eisenhower Library, Johns Hopkins University.

15. *Bulletin of the New England Meteorological Society* 1, no. 1 (1885): 1; "Circular Lately Issued by the New England Meteorological Society," *American Meteorological Journal* 3, no. 4 (1886): 151–53; "The Work of the New England Meteorological Society," ibid., 5, no. 3 (1888): 133–36; "The New England Meteorological Society," ibid., 9, no. 2 (1892): 93; *Bulletin of the New England Weather Service* 1, no. 1 (1892): 1; William Morris Davis, introduction to J. Warren Smith, "Five-Year Tables of Temperature and Precipitation for New England," *Annals of the Astronomical Observatory of Harvard College* 31, pt. 2 (1892):95.

16. Richard J. Chorley, Robert P. Beckinsale, and Antony J. Dunn, *The History of the Study of Landforms, or the Development of Geomorphology*, vol. 2, *The Life and Work of William Morris Davis* (London: Methuen 1973), passim and appendices 3 (Davis's bibliography) and 5 (general references).

17. Cleveland Abbe, "The Present Condition in our Schools and Colleges of the Study of Climatology as a Branch of Geography and of Meteorology as a Branch of Physics," *Bulletin of the American Geographical Society* 38 no. 2 (1906): 121. Davis's first advanced course in this area, "Natural History 20," which gave students the opportunity to investigate special problems in physical geography, was offered initially in the 1885–86 academic year, after he had been appointed assistant professor.

18. *American Meteorological Journal* 10–12 (1893–96), passim; Robert DeCourcy Ward, "Editorial Note," *American Meteorological Journal* 11, no. 12 (1895): 434–35. See also William Morris Davis, "Meteorology in the Schools," *American Meteorological Journal* 9, no. 1 (1892): 1–21; and Robert DeCourcy Ward, *Practical Exercises in Elementary Meteorology* (Boston: Ginn and Company, 1899); Ward to Rotch, 13 December 1896, BHMO, Office Files. After the society had disbanded, its remaining funds were used to award prizes for the best work in weather and climate done in any New England grammar school. See "Meteorology in the Public Schools," *Monthly Weather Review* 25, no. 1 (1897): 17–18.

19. Robert DeCourcy Ward, "Editorial Note: A Word of Farewell," *American Meteorological Journal* 12, no. 12 (1896): 367–71; Ward to Rotch, 9 August 1895; Harrington to Rotch, 9 September 1895; Rotch to Ward, 16 October 1895; Ward to Rotch, 22 November 1895, 13 December 1895; Ward to "My Dear Sir," 1 March 1896; Ward to Rotch, 13 March 1896, BHMO, Office Files.

20. Niles to [Members of Council], 21 February 1896, BHMO, Office Files.

21. "New England Meteorological Society," *American Meteorological Journal* 12, no. 12 (1896): 392–93; "The New England Meteorological Society," *Monthly Weather Review*, 24, no. 1 (1896): 13; "Dissolution of the New England Meteorological Society," *Climate and Crops* (U.S. Department of Agriculture, Climate and Crop Service, New England Section) 1, no. 3 (1896): 3.

22. William Morris Davis, "The College Life of Robert DeCourcy Ward," *Annals of the Association of American Geographers* 22, no. 1 (1932): 30.

23. Edwin Willets, assistant secretary of agriculture, to Mendenhall, 13 June 1891, Mendenhall Papers; Ward to Rotch, 19 June 1896, BHMO, Office Files; Davis, introduction to J. Warren Smith, op. cit., 95.

24. Miller, *Dollars for Research*, pp. 82–83; Margaret W. Rossiter, *The Emergence of Agricultural Science: Justus Leibig and the Americans, 1840–1880* (New Haven: Yale University Press, 1975), chapters 3 and 4. A copy of the *Journal* with original covers was located in the Research Department of the Boston Public Library; the set in the Clark University Library lacks this extra feature.

The Scholars

W.M. Davis and American Geography: 1880-1934

Robert P. Beckinsale

Rise of a "New Geography": The Uniqueness of the United States

Of the chief countries in which a "new geography" arose after the mid-nineteenth century, only the United States seems to have been dominated by largely or purely pedagogic aims and principles. In Britain the geography advocated by H. J. Mackinder was fitted to a worldwide empire and was rich in chauvinistic and global overtones. On the European mainland the Franco-Prussian war of 1870–71 had a considerable effect on academic geography. The unified German empire within a short period set up twelve additional chairs in geography under a strong military influence—Ratzel was twice wounded in the war—and its geographers were intensely interested in possible colonial tracts and in German-speaking peoples living outside Germany. But the victorious nation could afford to be innovative, informative, and discursive; and provided, among other valuable themes, spatial ideas such as lebensraum.

In France, the loser, the war debacle was blamed partly on the inferior quality of its officers, a failing which could be remedied by better geographical education. True there was also among their geographers a conviction that other countries of the world would benefit from experiencing French civilization, but the geography that developed was dominated by domestic needs and was strongly influenced by traditional Descartesism and the new philosophy of Henri Bergson, both of which placed high value on intuition and deduction. Thus the stark geographical determinism then rampant in some other nations was modified into a form of "possibilism," and a country which had been affected by strong centripetal functions since the seventeenth century experienced an upsurge of studies on natural or geographical regions (*pays*) in which, with due regard to intuitive and informed selection, culture and nature were symbiotic. Simultaneously there developed in the new German

107

empire, created from a mosaic of smaller centralized states, a tendency toward *Landschaftskunde* and a chorological geography or, in the modern idiom, *landschaftökologie*.[1]

In academic geographical teaching and institutions, these relatively small European countries were well ahead of the United States which covered half a continent and was socially or racially still uncongealed. When Davis was born geography was taught in only one college, Harvard, where it was introduced in 1841. By 1875 it had been introduced also at Princeton (1854), Cornell, the University of Wisconsin (1868), and Yale. But in some of these places it was taught, not necessarily every year, by the professor of geology, zoology, or some other subject and in some was combined with history.[2]

However, the uniqueness of the United States rested also on the explosive growth, westward expansion, and multiracial composition of its population. In Davis's lifetime (1850–1934), the United States grew in population by over a hundred million and received all told thirty-five million foreign immigrants. When he was born, there were very few states west of the Mississippi and about 85 percent of the population was rural; when he died, the national center of population had shifted westward from West Virginia near Huntington to the Indiana-Illinois boundary south of Lake Michigan, and more than half was urban. The contacts of new settlers with nature were direct and harsh, and it seems reasonable to assume that in the nineteenth century the majority of Americans were more interested in their physical environment than in their social conditions or human geography. Propably only truly servile or highly sophisticated societies tolerate investigations into their private affairs, and surely Frédéric Le Play would have died prematurely if he had pursued his detailed family surveys in the American West! Millions of Americans, who would have welcomed themes on their natural environment, would not have tolerated comments on their own life-style nor would have wished to read impracticable or unacceptable advice on the dangers of soil erosion and environmental exploitation, such as were expounded so clearly by George Perkins Marsh and other residents of the eastern seaboard.[3] With hindsight, it seems more than probable that in nineteenth-century America the only geography capable of attracting a wide following would have to have been dominantly physical. Davis was a realist; he instinctively sensed the right approach to create a wide following.

By the early twentieth century, America had changed more rapidly than Davis. The explosive development of the central states had created a new sphere of influence and there now existed in the American stream of consciousness two voices, that of the eastern seaboard and that of the central lakeside. Each was a mighty voice. The geographical milieu then began to embrace a traditional East and recalcitrant center; the former showed a growing interest in commercial themes, while the latter evolved a mind of its own and was not slow in expressing disapproval of Davisian themes.

The Unique Qualities of W. M. Davis (1850–1934)

The offspring of a well-known Philadelphian Quaker family, Davis in 1866 at the age of sixteen entered the Lawrence Scientific School at Harvard and graduated S.B. (magna cum laude) three years later.[4] During the following year he took a degree in mining engineering (summa cum laude). Among the Harvardians who influenced him most was Nathaniel Southgate Shaler. From late 1870 to 1873, Davis worked at the astronomical observatory at Cordoba in Argentina and used his off-duty days mainly for travel and the detailed investigation of insects. In 1877 he traveled round the world and then lectured at Harvard, with breaks abroad, until 1912, being for long periods professor of physiography and professor of geology. He published his first article in 1880, was smitten with the idea of a cycle of erosion when working in Montana in 1883, outlined it in 1889, and developed it fully in 1899. At the same time he wrote many excellent articles and a long-lived textbook on meteorology. During the early twentieth century he expanded, propaganded, and defended the cyclic concept and, more importantly, developed his themes on explanatory scientific description and methods of regional description. He used these concepts to boost the status and popularity of geography at all levels of education. From his professional retirement in 1912 to his death in 1934, he produced his best geographical and geomorphological works which show a distinct versatility of thought and often reveal the modified views of a formerly overdogmatic campaigner.

Davis was over thirty years old when, having been warned of his incompetency as a lecturer, he deliberately set out to turn himself into a most proficient educator.[5] At the same time he seized the chance to improve geographical education as a whole. He became one of the few professional geographers who realized the need for simplicity and general attractiveness based on a sound methodology. Among geographers he is rightly regarded as the master of method.

He found geography a chaos of facts and surmises, and saw that its physical side at least could be systematically arranged so as to allow it to compete with other disciplines all the way from grammar school to college. Such an explanatory scientific treatment of the physical environment would provide a satisfactory basis for studying the relationships between the inorganic and the organic world. Davis lived to see much of his "system of physiographic instruction and research adopted in colleges, gymnasia, lycées, and universities of every continent"[6] both for geography and geology. In respect to the latter we must notice that he was a close friend and colleague of the western geologists, such as J. W. Powell, G. K. Gilbert and T. C. Chamberlin, who steadfastly used their *Reports* and other writings to convey both factual information and their ideas on methods of scientific analysis. But only Davis roamed over the whole gamut of education in his subject.

Davis's Methods of Promoting Geography

The advancement of Davis and of geography are coincidental. He had no conflicting interests and disliked noncultural pursuits almost as much as he detested martial activities and colonialism. To him, life was an opportunity for the scientific investigation of natural science; his work was his hobby and during a long life he devoted an extraordinary number of hours to it. For over forty years he used his acumen in physical geography to advance the cause of academic geography as a whole in the United States. This he did in six main ways: by adding to its factual knowledge; by popularizing the need for a more scientific approach; by propounding its chief educational methods and popularizing new techniques; by fostering its independence as an academic subject; by providing a professional personnel; and by raising its general status or standing both at home and abroad. Obviously these avenues converge and carry much the same traffic.

Davis's Publications

After 1880 Davis's rule was "if it's worth writing, it's worth printing," and he wrote profusely and edited widely for scientific and educational journals. For over half a century he never failed in any single year to produce a few learned articles, and his peak annual production amounted to 25 separate works, totalling well over 800 pages, irrespective of numerous reprints. In at least twenty-five of those years he published some matter connected mainly with geographical education, and he seized on any opportunity to expound his favored methodology. His publications, exclusive of brief reviews, exceeded 500 sizeable articles and books and appeared all told in 48 different journals.[7] At various times he was associate editor of *Science, American Naturalist, Journal of Geography, American Journal of Science,* and the *American Meteoro-*

logical Journal, as well as being a member of other learned societies at home, and correspondent or honorand of sixteen academies or societies abroad.

He was a great promoter and encourager of new journals and contributed to twelve of them, including eight that still survive. For example, he contributed to the *Journal of School Geography* founded in 1897 by Richard E. Dodge, one of his former students who was lecturing at Teachers College, Columbia. In 1902 on Davis's advice this periodical was refounded as the *Journal of Geography.* Or again, it was Davis who first suggested privately and formulated publicly at St. Louis in 1903 the ideas that led to the foundation of the Association of American Geographers, now happily celebrating its seventy-fifth birthday. Those not acquainted with Davis's articles in this journal have missed some of the finest advocative writing in geographical literature. Today geographers may dislike their Davisian content, but their quality should be seen within the context of the "new geography" of the nineteenth century rather than in that of the "new geography" of modern times. Davis's reputation is at a disadvantage today because his *Geographical Essays* of 1909 are commonly thought to represent his conclusions whereas they represent his beginnings, and most of his finest articles came later. Whatever view is taken of the modern relevance of his publications, they form a corpus of quite exceptional length and excellence.

Popularization of a More Scientific Approach

Davis made a prolonged effort to improve the quality of geographical teaching in elementary schools, and to win a secure place for geography in the higher levels of education. In 1894 the *Report of the Committee of Ten on Secondary School Studies* affirmed that geography has long been a subject of recognized value in elementary schools and "that a considerable proportion of the whole school time of children" has long been devoted to it. Davis set out to rescue all precollege geography from uncoordinated factual memorization (mnemonics), and replace mnemonics with description or explanation based on a "scientific" or "rational" sequence of related statements. His great opportunity came in 1892, when the National Educational Association undertook to investigate the relationship between elementary and higher education as expressed in the content of school syllabuses and college entrance examinations. The association appointed a Committee of Ten under the leadership of President Eliot of Harvard, and they organized conferences to study nine different academic subjects. The conference on geography was chaired by T. C. Chamberlin, head of the geology department at the University of Chicago. Its other members included George L. Collie of Beloit College;

W. M. Davis of Harvard University; Delwyn A. Hamlin of Rice Training School, Boston; Mark W. Harrington of the Weather Bureau, Washington, D.C.; Edwin J. Houston of Philadelphia; Charles F. King of Dearborn School, Boston; Francis W. Parker of County Normal School, Chicago; and Israel C. Russell of Michigan University.

There is no doubt that Davis was mainly responsible for the report that was sent to the committee. It stressed that "physical geography should include elements of botany, zoology, astronomy, commerce, government and ethnology," and that it should assume a "more advanced form" and should relate more specifically to the features of the earth's surface, the agencies that produce or destroy them, the environmental conditions under which these act, and the physical influences by which the creatures of the earth are so profoundly affected. Although the committee members were surprised at the radical nature of the proposed changes, they adopted the report. Numerous schools now introduced a "new geography" and many new textbooks took up the theme, among them being A. E. Frye's *Elements of Geography* (1895), and T. W. Redway and R. Hinman's *Natural Advanced Geography* (1897). As usual Davis soon joined the van and in 1898 published *Physical Geography*, written with the aid of William Henry Snyder of Worcester Academy, Massachusetts, whose teaching experience was valuable in adapting the text to the needs of secondary schools. This popular textbook states unequivocally that

> the successful development of Geography, considered as the study of the earth in relation to man, must be founded on Physical Geography.... No rational or scientific advance can be made in the former without appropriate preparation in the latter.

The earth's physical features must be explained so that understanding aids the memory. They must not be presented apart from the manner in which they affect humanity's way of living, and "the organic environment of man, a large subject in itself," should by no means be neglected.[8]

Although these Davisian ideas met traditional resistance to change and took several decades to permeate widely the American educational system, their ultimate effect was large, especially in the East. Some of this influence may be glimpsed in the spread of climatology, in which

> the great pioneer in school and college work was.... Professor William Morris Davis, who made his elective courses for Harvard freshmen so thorough and so attractive, that they became the ideal model for all others. The influence of the Harvard school of Meteorology has been felt everywhere.[9]

In 1906 a thousand grade schools in the United States were teaching the elements of climate and using daily weather charts for simple forcasting. Most normal schools studied climatology, and no less than 144 colleges and universities had some meteorological instruction.

There can be no doupt that in America outside the eastern states the spread of Davisian physiography was relatively slow, as it required expertise and was expensive of time and equipment. Some areas obviously neglected the Davisian method and in others it was, as Preston James says, "gradually pushed out by general science, social studies and commercial geography,"[10] but the general causal relationship theme as preached by Davis—and numerous others—was too fundamental to be stifled. Take for example, the advice in *Principles and Methods of Teaching Geography* by Frederick L. Holtz, A.M. of New York (New York: MacMillan, 1926). Here a long chapter (pp. 120–41) is devoted to the causal relation, or the application of the scientific method, the explanatory principle that unifies modern geography. This praiseworthy principle transcends all others expecially if used with restraint because human reason, inclination, and even whim may occasionally be more important factors than the natural conditions. One important method of pointing out the more obvious geographic influences is by topics in causal sequence, thus aiding the memory and enabling students to work out little geographical problems. The author admits that this logical treatment "may become tedious even in higher grades."

The Davisian scientific physiography was undoubtedly dull for the unenthusiastic, yet we doubt if it was much more depressing than the interminable lists of national products—animal, vegetable, and mineral—that comprised commercial geography. The causal method in geography as a whole proliferated until modern times when the problem progressed from "Why?" to "How?" and "How much?" By restricting his vision largely to physical geography, Davis managed to avoid the grossly overdeterministic tendencies of some of his comtemporaries in America and in Britain. He never asked questions such as "Why do coastal dwellers have weak and flabby leg muscles? Why did the Swedes invent cream separators? Why are Portuguese women ugly?

Fostering Geography as a Specialized Field of Study

In Davis's heyday there was a notable lack of continuity between school and professional (higher) geography in American education. The geography of early years usually disintegrated into the study of its various components—geology, botany, etc.—at higher levels. Consequently at college and university level Davis saw the need both to reform existing curricula and to establish a much wider foothold for an independent geography. The core of geography was, he thought, worthy of broader treatment in colleges and of investigation in universities as may be seen in physiography, economic geography, and, for example, the "grand divisions of the lands" such as is studied in some German gymnasia and universities. "In all this we are not behind the English Universities, but we are far behind those of Germany, where professorships in geography are not uncommon."[11] There was, he continued, a great national need for professional geographers, especially for those willing to serve as topographical surveyors, cartographers, and explorers.

To promote geography Davis had to free it from its geological barnacles and its strictly meteorological and astronomical enmeshments. As a famous practitioner of these sciences, he had a most difficult task in trying to filch from them all mention of the human response or organic undertones. Whether the cause-consequence, earth-human relationships appropriated from these and other natural sciences formed a distinct geography was another matter. Ultimately his great achievement was to create an almost independent science of geomorphology, but in the shorter term he helped the whole geographical field by enhancing its status and ensuring it a new popularity. Geographers thoughout America and much of the remainder of the world survived and multiplied by riding on the Davisian bandwagon.

Davis constantly stressed the irrelevancy to geography of all scientific aspects that did not affect phenomena on the earth's surface. That the disentanglement was slow may be judged from his later advice:

"It is a sound principle of geographical description to omit all geological matter, however important it may be in some other relation, if it does not aid in picturing existing features.... It is only by attending scrupulously to details of this kind that a strong geographical discipline can be developed and maintained."[12]

Davis's advocacy of geography as an independent discipline in higher education is shown clearly in a long letter to President Faunce of Brown University, suggesting that he should establish a new geography department on an equal footing with the existing Geology Department.

Geology has a traditional position in our universities.... The science fully deserves the position that it has thus won.

Geography has no such position. It is still regarded by most persons in this country, even by most educated persons, as a school subject, not needing, indeed not capable of filling a place in our colleges. But the progress made by Geography in this country during the last 30 years, and in Europe during a longer period, suffices to show that this opinion is erroneous. Geography, properly presented, would be today of more general usefulness than Geology in a college education.

He goes on to commend general courses on geology with some field excursions, but considers that petrography and paleontology, as well as courses on historical geology, are essential only for professional geologists and are not suitable for general education.

The development of such courses, while geography remains undeveloped is, in my opinion, an educational mistake. General courses on the Geography of the United States and of Europe, each occupying half a year or more ... would not only have large educational value in general, but also larger application in other studies, such as engineering, history, and economics, which draw large numbers of students. It is indeed unfortunate that most college students in this country have no college opportunity of gaining a better knowledge of their home country or of Europe than was given them by (mostly very inexperienced) teachers in their preparatory years—if indeed they studied geography at all after leaving elementary schools.... The above mentioned general courses on the Geography of the United States and of Europe should be untechnical ... with no special emphasis on scientific physiography but with much attention to the present lay of the land, to climate factors, to natural resources, density of population, lines of movement, industries—all presented rationally, as a complex of interdependent facts. Further, these courses should be associated with other courses for more senior students, on physical geography, climatology, economic geography, and on other continents, especially at present South America.

They should be taught by people who had visited the countries, by professionally trained geographers not necessarily geologists.

Geographical courses have a distinct advantage over geological courses, in that the topics they teach are much more easily visible to the general, nonprofessional traveller. In his later life he can recognize many of them from a train window .... But more than this, Geography is destined to have an immensely larger economic use than geology in the coming half century and thus to extend more and more into the natural and commercial worlds ... geographical expertness, that is, a competent knowledge of various contries, will be called upon much oftener in the expansion of our commercial relations.... For all those reasons, I am convinced that Geography should be given at the earliest possible date, a position as good as that which Geology has so well won for itself in Brown University.[13]

These wise suggestions of a septuagenarian may surprise anyone familiar only with the professional Davis of twenty years earlier militantly propagandizing for a physiographic-dominated geography. In his old age, he had a finger in the creation of several chairs of geography and in the election of many professors.

The Provision of a Professional Personnel

In addition to lecturing to geography teachers at summer schools and conferences, Davis during three decades at Harvard tutored many students who later became famous in geographical circles. Academically he set a standard that only the ablest did not find discouraging, but which even the weaker admired. This academic Davisian ancestry played a major role in American professional geography until 1940, and remained important until at least 1950. Among the outstanding Harvard graduates trained under Shaler and Davis, and after 1906 under Davis alone, were (with the date of death in parentheses): Isaiah Bowman (1950); A. P. Brigham (1932); A. H. Brooks (1924); R. E. Dodge (1952); J. W. Goldthwaite (1948); Ellsworth Huntington (1947); Mark Jefferson (1949); D. W. Johnson (1944); C. F. Marbut (1935); R. de C. Ward (1931); and L. G. Westgate (1948).

Brigham summed up the situation nicely:

It has been his privilege to train a larger share of the teachers of physiography and scientific geography in the United States; every worker in these fields is daily making use of the results of his labour. He is the leading American specialist in land forms, and led by a masterly knowledge of the methods of pure science has become a leader in the wider field of geography.[14]

His students taught in many colleges and universities, but probably two were preeminent in recruiting adherents to geography—Mark Jefferson and Isaiah Bowman.[15] Jefferson was a superb teacher who for thirty-eight years (1901–38) was professor of geography at Michigan State Normal College in Ypsilanti. He took a wide view of the content of geography,

116

and worked to fill notable gaps deliberately avoided or ignored by the Harvard maestro in his professional days. Isaiah Bowman, who was a conjoint product of Jefferson and Davis, has won wide acclaim for his acumen in human geography but none, except his latest biographer, has given him full credit for his great skill in physiography. We cannot refrain from also mentioning the scholarly, wide-angled work of Ellsworth Huntington, if only to remind the reader of Davis's own great contributions to meteorology and of the interesting reception of Huntington and Cushing's *Principles of Human Geography*(1920)— which was severely criticized by Davis in private for its inadequate physiography, and Harlan H. Barrows in public for its inadequate human ecology. The Yale research professor had fallen between the traditional East and the innovative center.

Raising the Status of American Geography

Prior to Davis, geographical teaching in the United States was based largely on the writings of European scholars and on the work of professors who had migrated from Europe. Arnold Guyot, a Swiss emigré who was professor of physical geography and geology at the College of New Jersey from 1854 to 1884, comes readily to mind. A keen disciple of Carl Ritter, he was so teleological that he inadvertently boosted the spread of Davisian scientific explanatory geography. During the nineteenth century many famous European scholars, such as Charles Lyell, Archibald Geikie, and Friedrich Ratzel, visited America, but they came to see the country rather than to sit at the feet of its scholars. In the twentieth century the movement was reciprocated and American professors went to Europe to lecture and instruct in geography. W. M. Davis had an unequalled worldwide influence, and that of his disciples was also great. Because his international influence has recently been described elsewhere, we will here only attempt to assess the growing impact of American scholars on world academic geography as revealed by their attendances and contributions to early international geographical congresses.[16]

The five congresses between 1871 (Antwerp) and 1891 (Berne) were dominated by French, German, and Swiss geographers and, all told, only fifty-seven Americans attended or subscribed. In 1895 at London the American interest increased to forty persons, but European scholarship remained dominant. Physical geographers, especially geomorphologists, played a relatively insignificant part although William Libbey, professor of physical geography at Princeton, gave a remarkably fine lecture on the relations of the Gulf Stream and Labrador Current. In 1899 both Berlin and Washington, D.C., offered to house the congress, but the former was chosen as more convenient. Here the tide began to turn away from the massive matrices of pedagogical *landerkunde* and *volkerkunde* themes, toward physical geography and toward American geographers. Agassiz, Pumpelly, and Davis were among the twenty-four contributors and subscribers from the United States. In a discussion on peneplains, Albert C. de Lapparent showed how strongly the French had supported the subaerial concept of Davis as opposed to the older marine planation hypothesis. However, Davis spoke for himself in his famous address on "The Geographical Cycle." There are today, he said, as Albrecht Penck has shown, three distinct schemes of terminology which serve the purpose of geographical description. The first employs empirical terms only, the second uses a structural terminology, while

> the third method may be called explanatory, rational or genetic; here the effort is made ... not merely to describe the existing forms of the land, but to recognize the universally admitted fact that existing forms have been developed from earlier forms by the action of natural processes.[17]

In 1904 from 8 to 22 September, the Eighth International Geographical Congress was held in the United States under the presidency of Adm. Robert E. Peary. No less than 442, or nearly two-thirds, of the total participants came from the host country. The meeting was peripatetic with the work grouped under eight main classes headed by physical geography, which itself was subdivided into physiography of the land (chaired by Davis); volcanoes and earthquakes (C. H. Hitchcock); glaciers (H. G. Reid); oceanography (W. Libbey); and biogeography. G. K. Gilbert, in one of the general addresses of welcome, wisely said that "in the field of physical geography we have long been active and we have felt that we were reasonably in touch with the geographic scholars of other lands," but in nonphysical aspects "we are the merest tyros." Davis presented "The Complications of the Geographical Cycle," and physical geography supplied about 43 percent of the articles and printed text, over half of that being geomorphological. But the personal repercussions of this congress were perhaps equally important. Davis played a large part in its organization and participated in excursions to the Colorado canyon and Mexico. On these he won the admiration of Emmanuel de Martonne, who became enamored of Davisian geographical methods as well as of the work of G. K. Gilbert and R. D. Salisbury. On the Mexican journey, Vidal de la Blache strongly recommended to Davis—"the most Europeanized of all the Americans I have met here"[18]—one of his Parisian protégés, Henri Baulig, a serious and persevering student trained mainly in historical methods. After their meeting Baulig, then aged twenty-seven, found a lifelong interest in Davisian geomorphology and methodology, and his first visit to the United States lasted eight years. Not surprisingly it was this 1904 American congress that recommended that history and geography, two distinct disciplines, should be taught by different professors.

Davis now determined to test his cyclic ideas among foreign scholars, and for the next eight years led a great propaganda campaign at home and abroad. He toured and lectured widely in Europe, including Germany, where he met his chief opponents; and France and Britain, where he was a total success. He made it quite clear that his scheme of landform description

> really contains five elements: structure, process, stage, relief and texture (that is the spacing of the streams and their valleys, and the resultant breadth of the hills and spurs); all require consideration but the first three suffice when giving the scheme a name.[19]

In 1912 he directed a perfectly planned transcontinental excursion in the United States, which covered about thirteen thousand miles in fifty-seven days and delighted forty-three European geographers from fourteen different countries. The international popularity of American geography was now at its peak and although Davis won few new important adherents at home—except among geologists—his world status grew, especially with the help of Charles Andrew Cotton from New Zealand, who after 1922 produced a remarkable flood of Davisian geomorphological literature.

From 1912 to 1924, Davis spent much of his time in defending his simple cyclic concept against German opposition and in studying the coral reef problem. Simultaneously he did his best to promote geography as a whole. His *Principles of Geographical Description* (1915) was carefully vetted by several advisers, and represents a fair cross-section of contemporary American professional opinion.[20] It reviews at length the differences between empirical and explanatory descriptive methods. The latter, he admits, does risk errors, but the main risk to geography is the distraction arising from the introduction of complicated and irrelevant discussions on geological, biological, and historical matters. All geographical study aims at the description of existing landscapes, districts, and regions. Regional geography

> is synthetic in combining the helpful results of all other modes of presentation in a vivid description of a part of the earth's surface, so

that all the geographical elements and activities there occurring, inorganic and organic, shall be appreciated in their true spacial relations ... regional geography is the final object of a geographer's efforts [p. 62].

Davis's eulogy of regional geography contrasts with his disapproval of complicated and novel analytical explanations which, he thought, should be made simpler and familiar by "*SYSTEMIZATION*" as he had done with the simple "structure, process, stage" method.

We can sense that Davis was already beginning to take a wide view of geography as an academic study. By 1924 he suggested that, despite slow progress,

we have advanced from a day when geographical knowledge was gatherd in an almost unconscious, accidental manner by untraind travellers, to a day when it is consciously and intentionally gatherd by traind experts and when its different aspects and various appropriate ways of treating them are coming to receive deliberate attention.[21]

Five years later Davis received high praise for his account of the human geography of the United States, and his encouragement and appreciation of "every phase of geography."[22] In his final retrospect of American geography (1932), he suggested that the swing away from physiography toward commercial geography from about 1912 onwards had been so violent that it had "almost uprooted the Geo- from Geography," and needed some correction just as the earlier swing to physiography should have paid more attention to the human element.[23] In his old age, Davis continued his landform studies with and for the benefit of geologists who encouraged him in his explanatory deductive schemes, but he retained to the end his interest in geographical methods and presentation. "To him the method was, if anything, more important than the result."[24]

Notes

1. H. Leser, *Landschaftökologie* (Stuttgart: Ulmer Verlag, 1976).
2. Vera E. Rigdon, *The Contributions of William Morris Davis to Geography in America* (Ph.D. diss., University of Nebraska, 1933).
3. G. P. Marsh, *Man and Nature, or Physical Geography as Modified by Human Action*, ed. D. Lowenthal (1864; reprint ed., Cambridge, Mass.:

Harvard University Press, 1965); idem, *The Earth as Modified by Human Action* (New York: Scribner, 1874).

4. R. J. Chorley, et al., *The Life and Work of William Morris Davis*, The History of the Study of Landforms, vol. 2 (London: Methuen, 1973); see also vol. 1, (London: Methuen, 1964), pp. 621–41, which contains a photograph of President Eliot's letter to Davis (p. 623).

5. Ibid.

6. *Harvard University Gazette*, 31 July 1934, p. 149.

7. See note 4 above.

8. *Physical Geography* (Boston and London: Ginn, 1898).

9. C. Abbe, "The Present Condition in Our Schools and Colleges of the Study of Climatology . . . ," *Bulletin American Geographical Society 38 (1906): 121.* See also Dr. W. A. Koelsch's account of the New England Meteorological Society in the present volume.

10. P. E. James, *All Possible Worlds* (New York: Odyssey Press, 1972), p. 362.

11. W. M. Davis, "The Need of Geography in the University," *Educational Review* 10 (1895): 22–41. Reprinted in idem, *Geographical Essays* (1909; reprint ed., New York: Dover Publications, 1945), pp. 146–92, quote from p. 149.

12. W. M. Davis, "The Principles of Geographical Description," *Annals Association American Geographers* 5 (1915): 91. The whole article occupies pages 61–105.

13. W. M. Davis to W. H. P. Faunce; 2 March 1920. Reprinted in full in Chorley, *Davis*, pp. 473–75. Davis probably wrote this letter as chairman of the Committee of Five on the Promotion of Geography.

14. A. P. Brigham, *Geographen Kalender*, vol. 7 (Gotha: Justus Perthes, 1909), p. 66.

15. G. J. Martin, *Mark Jefferson: Geographer* (Ypsilanti: Eastern Michigan University Press, 1968); idem, *Isaiah Bowman* (Hamden, Conn.: Archon, 1980); see also idem, *Ellsworth Huntington: His Life and Thought* (Hamden, Conn.: Archon, 1973).

16. *Geography through a Century of International Congresses* (Paris: International Geographical Union, UNESCO, 1972). See R. P. Beckinsale, "The Development of Physical Geography," in *Geography through a Century*, pp. 114–30.

17. Ibid.

18. P. Vidal de la Blache to H. Baulig, 9 October 1904. Reprinted in full in Chorley, Davis, p. 444.

19. W. M. Davis, "The Systematic Description of Land Forms," *Geographical Journal* (London) 34 (1909): 308.

20. See note 10 above.

21. W. M. Davis, "The Progress of Geography in the United States," *Annals Association American Geographers* (1924): 214–15. Notice the reformed spelling being advocated by Davis.

22. A. P. Brigham, "An Appreciation of William Morris Davis," *Annals Association American Geographers* 19 (1929): 61–62; Davis, "The United States," in *International Geography*, ed. H. R. Mill (London: Newnes, 1899), pp. 710–73.

23. W. M. Davis, "A Retrospect of Geography," *Annals Association American Geographers* 22 (1932) 211–30.

24. K. Bryan, "William Morris Davis," *Annals Association American Geographers* 25 (1935): 23–31. For reference to methods: R. P. Beckinsale, "The International Influence of William Morris Davis," *Geographical Review* 66 (1976): 448–66; Chorley, *Davis*, pp. 746–49; H. Baulig, "William Morris Davis, Master of Method," *Annals Association American Geographers* 40 (1950): 190–92.

Environment and Inheritance: Nathaniel Southgate Shaler and the American Frontier

David N. Livingstone

For generations the North American frontier has been a source of almost hypnotic fascination, and a stimulus to speculative imagination for students of history and society alike. Nevertheless, although over thirty years have elapsed since J. C. Malin wrote of Nathaniel Southgate Shaler that "in his use of the frontier concept as applied to American history, he appears to have been original, and in some respects his application was more significant and enduring than Turner's," the wealth of his thinking has, in the interim, continued to be largely ignored, unappreciated and unexplored.[1] Born in Kentucky in 1841, Shaler spent most of his life at Harvard University, in Cambridge, where, having studied under the renowned naturalist Louis Agassiz, he became professor of paleontology (later changed to geology) and dean of the Lawrence Scientific School.[2] An outstandingly successful university teacher, he made original contributions not only to frontier theory, but also to conservation, evolutionary perspectives on race relations, and the development of the American summer school–an eclecticism which highlights his proficiency as geographer, historian, and social philosopher, and which his frontier views amply reveal.

To the first European pioneers however, the frontier's presence was more of a physical threat than an intellectual enigma. Since in colonial days securing the basic necessities of life depended on overcoming a wild environment, it was appropriate that the broadax should be viewed as the symbol of early American attitudes toward nature.[3] Animated further by a western tradition that envisaged untamed nature as cursed and chaotic, frontier dwellers struggled with wild country in the name of nation, race, and God, while poets employed evocative and terrifying images in their portrayal of a "howling wilderness" inhabited by

> hellish fiends, and brutish men
> That devils worshiped.[4]

Nonetheless, despite almost uniformly adverse wilderness images, few English-speaking colonists had reliable knowledge of the interior of the continent at the opening of the eighteenth century, for, under British policy, settlement in the interior was regarded purely as a means of forestalling the French.[5] But the American West remained, with all its pristine glory and potential agricultural wealth, and soon generated a vision which was reinforced by the achievement of American independence, its attendant, emerging nationalism introducing belief in a continental destiny as its principal article of faith. This new empire of the future, which Freneau felt would bring agriculture to the summit of perfection and make the nations brothers by disseminating the riches of the New World throughout the earth, was reflected in the thinking of Benjamin Franklin and in the writings of St. John de Crévecoeur who, in espousing an Arcadian view of America as a modern Garden of Eden, believed that the West would remain an agrarian refuge retaining an ideal simplicity and virtue as society spread westward.[6]

Following his inauguration as president in 1801, Thomas Jefferson, who believed that those "who labor in the earth are the chosen people of God, if ever he had a chosen people," became the intellectual father of the advance to the Pacific by sending Lewis and Clark up the Missouri and over the Rocky Mountains on a government exploration. As a consequence of this and two other expeditions—those by Pike (1806–7) and Long (1819–20)—there began to emerge the concept of a western desert to the east of the Rockies, a designation partly based on personal observation and partly quarried from impressions of earlier French, British, and Spanish pioneers.[7] However, during the 1840s the explorations of Frémont gave rise to a new concept which largely replaced the idea of a Great American Desert and became the driving force behind westward expansionist policy. This was the idea of the Great Plains, promulgated by William Gilpin, and eagerly promoted by railroad companies after the Civil War. Gilpin rejected the easterner's image of the West by affirming its agricultural significance in superlative terms; and in going beyond a recognition of the potentialities of the region to a belief in the inevitability of its development, he assumed the role of a bardic seer and strove to convey to his audience the contagion of his own ecstatic vision.[8]

With the frontier of agricultural settlement now lying along the ninety-sixth meridian, the end of the Civil War heralded the potential realization of an agrarian Utopia in the West. The westward surge in the postbellum years, under the stimulus of the Homestead Act (1862), soon pushed the frontier out upon the subhumid plains, so that by the 1870s lands were being occupied where rainfall was inadequate for traditional farming techniques. Once special seeds and new cultivation methods were successfully employed, the desert concept rapidly evaporated, agriculture became feasible on a large scale beyond the hundredth meridian, and the term *Great Plains* was readily adopted by men like J. W. Powell, F. V. Hayden, H. Gannett and W. M. Davis.[9]

The United States Census Report of 1870 represents the birth of a more conscious exposition of the frontier by several scholars. Its particular significance lies in the fact that its compilers, without instructive comment, incorporated a map which exhibited the very first representation of a frontier line. In particular, Francis A. Walker, who stressed the railroad's importance in accelerating population expansion westwards, must be identified as the major contributor to the frontier concept throughout the 1870s.[10] Like Henry Gannett, chief geographer of the United States Geological Survey under Powell, he recognized the dynamic, processual nature of the frontier by emphasizing the multi-directional and irregular character of settlement penetration.[11]

It was, however, through the work of Frederick Jackson Turner that intellectual America became most conscious of its own frontier experience. Although it is true that Turner repeatedly repudiated simple, one-factor, historical causation, it was the frontier as a many-sided process, described in 1893 as "this perennial rebirth, this fluidity of American life, this expansion westward with its new opportunities, its continuous touch with the simplicity of primitive society," which furnished "the forces dominating American character."[12] Largely reversing the emphasis of the Teutonic School's "germ theory" of American history, Turner employed the metaphor of the social organism's intrinsic plasticity as the central theme of his frontier hypothesis; and with similar biological analogy, he perceived in American frontier history a society recapitulating the stages of evolutionary advance from hunting through settlement to urban manufacture.[13] In his analysis, therefore, bio-social inheritance was envisaged as subservient to the influence of the physical environment in shaping the American nation.

In his evaluation of the West, Shaler exhibited that same inconstancy of attitude displayed by both his predecessors and his contemporaries. His first expressed opinion, to be found in a short 1883 article, indicates his early acceptance of the "well known fact, that the greater part of the

United States west of the meridian of Omaha is unfit for tillage."[14] Although a few isolated areas in this region could conceivably be cultivated, as a whole the only use he could envisage for it was as pasture; and since the inadequacy of water supply could be remedied by wells or storage reservoirs, the only limitation to an increase in the area's livestock-carrying capacity lay in the scarcity of herbage—a problem which could be solved by the introduction of forage plants indigenous to regions climatologically akin to the West. Some five years earlier, in 1878, Powell had proposed, inter alia, a revision of the near-sacred 160-acre formula of the Homestead Act in favor of smaller irrigated farms and very much larger grazing farms for the lands beyond the hundredth meridian.[15]

Shaler again assessed this area in "Physiography of North America," which appeared as the introductory essay to the fourth volume of Justin Winsor's monumental eight-volume treatise, *Narrative and Critical History of America.* Having divided the continent into six "fairly distinct regions,"[16] he examined each in turn, evaluating the "Cordilleran region" beyond the Mississippi Valley as an excellent mineral source; but in view of "the cold and dryness which their height entails," the Cordilleras were a curse to the nation by reducing one-third of the continent to sterility.[17] By 1887, however, the hint of a more positive appraisal can be detected for, keenly aware of the seriousness of forest depletion in this region, he suggested that the loss was particularly regrettable due to the absence of spontaneous timber replacement.[18] Moreover, three years later, he devoted the last of three articles on "Nature and Man in America"[19] to that section of North America west of the Mississippi where he now identified two regions in terms of economic potential. The eastern part, incorporating eastern Nebraska, Iowa, Missouri, eastern Kansas, Arkansas, and eastern Texas, offered excellent soils well suited for agriculture, but to the west lay an area of low, unreliable rainfall which, without irrigation, was suitable only for livestock. In 1894 appeared his most elaborate treatment of regionalism, expounded in *The United States of America,* a three-volume work of which Shaler was editor.[20] Here the arid west—that area between the hundredth meridian and the narrow Pacific coastlands—was examined in more detail. Those states stretching south from North Dakota to Texas represented a zone of transition comprising a belt of scantily watered lands about two hundred miles in width, beyond which lay the "desert region" of the Upper Missouri and the Cordilleran Plateau. The characteristics of the plateau would, he felt, bring about the social evolution of a new, nomadic human type whose mind and body would be adapted to the necessities of life which the herdsman's primitive occupation entailed. In contrast, the Cordilleran region—that area between the eastern face of the Rocky Mountain Front and the chain of the Sierra Nevada—was on many accounts the most interesting portion of the United States. Thus, whereas the whole region, some ten years earlier, had been rejected as a "curse to the continent," Shaler now issued an appeal for a detailed study of its potentially great mineral wealth, concluding that:

> It seems likely that in twenty years from the present time the aggregate of commercial values which will thus be won from this "Great American Desert" will be as large as that obtained in any equal area of the continent.[21]

Following his own move away from a cavalier dismissal of the West as a desert to this modified evaluation—"a revision which might be called a forest man's apology for his former misunderstanding"[22]—Shaler, in turn, likewise accounted for the earlier development of a desert concept as the perceptual response of pioneers and explorers nurtured in a forest environment:

> The American desert of our older geographies was pictured as the most inhospitable realm, fit to be compared in sterility with the arid wilderness of Asia and Africa. In part, the impression it made upon the early explorers was due to the fact that they went forth into its fields from the densely forested and superabundantly watered district of the eastern part of the continent . . . In a word, the name of desert, which was applied to the district, is to a great extent a misnomer; it might be better termed 'the arid region,' or, better still 'the country of scanty rain.'[23]

Fundamental to Shaler's differing appraisals of the West, and its potential, was a basic distinction between the forest and prairie frontiers, hinted at as early as 1884 and made explicit in the early 1890s. Attributing the timberless character of the western prairies to Indian firing,[24] he suggested in 1884 that, although the open prairies did have the temporary advantage that they could be more easily brought under cultivation than wooded regions, a forest environment so largely contributed to humanity's well-being that without it the structure of existing civilization could scarcely be maintained. And yet, contrarily, in this same paper Shaler remarked on the international significance of the rapid progress on the prairies and its associated swift tillage extension.

We are now in the midst of the great revolution that these easily won and very fertile lands are making in the affairs of the world. For the first time in human history, a highly skilled people have suddenly come into possession of a vast and fertile area which stands ready for tillage without the labor that is necessary to prepare forest lands for the plough.[25]

Demurring from this judgment some three decades later, Carl Sauer was to emphasize the problems and hardships experienced in extending settlement from the forest out onto the prairie. Early superstitions of the prairies as a virtually woodless desert with severe winter climates, together with the danger of fires, an apparent lack of water, and primitive transportation methods were some of the reasons Sauer identified as discouraging prairie homesteading.[26]

The basic forest-prairie distinction, subsequently developed in *The United States of America*, was made explicit in Shaler's famous 1891 monograph "The Origin and Nature of Soils"—"a landmark in the history of soil concepts."[27] Only those who had actively participated in clearing away a primeval wood could conceive how onerous was the task of preparing fields "for the uses of civilization." In contrast, the prairies were "holiday work" for those who, for generations, had battled with the primitive forests of the Atlantic coast; the open character of the country and its rapidly increasing accessibility by railroads, meant that the rate at which the frontier line moved to the west became vastly greater than before. Whereas it had taken the English-speaking pioneers a century to establish settlement as far west as the eastern front of the Appalachians and another hundred years before they could attain the border of the prairies, widespread occupancy of the Mississippi Valley took less than fifty years. This forced Shaler to conclude that "after 1830 the frontier ceased to have anything like a definite line, for the immigrants swarmed to the westward all along the ways of communication."[28] Thus, whereas Turner viewed the frontier in idealized terms as one continuous process through to its official closure in 1890, Shaler, who had corresponded and worked with Henry Gannett,[29] perceived it as a twofold advance. For Shaler then, the orderly line of wilderness penetration up to 1830 was a forest process, slow, dogged, and persistent; while the open grassland brought much more rapid, if irregular, settlement advance.

Similarly, while Shaler emphasized the importance of the railroad and steamboat in accelerating the westward movement (ideas perhaps derived from Walker), Turner, in overlooking the transportation and communication revolution of late nineteenth-century America, failed to realize how profound was the influence of accessibility on the pace of frontier settlement. For Shaler this was of particular significance for the advance of the northwestern frontier.

> The peculiarly rapid advance of these Northwestern settlements is undoubtedly due to the singularly perfect organization of the ways 'by which the people were brought to the country. The waters of the Great Lakes, of the upper Missouri and of its navigable tributaries, with the aid of cheap steamboats, at once laid open a large portion of the area to settlement, under conditions which permitted the incoming people to bring an abundant store of household comforts with them. The rapid construction of railways, which under our system of Government land grants had their termini generally on the very frontier, afforded a yet more convenient method of access to the land. The prairie character of the surface made it possible for the tillage swiftly to occupy so large a part of the area that the people at once won their way to wealth through their exports of grain and cattle.[30]

And so, looking inward on America's domestic historical scene, Shaler focussed on the twin themes of grassland and transportation as key elements in the changing subjugation process of the continent—elements so vital that failure to perceive them meant that, as Malin says, Turner never really got his frontier out of the woods.

Shaler, however, did not find these factors sufficient as exhaustive causal explanations for the complex, yet successful, westward movement, and so from time to time he directed his readers to features of a more sociocultural nature. Like Herbert B. Adams, Woodrow Wilson, and John Fiske, Shaler adopted the "germ theory" which posited a Teutonic origin of American democratic institutions in the English shire and ultimately in the *Volkmoot* of the German forests.[31] To this he wedded ideas of Aryan supremacy and immigration restriction, and interpreted American history in terms of persistent racialnational traits deemed characteristic. Such inherited institutions and skills had so largely determined the advance of the American people that Shaler could assert:

> All the progress of our people has been shaped and controlled by the inherited traditions which they brought from the Old World. This accumulation of motives which determined the spirit of individual and associated action, and has been manifested in the morals, religion, and politics, of this country, is the aggregation of experience extending over thousands of years.[32]

In *Nature and Man in America* (an exceptionally popular work first published in 1891 and reappearing in new editions until well into the twentieth century), Shaler conceded the unsuitability of the North American continent as a cradle for civilization, but contended that it provided unparalleled opportunities for the dissemination of racial characteristics bred elsewhere; in fact, it brought "those characteristics into interaction on a field favorable for their best development."[33] The United States, therefore, was in no way inferior to the Old World; and, in contrast to Buffon, Shaler protested that in its transplantation from Europe to America the Aryan race had not deteriorated, but had probably benefitted. Ostensibly Frederick J. Turner pursued this form of argument, but without Shaler's overt racism,[34] by showing that America meant generation, not degeneration. Combining the influence of inherited traditions and environmental conditions, he suggested that each frontier furnished "a new field of opportunity, a gate of escape from the bondage of the past." Nonetheless, writing in the Chicago *Record-Herald* in 1901, Turner expressed the conviction that the coming of Italians, Poles, Russian Jews, and Slovaks was "a loss to the social organism of the United States." While the immigrants in general were of doubtful value compared with the ethical excellence of those stocks which had hitherto made the nation, the Jewish people in particular disturbed him greatly. The social fabric of the Jews, evolved through generations of life in crowded inner-city ghettos, had produced, Turner maintained, "a race capable of living under conditions that would exterminate men whom centuries of national selection had not adapted to endure squalor and the unsanitary and indecent conditions of a dangerously crowded population."[35]

Although Turner, in a reply to Merle Curti, insisted that he had not been influenced by Shaler,[36] he is known to have used for his student dissertation an article published in the same volume of Winsor's *History* as Shaler's "Physiography of North America"; moreover E. D. Neill, author of this article, had referred his readers to Shaler's introductory essay. Certainly *Nature and Man in America* was familiar to Van Hise and Chamberlin, both intellectual colleagues of Turner at Wisconsin; indeed Shaler's friendship with Chamberlin, revealed in the latter's acceptance of an invitation to spend the summer of 1888 with him in his retreat on Martha's Vineyard, could well indicate an indirect influence on Turner's thinking.[37]

Shaler also acknowledged the importance of those skills acquired through the frontier experience of the New World itself. The long educational experience of subjugating a new country had induced not only that training in self-reliance which was essential for the frontier dweller, but also the ability to frame and consolidate both social and governmental systems. In fact, the terrain characteristic of the forest frontier had brought about the development of this new kind of social being, "that essence of the practical man" who, still a slayer of woods, believed he served the "god of progress by the sacrifice of the forest."[38] This individual found a place in Shaler's evolutionary forest model of human development. In this scheme mankind, originating in the trees and then dwelling on the forest floor, eventually emerged from his ancestral woods as a forest-destroying, frontier farmer who was coming to see the need for developing a conservation program. While others denounced the system of pioneer farming as wasteful, myopic, or immoral, Shaler instead conceived of it as an inevitable stage in the nation's historical process. Indeed it was the colonists' ready adoption of the strong-rooted Indian corn or maize, an agricultural modification later stressed by Carl Sauer,[39] which Shaler felt provided part of the foundation of the rapid advance of early settlement. While the crop species and tillage traditions developed in northern Europe were satisfactory for life on the Atlantic seaboard, Shaler appreciated their inadequacy with interior penetration, and from this extracted a general frontier principle which encompassed both the pioneers' initial response to their environment and the subsequent modification of farming methods. Like Turner, who observed that "at the frontier the environment is at first too strong for the man,"[40] Shaler concluded:

> The result is, that when a new portion of our frontier is occupied there is apt to be a period of rude and painful experience in which there is a frequent loss of crops, leading to the impression that the area is more or less unsuited to the needs of agriculture. After a time the culture becomes more or less reconciled to the environment, and the people become more hopeful for their future.[41]

Also like Turner, Shaler found the biological sciences a rich source of metaphorical inspiration[42] and, to the dismay of his teacher Louis Agassiz, adopted not only Darwinism as an all-embracing *Weltanschauung,* but a more specific neo-Lamarckian version of evolutionary thinking.[43] From the early 1860s, Shaler had entertained doubts about the efficacy of natural selection alone in accounting for evolutionary development, and in a paper reporting his research on brachiopoda showed that several of the series had developed features at great organic cost which, far from having any survival value, rather appeared disadvantageous.[44] In essence, neo-Lamarckism was an attack upon monistic interpretations of evolution by natural selection, in that natural selection per se could not originate anything, but only came into operation as a mechanism after some feature had been developed through direct environmental experience and passed on by heredity. Characterizing organic life by its ability to inherit features acquired through such immediate environmental adaptation, Shaler could assert that organisms

> adapt themselves in an immediate manner to the peculiarities of their environment. Those conditions which surround them make an impression on their bodies which is transmitted to their progeny, and those influences, accumulating from age to age, become the precious store of influences which lead organisms ever upward to higher planes of existence.[45]

Furthermore, Shaler's interest in the biological phenomena of atavistic reversions to characters of lower ancestral types, the retrogression inherent in blending hypotheses of inheritance, and his advocacy of "stirpiculture" or eugenics in terms of selective breeding to retain hereditary talent, reflect the pervasive influence of Francis Galton's work in *Hereditary Genius* (1869).[46]

Since neo-Lamarckism provided a link between social and intellectual progress and organic mental evolution, it was not difficult for Shaler to extend his biological thinking into the mental, moral, and social realms. The organism's response to those difficulties posed by the physical environment was a cornerstone in his concept of the evolution of mind. Whereas the superb physical adaptation of bees and ants to environmental conditions meant that their mental operations were purely instinctive and automatic, it was the physical inefficiency of human beings which forced them to use the hand. If, however, humans had been as amply provided with instruments suited to their needs as had bees, Shaler believed that the quality of human intelligence would have been no more rational than that of the insects.

For his views on moral evolution Shaler relied on John Fiske, who accounted for the qualities of sympathy and cooperation by prolonged infantile dependence, and argued that the first step toward civil society came with the extension of the maternal instincts to family and clan. Although at the individual level altruism seemed inconsistent with natural selection, when the group was viewed as the basic unit of evolution, communal solidarity had survival value. Thus those clans in which the primeval selfish instincts were subordinated to group needs would prevail in the struggle for life. Echoing Wallace, however, Shaler held that with the emergence of civilization, humanity was freed from the workings of natural selection—overall an essentially two-stage interpretation of human evolution, in which cooperation and competition, sympathy and struggle, each played a part.[47]

For Shaler, man's mental characteristics (that "capacity to plan actions in relation to his needs") and his moral attributes (derived from the progressive extension of sympathy from family to clan and race) not only differentiated him from the rest of the animal kingdom, but formed the basis of social evolution. The extrapolation of family relationships, as an organizational model, to the tribal level, and the invention of weapons and tools as property, became the institutional bases of the inauguration and development of social government.[48] Mental, moral, and social evolution were thus not only intimately related, but were superstructures erected on an environmental foundation.

In America, the decisive environmental reality was the frontier and it had, therefore, a profound influence on the evolution of the nation's political institutions and social traits. The conditions of life on the frontier had always forced settlers to devote their energies to practicalities rather than to abstract, theoretical issues, and had produced that "inventiveness" which was a major quality of the "American spirit." While every member of the Aryan race had innovative capacities, Shaler believed that "their efficiency in this work depends upon the stimulus that comes to them from their surroundings."[49] Significantly, Shaler emphasized that American inventiveness was manifest not only in technological ingenuity, but more especially in the institutions evolved by the American people to meet their social and governmental needs. Their intellectual practicality and pragmatic inventiveness were the result of their participation in a metaphorical military conquest of the frontier wilderness which left little time for meditation.[50]

For Shaler, as for Turner, such colonial conditions were peculiarly adapted to be "the nursery of freedom" by presenting possibilities for emancipation from the tyranny of ancient institutions. In coming to such a wilderness affording abundant opportunities for agriculture and enterprise, the settlers threw off the shackles of the "cramping influences of their ancient life"[51] and "became accustomed to think and act freely, guided only by the ideals which their religious and social traditions and their written law enjoined upon them."[52] Indeed for Shaler, it was this very emancipation from the methods of the Old World that brought about the American rebellion against the tightening reins of authority, and showed that the nation had outgrown the system of the mother country. Forged on the anvil of frontier experience, the American Declaration of Independence was thus a clear and masterful statement of their emancipation from hampering systems. So the frontier was preeminently a place of freedom—both political and social—and, for Shaler and Turner alike, was a region of religious independence. But while Turner saw the multiplicity of religious sects as a reflection of the contest for power and the expansive tendency of the frontier issuing in church rivalry, Shaler felt that such ecclesiastical patterns were more a reflection of their freedom from the influence of tradition.

Shaler's thinking on the frontier was largely premised on the twin themes of nature and nurture—environmental conditions and inherited traditions—which interacted in the historical process of the New World to evolve the features of the American character. Although reflecting some of the major intellectual currents of his day, Shaler's original contribution to the frontier theme lies in his imaginative, eclectic synthesis. A lack of systematic exposition and absolute consistency in his emerging frontier philosophy in no way detracts from the essential underlying tenets which were among the basic presuppositions of his conceptual framework, but reveals the progressive evolution of his own fertile mind. Carefully distinguishing the frontier experience of the eastern forest pioneers from that of the settlers on the open prairie grasslands, he stressed the importance of soil fertility, agricultural and technological innovations, and acquired educational experience in the rapid westward movement. Holding the themes of inheritance and environment in balance, Shaler, from an evolutionary viewpoint, assessed the influence of the frontier as a major factor in the social evolution of the American people.

Acknowledgements

I should like to express my thanks to Mr. J. A. Campbell for many valuable comments on an earlier version of this paper, and to Dr. R. H. Buchanan for his helpful observations. References to and quotations from manuscripts are by permission of the Harvard University Archives.

Notes

1. James C. Malin, *Essays on Historiography* (Lawrence: University of Kansas Press, 1948), p. 45.
2. John E. Wolff, "Memoir of Nathaniel Southgate Shaler," *Bulletin of the Geological Society of America*, 18 (1906): 592–609; Nathaniel S. Shaler, *The*

Autobiography of Nathaniel Southgate Shaler (Boston and New York: Houghton Mifflin Co., 1909); Walter Berg, "Nathaniel Southgate Shaler: A Critical Study of an Earth Scientist" (Ph. D. diss., University of Washington, 1957); William A. Koelsch, "Nathaniel Southgate Shaler," in *Geographers: Biobibliographical Studies*, ed. T. W. Freeman and Philippe Pinchemel (London: Mansell, 1979), pp. 133–39; James Lee Love, *The Scientific School in Harvard University* (Burlington: privately printed, 1944).

3. Roderick Nash, *Wilderness and the American Mind* (New Haven: Yale University Press, 1967); Hans Huth, *Nature and the American: Three Centuries of Changing Attitudes* (Berkeley: University of California Press, 1957); J. Wreford Watson, "The Image of Nature in America," in *The American Environment*, ed. W. R. Mead (London: Athlone Press, 1974), pp. 1–20.

4. Michael Wigglesworth, "God's Controversy with New England," quoted in Henry Nash Smith, *Virgin Land: The American West as Symbol and Myth* (New York: Vintage Books, 1950), p. 4.

5. Henry Nash Smith, *Virgin Land: The American West as Symbol and Myth* (New York: Vintage Books, 1950); John F. Davis, "Constructing the British View of the Great Plains," in *Images of the Plains: The Role of Human Nature in Settlement*, ed. Brian W. Blouet and Merlin P. Lawson (Lincoln: University of Nebraska Press, 1975), pp. 181–85.

6. Arthur A. Ekirch, Jr., *Man and Nature in America* (New York: Columbia University Press, 1963).

7. See G. Malcolm Lewis, "Three Centuries of Desert Concepts in the Cis-Rocky Mountain West," *Journal of the West* 4 (1965): 457–68; Ralph C. Morris, "The Notion of a Great American Desert East of the Rockies," *Mississippi Valley Historical Review* 13 (1926–27): 190–200; G. Malcolm Lewis, "First Impressions of the Great Plains," in *The American Environment: Perceptions and Policies*, ed. J. Wreford Watson and Timothy O'Riordan (London: John Wiley and Sons, 1976), pp. 37–45.

8. G. Malcolm Lewis, "William Gilpin and the Concept of the Great Plains Region," *Annals of the Association of American Geographers* 56 (1966): 33–51.

9. G. Malcolm Lewis, "Changing Emphases in the Description of the Natural Environment of the American Great Plains Area," *Transactions of the Institute of British Geographers* 30 (1962): 75–90.

10. Fulmer Mood, "The Development of Frederick Jackson Turner as a Historical Thinker," *Publications of the Colonial Society of Massachusetts* 34 (1943): 306; item, "The Concept of the Frontier, 1871–1898," *Agricultural History* 19 (1945): 24–30; Carl O. Sauer, in his paper "On the Background of Geography in the United States" (in *Heidelberger Studien zur Kulturgeographie: Festgabe für Gottfried Pfeifer*, Heidelberger Geographische Arbeiten, vol. 15, [Wiesbaden: Franz Steiner Verlag, 1966], pp. 59–71), emphasizes Walker's importance in American geography, extolling in particular his organization of the massive census of 1880 which, he asserts, "is the greatest single contribution to the historical geography of the United States."

11. Francis A. Walker, "The Indian Question," *North American Review* 116 (1873): 329–88; Henry Gannett, "The Settled Area and the Density of our Population," *International Review* 12 (1882): 70–77.

12. Frederick J. Turner, "The Significance of the Frontier in American History," *Proceedings of the State Historical Society of Wisconsin* 41 (1894): 79–112.

13. William Coleman, "Science and Symbol in the Turner Frontier Hypothesis," *American Historical Review* 72 (1966): 22–30; Robert F. Berkhofer, Jr., "Space, Time, Culture and the New Frontier," *Agricultural History* 38 (1964): 21–30; Ray A. Billington, *Genesis of the Frontier Thesis: A Study in Historical Creativity* (San Marino, Calif.: The Huntington Library, 1971).

14. Nathaniel S. Shaler, "Improvement of the Native Pasture-Lands of the Far West," *Science*, 23 March 1883, pp. 186–87.

15. John W. Powell, *Report on the Lands of the Arid Region of the United States* (Washington, D.C.: Government Printing Office, 1878).

16. The six physiographic regions identified were: (1) the eastern lowlands between the shore and the Appalachians; (2) the lowlands of the Gulf States; (3) the Mississippi Valley Plain; (4) the Appalachian Mountains; (5) the Cordilleras; (6) the Pacific Shoreland Fringe.

17. Nathaniel S. Shaler, "The Physiography of North America," in *Narrative and Critical History of America*, ed. Justin Winsor, (Boston: Houghton Mifflin Co., 1884–89), 4:i–xxx.

18. Nathaniel S. Shaler, "The Forests of North America," *Scribner's Magazine* 1 (1887): 561–80.

19. Nathaniel S. Shaler, "Nature and Man in America," *Scribner's Magazine* 8 (1890): 360–76, 473–84, 645–56.

20. Nathaniel S. Shaler, ed., *The United States of America*, 3 vols. (New York: Appleton and Co. 1894). Lewis Mumford in *The Brown Decades: A Study of the Arts in America 1865–1895* (New York: Dover Publications, 1955) says: "In the compendious survey of the country which closed the period, the book Shaler edited on the United States, the land was for the first time given its due place" (p. 29).

21. Shaler, *The United States of America*, 1:168.

22. Malin, *Essays on Historiography* p. 61. In his monograph "The Origin and Nature of Soils" (*United States Geological Survey, 12th Annual Report* [1890–91], pp. 219–345), Shaler viewed forest soils as the criterion against which other soil types were to be judged, and thus considered prairie soils under the heading "Certain Peculiar Soil Conditions."

23. Shaler, *The United States of America*, 1: 145–46.

24. Carl O. Sauer supported this explanation in "The Agency of Man on the Earth," in *Man's Role in Changing the Face of the Earth*, ed. William L. Thomas, Jr. (Chicago: University of Chicago Press, 1956), pp. 350–66.

25. Shaler, "The Physiography of North America" pp. xiv, xv.

26. Carl O. Sauer, "Conditions of Pioneer Life in the Upper Illinois Valley," in *Land and Life: A Selection from the Writings of Carl Ortwin Sauer,* ed. John Leighly (Berkeley and Los Angeles: University of California Press, 1963), pp. 11–22.

27. Clarence J. Glacken, "Changing Ideas of the Habitable World," in Thomas, *Man's Role*, p. 84. For Shaler's role as one of the pioneers of soil science along with Dokuchaev, and his concept of the soil as an organism, see C. C. Nikiforoff, "Reappraisal of the Soil," *Science* 129 (January 1959): 186–96.

28. Shaler, *The United States of America*, 1:47.

29. There are several letters from Henry Gannett, chief geographer of the United States Geological Survey, to Shaler concerning maps for the Census Reports

between 1885 and 1887 in Harvard University Archives, Shaler Box File, HUG 1874.10.

30. Shaler, *The United States of America*, 1:134, 135; also 3: 1270, 1271. The importance of these means of communication was stressed by Carl O. Sauer in "Pioneer Life in the Upper Illinois Valley," in *Land and Life*, ed. Leighly, pp. 20–22.

31. Richard Hofstadter, *Social Darwinism in American Thought* (Philadelphia: University of Pennsylvania Press, 1944); item, *The Progressive Historians* (New York: Vintage Books, 1970); Gene M. Gressley, "The Turner Thesis— A Problem in Historiography," *Agricultural History* 32 (1958): 227–49.

32. Shaler, *The United States of America*, 3: 1272.

33. Nathaniel S. Shaler, *Nature and Man in America* (New York: Charles Scribner's Sons, 1891), p. 164.

34. The significance of immigration restriction and racial thinking in the thought of the period is traced in Barbara M. Solomon, *Ancestors and Immigrants: A Changing New England Tradition* (Chicago: University of Chicago Press, 1956); John Higham, *Strangers in the Land: Patterns of American Nativism* (New York: Atheneum, 1973).

35. Quoted in Thomas F. Gossett, *Race: The History of an Idea in America* (Dallas: Southern Methodist University Press, 1963), p. 293; see also Gilman M. Ostrander, "Turner and the Germ Theory," *Agricultural History* 32 (1958): 258–61.

36. Billington, *Genesis of the Frontier Thesis*, p. 272; see also Robert P. Block, "Frederick Jackson Turner and American Geography," *Annals of the Association of American Geographers* 70 (1980): 31–42.

37. A letter from T. C. Chamberlin, 8 December 1887, office of the president, University of Wisconsin, to Shaler says: "Nothing would give me more pleasure than to take a vacation with you next summer in your charming retreat on Martha's Vineyard." Harvard University Archives, Shaler Box File, HUG 1784.10.

38. Nathaniel S. Shaler, "The Forests of North America," *Scribner's Magazine* 1 (1887): 561.

39. Carl O. Sauer, "The Settlement of the Humid East," in *Yearbook of Agriculture* (Washington, D.C.: Government Printing Office (1941), pp. 157–66.

40. Frederick Jackson Turner, *The Frontier in American History* (New York: Henry Holt and Company, 1920), p. 4.

41. Shaler, *The United States of America*, 1: 408, 409.

42. Coleman, "Science and Symbol"; Rudolf Freund, "Turner's Theory of Social Evolution," *Agricultural History* 19 (1945): 78–87.

43. Edward J. Pfeifer, "The Genesis of American Neo-Lamarckism," *Isis* 56 (1965): 156–67; George W. Stocking, Jr., "Lamarckianism in American Social Science: 1890-1915" *Journal of the History of Ideas* 23 (1962): 239–56. Shaler's close friendship with A. Hyatt, subsequently the father of American neo-Lamarckism, is recorded in A. E. Verrill, "Diary 1860–63," Harvard University Archives, HUD 860.90.5F; see also Ralph W. Dexter, "Three Young Naturalists Afield: The First Expedition of Hyatt, Shaler, and Verill," *The Scientific Monthly*, July 1945, pp. 45–51.

44. Nathaniel S. Shaler, "Lateral Symmetry in Brachiopoda," *Proceedings of the Boston Society of Natural History* 8 (1861–62): 274–79.

45. Nathanial S. Shaler, *The Interpretation of Nature* (Boston and New York: Houghton Mifflin Co., 1893), p. 146; see also idem, *The Neighbor: The Natural History of Human Contacts* (New York and London: A. P. Watt, 1904), pp. 3, 4.

46. In "European Peasants as Immigrants" (*Atlantic Monthly* 71 [1893]: 651), Shaler remarked: "The researches of Mr. Francis Galton, and of the other investigators who have followed his admirable methods of inquiry, have clearly shown that the inheritance of qualities in man is as certain as among the lower animals."

47. Nathaniel S. Shaler, "The Natural History of Politics," *Atlantic Monthly*, March 1879, p. 304.

48. Nathaniel S. Shaler, *The Citizen: A Study of the Individual and the Government* (New York: A. S. Barnes, 1904), p. 16. Institutions were used by early anthropologists as criteria for interpreting the psychogenetic development of human culture. See F. W. Voget, "Man and Culture: An Essay in Changing Anthropological Interpretation," *American Anthropologist* 62 (1960): 943–65.

49. Shaler, *The Citizen*, pp. 320, 321.

50. This emphasis in Shaler's thought reflects the influence of Pragmatism, the new American school of philosophy emerging from the work of his four personal friends, Josiah Royce, Charles Peirce, Chauncey Wright, and William James. See Morton White, *Science and Sentiment in America: Philosophical Thought from Jonathan Edwards to John Dewey* (New York: Oxford University Press, 1972).

51. This shows the inadequacy of Gulley's remark that "Shaler concluded that American ideals of family, church and political organization were an inheritance from the Old World." J. L. M. Gulley, "The Turnerian Frontier," *Tijdschrift voor Economische en Sociale Geografie* 50 (1959): 68.

52. Shaler, *The Citizen*, p. 30.

William Morris Davis—The Course of Development of His Concept of Geography

Richard Hartshorne

In discussions of the history of geographic thought in the United States it is generally accepted that William Morris Davis played the leading, if not the dominant, role during the first quarter of this century. It is also common to present his view of the scope and purpose of geography as an unchanging position, much as we find it in his address in 1905 as first president of the Association of American Geographers. It would be ironic if this were really the case, when one remembers Davis's repeated theme of the evolutionary principle in explanation.

John Leighly observed years ago, in a paper concerned primarily with a different topic, that Davis's view of the purpose of physical geography had changed at some time in the 1890s, but he had not studied the material in sufficient depth to permit reliable conclusions.[1] The superb biographical study by Beckinsale and his colleagues is rich with information on Davis's work in geography, which however is not presented in chronological order.[2] In a paper read at a recent meeting of the Association of American Geographers, Beckinsale pointed directly to changes in Davis's thinking in the latter part of his career.

For the present study, I have sought to follow Davis's evolutionary principle by examining chronologically the record of his writings about the nature,scope, and purpose of geography. By noting progressive changes in the thoughts expressed and comparing them with writings of likely sources, it may be possible to conjecture what factors may have influenced the course of his thinking.

In the first decade or so of his career, Davis reported later, he had shared the indifference of some geographers to abstract inquiries into the general content of the field in which they were engaged; like them he was "content to get on with the work."[3] For Davis then, and subsequently, the work he was doing was almost entirely in physical geography, which for him—inspired and trained by the scientific exploration of largely unsettled lands in the West—meant the geography of the inorganic earth: land, air, and water. It was only after he had published nearly a hundred substantive papers, that we find him writing what may be called methodological papers. The stimulus to do this apparently came from experience in teaching summer school courses at Harvard, attended largely by schoolteachers, and in addressing teachers' institutes in New England, New York, and Washington, D.C.[4]

In these discussions, as well as in his substantive papers, Davis frequently used the single word *geography* to mean physical geography, illustrated most commonly by discussion solely of land features. It comes as a surprise therefore to read, in his talk to a teachers' institute in July 1892, that physical geography "includes a consideration of the occupation of the earth by man as one of the most interesting chapters in natural history, and it therefore takes particular care to distinguish those conditions which determine man's settlement and occupation."[5]

To show what he meant by this, he included in his analysis of the physical geography of southern New England such items as the location of manufacturing cities on water power sites resulting from glaciation, and of commercial cities on the harbors that resulted from the drowning of coastal river valleys. But these are so briefly mentioned as to seem of little more than passing interest. Only three months later he discussed the same topic at another teachers' meeting with no mention of any relation to man.[6] Certainly in no later paper did he refer to the occupation of the earth by man as a chapter in natural history.

In December 1892 Davis became involved, probably for the first time, in group discussion of the scope and purpose of geography with colleagues from other colleges and teachers from secondary and normal schools. The National Education Association, with the support of the United State commissioner of education, had named a special committee known as the Committee of Ten, under the chairmanship of President Eliot of Harvard, to consider course programs in secondary schools, both public and private.[7] The Committee of Ten set up a number of "conferences," each for a particular field, appointing ten members for each field (pp. 3–5).

Reflecting the situation of geography in colleges at the time, the four college members of the geography conference came from departments of geology. One member was a professional in the United States Weather Bureau, who had formerly taught at the college level (p. 11). Four were principals or teachers of geography or natural history in normal schools. Six schoolmen had originally been appointed, but one was unable to accept and his place was filled by a college teacher; another who accepted appointment did not attend, so only nine met in conference (pp. 9, 236, 249).

The most notable members, along with Davis but somewhat older, were T. C. Chamberlin and Francis W. Parker. Chamberlin had just resigned from the presidency of the University of Wisconsin to head the department of geology at the new University of Chicago. Parker, principal of the Cook County Normal School at Chicago, had studied geography under Kiepert, Ritter's successor at Berlin, and was well known among schoolmen for his writings in promotion of progressive education and of the geographical viewpoint of Carl Ritter and Arnold Guyot.[8] The conference selected Chamberlin as its chairman and a secretary, not named in the report but evidently one of the schoolmen. Parker functioned as host for the meetings which were held for three days during the Christmas vacation of 1892, in his school and also in his residence. A report was first drafted by Chamberlin and one other, unnamed but presumably the secretary; additions sent in by others were interwoven, without indication of authorship, so that the majority report, as approved by all but one member, was very long and in some respects appears self-contradictory (p. 237). Judging from the ideas and the phrasing, it seems probable that both Davis and Parker made important contributions.

A major theme of the report stressed the use of rational explanation of earth feature, as had been developed in the past few years especially in the study of land forms (p. 205). Physical geography at this evolutionary level of thought should be distinguished by the term *physiography*, a suggestion on which Davis voted in the negative, but went along with the majority.[9] There is little doubt that he supported the majority in urging specialization in but one branch of physical geography (pp. 207, 209, 223–25). This recommendation was strongly opposed in the minority report of one of the schoolmen (pp. 246–47). Since most of detailed treatment referred to topics of features of the land, the term *physiography* inevitably became ambiguous.

In terms of quantities of words used, the report seemed to emphasize physical geography for the high schools to the practical exclusion of human geography. But in fact the report specifically included "the physical influences by which man and all the creatures of the earth are so profoundly affected" (p. 205). Mention of these is noted in a dozen or more brief passages scattered through the report (pp. 206–9, 211–16, 226–27, 234). This was most simply expressed in a statement which the overall Committee of Ten adopted in its summary statement: what was proposed for study "may be broadly charactereized as that which relates to the physical environment of man" (pp. 32, 206).

This principle was emphasized by both Chamberlin and Parker, each in different words, speaking some months later and without mention of the work of the conference, in papers read at another meeting of geographers. Parker's paper also included statements about geography as "the study of the earth as the home of man and the influence of that home on man's growth," together with other views of Carl Ritter. While none of these appear in the report of the conference, one may well suppose they had been presented in its discussions.[10]

In contrast, Davis's publications in the next two years reflect little change in his thinking.[11] But a series of papers beginning late in 1895 and continuing through the next decade show very significant changes. In a paper read in October 1895, as well as another published sometime in the same year, he spoke of geography as "the study of the earth in relation to man."[12] This expression, so far as I can find, Davis had never used before. It had been used by Parker and other schoolmen. In the following decade Davis used it in a dozen or more papers—with one modification to be noted later. In the first several cases he mentioned no source, but beginning with his address to the University of the State of New York in July 1897, he named Ritter as the source.[13]

It is significant to note the use Davis made of this concept in his talk in October 1895: "Geography being the study of the earth in relation to man, physical geography is the study of those features of the earth which must be understood in order to appreciate its relation to man." He thus provided a logical basis for the concept of physical geography which the conference of 1892 had stated without explanation.

In 1898 when physical geography was considered by another subcommittee of the National Education Association, Davis was a member and the other four members, including the chairman, had all studied with him. Their report asserted, even more definitely than the conference of 1892, the identification of physical geography as "the physical environment of man."[14] Writing shortly after, without mentioning his role on the committee, Davis strongly supported this "limitation of the subject" as a logical deduction of "Ritter's teaching that geography is the study of the earth in relation to man." Similarly he drew on Guyot's famous sentence about "causes" and "consequences" to conclude that "explanatory treatment" should be balanced by "applied treatment": "every item is to be presented as an element of the environment in which the life of the earth has been developed and by which it is conditioned."[15]

In his writings on the subject in this period Davis gives no references to contemporary discussions by others on the same subject; we can only conjecture what may have influenced his thinking. In one case it is evident that a relationship developed with Carles A McMurry, a normal school teacher in Illinois. McMurry had received a doctorate in education at Halle, Germany, where there is reason to believe he heard lectures on geography by Kirchhoff, an exponent of the views of Ritter.[16] The *Educational Review*, which had published a series of discussions of the report of the Committee of Ten, carried in its issue of May 1895 a paper by McMurry on "Geography as a School Subject—Propositions and Criticisms."[17] His positive statements were based on Ritter's expression of geography as "the study of the earth as related to man," which we noted Davis used in an address seven months later. More striking is the comparison of other statements in this paper by McMurry in 1895, with those of Davis in 1897.[18]

McMurry: Every topic in geography has a double footing in natural science and history. It has two faces—one toward nature and one toward man.

Davis: Geography is concerned with two classes of facts. The first class embraces all necessary facts about the inorganic earth . . . and all about plants and animals considered as the non-human inhabitants of the earth; the second includes the necessary facts as to the manner of man's living. . . .

McMurry: This double or complex character is the distinguishing trait of a strictly geographical topic.

Davis: The matter of relationship then becomes the very soul of geography . . . relationship between man and his natural environment.

In 1898 the *Yearbook of the National Herbert Society*, of which McMurry was editor, contained a discussion by Davis of a paper by another writer on the "Social Function of Geography." Davis welcomed the paper with the statement that "Ritter's desire to study the earth in relation to man is still the chief desire of the modern geographer."[19] In 1902, Davis published one of his longest papers about geography, "The progress of Geography in the Schools," in the yearbook of the same society—now under a different name, but with McMurry still as editor.[20] This provides the following comparison:

McMurry (1895): The moment a topic becomes purely scientific or purely historical it loses its geographical character.

Davis (1902) (following statements concerning "the two great classes of facts"): . . . neither alone is geography proper. . . . It is essentially the factor of relationship of the earth and inhabitants that characterizes geography as a subject apart from other sciences.

Davis was also, of course, aware of new developments during those years in geography at the college level. His own teacher, Shaler, had had a strong interest in the relation of man to the earth and several of Davis's former students, notably Mark Jefferson and A. P. Brigham, were emphasing the human aspect of geography. A program in economic geography was being developed at the University of Pennsylvania, and the University of Chicago was about to set up an autonomous department of geography which would combine both physical and human geography.[21] In 1903 Davis issued a call for the establishment of a new professional society to include scholars concerned with the advancement of whatever branches of geography.

Essentially Davis's picture of the field of geography was dualistic, but unified by the principle of multiple relationships between the two halves.[22] But he insisted—notably in a brief review of Hettner's fundamental paper of 1905—that reliable study of the relationships between the two halves required concentration first on the development of each half separately.[23] Evidently it did not occur to him that this could only accentuate the division. The only objections to the dichotomy that I have found were in two short papers by Fred J. Breeze, a high school teacher in Indiana, and by Martha Krug-Genthe, who had studied under Hettner.[24]

For some time Davis was uncertain as to just where the division should be drawn. For several years he went along with Ritter, Guyot (and Marsh), and their followers in thinking in terms of "man" and "nature" (or, if one will, the rest of nature). But this made it difficult to place plant and animal life, since he had never included those as parts of the "physical environment." Then he gradually shifted. First he changed Ritter's phrase, without explanation, from "the earth and man" to "the earth and its inhabitants"; two years later he explained that this was based not "on the old doctrine of teleology" but "on the modern principle of evolution." This he evidently felt provided a more logical division between the physical or inorganic earth and all organic life, a contrast which thereafter he expressed in terms of a new meaning for the old word *physiography*, and a new word *ontography*.[25]

This period of development of Davis's thinking about geography culminated in his classic address in 1905 as first president of the new Association of American Geographers. If one compares that with the views he had expressed before 1892, one might well conclude that he had moved more than halfway toward the views which the schoolmen had inherited from Guyot and Ritter.

At the time teachers concerned with geography in the schools were becoming increasingly dissatisfied with the virtual limitation of geography in the high schools to physical geography, even if it included scattered examples of the consequenses of physical features for human activities. In the years following the report of the Committee of Ten, more than a score of teachers, including a number from the college level, wrote no fewer than thirty-five papers published in a wide variety of educational journals either directly opposing the limitation to physical geography or at least stressing the importance of the human side of geography. This widespread discussion was brought to focus in the new *Journal of School Geography*, which Richard Dodge, a former student of Davis, had founded in 1897, with the latter's blessing.

In response, the science section of the National Education Association in 1908 appointed a new special committee to consider the geography curriculum in the high schools.[26] At least three of the six were members of the Association of American Geographers: Martha Krug-Genthe, a charter member who had come from Germany shortly after taking her doctorate under Hettner, at Heidelberg in 1901; Mark Jefferson, who had studied under Davis; and Ray Whitbeck, who had just transferred from a normal school in New Jersey to the University of Wisconsin.

The Association of American Geographers also set up a committee on school geography. Davis, who happened to be president that year (for the second time), appointed Richard Dodge as chairman, and several other of his former students; all but one of the members were persons who had developed a major interest in geography in the schools.[27]

Both committees in their reports called for a major rôle for human geography in the high schools. Writing a decade later, Whitbeck—who had served on both committees—noted that in that time "there had been relatively little defense of pure physical geography for high school purposes."[28]

In the meantime, Davis's interests had shifted away from the schools. New experiences and new associations were leading him to different efforts in his substantive writings and a different view of the purpose of geography in general. In 1908–9 he was visiting professor at the University of Berlin and the next several years he made successive trips to Europe, meeting European geographers in the field there, and in this country during the famous transcontinental trip which he organized in 1912. His protracted and mutually vehement debate with Hettner over his theory of the cycle of erosion apparently led him to read, or reread, Hettner's general views on geography. Whatever the influences, the consequence may be traced through a series of papers emphasizing increasingly the ultimate role of regional geography.

In 1911 Davis wrote: "In regional description, the climax of geographical work is reached; here the attempt is made to describe, in their actual spatial relations, all the geographical features which occur together in a given district."[29] In 1914, in his paper on "Der Valdarno ...," published in German in the *Zeitschrift der Gesellschaft für Erdkunde zu Berlin*, he wrote: "Die regionale Beschreibung stellt, wie Hettner sehr klar dargelegt hat, in einem Gesamtbild, alle die verschiedenen Züge eines Gebietes in ihrem räumlichen Zusammenhang dar. Sie ist die höchste geographische Aufgabe, zu der alle anderen beitragen."[30]

The next year he said much the same to American geographers, again in terms reflecting Hettner's writings, but this time without mention of source: "The description of existing landscapes, districts, and regions of the earth surface is the goal toward which other phases of goegraphic study all lead.... Pure regional geography is the final object of a geographer's efforts."[31] He returned to this theme in an address at Clark University shortly after the opening of its graduate school of geography,[32] and once more in addressing American geographers in 1923, on "The Progress of Geography in the United States."[33]

In that paper Davis paid tribute, in greater measure than he had ever before, to the work of Arnold Guyot, "through which the rational or causal notion, which has in later years so largely characterized our treatment of the Earth as the home of man, was implanted in our concept of goegraphy" (pp. 165–69). (Apparently Davis forgot that years before he had named Ritter as "the originator of the causal notion in geography, and therefore the greatest benefactor of geography in the nineteenth century."[34])

Likewise Davis wrote, in the same paper, of "the long established tradition that defines the object of our study to be a description of the regions of the earth" in which "all the constituents and occupants of a region are described in their actual combination or inter-mixture." But again in expressing this in terms of "the material filling of terrestrial spaces" ("die dingliche Erfüllung der Erdräume"), he ascribes the phrase to Hettner, apparently unaware that it was the classical phrase of Carl Ritter (pp. 204, 209–10).

William Morris Davis in that last address to the Association of American Geographers had come a long way in his view of geography since the days when he worked in it without thought of defining its content, and even a long way since formal exposition of his position in his most often quoted presidential address of 1905. In doing this, he seems never to have dug into the writings of past students of geographic thought before writing his own. Rather, his thoughts about geography came to him from thinking about his work and considering what his contemporaries were saying and writing. But from these he did learn.

Notes

William Morris Davis's *Geographical Essays* (Boston: Ginn and Company 1909) includes twelve of his educational papers published before that date, selected and edited by Douglas Johnson. Where this is the case in respect to a paper cited in these notes, that is indicated by the word *Essays*, followed by the specific pages in that volume.

1. John Leighly, "What Has Happened to Physical Geography?" *Annals of the Association of American Geographers* 45 (1955): 309–13.
2. Richard J. Chorley, Robert P. Beckinsale, and Antony J. Dunn, *The Life and Work of William Morris Davis*, The History of the Study of Landforms, vol. 2 (London: Methuen, 1973).
3. W. M. Davis, "An Inductive Study of the Content of Geography," *Bulletin of the American Geographical Society* 38 (1906): 67–84 (also in *Essays*, p. 22).
4. A. P. Brigham, "William Morris Davis," *Geographen Kalender*,vol. 7, (Gotha: Justus Perthes, 1909), p. 34.
5. W. M. Davis, "Geographical Illustrations: Suggestions for Teaching Physical Geography Based on the Physical Features of Southern New England," *Proceeding, Americans Institute of Instruction* (1892): 22.
6. W. M. Davis, "The Extension of Physical Geography in Elementary Teaching," *School and College* 1 (1892): 599–608 (also in *Essays*, pp. 105–14).
7. National Education Association, *Report of the Committee of Ten on Secondary School Studies; with the Reports of the Conferences arranged by the Committee* (New York: American Book Co. for the National Educational Association, 1894); Israel C. Russell, "Report of a Conference on Geography," *Journal of The American Geographical Society* 27 (1895): 30–41; William T. Harris, "The Committee of Ten on Secondary Schools," *Educational Review* 7 (1894): 3.
8. Samuel C. Parker, *History of Modern Elementary Education* (1912; reprint ed., Totowa, N.J.: Littlefield, Adams, 1970), pp. 348 ff., 470-73. Francis W. Parker, *How to Study Geography,* Boston, 1890.
9. W. M. Davis, "A Retrospect of Geography," *Annals of the Association of American Geographers* 22 (1932): 220.
10. T. C. Chamberlin, "The Relations of Geology to Physiography in our Educational System," and Francis W. Parker, "The Relations of Geography to History," both in "Proceedings of the International Geographic Conference in Chicago, July 27–28 1893," *National Geographic Magazine* 5 (1893): 154– 60 and 125–31.
11. W. M. Davis, "Geography in Grammar and Primary Schools," *School Review 1* (1893): 327-39 (also in *Essays,* pp. 115-28); idem, "The Improvement of Geographical Teaching," *National Geographic Magazine 5* (1893): 68-75; and idem, "Physical Geography as a University Study," *Journal of Geology 2* (1894): 66-100 (also in *Essays,* pp. 165-92).
12. W. M. Davis, "Physiography as an Alternative Subject for Admission to College," *School Review,* 3 (1895): 633; and idem, "The Physiography of Southern New England," in *The Physiography of the United States*, National Geographic Society, monograph 1, 9 (New York: American Book Co., 1896), p. 304.

13. W. M. Davis, "The Present Trend of Geography" (Address delivered 29 June 1897), in *IIIth Annual Report of the University of the State of New York*, published in *Documents of the Senate of the State of New York* 8, no. 46 (1898): 192–202; specific reference, pp. 193 ff.

14. "Report of the Committee on College Entrance Requirements," *Proceeding, National Education Association*, 1899, pp. 652 and 780–92 (also in *Journal of School Geography* 2 [1898]: 248–62).

15. W. M. Davis, "Physical Geography in the High School," *School Review* 8 (1900): 388–404 and 449–56 (also in *Essays*, pp. 129 ff., 132).

16. Willi Ule, "Alfred Kirchhoff," *Geographische Zeitschrift* 13 (1907): 538–43.

17. C. A. McMurry, "Geography as a School Subject," *Educational Review* 9 (May 1895); 448 ff., 452.

18. W. M. Davis, "Home Geography," *Journal of School Geography* 1 (1897): 3.

19. W. M. Davis, "Discussion—Systematic Geography," *4th Yearbook of the National Herbert Society* (Chicago: University of Chicago Press, 1898), p. 81.

20. W. M. Davis, "Progress of Geography in the Schools," *First Yearbook of the National Society for the Scientific Study of Education*, Part II (Chicago: University of Chicago Press, 1902), p. 19 (also in *Essays*, p. 36.)

21. P. E. James and G. J. Martin, *The Association of American Geographers— The First Seventy-Five Years* (Washington, D.C.: Association of American Geographers, 1979), pp. 17–26.

22. W. M. Davis, "The Progress of Geography in the Schools," *Essays*, pp. 36 ff., idem, "An Inductive Study of the Content of Geography," *Essays*, p. 8.

23. W. M. Davis, "Hettner's Conception of Geography," *Journal of Geography* 6 (1907): 49–53.

24. Fred J. Breeze, "High School Geography," *School Science and Mathematics* 5 (1905): 516–19; Martha Krug-Genthe, "Results to be Expected from School Courses in Geography," *Journal of Geography* 4 (April 1905): 155–59.

25. W. M. Davis, "The Physical Geography of the Lands," *Popular Science Monthly* 57 (1900): 158 (also in *Essays*, p. 71); idem, "Progress of Geography in the Schools," p. 16 ff. (also in *Essays*, p. 71 ff.); idem, "Systematic Geography," *Proceedings of the American Philosophical Society* 41 (1902): 239ff.

26. James F. Chamberlain, *"Report of the Committee on Secondary Geography," Journal of Geography* 8 (1909): 1–9.

27. "News Items," *Journal of Geography* 7 (1909): 192 Richard Elwood Dodge, "Report of Committee on Geography for Secondary Schools," *Journal of Geography* 8 (1910): 159–65.

28. Ray H. Whitbeck, "Thirty Years of Geography in the United States, " *Journal of Geography* 20 (1921): 123–26; idem, "The Journal in the Field of Education," *Journal of Geography* 21 (1922): 7 ff.

29. W. M. Davis, "The Colorado Front Range—A Study in Geographic Presentation," *Annals of the Association of American Geographers*, 1 (1911): 24; similarly in idem, "The Disciplinary Value of Geography," *Popular Science Monthly* 78 (1911): 233.

30. W. M. Davis, "Der Valdarno: eine Darstellungsstudie," *Zeitschrift der Gesellschaft für Erdkunde zu Berlin*, 1914, p. 615.

31. W. M. Davis, "The principles of Geographical Description," *Annals of the Association of American Geographers* 5 (1915): 62.

32. W. M. Davis, "A Graduate School of Geography," *Science* 56 (1922): 121–34.

33. W. M. Davis, "The Progress of Geography in the United States," *Annals of the Association of American Geographers* 14 (1924): 165–69.
34. W. M. Davis, "Geography in the United States," *Proceeding of the American Association for the Advancement of Science* 53 (1903): 482.

Rollin Salisbury and the Establishment of Geography at the University of Chicago

William D. Pattison

Rollin D. Salisbury was for many years a leading figure in American academic geography. He founded the first department of graduate studies in geography, at the University of Chicago (1903); he was a charter member of the Association of American Geographers (1904); and he served as president of that society (1912). Most often remembered by geographers today for his teaching, he was a master of the Socratic method.

Writers who knew Salisbury[1] have presented a portrait of an intensely dedicated academician who came to the University of Chicago at its opening in 1892, to join in creating the Department of Geology with Thomas C. Chamberlin, the department's head. Later appointed dean of the Ogden Graduate School of Science, he held that post until his death in 1922. His career was marked by a helping relationship to Chamberlin, probably the greatest American geologist of his time. Their association had begun at Beloit College, where Salisbury had been Chamberlin's student, and it continued throughout the Chicago years. Succeeding Chamberlin at Beloit, Salisbury taught for nearly a decade there (save for a year in which he studied at Heidelberg University); he served briefly with the geology department of the University of Wisconsin, during Chamberlin's presidency of that institution; and he was invited to Chicago at Chamberlin's request.[2]

The premise on which the present paper rests is that the relation of Salisbury to geography remains at best only partially understood. Taking a fresh approach to the entirety of geography's preprofessional and professional past in which Salisbury was active—about 1890 to about 1920—I propose that it be thought of as an episode in the life of an idea. Ultimately, this approach raises the question "What is the significance of earth conditions to human affairs?"—the query that Clarence Glacken has resolved into (1) the idea of a designed earth, (2) the idea of environmental influence, and (3) the idea of humanity as a modifier of the environment.[3] The episode was a particular sequence of events in American academic history pertaining to the second of these conceptions.

In the pages that follow, better understanding of the episode is sought through a new look at Salisbury's opinions and actions, while better understanding of Salisbury is aimed at through a new analysis of the episode. For both purposes, reliance is placed upon Salisbury's published writings and upon archival materials, especially University of Chicago records and a collection of papers left by Salisbury, largely made up of letters he had received.[4]

Invisible College

To read the papers of Salisbury for the years around 1890 is to become aware of his prominence in something known in our day as an invisible college. True to definition, it was an association of researchers held together by an intellectual interest, unassisted by common institutional ties or shared location.[5] The work of the college was directed toward an understanding of surface materials and landforms. Membership came from state geological surveys, the United States Geological Survey, and universities; the roster included, besides Salisbury, G. K. Gilbert, Frank Leverett, and William Morris Davis. The ranks merged into those of the generality of geologists.

The tone of the college is struck in selections from two letters. In the first, Salisbury is confiding to a friend (outside the circle):

> Well, I have had a good summer. Fortune has favored me . . . and as a result I am credited with some discoveries. . . . I have had the same experience several times within a few years. . . . This year a second driftless area down in Illinois was found, and also some clinchers for the orange sand argument. . . . In New Jersey I was fortunate again. I have demonstrated that the drift limit as heretofore given is incorrect . . . for the very states in which most work on the drift has been done. . . . To upset the old conclusions was not altogether unpleasant, you may be sure.[6]

In the second excerpt, G. K. Gilbert is writing to Salisbury, regarding some kames near Rochester, New York:

> They have always been a puzzle to me and a recent examination left

them still problematic. . . . I can exhibit them to geologists only as a conundrum, but your special studies may enable you to suggest an explanation.[7]

The activities of Salisbury and company, it must be emphasized, were wholly integrated into geology, a field that had been undergoing systematic reconstruction on historical principles from at least the time of Charles Lyell, two generations earlier. After Lyell, Joseph Le Conte had said, "Geology may be defined as the history of the earth as revealed in its structure, and as interpreted by causes still in operation."[8] The great intellectual gain arising from historicization could be found in the opportunities for inference that it opened to investigators. The landform-studying geologists held, as indispensable assumptions, that the problems they attacked were historical problems, and that they were looking into the latest chapter in the history of the earth.[9] Parenthetically: Davis set himself apart by bringing into the dialogue of the company, and insisting upon, a cyclical scheme for imposition on that history.[10]

I suggest that *physical* history was central to the geologists' pursuit of earth history, and that this pursuit qualified geology, if anything did, for consideration as a "rational enterprise." In this inquiry were to be discovered, to quote from Stephen Toulmin, the "conceptual aggregates, systems, or populations employed on a collective basis" that distinquished the geologist's search for understanding.[11] Accordingly, the subject matter of the landform-studying college lay within the scope of a geophysical rationale, and so did that of an expansive teaching venture of theirs, called by many of them physiography—a term taken over from Thomas Huxley. The striking efflorescence of turn-of-the-century texts representing the venture came almost entirely from the college. Said Salisbury, in a two-page review of meanings introducing his own *Physiography*, "The study has to do primarily with the surface of the lithosphere, and with the relations of air and water to it. Its field is the zone of contact of air and water with land, and of air with water."[12]

Given this limitation on primary scope, I argue that, when the question of the relation of contemporary life to earth conditions came up among the landform-studying geologists, it was appropriate to opt not for pursuit of it but rather for sponsorship of its pursuit by others. This was the option taken by Salisbury; it was, for him, a commitment. Because the period of his sponsorship corresponded closely with the years in which Davis was similarly active, I am designating it the Davis-Salisbury Episode.

Guide to the Episode

The dominating question of the Davis-Salisbury Episode had two versions, one of sweeping inclusiveness, the other of specifically human reference. It ran, in the comprehensive version, as posed to the mind of Salisbury, what should be believed about "the influences of earth features and earth resources on the distribution, character, and activities of life— life of all kinds?"[13] As posed for Davis, it went, what should be believed about relations between "the physical environment of life ... and responses which life has made to the physical environment?"[14] In the version confined to humanity, the question for Salisbury was, what should be believed about "the influence of the [terrain], the climate, and the natural resources of [various] lands on their settlement, development, and present commercial and industrial status?"[15] For Davis, it was, what should be believed about "the controls that [the fundamental facts of earth] exercise on human conditions?"[16]

That their chosen issue, in either version, expressed the idea of environmental influence—as carried into their own time, society, and conceptual frame—should not be surprising, if only because it reserved to objects in which they had a vested interest the position of independent variable. It imparted justification to the pursuit of their science. Still, we should be reminded that both the idea of a designed earth and that of humanity as a modifier of environment were consciously selected against, by them. The rejection of the first has been long recognized; I can now confirm from a letter by Salisbury that the second, as found in the work of George Perkins Marsh, was thought about, too, but passed over.[17]

Pursuit of the environmental influence idea—with variable emphasis on each of the two versions—occurred in phases, a key to which may be found in Merle Curti's *The Growth of American Thought*, where impulses toward professionalization and popularization in the late nineteenth and early twentieth centuries are detailed.[18] Application of the key follows.

In the opening phase—roughly the 1890s—the impulses found expression concurrently, as follows: (1) landform study, having achieved a research-defined professionalization in the late 1880s, was continuing to progress; (2) an associated effort to popularize landform awareness, by preachment and demonstration, was being pressed; (3) *the idea of environmental influence was invoked as a strategem of the popularization campaign;* and (4) tentative moves were made toward securing to that idea a professionalized, research approach.

In the next phase, all of these lines of work and thought continued, but with significant changes in standing: (1) landform science was, at the opening of the phase, nearing the crest of its excitement, as then formulated; (2) the program for popularization of landform awareness, with its subtheme of environmental influence, kept making headway for a while after the opening; (3) *a concerted attempt was made to establish professional pursuit of the environmental influence idea*; and (4) as a consequence, efforts to popularize that pursuit came into prominence.

Both Davis and Salisbury played a part in popularizing landform awareness through the environmental influence idea, with Davis registering a far greater impact, especially in the 1890s. And both invested their reputations in the credibility of the idea as a broad research challenge, eligible for professionalization. In the latter interest, Davis's leadership went to the founding of a national society, Salisbury's to the creation of a university department.

The Chicago Venture: School of Thought

Salisbury's commitment, at Chicago, was to the sponsorship first of a faculty which, however provisionally qualified, would be ready to teach and write in furtherance of the environmental influence idea. Beyond that, it was a commitment to graduate students who would be, theoretically, the first generation with adequate education and credentials for the research and teaching that the idea demanded.

Thanks to a document discovered about two years ago, we know that courses believed to embody the environmental influence idea were already being taught at Chicago when Salisbury's new department was in the planning stage.[19] In a sense, then, although the courses concerned spread across six departments, a "department" on the environmental question already existed. This shadow department was most evident in botany and zoology, where appropriately oriented courses were prominent. Of the two individuals chiefly responsible—Henry C. Cowles and Charles M. Child[20]—it was Cowles whose direct connection with the geophysical program at Chicago can be more readily demonstrated.[21] He had first studied under Salisbury and Chamberlin, then proceeded to take a doctorate in the botany department, where he stayed to teach.[22]

Also to be reckoned into the shadow department were history (for its offerings on European and American expansion), sociology and anthropology (for studies in ethnology and early social history), and political economy (for courses in railway transportation, industrial development, commerce, and agriculture).[23] The record leaves no doubt about awareness of and interest in these departments, in the Salisbury-Chamberlin purlieu. Salisbury's correspondence reveals, for example, that he was giving attention as early as 1893 to the recruitment of an instructor for political economy, a William Hill, who had been trained in economics at Harvard.[24].

The shadow department, however, could not have achieved the focus required for an attempt at professionalization. For this purpose, an independent department to be led by Salisbury was proposed, gaining approval in time for the university announcements for 1903-4. Salisbury, who was by now dean of the school to which both geology and the new department were assigned, was proud of what he had instituted. Today, the critical reviewer must ask what he had brought into being. It was at first an educational venture, comprising an environmentally defined variant on the social studies.

To follow the experience of two of the earliest candidates for a graduate degree—Chessley Posey and Helen Collins[25]—a core of studies was surrounded by courses in geology, *mainly taught by Salisbury*, where knowledge of the geophysical environment was developed; and by courses in botany and zoology, where nonhuman life was interpreted with special reference to that environment. The core itself, taken in the new department, consisted of courses in which human life received a comparable interpretation. Through the program, students were inducted into the point of view for which the new department had been opened: an earth-referring environmentalist school of social thought. In his M.A. thesis, Posey validated his membership in the school by writing on irrigation in the American West; in hers, Collins did the same by writing on the settlement history of Illinois.[26]

For the center to hold, in the beginning, the will and spokesmanship of Salisbury may have been necessary, but the substance of the center—the content of the five or so essential courses of the new curriculum—was owed to two students of his, J. Paul Goode and Harlan H. Barrows. Adding to what has been published already about these men, perhaps most memorably by William Koelsch about Barrows, I point to the fact that the professionalization which they were helping to initiate largely depended upon a special relation to teachers. They were teachers themselves, to be sure; but as theologians are to ministers, so they were consciously striving to become to teachers in the schools. A document from the hand of Goode firmly establishes this aim.[27]

Finally, note should be taken of the popularizing side of the early Chicago effort. To the popularization through teachers that was implicit in the Chicago approach to professionalization must be added the rôle filled by Goode from his first year onward as public lecturer in university extension, and the department's very close relations with a new citywide layman's society.[28] I suggest that even the part-time engagement of Ellen Semple, beginning in 1906, be regarded as a popularizing contribution, considering the manner in which she developed her themes on American history.

The Chicago Venture as "Geography"

Until now, I have refrained from referring to the new department by its title, "Geography." My aim has been to sharpen recognition, through the Chicago case, that the Davis-Salisbury Episode is to be remembered for *two* debatable legacies, the first a school of thought, the second an adopted name.

What was believed to be geographical about the venture? From statements by Salisbury, his faculty, and their students comes the answer that it was geographical insofar as conditions and events of recent earth history were related to its work. The frame in which "geography" referred to recent earth history had been operative already in the 1850s, when a chair for Arnold Guyot at Princeton was announced as a professorship in geography and geology. In the late 1880s, Davis had been thinking in the same frame when he spoke of geography as the study of the present in the light of the past, and of geology (or better, the rest of geology) as the study of the past in the light of the present.[29] At the opening of the University of Chicago in 1892, it had been expressed in the designation of Salisbury as professor of geographic geology, and in the description of geology as a field composed of three sciences: geography, mineralogy, and petrology.[30]

With the founding of the Department of Geography under Salisbury, in 1903, the title served as an indicator by which new courses could be known to differ from those of other departments of social thought. Terms of discourse signalizing the difference at that time—and causing most geographers to wince today—were "geographical influence," "geographic factor," and "geographic conditon." A minor monument to this usage was Harlan Barrows's study of the middle Illinois Valley, completed in 1908. Salisbury, as approving sponsor, is directly tied to it by a letter of that year.[31]

This dimension of the Salisbury commitment showed the innocence of a generation long immersed in earth science. Salisbury was spared anxiety over the existence of an alternative tradition in which "geography" was understood to stand for knowledge organized around a locative principle. To quote from an important contemporary source, which was ignored with apparent equanimity, "That which distinguishes geography ... is that it localizes objects ... it indicates ... the distribution of being, organic and inorganic, upon the earth.[32]

Where else were university voices applying the name "geography" to an earth-referring environmentalist school of social thought that was only incidentally concerned with place, location, and distribution? At Nebraska, George Condra was doing this, in a program whose early growth was contemporaneous with that at Chicago. At Cornell, a corresponding adopter was Ralph S. Tarr; at Yale, Isaiah Bowman. Indeed, the potential for emergence of the name in this meaning was present wherever there were geology faculties. The potential existed, too, where faculties with no vested interest in earth science saw an advantage in exploiting the pattern set by the geologists. The most notable demonstration came from the University of Pennsylvania's Wharton School, where an economics faculty recommended candidates for degrees under the same appellation.

As the Davis-Salisbury Episode reached about the halfway mark in its later phase, the naming legacy, regularly attached to the school-of-thought legacy, had become observable in many universities; but the Chicago case remained the one to watch especially, because there alone the name was borne by an autonomous department.

How, at Chicago, the Episode Came to an End

Over the succeeding years, Salisbury held to his vision of what a pursuit of knowledge called "geography" should be, confirming and clarifying it on two important public occasions.[33] As applied at Chicago, it had resulted in the allocation of the study in its human concern to the Department of Geography, in its concern with nonhuman life, to zoology and botany.

Meantime, as that ideal was being maintained by Salisbury, at a level of general management and elder statesmanship, a new generation in geography was coming up, providing a chance to test decisively the professionalizing capability of it. Graduate students were presenting themselves for work on the doctorate, while holding hopes for careers in universities. At this juncture, one observes a turn toward self-consciousness at Chicago, as though these students and the younger faculty (a category that included Barrows, but not Goode) were asking themselves, "What ought being a member of a university department of geography mean?"

158

The most evident innovations came in the years 1913 and 1914, when the departmental announcements spoke for the first time of training for research, when the first field courses were offered *in geography*, and when Salisbury made a limited entry into the department's teaching by convening a student-staff weekly seminar.[34] These three breaks with custom signified that the group as a whole was not only following through in earnest on the idea of geography as research, but was also embracing the proposition that the best geographic research takes place in the field. Until now, typical geographic research had been literary. Thus it was with an isolated doctorate of 1907, and with the preponderance of master's level work.[35] The leading purpose of the new seminar was to think together about geography as field research.

The Salisbury seminar, which was later made famous by its participants, ran from 1913 to 1919. It yielded a substantial corpus of field-based research, including doctoral dissertations by Stephen Visher, Wellington Jones, Carl Sauer, Charles Colby, and Robert Platt.[36] The product was highly orthodox, and it gave warning of the end of the episode.

Reading the seminar output, one gets the impression that the environmental school of social thought, which continued to hold for Salisbury great intellectual promise, was becoming for the new generation an uncomfortably restrictive frame of reference. Sooner or later, all but one of the named alumni—the exception being Visher—were to assert their dissatisfaction. Sauer and Barrows would take revisionist positions, each in his own fashion rejecting the geologist's way—Salisbury's way— of asking the question with which the present paper began, while continuing to find his identity as a geographer in the question itself. Jones, Colby, and Platt were to become reconstructionists, moving slowly away from the question, and eventually finding their identities as geographers in the great tradition of locative pursuits to which Salisbury—along with Davis and others of his generation—had denied a defining function. Their vehicle of departure was to be the series of spring field conferences to which Preston James has been directing the attention of our profession in recent years.

Of the outright declarations of independence issuing from this company, the earliest—by Barrows—fittingly brings the present paper to a close. It was the presidential address "Geography as Human Ecology," given before the A.A.G. in 1922, three years after Salisbury had relinquished to Barrows leadership both of the Chicago seminar and of the Chicago department itself. This is the speech in which geographers everywhere were advised to limit themselves to human problems, formulating them "from the standpoint of man's adjustment to environment, rather than from that of environmental influence." Said Barrows, "The former approach is ... likely ... to minimize the danger of assigning to the environmental factors a determinative influence which they do not exert."[37]

When read in the light of the present paper, this celebrated statement conveys a meaning interestingly different from that ordinarily drawn from it. Attention goes not only to "adjustment" (the usual object of interest), but also to "environment." It has generally escaped notice that Barrows, in nearby lines, undercut the motivation behind the Davis-Salisbury Episode by saying that geographers of his persuasion "of course mean [by environment] the combined physical and biological environments."

By this simple restatement, the reference base of the geographer ceased to be confined to the subject matter of Salisbury's old invisible college; geophysical facts lost their privileged position. The college itself, we must understand, had been maintaining a life of its own since the 1890s in any event, adding to its membership through departments of geology at Chicago and elsewhere. The Barrows address gave notice that the Department of Geography at Chicago would continue to represent an environmental approach to social thought, if under altered conceptual conditions that weakened the connection with geology. It also signified that scientists from botany and zoology could no longer be counted, in prevailing theory, as members of the geographic fellowship.

Would Salisbury, who had died less than six months before the Barrows address, have been disappointed? Beyond any doubt he would have been. Yet, to judge by the generosity and hopefulness toward younger workers frequently reflected in his correspondence, I wonder if he would not have been ready to say to Barrows and others whom he had sponsored, "It is your turn now; you should not be deterred by what I believed was the right thing to do, when it was mine."

Notes

1. For overall apapreciations of Salisbury (1858 -1922), see Stephen S. Visher, "Rollin D. Salisbury and Geography," *Annals, Association of American Geographers* 63 (1953): 4-11, and Rollin T. chamberlin, "Memorial of Rollin D. Salisbury," *Bulletin, Geological Society of America* 42 (1931): 126-138.
2. On the symbiotic relationship between Chamberlin and Salisbury, see George L. Collie and Hiram D. Densmore, *Thomas C. Chamberlin, Ph.D., Sc.D.,*

LL.D. and Rollin D. Salisbury, LL.D.: A Beloit College Partnership
(Madison: State Historical Society of Wisconsin, 1932).

3. Clarence J. Glacken, *Traces on the Rhodian Shore: Nature and Culture in Western Thought from Ancient Times to the End of the Eighteenth Century* (Berkeley: University of California Press, 1967), pp. vii, 5, and 706-13.

4. The Papers of Rollin D. Salisbury, University Archives, Department of Special Collections, Joseph Regenstein Library, the University of Chicago. Occupying five linear feet and stored in eleven boxes, this collection is grouped in the following categories: correspondence; lectures and notes; speeches; legal and financial papers; clippings; reviews and memorabilia; notebooks; and photographs. Reference will be made below to "Sal. Papers," and to box and folder by number.

5. An essay briefly characterizing invisible colleges appears in John Ziman, *Public Knowledge: The Social Dimension of Science* (Cambridge: Cambridge University Press, 1968), pp. 130-38. Salisbury's college was kept together by publications, correspondence, and national conferences. He played a key role from 1893 onward as editor for "the physiographic aspects of geology" of the *Journal of Geology*.

6. Copy of Salisbury to Horace Fiske (poet and scholar of American literature), 14 September 1891, Sal. Papers, Box 1, Folder 1.

7. G. K. Gilbert to Salisbury, 1 July 1892, Sal. Papers, Box 1, Folder 5. Gilbert was at this time chief geologist, U.S. Geological Survey.

8. Joseph Le Conte, *Elements of Geology*, rev. and enl. ed. (New York: D. Appleton and Co., 1882), p. 2.

9. These assumptions are evident in the account of Salisbury's most ambitious research project, *The Physical Geography of New Jersey*, Final Report of the State Geologist, vol. 4 ((Trenton: Geological Survey of New Jersey, 1898). A contemporary tribute to the landform-studying geologists is in T. C. Chamberlin, "The New Geology," *University of Chicago Weekly*, no. 1 (October 1892): 7-9.

10. For definitive treatment, see "The Cycle of Erosion," chapter 10 of Richard J. Chorley, Robert P. Beckinsale, and Antony J. Dunn, *The Life and Work of William Morris Davis*, The History of the Study of Landforms, vol. 2 (London: Methuen, 1973), pp. 160-97. Salisbury as adversary to the Davisian system appears in the same volume, pp. 428-29 and 442.

11. See "Rational Enterprises and Their Evolution," section B of Stephen Toulmin, *Human Understanding: The Collective Use and Evolution of Concepts* (Princeton: Princeton University Press, 1972), pp. 133-356.

12. Rollin D. Salisbury, *Physiography* (New York: Henry Holt and Co., 1907), pp. 3-4.

13. Rollin D. Salisbury, "Geology in Education," *Science, n.s., 47 (1918): 325-35.* The quotation is from p. 334.

14. William Morris Davis, "Systematic Geography," *Proceedings, American Philosophical Society* 41 (1902): 235-59. The quotation is from p. 240.

15. From a statement on courses in economic geography included in "Geography at the University of Chicago," *Bulletin, American Geographical Society* 35 (1903): 207-8.

16. William Morris Davis, "The State Map of Massachusetts as an Aid to the Study of Geography in Grammar and High Schools," *Sixtieth Annual*

Report of the ₍Massachusetts₎ *Board of Education, 1895-1896* (Boston: Wright and Potter Printing Co., 1897), pp. 482-500. The quotation is from p. 485, with bracketed insert from p. 484.

17. Draft of letter from Salisbury, addressee not named, 9 March 1893, Sal. Papers, Box 1, Folder 7.

18. "Professionalization and Popularization of Learning," chapter 23 in Merle Curti, *The Growth of American Thought* (New York: Harper and Brothers, 1943), pp. 580-604.

19. William D. Pattison, "Goode's Proposal of 1902: An Interpretation," *Professional Geographer* 30 (1978): 3-8.

20. In the spring of 1903, relevant courses were being offered by Cowles under the titles "Geographic Botany," "Physiographic Ecology," and "Field Ecology"; by Child under the title "Field Zoology." *Circular of Information, The Graduate Schools* (Chicago: University of Chicago, April 1903).

21. Of the thirteen courses taken by Cowles during his first years of graduate studies (1895-96) at Chicago, twelve were in geology. "Records of Work, Henry Chandler Cowles," Office of the Registrar, University of Chicago.

22. The effects of geological training are displayed in Henry C. Cowles, "The Physiographic Ecology of Chicago and Vicinity; a Study of the Origin, Development, and Classification of Plant Societies," *Botanical Gazette* 31 (1901): 73-108.

23. The courses are listed in *Circular of Information, The Graduate Schools* (Chicago: University of Chicago, April 1903).

24. Henry K. White to Salisbury, 5 and 18 March 1893, Sal. Papers, Box 1, Folder 7.

25. "Record of Work, Chessley Justin Posey," and "Record of Work, Helen Marr Collins," Office of the Registrar, University of Chicago.

26. Chessley Justin Posey, "Geographic Factors in the Irrigation of Our Arid Regions," and Helen Marr Collins, "Geographis Influence in Illinois History" (M.S. University of Chicago, 1905 and 1908).

27. J. Paul Goode, section titled "Advantages" in typescript titled "Courses in Geography," dated 17 July 1902, Geography Collection, University Archives, Department of Special Collections, Joseph Regenstein Library, University of Chicago.

28. The organization was the Geographic Society of Chicago, founded in 1898 by Zonia Baber, then of Cook County Normal School, with the cooperation of Goode and Salisbury. Conditions at the time of founding are evidenced in Baber to Salisbury, 14 March and 5 April 1898, Sal. Papers, Box 3, Folder 1.

29. William Morris Davis, "Geographic Methods in Geologic Investigation," *National Geographic Magazine* 1 (1888): 11-26. the quotation is from p. 12.

30. *Programme of Courses in Geology, The University of Chicago, 1892-3* (Chicago: University of Chicago Press, 1892). The copy consulted is in folder titled "Geology Department," University Archives, Department of Special Collections, Joseph Regenstein Library, The University of Chicago.

31. Copy of Salisbury to H. Foster Bain, director of Illinois State Geological Survey, 11 November 1908. The study was published as H. H. Barrows, *Geography of the Middle Illinois Valley,* Bulletin no. 15, Illinois State Geological Survey (Urbana: University of Illinois, 1910).

32. [Extracts from resolutions of the congress] in George M. Wheeler, *Report Upon the Third International Geographical Congress and Exhibition at*

Venice, Italy, 1881, (Washington, D.C.: War Department, U.S. Army Corps of Engineers, 1885), pp. 35-41. The quotation is from p. 40.

33. See address by Salisbury in "The Dedication of Julius Rosenwald Hall," *The University Record*, n.s. 1, no. 2 (April 1915): 76-87; and his statements on geography made as chairman of Section E, American Association for the Advancement of Science, in "Geology in Education," *Science*, n.s., 47 (1918): 325-35.

34. See entries under "The Department of Geography," in *Circular of the Departments of Geology, Geography and Paleontology* (Chicago: University of Chicago, 1913 and 1914).

35. The isolated doctoral dissertation was published as Frederick V. Emerson, "A Geographic Interpretation of New York City," *Bulletin, American Geographical Society* 40 (1908): 587-612, 726-38 , and 41 (1909): 3-21. Of the eleven pre-1913 studies for the master's degree at Chicago, only two were field based.

36. In order of completion, these were the dissertations: Stephen S. Visher, *The Geography of South Dakota* (1914), published as Bulletin 8, South Dakota State Geological Natural History Survey (1918); Wellington D. Jones, "Geography of Northern Patagonia" (1914); Carl O. Sauer, *Geography of the Ozark Highland of Missouri* (1915), published as bulletin no. 7, Geographic Society of Chicago (Chicago: University of Chicago Press, 1920); Charles C. Colby, "Geography of Southeastern Minnesota" (1917); and Robert S. Platt, "Resources and Economic Interests of the Bermudas" (1920). Productions directly bearing on the work of the seminar were an unpublished outline by Barrows for a field course in the Cumberland Plateau and southern Appalachians, and Wellington D. Jones and Carl O. Sauer, "Outline for Field Work in Geography," *Bulletin, American Geographical Society* 47 (1915): 520-525. Sauer with G. H. Cady and H. C. Cowles, *Starved Rock State Park and Its Environs*, bulletin no. 6, Geographic Society of Chicago (Chicago: University of Chicago Press, 1918) was also seminar related.

37. Harlan H. Barrows, "Geography as Human Ecology," *Annals, Association of American Geographers* 13 (1923): 1-14. Address given in December 1922. Salisbury, who had been functioning as managing head of geology for many years, succeeded to the headship upon Chamberlin's retirement in 1919.

Carl O. Sauer

David Hooson

The name Carl Sauer is one to conjure with. Raised in a small midwestern town and educated for a few years in Germany, he began graduate studies in geography in the first decade (what he called "the Golden Age") of the department of geography of the University of Chicago and in the first decade of the life of the Association of American Geography. He died in 1975 at the age of eighty-five in Berkeley, California, where, over fifty years earlier, he had begun to develop one of the most distinctive of the schools of thought in American geography.

What was he really like and what did he contribute to American geography? The man I knew, in the last decade of his life, is the benign, impressively wrinkled Einsteinian old gentleman as photographed in the *Annals of the Association of the American Geographers* for September 1976, and also the one captured as the centerpiece of the Geographers on Film Series. In this late period, I became curious about the distinction between the man and the legend, between his early pronouncements and the man who later disowned them, between the "Berkeley school" and the present Berkeley department, and so on. A nagging regret is that I did not make more time for leisurely chats with him in the last five years of his life, when I was unfortunately department chairman at Berkeley and did not always feel able to follow his advice to use the wastebasket as liberally as he had apparently done during his three decades in that office. It seemed then that he would probably still be pottering about ten years on, mellowing, reminiscing, writing his books.

If Winston Churchill had died in 1939, when he had reached normal retiring age, he would probably have gone down in history as a somewhat wayward and cantankerous politician, adventurer, and gadfly—a colorful but essentially minor figure. Similarly it occurs to me that when I was a student in Britain around 1950, when Sauer was coming close to retirement, he was anything but a household word in geographical circles there and, in fact, was rarely mentioned or quoted in the literature. Maybe this was because his monographs and many of his articles had appeared in rather obscure house-organ types of series, which had incidentally helped to put him somewhat off to one side even in American geography. But there was also the curious fact that, while in American geography he was identified as being, as much as anyone, in the European tradition, he had not visited Europe at all in the half century or so since his school days in southern Germany.

However, when I first visited Berkeley in the late fifties, by which time Sauer had retired and had returned from an extended trip to Europe, I found that the aura of sage, philosopher-king, and even oracle surrounded him. Maybe this apparent transformation of his image during the 1950s was partly an illusion attributable to my own spotty education, but my impression is that the publication of his book *Agricultural Origins and Dispersals* and of the Princeton Symposium volume *Man's Role in Changing the Face of the Earth*, plus a number of wide-ranging articles including his second presidential address to the Association of American Geographers had suddenly promoted the diffusion of his thought and caused his international reputation to take off. There followed an unusually productive twenty-year nominal "retirement," during which four books and a score of articles appeared—fruits of a lifetime's reflective and unhurried gathering.

For all his simplicity, genuine and contrived, and his sympathy for those living apparently simple lives, he was a complex man, surrounded not only by his well-known ruminative cloud of pipe smoke but also by more than a few paradoxes. He was a continuously committed, broad-ranging speculative scholar, but he was by no means unpractical or softheaded with it. He was both a rock-ribbed conservative and a congenital nonconformist. He was profoundly concerned with a conservationist ethic in respect to human "stewardship" of the earth, yet had "an ineradicable distrust of political solutions," in the New Deal and after, and cast a "fishy eye" toward "applied geography" or government employment. He always maintained an incurably romantic vision of his "country-bred" origins and "the native virtues of rural life," (in contrast to Marx's "imbecility of rural life"), while choosing to live amongst city folks most of the time. While cursing the darkness of western urban culture, he did not get around to lighting a candle to point the way to what might be called a "natural way to live" in the cities which most of us perforce inhabit. He disparaged the study of urban geography, as well as political and sometimes even economic, although oddly enough his first two Ph.D. students wrote their dissertations on urban topics. His attitudes toward American blacks were more ambivalent than those toward American

Indians, and his view of modern sex rôles in some ways had not changed from the imaginative picture he built up of early woman as a nurturing, conservative, locational decision maker, providing "bed and board" for her man. Although he had a consuming life-long concern with the origins of humanity and of agriculture, he never went to Asia or Africa. Although contemptuous of twentieth-century American civilization, he is also said to have doubted in 1950 whether Europe had "anything to teach us."

While disparaging the attempts of others to hammer out a logical, methodological framework for the discipline, he added substantially and fruitfully to the literature along these lines himself. A true intellectual, he was in some ways more at home, and more patient, with "ordinary folk" than with his fellow intellectuals. He had an increasing distaste for the way in which the university and its scholars were organized and motivated, and yet he had a somewhat cavalier attitude to service on committees in an academy where this was the only practicable way open to improve things. The corollary of his apparent deep distrust of institutions was that he cherished individualism but, as one of his early students once observed, "his taste for it in practice was not infinitely extensible." Like many powerful strong-minded men, he always seemed to have confidence in his own judgments, and although he liked the informed dissenter, one could be forgiven for getting the impression that there were indeed limits to his tolerance. But then he was equally scathing about some of his own former ideas and pronouncements, and about the poor benighted people who had apparently swallowed them. Finally his warmth; wry, dry, and occasionally lethal sense of humor; depth of human understanding; and quiet aura of learning were always there to overcome and redeem all but the most difficult of contretemps, resulting from these contradictions.

We may at this point take note of his dictum that "we shall not get far if we limit ourselves in any way as to human time in our studies," and proceed to look briefly into the origins and stages of development of this complex man. When he arrived, at the age of thirty-three, to take up his new job at Berkeley, he was, of course, carrying a motley baggage of ideas which had sprung from a variety of experiences and environments. Although he was to change these ideas considerably over the next half century in the new intellectual atmosphere of Berkeley and his field experience in Latin America, the formative elements were at least as important to Sauer as to others of us, even if only to react against, and he was always very conscious of his own history, not merely that of humanity in general. The first element was his perception of himself as "country-bred" (his father was, however, a college professor, and Sauer was not raised on a farm, although he did inherit farms later and took a keen interest in them). His sympathy, if not identification, with rural "home folks," was genuine and was transferred naturally to the peasants of Latin America and to people struggling close to the land throughout history. Secondly, because he had regarded the land clearance and use of the "prairie and woodland soils" of his native Missouri as harmonious and somehow natural, his later experience of the destructive land use on deforested pinelands in Michigan made a deep impression on him. Apart from leading him to help found the Michigan Land Economic Survey to help heal and prevent such abuse, it deepened his interest in soils as a critical focus of geographical study, a sensitive indicator of the complex physical conditions, and a pointer to wise rural land use. He had already been particularly influenced by the soil scientists Hilgard and Marbut, the latter reflecting the ideas of the Russian Dokuchaev about climatically induced soil-vegetation zones. This led to an integrated, human-related physical geography, much more in the line with Sauer's needs and philosophy than Davisian geomorphology had been.

The experience in Michigan helped him to perfect the survey method in geography which he had begun to develop with Wellington Jones at Chicago, and also to exorcise the remnants of an environmentalist way of thought, expressed in simple terms like influence, control, response, or even adjustment, which had been instilled in him in Chicago, and buttressed by the ex cathedra pronouncements of W. M. Davis. Such mind-sets were evident in Sauer's early work in regional and political geography, such as those on the Upper Illinois Valley and on "Geography and the Gerrymander."[3] This methodological restructuring and philosophical reversal soon crystallized into formal, well-argued statements such as "The Survey Method"[4] and "The Morphology of Landscape"[5] which I had found reasonably sensible, and as a matter of fact still do, more or less, even after being told by Sauer himself that they should be consigned to the wastebasket. Although these seemed to have a certain family resemblance to Harlan H. Barrows's (1877–1960) immediately preceding presidential statement advocating geography as human ecology, there are subtle differences, which grew clearer as time passed.[6] In fact, it is odd and rather sad that Barrows, who supervised Sauer's dissertation and reportedly helped him get the job at Berkeley, apparently never communicated with Sauer thereafter (and vice versa) although they were simultaneously chairmen of two of the most important departments in the country over a period of two decades.

The seachange in Sauer's thought structure was also to lead inexorably to a preoccupation with the general problem of humanity's rôle in changing the face of the earth. One index of the previous neglect of that theme was that Sauer had not come across the works of George Perkins Marsh at all when undergoing his personal metamorphosis.

In this, for him, transitional period of the early 1920s, Sauer obviously gained much inspiration and guidance from broad and careful reading not only in German but also in the French classics. From it emerged a reaffirmation of the old principle of a regional geography as the core of the discipline, but one soundly based on field work, a broadly social science focus, and significant problems and themes. Though he later deplored, in an inference which now seems condescending, that his programmatic statements, notably "The Morphology of Landscape," had spawned many soulless, wooden regional studies, he really continued to live by and practice the true spirit of a living regional geography in his teaching and writing for the rest of his life, as he affirmed to me a few weeks before he died.

In this climate the first few years at Berkeley, when he was finding his feet, building the foundations of the infant department, and before he had charted his new direction into Latin American and historico-cultural geography, were rather becalmed and uncertain. While he actively cultivated connections with social science, notably economics, he was actually doing work in geomorphology and his first two Ph.D. students were future climatologists working on urban topics. By the early thirties he had become disillusioned with the economic connection, as he had earlier with the geological, and had found his natural soul mates in anthropology, history, and economic botany for the broad-ranging studies of people and nature on which he was about to embark.

Increasingly all geography henceforth became historical for him and, after a decade of field seasons and research in Mexico he delivered his revised, remarkably inclusive and powerful, testament of faith and blueprint for future work in his presidential address to the AAG, "Foreword to Historical Geography."[2] Sauer was in many ways at the height of his powers then, at fifty.

In the decade or so after the war he gradually wound down his visits to Mexico and his work broadened into general investigations of early humans, particularly their symbiosis with plants and their transformation of the landscape. These large endeavors culminated with the publication of *Agricultural Origins and Dispersals,* and of *Man's Role in Changing the Face of the Earth*, which put him at the center of an international, interdisciplinary circle at a critical juncture in world development. He also continued to speak up on the condition and future of geography and related fields. In this repect, his cautionary address "Folkways of Social Science"[8] in 1951, warning against the sophistries which he had seen developing in other fields and which were about to diffuse into geography, was at least as prescient, powerfully written, and influential as his second presidential address to the A.A.G., "The Education of a Geographer."[9]

In the last decade of his life, although he continued, of course, to be interested in, and to pursue, these universal themes, he focused in particular upon the earliest European encounters with the natives of the New World, the impact of the new environments and the challenges attending the initial establishment of permanent settlements. In spite of the intrinsic interest of these books—*The Early Spanish Main,*[10] *Northern Mists*[11], and *Sixteenth Century North America*[12], all produced in retirement—they have not yet, at least, been received with the interest and approbation, or even critical attention, that attended much of his earlier work.

So a further paradox is that while he has been quoted far more in the geographical literature and elsewhere, both here and abroad, in the sixties and seventies, than he was before, the references are largely to his previous work on early humanity and agricultural origins and his ecological, cultural, and methodological pronouncements. At this period he has also been taken up with enthusiasm and even reverence by a group of avant-garde poets and literary people in the San Francisco Bay area and elsewhere. This might until recently have been considered surprising, but Sauer obviously touched a vital chord there, not only because of his evocative, simple, and expressive language, but because of his speculative bent and his broad and imaginative sweep, back into prehistory. These people apparently view his work as a semiscientific check on unnecessary poetic license, but at the same time a suggestive source of inspiration for their own work. In a recent issue of the *Geographical Review* his philosophy and "imagination" has been compared with that of John Ruskin, converging on the perception of cultural landscapes.[13]

Faced with such a wide range of interests and published work as well as its appreciative audience, it is not easy to "place" Carl Sauer in the history of art, science, and learning, not to mention in that of geographical thought. He was indeed a polymath, recalling great free-ranging scholars of the nineteenth or even earlier centuries. He transcended academic geography as such, though virtually all of his work was geographical in spirit and in the broadest sense contributed to the illumination of basic geographical questions. It might be viewed as a philosophy of humanity, considered as inhabitants and transformers of the earth, with nature itself always considered as a living and changing thing of its own, inseparable from humans and integral to them—not just an inert "stage." In this context Sauer can be classified with those who have come from different intellectual origins toward a comprehensive synthesis of humans and their world in this century, such as Lewis Mumford, Nathaniel Shaler, Julian Huxley, or Arnold Toynbee. That Sauer is less of a household word than are some of them, or than some of the doom-saying ecologists or futurists of today, is perhaps a function of where he chose to publish or speak, and of the fact that he has been almost deliberately low-key and tentative. My sometime teacher Dudley Stamp even went so far, in a review of *Land and Life*, to describe Sauer as "something of an academic recluse ... avoiding the cut and thrust of public debate or private discussion," presumably outside Berkeley.[14] There is just a grain of truth in this—for instance, he would not agree to review a book he could not speak well of, in marked contrast to his colleague John Leighly.

Among geographers Sauer deserves to be placed alongside those select scholars who have had large ideas, wide erudition, literary flair, a speculative bent, and a worldwide perspective. He does not quite fit into the comprehensive, almost encyclopaedic cast of mind of Humboldt, Ritter, or Reclus, however humane or scientific they were, and he transcends those who tended largely to grind one axe, such as Davis or Huntington. I would mention in the same breath as him Ratzel, Vidal de la Blache, Jean Brunhes, George Perkins Marsh, and H. J. Fleure. According to these criteria, Halford Mackinder and Patrick Geddes of Britain, Frederic LePlay of France, Alexander Voeikov of Russia, and perhaps Sten de Geer of Sweden could also be added. Although comparisons and pecking orders are known to be odious, and one has to be very careful about building anyone up unduly, I find it difficult to think of another American geographer in this century who stands higher in intellectual grasp and general fertility and breadth of mind, and who is more likely to last into the next. Which is not to ignore his prejudices and shortcomings, many of which are traceable, as in the case of all of us, to his background and early experiences.

What, in sum, is the legacy Carl Sauer has bequeathed us? Most concretely there are the three dozen Ph.D.'s who graduated under his tutelage and have made up a distinctive group of leaders in American geography and other parts of the world, which became loosely known elsewhere as the "Berkeley school," though they are by no means in a restricted mould in respect to specialty or even method. Sauer was the patriarch of this closely knit clan, which of course included, to greater or less degree, large numbers of undergraduates and others who came under his influence.

Although much of his work was directed partly to a larger audience beyond academic geography, he has had an influence on the evolution and spirit of geography in America as powerful over the last half century in the life of the A.A.G. as Davis had in the first quarter and, to my mind, more wise and lasting. Sauer's early methodological statements, whatever he may have said about them later, were effective in dealing the coup de grace to the twin beguiling doctrines which, by their persuasiveness, almost drove the discipline into a dead end—environmentalism and the cycle theory of geomorphology. His role in slaying the environmentalist dragon is the more well known, but his elaboration of an integrated functional physical geography, focusing on climate, soils, and vegetation along the Russian model, and always including the impact of humanity, helped cut geomorphology down to size, forcing it also to dovetail its theories with those of environmental systems in general.

To my mind, the most influential of Sauer's general precepts in geography, the one which most identifies the common denominator of the "Berkeley school" and even the present Berkeley department (a different thing) is the fundamental value and necessity of a historical, process-oriented approach in virtually all subfields. There would be much less universal agreement about the focal indispensability of the concepts of landscape and culture as the other distinctive elements of the Sauer tradition, since they are at the same time too specific for some and too vaguely defined for others, and have not found such deep roots in our field. While I would agree with him that the geographer who focuses exclusively on the contemporary scene is not only "held by a peculiar obsession,"[15] but may often be expected to fall in through his own thin ice, I also feel that an undue preoccupation with origins to the neglect of insistent contemporary problems and questions could also arguably be labeled as perverse, if not reactionary.

Whatever caveats there may be about his emphases, Carl Sauer's breadth of mind and the range of his inquiries—blending historical, ecological, and cultural ways of thought; field work with library study; habit with habitat; regional with topical; maps with values—are impressive and ultimately satisfying. In what might be called, with due caution, the "greening" of American geography in the seventies, these qualities have returned to favor following what is now widely viewed as an excessive preoccupation with technique, precision, "optimal" solutions, and a narrowly spatial analysis in the sixties. Geography now needs to nurture all the more what may broadly be called the humanities approach, alongside the more strictly scientific and policy-oriented approaches, because it remains, I believe, primarily a cultural-educational subject (not excluding, of course, the education of policy-makers). Sauer would probably agree that it comes closest philosophically to the broad humane disciplines of history and anthropology, the latter also having a strong physical component. He seemed, through his writings, and in

172

conversations I had with him in the last years of his life, to regard geography as a kind of philosophy of humanity viewed as inhabitant and transformer of the earth, fully involving analysis of environmental and spatial systems alongside a historico-cultural approach. What he helped to teach us was to value the art of understanding at least as much as a presumed science of "explanation," humane scholars at least as much as research analysts, and to cherish the world's cultural and environmental diversity. In all of this, and beyond any blind spots he may have had, ring out the authentic tones of his evocative and vivid—yet accurate and simple—prose, the fruits of his constant curiosity, exploration, speculation, and wisdom about questions of universal interest and concern.

Notes

1. Carl Ortwin Sauer, *Agricultural Origins and Dispersals* (New York: American Geographical Society, 1952).
2. William L. Thomas, ed., *Man's Role in Changing the Face of the Earth* (Chicago: University of Chicago Press, 1956).
3. Carl Ortwin Sauer, "Geography and the Gerrymander," *American Political Science Review* 12 (1918): 403–26.
4. Carl Ortwin Sauer, "The Survey Method in Geography and Its Objectives," *Annals of the Association of American Geographics* 14 (1924): 17–33.
5. Carl Ortwin Sauer, "The Morphology of Landscape," in Berkeley, University of California Publications in Geography, vol. 2, no. 2 (Berkeley: University of California, 1925), pp. 19–54.
6. Harlan H. Barrows, "Geography as Human Ecology," *Annals of the Association of American Geographers* 13 (1923): 1–14.
7. Carl Ortwin Sauer, "Foreword to Historical Geography," *Annals of the Association of American Geography* 31 (1941): 1–24. For more information regarding Sauer's Latin America fieldwork, see Robert C. West, *Carl Sauer's Fieldwork in Latin America* (Michigan: University Microfilms International, 1979).
8. Carl Ortwin Sauer, "Folkways of Social Science," in *The Social Sciences at Mid-Century: Papers at the Dedication of Ford Hall, 1951* (Minneapolis: University of Minnesota, 1952), pp. 100–109.
9. Carl Ortwin Sauer, "The Education of a Geographer," *Annals of the Association of American Geographers* 46 (1956): 287–99.
10. Carl Ortwin Sauer, *The Early Spanish Main* (Berkeley: University of California Press, 1969).
11. Carl Ortwin Sauer, *Northern Mists* (Berkeley: University of California Press, 1968).
12. Carl Ortwin Sauer, *Sixteenth Century North America* (Berkeley: University of California Press, 1971).
13. Denis E. Cosgrove, "John Ruskin and the Geographical Imagination," *Geographical Review* 69, no. 1 (1979): 43–62.

14. L. D. Stamp, review of *Land and Life: A Selection from the Writings of Carl O. Sauer* (edited, with an introduction by J. Leighly [Berkeley: University of California Press, 1963]), in *Geographical Journal* 132, no. 1 (1966): 145–46.
15. Sauer, *Land and Life,* p. 366.

The Midwest as a Hearth Area in American Academic Geography

Dean S. Rugg

An intriguing problem in the history of American academic geography is the influence exerted by different regions on the development of the discipline. Even brief study of this problem reveals that the Midwest has been an important hearth or source area for the diffusion of geographical ideas. In an effort to document this specific regional influence, I have examined systematically the academic history of two major groups of geographers who were important before 1946. The first major group consists of the 337 Ph.D.'s granted between 1893 and 1946 as listed by Whittlesey[1] and Hewes.[2] However, since the production of such degrees was sporadic in the early years of this century, a second, selective group of 41 people, who either lacked the Ph.D. or who had gained it in another field or from a foreign area, also is included. These two groups are analyzed in terms of their academic origin, destination, and topic specialty. Major questions are: (1) Where were these people trained and where were they employed academically? (2) What areas provided the members of principal departments? and (4) What major dissertation topics were chosen, and how do they indicate regional influence in the field of geography? The primary hypothesis is that the Midwest served as a hearth area in terms of these three criteria. The focus, therefore, is regional and differs from that of Bushong's paper, included in this volume, which places the emphasis on individual geographers and their connections through their mentors.

The basic sources for Ph.D.'s granted are the two lists prepared by Whittlesey and Hewes for the 1893-1935 and 1935-46 periods, respectively.* A total of 337 persons are listed as having received Ph.D.'s in

* Although fairly inclusive, these two lists exhibit some omissions and inconsistencies. Four geographers with Ph.D.'s before 1946 are omitted by Whittlesey and Hewes but are included in my analysis. Certain geologists are shown as geographers, but are primarily physiographers from Harvard. In addition, some geologists are included (e.g., R. Goldthwait), but others are not (e.g., R. Russell). Dunbar, in an article in this volume, mentions certain other omissions.

this period of fifty-three years, 176 up to 1935 and 161 in the following decade. I was able to trace the movement of 312 of these persons, and their distribution—162 from the early list and 150 from the later one—constitutes a good sample of the origins, destinations, and basic research of Ph.D.'s in the early days of expansion in our discipline. The data for this diffusion of geographers came from membership lists of the Association of American Geographers, volumes of *American Men of Science,* and major journals in the field.

The pattern of Ph.D.'s by institutions as shown in Table 1 reveals that Clark and Chicago dominate with eighty-two and sixty-one, respectively. Wisconsin is third with thirty-four, followed by Michigan with twenty-three and Berkeley with twenty. The eastern schools decline in the second period, especially Yale, Pennsylvania, and Cornell, while a southern school, Peabody, picks up. Nebraska, on the edge of the midwestern region, has been consistent since the early 1930s. However, the most important figure is that 149 out of 337 dissertations were written at midwestern institutions. Bushong, in an article in this volume, emphasizes the importance of midwestern mentors in directing these dissertations.

Supplementing the 337 Ph.D.'s in geography is a second group of 41 people who exerted an early influence on our discipline, either without a Ph.D. or possessing this degree in another field or from a foreign area. These people, shown in Table 2, are recognized in general as geographers. Admittedly, the list is selective but seems to be representative for these categories. Some of them are listed by Bushong in this volume as mentors; all of them, however, have made contributions in research and teaching. Those without Ph.D.'s, except for Parker, Miller, and Blair, were important in the days before doctoral degrees in geography were awarded; thus, it is not unusual that most of them were trained in the East. Parker and Miller made significant contributions to educational geography, while Blair, a meteorologist with the government, served at the University of Nebraska and was even a mentor to one student. The list includes nine geology Ph.D.'s who contributed significantly to geography —in fact, more than some physiographers mentioned by Whittlesey and Hewes. In addition, nine men with Ph.D.'s in other fields are included, all of them recognizable for their orientation toward our field. Finally, four foreign geographers, who spent periods as regular staff members in departments of geography, are mentioned.

The Origins and Destinations of Academic Geographers

Table 3 shows the origins and destination of the two groups of

176

geographers mentioned in Tables 1 and 2, and serves as an indicator of the diffusion of trained geographers from certain source areas. The table demonstrates that most Ph.D.'s originated at major universities while destinations are widely dispersed. Destinations are grouped into two categories, major universities and smaller colleges, which in turn involve major regional groupings—the Midwest, East, South, and West. In this arbitrary division, Nebraska and Missouri are included with the Midwest group. The West group comprises the area from the Great Plains to the Pacific Coast, since fewer institutions are represented here. It should be noted that some geographers moved one or more times, a factor which increased the totals in Table 3.

An analysis of Table 3 illustrates the importance of the Midwest as a hearthland in American geography in terms of both origins and destinations of Ph.D.'s. Of 400 total positions in academic geography up to 1946, 176 or 44 percent were filled from the region that extends from Ohio to Nebraska and from Minnesota to Missouri. The East, on the other hand, provided 172 (43 percent) positions while the West and South followed with 32 (8 percent) and 14 (4 percent), respectively. On the other hand, the Midwest was the destination of 187 (47 percent) Ph.D.'s, while the East, West, and South received 112 (27 percent), 70 (17 percent), and 31 (8 percent), respectively. So the midwestern hearth area of America stands out as the academic source and destination of more Ph.D.'s than other regions. Somewhat surprisingly, the South resembles an arid region with respect to geography, at least before 1946.

Although the Midwest and East placed about the same number of their Ph.D.'s in major universities, the pattern of each has been different. Of 264 positions in major American universities, 114 were filled by Midwestern Ph.D.'s while 117 came from the East, 26 from the West, and 2 from the South. However, 39 of those from the East were produced at Clark, while, except for Columbia, contributions from Ivy League schools dropped off after 1930 or were confined to geology or physiography (see Tables 1 and 3). The contrast between Chicago and Clark, the two major Ph.D.-granting sources in the Midwest and East, respectively, is also revealing. The former placed 53 of 75 graduates in major universities, with 37 in the Midwest itself. On the other hand, Clark placed only 39 of 82 at major institutions with many of the others going to small colleges, often teacher oriented, in various parts of the country. The other midwestern universities all followed the Chicago pattern, although to a lesser degree, with a higher proportion of Ph.D.'s going to major universities than to small colleges. The same pattern is true of the Ivy League schools and Berkeley, but is not true for George Peabody, which has been first and foremost a preparatory school for teachers. In examining the destinations of Ph.D.'s at major universities, the Midwest received 119, the East 79, the West 50, and the South 16.

Some of the outstanding names in the field of geography originated at midwestern institutions. The Chicago department produced Barrows, Wellington Jones, Colby, Platt, Whittlesey, Harris, Hartshorne, Sauer, Ullman, Clarence Jones, Fenneman, Atwood, Sr., and Whitaker. Wisconsin contributed Finch, Trewartha, Baker, Guy-Harold Smith, Ralph Brown, Weaver, and Murphy. From Michigan came Hall, Davis, Kohn, and Russell. On the other hand, in comparison with the large number of Ph.D.'s granted at Clark, outstanding names are not as numerous; Cressey, James, Van Royen, Bengtson, and Prunty come to mind. The Ivy League schools produced several, especially from the early part of the century, including Davis, C. Brooks, Jefferson, R. Dodge, Huntington, Bowman, Goode, J. Russell Smith, Lobeck, Raisz, Douglas Johnson, and Orchard; Ackerman, Stephen Jones, and Kollmorgan came later. Berkeley contributed, among others, Leighly, Russell, Hewes, Kniffin, and Clark. A primary spatial aspect of this distribution is that most of the well-known names in the profession came from relatively few major universities, while some of the early people either did not have the Ph.D. or received it in geology or in another field.

Not many geographers moved from one institution to another during the period of 1893 to 1946. However, some did and among the best known are Sauer from Michigan to Berkeley, Hartshorne from Minnesota to Wisconsin, Ullman from Indiana to Harvard (later Washington), Fenneman from Colorado to Wisconsin to Cincinnati, Atwood from Chicago to Harvard to Clark, James from Michigan to Syracuse, Whitaker from Wisconsin to Peabody, Whittlesey from Chicago to Harvard, Clarence Jones from Clark to Northwestern, and Van Royen from Nebraska to Maryland. Noteworthy about these moves is that many involved leaving the Midwest for other parts of the United States. These changes can be interpreted more as attempts to utilize midwestern talent in upgrading other institutions, rather than moves to existing important centers of geography. In other words, the Midwest created a surplus for diffusion.

Academic Origins of Staff Members in Major Departments of Geography

Supplementing this examination of the origins and destinations of Ph.D.'s is Table 4, which shows the academic origins of staff members for major departments of geography. These departments not only granted most of the Ph.D.'s in geography up to 1946 (303 out of 337; see Table 1), but also possessed the major names in the field. In general, only Ph.D.'s are included. However, in a few cases, non-Ph.D.'s or Ph.D.'s in other fields are listed because of their contributions to overall departmental activities, e.g., Salisbury and Barrows at Chicago, Atwood and Fenneman at several universities, Condra at Nebraska, and several specialists at Harvard. A comparison of Tables 1 and 4 reveals that before 1946, certain departments like Berkeley and George Peabody produced a good number of Ph.D.'s with small staffs. On the other hand, larger departments like Minnesota, Illinois, Indiana, Missouri, Syracuse, and UCLA produced very few or none at all.

Table 4 reinforces the importance of the Midwest as a hearth area: of a total of 176 staff members at major departments, about 60 percent (106) came from institutions in this area. Perhaps most significantly, all departments except Columbia had some members from the Midwest, thus illustrating the impact of this area. Clark had two Chicago Ph.D.'s (Atwood, Sr., and C. Jones), while Chicago had none from Clark however, Clark was represented on most large departmental staffs. Northwestern and Syracuse, expanding just after World War II, built their departments around midwestern doctoral personnel. Many departments kept some of their own Ph.D.'s, and Chicago, Wisconsin, and Harvard especially stood out in this respect. In addition, some of the eastern Ph.D.'s, like J. Paul Goode and Walter Tower of Pennsylvania, moved to midwestern schools in the early period when qualified personnel were lacking. On the other hand, Ohio State and Nebraska were built mainly around eastern Ph.D.'s, especially from Clark which sent Van Cleef and McCune to Ohio State, and Bengtson, Van Royen, and Anderson to Nebraska.

In the 1930s, traditional eastern departments began to show signs of weakness. At Harvard, only Whittlesey was oriented toward the human side of geography, while at Yale, Huntington held only a research appointment. Departments at Columbia and Pennsylvania were focused on the economic side of geography with the former also possessing a separate Teachers College group. Cornell and Johns Hopkins were insignificant in the field. Only Clark and Syracuse seemed to have solid bases that were to be built upon after World War II.

The midwestern persistence in the influence of its departments of geography is shown in rankings portrayed by Dickinson.[3] Chicago and Wisconsin appear in the top three for both 1925 and 1966, while Michigan is also mentioned in the top nine for both years. On the other hand, Columbia, Harvard, and Yale, all in the top eight in 1925, disappear by

1966. Clark, second in 1925, is also gone from the top nine by 1966 while Washington, Syracuse, Minnesota, and Northwestern appear. California is present in both lists.

A remarkable characteristic of academic staff composition up to 1946 was the large number of departments with very few Ph.D.'s in geography. For example, California and George Peabody, which had Ph.D.-granting programs, list only three Ph.D.'s each from American universities. Of the 154 universities and colleges before 1946 with either a Ph.D. on the staff or a person shown in Table 2, 87 had only one staff member—a lonely prospect for these academicians; many of these were located at either teachers colleges or small private institutions.

The Dissertation Topics of the Ph.D.'s

A major source for examining research foci of Ph.D.'s between 1893 and 1946 is the dissertation topic. Browning et al., have made an analysis of this subject, and the results as shown in Table 5 indicate a trend toward regional topics.[4] From the early part of the century to 1937, this topic led all others, but in the next years it declined slightly while social topics increased. These regional dissertations indicated no specific subject matter other than a particular location. For example, Robert Buzzard's topic at Clark University in 1925 was "The Geography of Cape Cod." However, the impression is that many of the topical studies were focussed as much on the region as on the topic, i.e., Herbert Burgy's 1930 dissertation, "The New England Cotton Textile Industry—A Study in Industrial Geography."

A survey of the topical divisions shows that (1) dissertations about cities were important from the beginning but increased steadily, thereby contributing to the importance of the social category; (2) physical geography was dominant up to 1922 and after that remained rather steady at about 10 to 12 percent of total dissertations; (3) economic topics were consistently popular, comprising between one-fourth and one-third of the degrees; and (4) political geography was almost entirely neglected.

The dissertation lists by Whittlesey and Hewes show that topics varied by institution. Regional geography was most important at Clark, Peabody, and Nebraska, but was only one of several important topics at Chicago, Michigan, Wisconsin, and Pennsylvania. Physical geography, actually physiography, dominated at Harvard, while historical geography was foremost at Berkeley. Topics were most diverse at Chicago, Columbia, Cornell, Yale, Ohio State, and Washington. Overall, however, many titles had a regional focus. Leighly states, for example, that "graduate students at Chicago were expected to write their dissertations on regions."[5] Sauer wrote his on the Ozark Highlands of Missouri.

An examination of the individual dissertation titles up to 1946 points to this importance of the regional concept as a theme. During the early period up to 1925, many regional studies were either deterministic or modified to place the emphasis on human response to the environment. In the 1930s, the more objective regional study generated by the land-use mapping of small areas was significant. In both cases, the Midwest, and especially Chicago, was a leader. Barrows's presidential address of 1923 on "human ecology" reflects the environmental focus, while Sauer's "Morphology of Landscape" in 1925 depicts the regional approach. In the case of human response, physiography was important as a background, a point supported by Fenneman when he wrote: "Logically it might be expected that a satisfactory development of areal physiography would lead to real scientific studies of the interrelations between physical conditions and human life, both in particular areas and in general."[6] However, the fieldwork emphasized by those geographers connected with the spring field conferences was a factor in changing this ecological thrust in academic geography. James and Mather state that Sauer's ideas, especially as incorporated in his "Morphology of Landscape," were eagerly adopted by young midwestern geographers after 1925 as an alternative to the human-response model.[7] The fieldwork thrust was not only basic to the more objective regional studies that appeared but also, when applied to concrete areas like Michigan and the Tennessee Valley, gave Chicago and other midwestern departments national prestige.

The diffusion of the regional idea from Chicago and the Midwest, however, was not consistent. It was apparently more important at Clark than at Berkeley. Etzel Pearcy, a geographer who received his Ph.D. at Clark in 1940, wrote to me that "due to the influence of Atwood, Jones, and others, just about every study made by a graduate student followed a pattern right out of Chicago with a physiographic background for any particular analysis."[8] However, at Berkeley the pattern by the mid-1930s was quite different. Sauer, by this time, had changed his ideas, abandoning both human response and regional land-use studies. For example, Leighly refers to Sauer's feeling toward regional studies by quoting him as saying in 1934, "I know that it was not a very good thing for me to do a regional thesis, though one was virtually forced to do so at my school and in my day." Leighly feels that Sauer's dissatisfaction with regional studies, including those involving land-use mapping, dates from the mid-1930s and stems from a lack of problems associated with them. He quotes Sauer as follows: "A thesis must have a thesis, and regional studies are likely to be pointless or diffuse as to formulation of

181

problems."[9] Leighly states, therefore, that regional studies became obsolete at Berkeley in the late 1930s. However, this change did not necessarily rule out field study there, which could be directed toward the solution of problems rather than the characterization of the area in which the work was done. The nature of these problems is well expressed in Sauer's 1940 presidential address to the Association of American Geographers entitled "Foreword to Historical Geography." In this paper he emphasized the localization of cultural phenomena over time, a theme that was related to work done earlier by Ratzel and Hahn. Leighly states that it is these two "authors whose points of view are recognizable for the longest time in Sauer's work."[10] Thus, although Sauer came to Berkeley from the Midwest with the themes of regional occupance and fieldwork, he retained the latter but in a culture-time context.

Prunty's statements regarding the teacher-training emphasis at Clark offers another explanation for the proliferation of regional studies there in this period. In this case, the midwestern influence is less evident. For example, Prunty finds the lack of research seminars particularly sporadic when he states:

> In retrospect, I fault Clark considerably for its limited emphasis on research training generally, particularly through problem-oriented seminars for doctoral candidates. ... To my knowledge, my seminar experience was not greatly different from that of students who preceded me at Clark. One has to wonder how the course of American geography might have differed, since World War II, if the Clark of the 1920s and 1930s had been more research-oriented and less teaching-oriented in its doctoral programs.[11]

Although it may be somewhat strong to emphasize a cause-and-effect relationship between regional topics and teacher training, such an influence seems to be implied in Prunty's words.

Factors Associated with Midwestern Influence

The data provided in this paper seem to point to the conclusion that the Midwest served as an important regional hearth area for American geography during the period up to 1946. The region served as both a primary academic source and destination of persons with Ph.D.'s, particularly at major universities. Midwestern Ph.D.'s were dominant on the staffs of most important departments. Finally, a persistent topic for dissertation research in the Midwest and at other institutions was the regional study. What were the factors that made the Midwest dominant, and why did regional studies become so significant? Three factors that seem to be significant are the influence of Salisbury at Chicago, the rôle of state institutions, and a central geographical location.

1. Influence of Salisbury. Sauer said in 1965 that "academic geography in the United States was shaped most strongly at the University of Chicago and through the personality of R. D. Salisbury."[12] This early leader of the Chicago school was a scholar of great prestige in both geology and geography. He had been brought to Chicago from Wisconsin by the outstanding geologist, T. C. Chamberlin, who encouraged the emergence of geography as an integral discipline. According to Visher, Salisbury was influential because of his excellent choice of staff, his position as dean of the graduate school, his teaching reputation, and his writing of important textbooks. Visher also states: "More members of the Association of American Geographers reported in a 1939 questionnaire that Salisbury had 'significantly influenced' them than gave that testimonial to any other person."[13] Since this date was seventeen years after his death in 1922, it is a significant testimonial to the importance of the man.

Salisbury's influence as an administrator and department head needs further comment. He was dean of the graduate school and was appointed chairman when the first independent department of geography offering a Ph.D. was established, quite in contrast to Harvard and Pennsylvania, where geographers operated within departments of geology and business, respectively. From 1903 to 1923, Chicago was the only school where a person could obtain a doctorate from a department of geography. Finally, during Salisbury's period, Chicago and other midwestern institutions were open to innovations, perhaps more so than Ivy League institutions where academic structure had already crystallized. For example, Pattison, in an article in this volume, emphasizes Salisbury's commitment to interdisciplinary study of the significance of earth conditions to human affairs.

Salisbury also contributed to the Chicago emphasis on regions. He was familiar with the regional concept as utilized in Germany, having spent a year in Heidelberg in 1887-88. His early focus on physiography was basic to the environment-response paradigm as it applied to regional study in the Midwest and in other parts of the United States. Later, however, the fieldwork emphasized by Salisbury and those connected with the spring field conferences was a factor in changing this ecological thrust in academic geography to one of regional studies based on land-use mapping. This later focus as applied in Michigan and Tennessee led to national recognition for geography.

One also should not ignore the traditional attempt to cover regions as well as topics in courses offered at Chicago. Salisbury had a strong influence on this staffing pattern and Barrows continued it. Harris, in an illuminating essay on the Chicago department, emphasizes the early importance of world-regional coverage in courses with the hiring of Morrison on the Soviet Union and Taylor for Australia to supplement the other regional classes taught by staff members.[14] As a graduate student at Maryland in the 1950s, I personally can recall Van Royen's attempt to cover the world with a teaching staff that included Hu, Augelli, Ahnert, Deshler, and Hooson.

This emphasis on regional studies, which started at Chicago and spread to other midwestern institutions, was also found at Clark and George Peabody. At Clark, Salisbury's influence may have been transmitted through Atwood and Clarence Jones, and at Peabody through Parkins. Parkins also attended the spring field conferences. However, at these two schools the emphasis on teacher training also seems to account for a regional bias in dissertations.

Finally, the importance of Salisbury seems to be reflected in the rise of the Midwest as a seat of American geography in the 1920s. The recently issued history of the Association of American Geographers reports that "transfer of control of the Association, from the disciples of William Morris Davis to those of Rollin D. Salisbury, was quietly and certainly one of the major developments of the 1924–1943 period."[15] At the same time, the decline of geography at Ivy League institutions is apparent in the number of dissertations and in staffing patterns. The reasons for this decline are hard to ascertain. Certainly Davis, unlike Salisbury, did not build a solid graduate department at Harvard that would stand the test of time. Dunbar, in an article in this volume, also mentions the failure of eastern institutions (except for Clark) to retain or replace outstanding people. Eventually, in the 1950s, geography departments at Harvard and Yale were abolished. A factor here may have been economics—the cost of maintaining numerous departments at a privately endowed university. It has been reported informally that the decision at Harvard to delete geography was influenced by the cost of building a first-rate department and dissatisfaction with anything less. It is interesting to speculate that if Salisbury had built his department at Harvard, it might still be there!

2. State institutions. A second major factor perhaps responsible for midwestern influence in geography is the ease of diffusing ideas through state universities, especially land-grant institutions. Admittedly, this is hard to prove. Certainly Chicago was not a state institution; yet those departments in midwestern universities adjacent to Chicago were leaders

in the diffusion of geographic ideas during the 1920s and 1930s. Wisconsin, Michigan (not a land-grant school), Ohio State, Illinois, Indiana, and Nebraska established significant departments and eventually produced many of the Ph.D.'s who influenced our field. One important characteristic of the state university is pragmatism. These universities are designed to provide service to their states and, although theory may also be emphasized, the applied aspects of any discipline remain important. In his paper "What's 'American' about American Geography?" John K. Wright refers to this penchant for the practical.[16] This inclination may have been a factor in the emphasis on fieldwork as applied in the Michigan Land Survey and the Tennessee Valley. It may also help to account for the focus on small, accurate, regional studies as building blocks in geographic research.

3. Location. Colby feels that, in part, American geography grew out of the advances in science associated with the opening of the West.[17] Chicago and the other midwestern institutions, centrally located in the United States, therefore, could partake of the interest generated in survey, cartography, and physiography by the four famous geographic expeditions under Powell, Hayden, Wheeler, and King. These institutions were also central for conferences. However, this focus on the Midwest in a locational sense also had its detractions in terms of regional bias. Spencer refers to the annoyance on the Pacific Coast at the eastern dominance— which included the Midwest—in the the location and timing of the annual meeting of the Association of American Geographers.[18] James and Mather also refer to the influence on A.A.G. policies in the 1920s by the small field-conference group and say that as the number of geographers in the profession grew, dissatisfaction with the concentration of power increased.[19] Even today, reference is made to the "midwest Mafia" and its control over the choice of national officers and the makeup of committees. However, any healthy discipline needs a hearth area and this midwestern bias, if it exists, helps to support my original hypothesis: the Midwest, for better or for worse, has served as a hearth area for American geography.

TABLE 1

DISSERTATIONS ACCEPTED IN AMERICAN GEOGRAPHY*

	To 1935	1935-1946	Total
Clark	46	36	82
Chicago	33	28	61
Wisconsin	22	12	34
Michigan	10	13	23
California	7	13	20
Harvard	5	11	16
Nebraska	7	8	15
Columbia	6	7	13
Cornell	10	1	11
Pennsylvania	10	0	10
Ohio State	1	9	10
George Peabody	0	9	9
Yale	7	0	7
Washington	2	5	7
Johns Hopkins	3	0	3
Washington, St. Louis	0	2	2
Louisiana State	0	2	2
Stanford	2	0	2
North Carolina	1	1	2
Illinois	1	0	1
George Washington	1	0	1
Missouri	1	0	1
Princeton	1	0	1
Minnesota	0	1	1
Marquette	0	1	1
Dropsie (Philadelphia)	0	1	1
New York University	0	1	1
	176	161	337

* Lists include 339 geographers but two are Canadian; in addition, John Adams, listed by Hewes, actually was granted the Ph.D. in 1930 and thus should have been in Whittlesey's compilation.

Sources: (1) Derwent Whittlesey, "Dissertations in Geography Accepted by Universities in the United States for the Degree of Ph.D. As of May 1935," *Annals of the Association of American Geographers* 25 (1935): 211-37.

(2) Leslie Hewes, "Dissertations in Georgraphy Accepted by Universities in the United States and Canada for the Degree of Ph.D., June 1935 to June 1946, and Those Currently in Progress," *Annals of the Association of American Geographers* 36 (1946): 215-47.

TABLE 2

SELECTED ACADEMIC GEOGRAPHERS EITHER WITHOUT THE PH.D. OR HOLDING IT FROM ANOTHER DISCIPLINE OR FROM A FOREIGN AREA

Without the Ph.D	Ph.D in Geology
Harlan H. Barrows, B.S., geol., 1903, Chicago	Wallace W. Atwood, Sr., 1903, Chicago
Thomas A. Blair, B.S., meteor., 1904, Stanford	George E. Condra, 1901, Nebraska
Albert P. Brigham, M.A., geol., 1892, Harvard	Nevin M. Fenneman, 1901, Chicago
William M. Davis, B.S., geol., 1869, Harvard	Herbert E. Gregory, 1899, Yale
Richard E. Dodge, M.A., geol., 1894, Harvard	William H. Hobbs 1888, Johns Hopkins
Charles R. Dryer, M.D., 1876, Buffalo	Douglas W. Johnson, 1903, Columbia
Daniel C. Gilman, M.A., geol., 1855, Yale	Lawrence Martin, 1913, Cornell
Mark S. Jefferson, M.A., geog., 1898, Harvard	William E. Powers 1931, Harvard
William Libbey, Sc.D., 1879, Princeton	Richard J. Russell, 1926, Berkeley
Charles T. McFarlane, B.A., 1892, New York St. Normal	
Curtis F. Marbut, M.A., geol., 1895, Harvard	
George J. Miller, M.S., geog., 1909, Chicago	*Ph.D. in Other Field*
Edith P. Parker, M.A., ed., 1920, Chicago	Oliver E. Baker, econ., 1921, Wisconsin
Rollin D. Salisbury, M.A., geol., 1884, Beloit	Charles C. Huntington, econ., 1915, Cornell
Ellen C. Semple, M.A., hist., 1891, Vassar	Earl E. Lackey, ed., 1933, Columbia
Nathaniel S. Shaler, B.S., geol., 1862, Harvard	Harold H. McCarty, econ., 1929, Iowa
Ralph S. Tarr, B.S., geol., 1891, Harvard	Howard H. Martin, econ., 1929, G. Washington
Robert D. Ward, M.A, meteor., 1893, Harvard	John E. Orchard, econ., 1923, Harvard
Ray H. Whitbeck, B.A., geol., 1901, Cornell	Homer L. Shantz, botany, 1905, Nebraska
	Carl F. Wehrwein, land econ., 1930, Wisconsin
	Derwent S. Whittlesey, hist., 1920, Chicago
Ph.D. from Foreign Area	
Jan O. Broek, Utrecht, 1932	
T. Griffith Taylor, Sydney, 1916	
Samuel Van Valkenburg, Zurich, 1918	
Joseph E. Williams, Vienna, 1932	

TABLE 3

ORIGIN AND DESTINATION OF AMERICAN Ph.D.'S, 1893-1946

Origin	Major				Destinations Small Colleges				
	M	E	S	W	M	E	S	W	Total
Midwest									
Chicago	37	10	1	5	11	5	3	3	75
Wisconsin	16	5	1	5	10	4	0	1	42
Michigan	8	3	0	1	5	2	1	0	20
Ohio State	2	1	1	1	2	0	0	0	7
Nebraska	7	0	1	2	8	0	0	3	21
Other [a]	7	0	0	0	3	0	0	1	11
	77	19	4	14	39	11	4	8	176
East									
Clark	13	11	6	9	18	15	4	6	82
Harvard	6	16	0	3	1	2	0	0	28
Yale	0	6	0	1	1	0	0	0	8
Cornell	6	3	1	0	1	0	1	0	12
Pennsylvania	2	7	0	0	0	0	0	0	9
Columbia	4	9	2	4	1	1	0	0	21
Other [b]	3	3	0	2	2	2	0	0	12
	34	55	9	19	24	20	5	6	172
South									
G. Peabody	1	0	0	1	3	2	4	2	13
North Carolina	0	0	0	0	0	0	1	0	1
	1	0	0	1	3	2	5	2	14
West									
Berkeley	4	4	3	11	1	0	0	3	26
Washington	1	0	0	2	0	1	1	0	5
Stanford	1	0	0	0	0	0	0	0	1
	6	4	3	13	1	1	1	3	32
Foreign [c]	1	1	0	3	1	0	0	0	6
Totals	119	79	16	50	68	34	15	19	400

Notes: [a] Minnesota/ Illinios/ Iowa/ Missouri/ Washington University St. Louis/ Beloit.

[b] Princeton; Johns Hopkins; Buffalo; Vassar; George Washington; New York University; New York St. Normal.

[c] Switzerland (2); Austria (2); Netherlands; Australia.

Sources: (1) Directories of the Association of American Geographers, 1932, 1945, 1946, and 1949.

(2) *American Men of Science.*

(3) Primary geographical journals.

TABLE 4

ACADEMIC SOURCES OF STAFF MEMBERS AT MAJOR DEPARTMENTS OF GEOGRAPHY, 1893-1946

	Own	M	E	S	W	Foreign	Total
Chicago	12	1	3			1	17
Wisconsin	7	4	5		1		17
Michigan	3	3	2				8
Ohio State		3	5		1		9
Nebraska	2	1	4		1		8
Minnesota	1	4	2		1		8
Illinois	1	9	3				13
Indiana		4	3				7
Northwestern		7	1				8
Missouri		8	2	1			11
Clark	4	3	2			1	10
Harvard	7	4	3				14
Columbia	5		3				8
Pennsylvania	5	2	1				8
Syracuse		4	2				6
George Peabody	1	2					3
Berkeley	3	1				1	5
UCLA		2	3		3		8
Washington	1	1	4		1	1	8
							176

Sources: (1) Directories of the Association of American Geographers, 1932, 1945, 1946, and 1949.

(2) *American Men of Science.*

(3) Primary geographical journals.

TABLE 5

SUBJECT MATTER OF DISSERTATIONS IN AMERICAN GEOGRAPHY TO 1953

	Pre-1922		1922-25		1926-29		1930-33		1934-37		1938-41		1942-45		1946-49		1950-53		Total	
	#	%	#	%	#	%	#	%	#	%	#	%	#	%	#	%	#	%	#	%
I. HUMAN GEOGRAPHY	9	32	13	46	20	53	22	47	27	50	42	63	24	55	53	60	84	58	294	55
A. *Social*	4	14	7	25	9	24	16	34	14	26	28	42	14	32	29	33	37	25	158	30
Urban	4	14	7	25	4	11	11	23	10	19	12	19	6	14	11	13	15	11	80	15
Settlement					2	5	1	2	3	6	10	15	4	9	8	9	11	8	38	7
Historical					2	5	3	6	1	2	3	5	2	5	2	2	6	4	19	4
Ethnic							1	2					2	5	2	2	3	2	11	2
Political					1	3			2	4	3	5	1	2	7	8	2	1	10	2
B. *Economic*	5	18	6	21	11	29	6	13	13	24	14	21	10	23	24	27	47	33	136	25
Agriculture	1	4	2	7	3	8	2	4	4	7	3	5	3	7	4	5	20	14	40	8
Land Use					2	5	1	2	7	13	5	8	3	7	9	10	9	6	36	7
Trade & Transport	2	7	2	7	3	8	2	4	2	4	2	3	2	5	2	2	4	3	17	3
Manufacturing	1	4	2	7	1	3			2	4	2	3	1	2	2	2	4	3	17	3
Extractive Indus.	1	4							2	4	2	3			5	5	5	4	13	2
Water Resources					2	5	1	2	2	4	2	3			1	1	5	4	13	2
II. PHYSICAL GEOGRAPHY	9	31	5	18	4	11	10	22	4	8	9	14	6	13	7	8	22	16	76	14
A. *Physical*	6	21	4	14	4	11	5	11	3	6	5	8	5	11	6	7	17	12	55	10
B. *Culture-Natural Environment*	3	10	1	4			5	11	1	2	4	6	1	2	1	1	5	4	21	4
III. REGIONAL	10	36	8	29	12	32	15	32	19	35	13	20	10	23	25	28	18	13	130	24
IV. ALL OTHER	2	7	2	7	2	5	5	11	4	7	2	3	4	9	3	3	18	13	35	7
Total No. Dissertations	28		28		38		47		54		66		44		88		142		535	

Sources: Browning, Clyde, et al., "Trends in Geographic Dissertation Subjects, 1906-1953," *Professional Geographer* 8 (1956): 9.

Notes

1. Derwent Whittlesey, "Dissertations in Geography Accepted by Universities in the United States for the Degree of Ph.D. As of May 1935,"*Annals of the Association of American Geographers* 25 (1935): 211–37.
2. Leslie Hewes, "Dissertations in Geography Accepted by Universities in the United States and Canada for the Degree of Ph.D., June 1935 to June 1946, and Those Currently in Progress," *Annals of the Association of American Geographers* 36 (1946): 215–47.
3. Robert E. Dickinson, *Regional Concept: The Anglo-American Leaders* (London: Routledge and Kegan Paul, 1976), p. 191.
4. Clyde Browning et al., Trends in Geographic Dissertation Subjects," *Professional Geographer* 8 (1956): 8–14.
5. John Leighly, "Carl Ortwin Sauer, 1889–1975," *Annals of the Association of American Geographers* 66 (1976): 338.
6. Nevin M. Fenneman, "The Place of Physiography in Geography," *Journal of Geography* 21 (1922): 21.
7. Preston E. James and Cotton Mather, "The Role of Periodic Field Conferences in the Development of Geographical Ideas in the United States," *Geographical Review* 67 (1977): 448.
8. Etzel Pearcy to me, 27 November 1978.
9. John Leighly, "Berkeley—Drifting into Geography in the Twenties," *Annals of the Association of American Geographers* 69 (1979): 8.
10. John Leighly, ed., *Land and Life: A Selection from the Writings of Carl O. Sauer* (Berkeley: University of California Press, 1963) p. 5.
11. Merle Prunty, "Clark in the Early 1940s," *Annals of the Association of American Geographers* 69 (1979): 44–45.
12. Carl O. Sauer, "On the Background of Geography in the United States," in *Festschrift Gottfried Pfeifer*, ed. Hans Graul and Hermann Overbeck, Heidelberger Studien zur Kulturgeographie no. 15 (Wiesbaden: Franz Steiner Verlag, 1966), p. 68.
13. Stephen S. Visher, "Rollin Salisbury and Geography," *Annals of the Association of American Geographers* 43 (1953): 4, 9.
14. Chauncy D. Harris, "Geography at Chicago in the 1930s and 1940s," *Annals of the Association of American Geographers* 69 (1979): 27–28.
15. Preston E. James and Geoffrey J. Martin, *The Association of American Geographers: The First Seventy-Five Years* (Washington, D.C.: Association of American Geographers, 1979), p. 69.
   John K. Wright, "What's 'American' about American Geography?" in *Human Nature in Geography*, ed. idem (Cambridge: Harvard University Press, 1966), pp. 124–39.
17. "A Half Century of Geography—What Next?" (Chicago: Department of Geography, University of Chicago, 1955), p. 8.
18. J. E. Spencer, "A Geographer West of the Sierra Nevada," *Annals of the Association of American Geographers* 69 (1979): 47.
19. James and Mather, "The Role of Periodic Field Conferences," p. 457.

Geographers and Their Mentors: A Genealogical View of American Academic Geography

Allen D. Bushong

The structure and development of geography as an academic discipline can be revealed or suggested in several ways. State-of-the-art assessments, analysis of the number and patterns of degrees awarded, and interpretation of the geographical literature have all been widely used to document disciplinary development. Citation analysis, studies of individual professional organizations and academic departments, and comprehensive book-length biographies of individual geographers have been less frequently used measures. This paper explores the structure and development of American academic geography from a rarely encountered genealogical perspective.

The convergence in the last quarter of the nineteenth century of academic specialization with its departmentalization within the university and the implantation of the German model of advanced scholarship at Johns Hopkins University set the pattern in American graduate education that has prevailed to this day. The acquisition of academia's highest earned degree, the Ph.D., awarded for broad mastery of a discipline and specialization in a segment of it, identifies the recipient as an approved member of a new generation of scholars in a defined discipline. This approval, a judgment of all of the graduate students' teachers, bears most directly on the one who supervises the single most significant and sustained requirement for the degree, the dissertation.

Whatever designation (supervisor, chairperson, director, sponsor, major professor) is applied to the teacher who oversees the dissertation, that person in most cases is the individual with whom the student elects to work, and from whom sponsorship in the profession is derived. The student is perceived as a disciple of that teacher, an inheritor and disseminator of the teacher's disciplinary beliefs. Such a person is not only a teacher to the student; he or she is a mentor, an established professional responsible for a neophyte professional. Mentors are thus at one and the same time a part of the discipline's structure and builders of it.

Given their key role, this study uses the mentors as the basis for the construction of an academic genealogy designed to demonstrate or to suggest the extent of their influence on the structure and development of American academic geography in the formative decades of its existence.[1] This formative period extended from 1907, when the first Ph.D. in geography was conferred, through 1946. This forty-year phase stands in clear contrast with the decades that followed. In the earlier years the core of professional geographers was relatively small, the annual output of Ph.D. degrees was limited and erratic, and the training of these new doctors of philosophy was concentrated in only a few schools. The membership of American geography's leading professional body, the Association of American Geographers (A.A.G.), likewise reflected that contrast. Before the Second World War, A.A.G. membership was small, slow growing, and exclusive; afterward much larger, faster growing, and less exclusive.[2]

General Patterns

In the years 1907–46, 294 doctor of philosophy degrees in geography were conferred by sixteen schools (Table 1). The leading schools in terms of number of degrees conferred, the private institutions of Clark and Chicago, granted exactly one-half of the 294 degrees. The addition of the next three schools, the state institutions of Wisconsin, Michigan, and Berkeley, accounted for another one-fourth of the doctorates granted. The remaining eleven schools collectively accounted for only one-fourth of all degrees conferred. Four of these first sixteen institutions no longer grant the Ph.D. degree in geography.

Of the degrees, 89 percent were awarded to men and 11 percent to women. Women received degrees at seven of the sixteen schools. Among the seven, three collectively awarded more than 75 percent of those conferred on women: Clark (39 percent), Chicago (21 percent), and Wisconsin (18 percent). The proportion of female to male Ph.D. recipients at each of these universities was: Clark, 15 percent; Chicago, 12 percent; and Wisconsin, 17 percent.

194

Student/Mentor Patterns

Among the fifty-three mentors, Colby (Chicago), Ekblaw (Clark), and Barrows (Chicago) were the mentors for one-fourth of all Ph.D. recipients in the period 1907–46 (Table 2). With the addition of the senior Atwood, Sauer, Clarence Jones, Finch, and Van Valkenburg, eight individuals were the mentors for more than half of all who received Ph.D. degrees in geography. Another nineteen mentors had only one student each, which collectively was less than the total for any one of the three leading mentors. Nine mentors had two students each. Only two of the fifty-three mentors were women, Ellen Churchill Semple and Frances Merritt Earle. Semple chaired two dissertations, Earle one; the remaining 291 Ph.D. recipients had male mentors, except for Ellsworth Huntington and Finch who had no mentors at all. Huntington and Finch received their doctorates on the basis of research already published.[3]

School/Mentor Patterns

The mentor function in most departments was dominated by one or two individuals (Table 3). Among the five leading schools in number of degrees conferred, this dominance was greatest at Berkeley, which had two mentors but where Sauer directed all but two of the twenty Ph.D.'s awarded, or 90 percent of the total. Chicago had eight mentors, but 80 percent of all Ph.D.'s in the study period took their degrees under the supervision of either Colby or Barrows. Clark, with eight mentors, had 70 percent of its degrees awarded under the direction of either Ekblaw, the senior Atwood, or Clarence Jones. McMurry, one of five mentors at Michigan, was the director for over one-half of that university's Ph.D.'s in geography. Close to half of Wisconsin's Ph.D.'s came under the guiding hand of Finch, one of eight mentors in that department. For most other schools with at least a half dozen Ph.D. recipients each, a single individual dominated in the mentor function. This was true for Nebraska (Bengtson), George Peabody (Parkins), Ohio State (Guy-Harold Smith), Columbia (J. Russell Smith), and Yale (Ellsworth Huntington).

Inbreeding Patterns

The widely deplored practice of inbreeding was widely practiced in the formative years of American academic geography. Nine of the sixteen departments engaged in it; that is, each appointed to their faculty individuals who received their highest earned degree at that school (Table 4). The initial widespread hiring by geography departments of some of their own graduates reflected the small number of Ph.D.'s available. This practice beyond the formative years, however, becomes far less justifiable as the number of Ph.D.-granting departments and their graduates increase. A reciprocity pattern wherein a given pair of Ph.D.-granting departments hire each other's Ph.D. graduates was nowhere in evidence insofar as the mentors were concerned. Such reciprocity did not appear until after World War II.

Chicago was the most inbred department, retaining four of its Ph.D. graduates who themselves became mentors. Another mentor, Barrows, also graduated from Chicago, though with a baccalaureate degree in geology as his highest earned degree. Only three Chicago mentors earned their degrees elsewhere. Half of Wisconsin's mentors earned their highest degree at Wisconsin, all Ph.D.'s in geography except for Wehrwein, whose doctorate was in agricultural economics. Three of Clark's eight mentors earned their Ph.D.'s in geography at Clark. Both of Yale's mentors held Yale doctorates in geography. Three other geography departments each retained one of their own graduates who subsequently became mentors: Hall at Michigan, Leighly at Berkeley, and Otte at Columbia. Two geography departments hired graduates of their school whose degrees were in geology, Ward at Harvard and Condra at Nebraska.

Diffusion Patterns

But if Chicago had the most inbred geography department, it was also the one whose Ph.D. graduates appeared as mentors in other doctoral granting departments of geography to a far greater extent than those from any other school (Table 5). Eight of the other fifteen Ph.D.-granting departments included mentors who earned their terminal degree at Chicago. At three schools (George Peabody, Washington—St. Louis, and North Carolina) all the mentors were Chicago graduates, and there were mentors with Chicago doctorates in geography at each of the top five Ph.D.-granting departments (Table 1) . This presence of Chicago geography graduates as mentors in the majority of Ph.D.-granting departments, including each of the top five producers, gave to that department in these formative decades a far greater potential influence on the development of American academic geography than that of any other department.

Six other geography departments placed their Ph.D. graduates in other Ph.D.-granting departments of geography, where they became mentors in this 1907-46 period. Clark graduates were mentors at Michigan (James), Nebraska (Bengtson), Ohio State (Van Cleef), and Washington—Seattle (Church). A Columbia geography Ph.D. (Renner) became a mentor at Washington—Seattle, while Lackey and Lobeck (Columbia Ph.D. graduates in education and geology, respectively) became geography mentors at Nebraska and Wisconsin. Wisconsin placed one of its Ph.D. graduates at Ohio State (Guy-Harold Smith) as did Harvard (Peattie), while Berkeley did similarly at Louisiana State University (Kniffen), and Michigan at Minnesota (Davis).

Genealogical Patterns

The genealogical patterns of mentors and students for the years 1907-46 are shown in Table 6. By the end of World War II, four generations of geographers had produced academic offspring; the fifth generation was launched but none among them had yet had any academic progeny. Only four of the fifty-three mentors had fourth generation descendants (Barrows, Finch, Salisbury, and Semple), but twenty-five of the thirty-two in that generation were directly descended from Barrows. Another ten mentors had descendants through the third generation, with Barrows having twice as many in the generation as any other single mentor. Equally striking is the fact that three-fourths of all mentors had no academic descendants beyond their own academic offspring. Of those mentors with a dozen or more students each, no more than one-fourth of any mentor's students became mentors themselves. The expansion of American academic geography's family tree has been mostly through the genealogical line of five mentors: Salisbury, Barrows, Finch, the senior Atwood, and Semple. No less than four out of every five geography Ph.D.'s graduated during and before 1946 can trace their academic lineage back to one of these five individuals.

Salisbury was mentor to only four students (Fig. 1). Two of his students, Wellington D. Jones and Platt, were retained as faculty at Chicago. A third, Sauer, was Salisbury's most productive student, the academic father of nineteen by the end of 1946. Through Sauer came four of Salisbury's five academic great-grandchildren.

With 104 academic descendants, Barrows had no near rivals (Fig. 2). Next, with 46, was Colby, one of his students. One-fourth of Barrows's students had Ph.D. students of their own. Eighteen of Barrows's twenty-five great-grandchildren (fourth generation) were the offspring of

197

Clarence Jones, one of Colby's students. Colby and Leppard, another Barrows student and subsequent mentor, were kept on the Chicago faculty after receiving their doctorates.

Trewartha and Guy-Harold Smith were the only two of Finch's thirteen students who had students of their own (Fig. 3). Each had six, of whom only one of these had a student.

Five of Atwood's nineteen students became mentors, of whom one was retained at Clark (Fig. 4). Not one of Atwood's twenty-two academic grandchildren were mentors. Half of those grandchildren were descended through one individual, Bengtson.

Semple had only two students, Ekblaw and Baugh, of whom only the former had academic offspring (Fig. 5). He remained at Clark. Only Warman among his twenty-five students had a student of his own. Warman, too, stayed on as a faculty member at Clark.

The genealogical pattern of American academic geography in the first four decades reveals a tightly knit group, nurtured in only sixteen institutions moderately well distributed across the country. Ten of the schools had graduated less than a dozen students each, while half of the students graduated from one of two schools. The 294 new geographers were approved by a comparative handful of fifty-one men and two women, the architects of the discipline. Who were these fifty-three architects of American academic geography, who comprised an elite corps within a small profession, and who controlled rites of passage into that profession?

The Mentors: A Collective Portrait[4]

Date and Place of Birth. More than one-half (53 percent) of the mentors were born prior tó 1890, the earliest in 1858 (Salisbury); almost one-third (32 percent) were born in the 1890s; the remainder (15 percent) were born in the twentieth century, the latest in 1907 (Warman). Their places of birth were both varied and concentrated (Table 7). As a group the mentors were overwhelmingly native born; only five of the fifty-three were born outside the United States. Two were natives of Canada (Bowman and Leppard), and one each was born in England (Taylor), Sweden (Bengtson) and the Netherlands (Van Valkenburg). However, Bowman came to the United States at the age of eight weeks and Bengtson at the age of two years so that their formative years were shared in the culture of the majority of mentors.

The American Midwest has long been identified as the core region for American geography. Several mentor characteristics reflect that fact. Of the forty-eight born in the United States, the Midwest was the birthplace for no less than thirty-one. Illinois was the homeland for nine, more than any other state, with five each coming from Michigan, Ohio, and Wisconsin. Three came from the Plains States. The Middle Atlantic and New England areas were home to seven mentors, while the south claimed six. Only one mentor hailed from the Southwest and none was born in a West Coast state. A minority of mentors, fifteen out of fifty-three, came from an urban environment.

Undergraduate Education Patterns. Twenty-four domestic and two foreign institutions of higher education conferred baccalaureate degrees on all mentors except Van Valkenburg (Table 8). Queen's of Canada and Sydney in Australia were the undergraduate schools for Leppard and Taylor, respectively. In addition, Taylor had another baccalaureate from Cambridge. Of the twenty-four U.S. schools that awarded fifty bachelor's degrees, twelve were conferred by Chicago, almost one-fourth of the domestic total. Wisconsin was the alma mater of five mentors, followed by Harvard, Michigan, and Nebraska with four each. Pennsylvania and Beloit were the undergraduate schools for two mentors each, while seventeen other schools each graduated one mentor. Thirty-one of the fifty mentors educated in the United States took their baccalaureate degrees at private institutions, and thirty-eight of all the mentors took their degrees in the same region where they were born and/or grew up. Only eleven pursued their undergraduate education in one of the Ivy League/Seven Sisters institutions, and two came out of Southern schools. Except for Stanford, no school west of Lincoln, Nebraska, was the alma mater for any mentor. Few mentors took undergraduate courses at teacher-oriented institutions. An outstanding exception among such schools was the Normal College at Ypsilanti, now Eastern Michigan University, where several mentors studied under Charles T. McFarlane or Mark Jefferson.[5]

For some mentors the undergraduate school was also the school where they later carried out their mentor functions. This, too, is an aspect of inbreeding, though in most instances the highest earned degree was taken elsewhere. In the case of Barrows, Colby, and Wellington Jones at Chicago; Durand, Trewartha, and Wehrwein at Wisconsin; Bengtson, Condra, and Lackey at Nebraska; Ward at Harvard; and Hall at Michigan, each supervised Ph. D.'s in geography at the school where he received his baccalaureate degree. and in the case of eight of these individuals (Colby, Wellington Jones, Durand, Trewartha, Wehrwein, Condra, Ward, and Hall), the undergraduate school was the same one which granted them their highest graduate degree (the Ph. D. for all except Ward). These eight individuals are the most inbred of all, for each passed his entire academic career from baccalaureate institution through graduate education and beyond to university teaching at a single institution. Finally, twenty-one out of fifty-three mentors earned their highest graduate degree at the same school where they earned their baccalaureate.

Graduate Education Patterns. Seventeen universities, including two foreign schools, were involved in training the mentors for their highest earned degree (Table 9). The top three schools—Chicago, Clark, and Wisconsin—were also the top three schools in Ph.D.'s awarded in geography (Table 1), though not in the same order. The median age at which mentors earned their highest degree was thirty-one, compared to a median age of thirty-three (thirty-two for men and thirty-eight for women) for their students.[6]

The highest earned degree for more than one-third of the mentors was in a discipline other than geography (Table 10). Eight earned that degree in geology, approximately one mentor in every six or seven. While geology was the leading field after geography, that proportion was far less than among the forty-eight charter members of the A.A.G., where approximately one-half would be classified as geologists by training.[7]

The terminal degree was not a doctorate for six mentors. For three individuals it was the master's (Salisbury, Semple, and Ward), and for three others it was the bachelor's (Barrows, Blair, and Whitbeck). For none of these six persons was geography the field of study for their highest earned degree. A higher proportion of mentors in this formative period of American academic geography had their final graduate study in a discipline other than geography than is true today, and a larger share then than now did not have an earned doctorate. The Ph.D. has long since become the passport to college teaching, and teaching is what most Ph.D. recipients in geography have always done. Having acquired the Ph.D. its bearer has, in Jacques Barzon's words, "paid his intitation fee into the most expensive and least luxurious club in the world."[8] It is also a far less exclusive club today than in the past. When Barzun made the above statement in the mid-1940s, the number of Ph.D.'s conferred annually in the United States was less than three thousand. By the mid-1970s that annual number exceeded thirty-three thousand.[9].

Out of this collective portrait emerges a "typical" mentor for the formative years of American academic geography. That mentor was male, native born and raised in the Midwest, and obtained both undergraduate and advanced degrees in that region. By these measures he was a parochial individual. That label applied indiscriminately to all fifty-three mentors would not be accurate, for some mentors studied or taught abroad, and a number of Ph.D. departments, especially the larger ones, broadened the outlook of their regular faculty and students with semester-long visits of geographers from overseas.

Conclusion

The student/mentor bond has long been a distinctive feature of academe. This study has charted that bond genealogically to gain a distinctive perspective on the growth and structure of American academic geography in its formative decades. Out of that perspective are revealed relationships and patterns both concrete and speculative. Student/mentor and school/mentor relationships, inbreeding and diffusion patterns, and the overall genealogical patterns confirm the tightly knit structure of the discipline in the years 1907-46. What the genealogical charts demonstrate about student-mentor influences and beyond through the genealogical line, however, can only be suggestive and speculative. It would be naive and untenable to assume solely on the basis of these genealogical patterns, for example, that the ideas of Rollin Salisbury were received, embraced, and promoted by his academic great-grandson, David Blumenstock, through the genealogical line by way of Sauer and Leighly (Fig. 1). Whether or not that was true would have to be verified by studying the intellectual links between individuals in the genealogical chain.

It is well to remember that just as children must assert their independence from their parents and strike out on their own self-determined course, yet retain earned respect for the parents, so too is this applicable to the student-mentor relationship. One of the better known examples of this is Carl Sauer, who, though respecting his mentor Salisbury, nevertheless needed to strike out on a new professional course at Berkeley. It is ironic that Sauer, who sent his students in whatever directions their intellectual labors required, has been viewed as the head of a "Berkeley school" whose offspring all carry intact and unaltered the ideas and beliefs of the patriarch. The validity of that conventional wisdom and the meaning of all such labels have been seriously questioned by one of Sauer's students.[10]

Mentors do take pride in the accomplishments of their students, and they would be only human to want to see their ideas and beliefs accepted and passed on through their students, but they would be wise to heed the advice of one of their own from the first generation of American Academic geographers, Ellen Churchill Semple:

In my opinion the profession critic of a doctor's thesis should drop
into the background as much as possible. For a master's thesis he

should suggest and criticize at every point, because he is training a novice in method of research and exposition. In either case he should give suggestions to clarify, but not to impose on the student a line of procedure. No scholar was ever made by slavish submission to the ideas of another.[11]

TABLE 1

NUMBER OF Ph.D.'S IN GEOGRAPHY IN THE UNITED STATES, BY SCHOOL AND SEX, 1907-46

School	Total	Male	Female
1 Clark (1922)#	86	73	13
2 Chicago (1907)	61	54	7
3 Wisconsin (1916)	35	29	6
4 Michigan (1923)	23	23	
5 Berkeley (1927)	20	20	
6 Nebraska (1909)	16	12	4
*7 George Peabody (1934)	11	10	1
8 Ohio State (1932)	10	10	
9 Columbia (1927)	9	9	
*10 Yale (1909)	7	6	1
10 Washington—Seattle (1930)	7	7	
*12 Harvard (1920)	4	3	1
*13 Washington—St. Louis (1937)	2	2	
14 Louisiana State (1938)	1	1	
14 Minnesota (1941)	1	1	
14 North Carolina (1945)	1	1	
	294	261	33

\# Date in parenthesis is year when first Ph.D. degree was conferred.

* Ph.D. degree in geography no longer offered. George Peabody conferred its last Ph.D. degree in 1942, Washington—St. Louis in 1950, Harvard in 1960, and Yale in 1966.

Source: For sources used in compiling this and all subsequent tables, see note 1.

TABLE 2

NUMBER OF Ph.D. RECIPIENTS IN GEOGRAPHY, BY MENTOR, 1907-46

1	C.C. Colby	25	26	J.B. Leighly	2
1	W.E. Ekblaw	25	26	A.K. Lobeck	2
3	H.H. Barrows	24	26	G.T. Renner	2
4	W.W. Atwood, Sr.	19	26	E.C. Semple	2
4	C.O. Sauer	19	26	L.F. Thomas	2
6	C.F. Jones	18	26	E. Van Cleef	2
7	V. C. Finch	15	26	D.S. Whittlesey	2
8	S. Van Valkenburg	13	35	T.A. Blair	1
9	K.C. McMurry	12	35	I. Bowman	1
10	N.A. Bengtson	11	35	P.E. Church	1
11	A.E. Parkins	8	35	G.E. Condra	1
11	J.R. Smith	8	35	D.H. Davis	1
13	G.-H. Smith	6	35	L. Durand	1
13	G.T. Trewartha	6	35	F.M. Earle	1
13	R.H. Whitbeck	6	35	S.T. Emory	1
16	C.F. Brooks	5	35	J.P. Goode	1
16	E. Huntington	5	35	R. Hartshorne	1
16	J.R. Whitaker	5	35	C.C. Huntington	1
19	W.W. Atwood, Jr.	4	35	F.B. Kniffen	1
19	R. B. Hall	4	35	H.F. Otte	1
19	P.E. James	4	35	R. Peattie	1
19	R.D. Salisbury	4	35	R.S. Platt	1
23	E.E. Lackey	3	35	T.G. Taylor	1
23	H.M. Leppard	3	35	R.D. Ward	1
23	H.H. Martin	3	35	H.J. Warman	1
26	S.D. Dodge	2	35	G.S. Wehrwein	1
26	W.D. Jones	2			

TOTAL — 292*

*To this should be added Ph.D. recipients Ellsworth Huntington and Vernor C. Finch, who did not have mentors, for a grand total of 294 recipients.

TABLE 3

NUMBER OF MENTORS AND STUDENTS, BY SCHOOL

Clark:			Berkeley:			Washington—Seattle:	
W.E. Ekblaw	25		C.O. Sauer	18		H.H. Martin	3
W.E. Atwood Sr.	18		J.B. Leighly	2		G.T. Renner	2
C.F. Jones	18			20		P.E. Church	1
S. Van Valkenburg	13					F.M. Earle	1
C.F. Brooks	5						7
W.W. Atwood, Jr.	4		Nebraska:				
E.C. Semple	2		N.A. Bengtson	11		Harvard:	
H.J. Warman	1		E.E. Lackey	3		D.E. Whittlesey	2
	86		T.A. Blair	1		W.W. Atwood, Sr.	1
			G.E. Condra	1		R.D. Ward	1
Chicago:				16			4
C.C. Colby	25						
H.H. Barrows	24						
R.D. Salisbury	4		George Peabody:				
H.M. Leppard	3		A.E. Parkins	8		Washington—St. Louis:	
W.D. Jones	2		J.R. Whitaker	3		L.F. Thomas	2
J.P. Goode	1			11			2
R.S. Platt	1						
T.G. Taylor	1						
	61		Ohio State:			Louisiana State:	
			G.-H. Smith	6		F.B. Kniffen	1
			E. Van Cleef	2			1
Wisconsin:			C.C. Huntington	1			
V.C. Finch	15		R. Peattie	1		Minnesota:	
G.T. Trewartha	6			10		D.H. Davis	1
R.H. Whitbeck	6						1
A.K. Lobeck	2						
J.R. Whitaker	2		Columbia:				
L. Durand	1		J.R. Smith	8		North Carolina:	
R. Hartshorne	1		H.F. Otte	1		S.T. Emory	1
G.S. Wehrwein	1			9			1
No mentor	1						
	35						
			Yale:				
Michigan:			E. Huntington	5			
K.C. McMurry	12		I. Bowman	1			
R.B. Hall	4		No mentor	1			
P.E. James	4			7			
S.D. Dodge	2						
C.O. Sauer	1						
	23						

TABLE 4

INBREEDING PATTERNS

Names under each school are those individuals whose highest earned degree was from that school and who were also mentors at that school. The figure after the school name denotes the total number of mentors at that school.

CHICAGO (8)
- H.H. Barrows
- W.D. Jones
- C.C. Colby
- R.S. Platt
- H.M. Leppard

MICHIGAN (5)
- R.B. Hall

COLUMBIA (2)
- H.F. Otte

CLARK (8)
- W.E. Ekblaw
- W.W. Atwood, Jr.
- H.J. Warman

BERKELEY (2)
- J.B. Leighly

YALE (2)
- E. Huntington
- I. Bowman

WISCONSIN (8)
- V.C. Finch
- G.T. Trewartha
- L. Durand
- G.S. Wehrwein

NEBRASKA (4)
- G.E. Condra

HARVARD (3)
- R.D. Ward

TABLE 5

DISTRIBUTION OF GEOGRAPHY MENTORS WHOSE HIGHEST EARNED DEGREE WAS FROM THE UNIVERSITY OF CHICAGO

MICHIGAN
- C.O. Sauer
- K.C. McMurry
- S.D. Dodge

BERKELEY
- C.O. Sauer

WISCONSIN
- J.R. Whitaker
- R. Hartshorne

GEORGE PEABODY
- A.E. Parkins
- J.R. Whitaker

HARVARD
- W.W. Atwood, Sr.
- D.S. Whittlesey

CLARK
- W.W. Atwood, Sr.
- C.F. Jones

WASHINGTON—ST. LOUIS
- L.F. Thomas

NORTH CAROLINA
- S.T. Emory

206

TABLE 6

MENTORS AND THE NUMBER OF THEIR DESCENDANTS*

1	2	3	4	Total	1	2	3	4	Total
W.W. Atwood, Sr.	19	22		41	H.M. Leppard	3			3
W.W. Atwood, Jr.	4			4	A.K. Lobeck	2			2
H.H. Barrows	24	55	25	104	H.H. Martin	3			3
N.A. Bengtson	11			11	K.C. McMurry	12	4		16
T.A. Blair	1			1	H.F. Otte	1			1
I. Bowman	1			1	A.E. Parkins	8			8
C.F. Brooks	5			5	R. Peattie	1			1
P.E. Church	1			1	R.S. Platt	1			1
C.C. Colby	25	21		46	G.T. Renner	2			2
G.E. Condra	1			1	R.D. Salisbury	4	22	5	31
D.H. Davis	1			1	C.O. Sauer	19	4		23
S.D. Dodge	2			2	E.C. Semple	2	25	1	28
L. Durand	1			1	G.-H. Smith	6			6
F.M. Earle	1			1	J.R. Smith	8	3		11
W.E. Ekblaw	25	1		26	T.G. Taylor	1			1
S.T. Emory	1			1	L.F. Thomas	2			2
V.C. Finch	15	12	1	28	G.T. Trewartha	6	1		7

TABLE 6
(continued)

	1	2	3	4	Total		1	2	3	4	Total
J.P. Goode	1				1	E. Van Cleef	2				2
R.B. Hall	4				4	S. Van Valkenburg	13	1			14
R. Hartshorne	1				1	R.D. Ward	1				1
C.C. Huntington	1				1	H.J. Warman	1				1
E. Huntington	5	1			6	G.S. Wehrwein	1				1
P.E. James	4				4	J.R. Whitaker	5				5
C.F. Jones	18				18	R.H. Whitbeck	6				6
W.D. Jones	2	1			3	D.S. Whittlesey	2				2
F.B. Kniffen	1				1	No mentor	2				2
E.E. Lackey	3				3	TOTAL	294	173	—	32	499
J.B. Leighly	2				2						

* Numbers across the top of the columns denote generations.

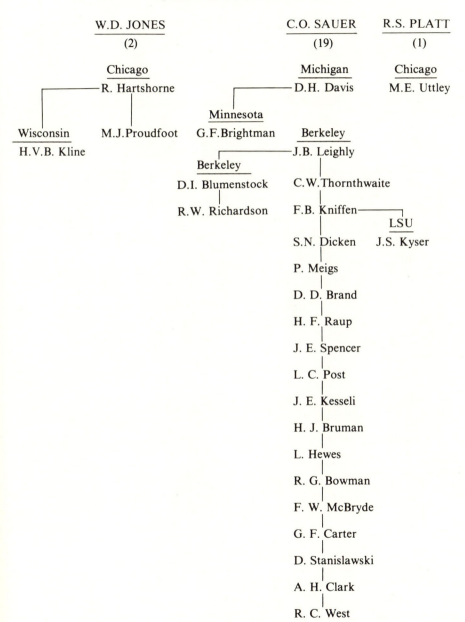

Figure 1
ACADEMIC GENEALOGY OF ROLLIN D. SALISBURY
(Total Number Of Students: 4)

209

Figure 2
ACADEMIC GENEALOGY OF HARLAN H. BARROWS
(Total Number of Students: 24)

A. E. PARKINS (8)
Geo. Peabody
- J. F. Glazner
- W. A. Browne
- W.W. Spellings
- L. C. Miller
- C. L. Stout
- J. W. Reid
- E. E. Hall
- J. Hodgson

C. C. COLBY (25)
Chicago
- H. M. Strong
- C. F. Jones — Clark
- J. B. Appleton — C. Gooze
- E. C. Case — M. M. Prator
- L. F. Thomas — J. H. Burgy
- C. M. Zierer — M. F. Burrill
- W. T. Chambers — E. F. Campbell
- L. G. Polspoel — S. D. Diettrich
- C. C. Cruz — H. P. Milstead

K. C. McMURRY (12)
Michigan
- R. B. Hall
- J. G. Thomas
- F. A. Stilgenbauer
- A. H. Meyer
- A. J. Wright
- C. M. Davis
- E. H. Faigle
- J. A. Russell
- J. E. Vanriper

S. C. DODGE (2)
Michigan
- H. M. Kendall
- C. F. Kohn

Michigan
- R. M. Glendinning
- L. D. Black
- G. Kish
- C. A. Manchester

H. M. LEPPARD (3)
Chicago
- J. H. Glasgow
- C. F. Carlson
- H. M. Mayer

J. R. WHITAKER (5)
Wisconsin
- J. R. Randall
- P. W. Icke

George Peabody
- R. L. Martin
- J. W. Morris
- P. W. Picklesimer

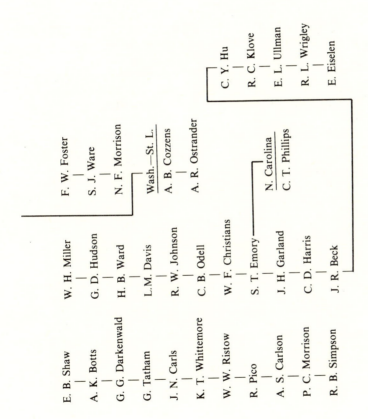

Figure 3
ACADEMIC GENEALOGY OF VERNOR C. FINCH
(Total Number of Students: 15)

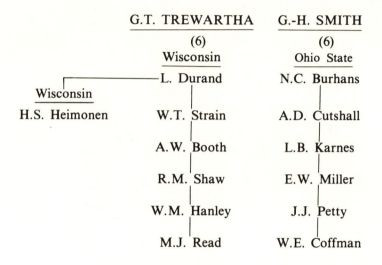

Figure 4

ACADEMIC GENEALOGY OF WALLACE W. ATTWOOD, SR.*

(Total Number of Students: 19)

R. PEATTIE	P.E. JAMES	E. VAN CLEEF	N.A. BENGTSON	W.W. ATTWOOD, JR.
(1)	(4)	(2)	(11)	(4)
Ohio State	Michigan	Ohio State	Nebraska	Clark
C.T. Heskett	O.E. Guthe	H.E. Stewart	F. Hurlbut	L.O. Quam
	H.T. Straw	W.G. Lezius	R.B. Clark	J.I. Culbert
	L.S. Wilson		C.L. Dow	B.W. Adkinson
	C.V. Crittenden		W. Hansen	V.H. English
			V.C. McKim	
			T.F. Barton	
			G.W. Schlesselman	
			G.D. Koch	
			H.E. Hoy	
			C.M. Wilson	
			I.A. Moke	

*The first of Atwood's nineteen students, Roderick Peattie, took his Ph.D. degree at Harvard. His was the first in geography at that school. All of Atwood's other students earned their Ph.D. degrees at Clark.

213

Figure 5
ACADEMIC GENEALOGY OF ELLEN CHURCHILL SEMPLE
(Total Number of Students: 2)

W. E. EKBLAW
_____
(25)
Clark
_____
J.M. Shipman

C.P. Barnes

O.W. Freeman

A. LaFleur

F.F. Cunningham

B. Hudgins

G.B. Cressey

E.J. Foscue

E.S. Anderson

G.H. Primmer

S.E. Ekblaw

J.S. Gibson

M.E. Lemaire

C.Y. Mason

A.R. Oliver

M.C. Roberts

R. Zeller

L.W. Fountain

J.R. Schwendeman

R.L. Parson

A.J. West

H.H. Balk

M.C. Prunty

H.J. Warman

Clark
_____
T.W. Chamberlin   J.G. Jensen

TABLE 7

MENTORS' PLACE OF BIRTH

MIDWEST	MIDWEST (cont'd)	SOUTH
Illinois:	**Missouri:**	**Virginia:**
W.W. Atwood, Sr.*	T.A. Blair	S.T. Emory
W.W. Atwood, Jr.*	W.D. Jones*	C.F. Jones
P.E. Church*	C.O. Sauer	J.R. Smith
W.E. Ekblaw		
E. Huntington	**Iowa:**	**Kentucky:**
K.C. McMurry	G.E. Condra	E.C. Semple*
H.H. Martin		J.R. Whitaker
E. Van Cleef*	**PLAINS**	
D.S. Whittlesey		**South Carolina:**
	Nebraska:	F.M. Earle
Michigan:	H.F. Otte	
H.H. Barrows	R. Peattie*	**SOUTHWEST**
C.C. Colby		
V.C. Finch	**Kansas:**	**New Mexico:**
F.B. Kniffen	G.T. Renner	R.B. Hall
A.E. Parkins		
	NEW ENGLAND	**FOREIGN**
Ohio:		
C.C. Huntington	**Massachusetts:**	**Canada:**
E.E. Lackey	P.E. James*	I. Bowman
J.B. Leighly	R.D. Ward*	H.M. Leppard
R.S. Platt*		
L.F. Thomas	**MIDDLE ATLANTIC**	**England:**
		T.G. Taylor*
Wisconsin:	**New York:**	
L. Durand	S.D. Dodge*	**Netherlands:**
R.D. Salisbury	A.K. Lobeck*	S. Van Valkenburg
G.-H. Smith	R.H. Whitbeck*	
G.T. Trewartha		**Sweden:**
G.S. Wehrwein	**Pennsylvania:**	N.A. Bengtson
	R. Hartshorne	
Minnesota:	H.J. Warman	
C.F. Brooks*		
D.H. Davis		
J.P. Goode		

* Urban birthplace.

215

TABLE 8

BACCALAUREATE ORIGINS OF MENTORS

1	Chicago	12	Atwood, Jr.; Atwood, Sr.; Barrows; Church; Colby; Dodge; C. Jones; W. Jones; Peattie; Van Cleef; Whitaker; Whittlesey
2	Wisconsin	5	Durand, McMurry, G.-H. Smith, Trewartha, Wehrwein
3	Harvard	4	Bowman, Brooks, James, Ward
3	Michigan	4	Davis, Hall, Kniffen, Leighly
3	Nebraska	4	Bengtson, Condra, Lackey, Otte
6	Beloit	2	E. Huntington, Salisbury
6	Pennsylvania	2	Martin, J. R. Smith
8	Antioch	1	C. Huntington
8	Central Wesleyan	1	Sauer
8	Columbia	1	Lobeck
8	Cornell (Iowa)	1	Renner
8	Cornell	1	Whitbeck
8	Denison	1	Thomas
8	Eastern Michigan	1	Parkins
8	Illinois	1	Ekblaw
8	Kalamazoo	1	Finch
8	Minnesota	1	Goode
8	Pennsylvania State College, Bloomsburg	1	Warman
8	Princeton	1	Hartshorne
8	Queen's	1	Leppard
8	Randolph-Macon	1	Emory
8	Stanford	1	Blair
8	Sydney	1	Taylor
8	Vassar	1	Semple
8	Winthrop	1	Earle
8	Yale	1	Platt

216

TABLE 9

SCHOOLS WHERE MENTORS OBTAINED
THEIR HIGHEST EARNED DEGREE

1	Chicago	16	Atwood, Sr.; Barrows; Colby; Dodge; Emory; Hartshorne; C. Jones; W. Jones; Leppard; McMurry; Parkins; Platt; Sauer; Thomas; Whitaker; Whittlesey
2	Clark	7	Atwood, Jr.; Bengtson; Church; Ekblaw; James; Van Cleef; Warman
3	Wisconsin	5	Durand, Finch, G.-H. Smith, Trewartha, Wehrwein
4	Columbia	4	Lackey, Lobeck, Otte, Renner
5	Harvard	3	Brooks, Peattie, Ward
6	Berkeley	2	Kniffen, Leighly
6	Cornell	2	C. Huntington, Whitbeck
6	George Washington	2	Earle, Martin
6	Michigan	2	Davis, Hall
6	Pennsylvania	2	Goode, J. R. Smith
6	Yale	2	Bowman, E. Huntington
12	Beloit	1	Salisbury
12	Nebraska	1	Condra
12	Stanford	1	Blair
12	Sydney	1	Taylor
12	Vassar	1	Semple
12	Zurich	1	Van Valkenburg

TABLE 10

MENTORS WHOSE HIGHEST EARNED DEGREE
WAS NOT IN GEOGRAPHY

(School after name is where that degree was conferred)

GEOLOGY
 W. W. Atwood, Sr. (Chicago)
 *H. H. Barrows (Chicago)
 G. E. Condra (Nebraska)
 A. K. Lobeck (Columbia)
 **R. D. Salisbury (Beloit)
 T. G. Taylor (Sydney)
 **R. D. Ward (Harvard)
 *R. H. Whitbeck (Cornell)

ECONOMICS
 F. M. Earle (Geo. Wash.)
 J. P. Goode (Pennsylvania)
 C. C. Huntington (Cornell)
 H. H. Martin (Geo. Wash.)
 J.R. Smith (Pennsylvania)

METEOROLOGY
 *T. A. Blair (Stanford)
 C. F. Brooks (Harvard)

AGRICULTURAL ECONOMICS
 G. S. Wehrwein (Wisconsin)

EDUCATION
 E. E. Lackey (Columbia)

HISTORY
 D. S. Whittlesey (Chicago)

SOCIOLOGY
 **E.C. Semple (Vassar)

* Highest earned degree was a bachelor's.
** Highest earned degree was a master's.

Notes

1. All of the dissertation supervisors for all of the recipients of Ph.D. degrees in geography awarded in the study period as well as the recipients themselves are included. Doctors of education degrees with a concentration in geography are excluded, as are interdisciplinary doctorates (area studies and social science, for example). These exclusions are deliberate in order that the data reflect as meaningfully as possible the structure of what is seen as a discrete field of academic study. The data for this study were derived from a wide variety of reference sources. *Comprehensive Dissertation Index, 1861-1972* (Ann Arbor, Mich.: Xerox University Microfilms, 1973), thesis issues of the *Professional Geographer*, and degree recipient lists from a number of individual geography departments provided the names of Ph.D. recipients in geography. From these sources a comprehensive list was compiled for each department and sent to that department for verification. Basic biographical data on each mentor was obtained from various biographical dictionaries and directories, obituaries, and memorials.

2. Allen D. Bushong, "Some Aspects of the Membership and Meetings of the Association of American Geographers Before 1949, *"Professional Geographer* 26, no. 4 (1974): 435-39.

3. Geoffrey J. Martin, *Ellsworth Huntington, His Life and Thought* (Hamden, Conn.: Archon Books, 1973), pp. 79-80. For Finch, the writer consulted the records in the University of Wisconsin Library in Madison.

4. For a large-scale example of a prosopographic study by a geographer, see Stephen Sargent Visher, *Scientists Starred 1903-1943 in "American Men of Science," a Study of Collegiate and Doctoral Training, Birthplace, Distribution, Backgrounds, and Developmental Influences* (Baltimore: Johns Hopkins Press, 1947).

5. Geoffrey J. Martin, *Mark Jefferson: Geographer* (Ypsilanti, Mich.: Eastern Michigan University Press, 1968), chapters 4 and 5, passim.

6. In more recent years the median age for male recipients has remained at thirty-two but dropped to thirty-six for women. For further discussion of this age differential among geographers, see Allen D. Bushong, "Women as Geographers: Some Thoughts of Ellen Churchill Semple," *Southeastern Geographer* 15, no. 2 (1975): 106-7.

7. Preston E. James and Ralph E. Ehrenberg, "The Original Members of the Association of American Geographers," *Professional Geographer* 27, no. 3 (1976): 327-35.

8. Jacques Barzun, *Teacher in America* (Boston: Little, Brown and Co., 1944), p. 196.

9. National Research Council, Board on Human-Resource Data and Analysis, *A Century of Doctorates* (Washington, D.C.: National Academy of Sciences, 1978), p. 7.

10. Joseph E. Spencer, "What's In A Name?—'The Berkeley School,'" *Historical Geography Newsletter* 6, no. 1 (1976): 7-11.

11. Ruth E. Baugh, "Ellen Churchill Semple, the Great Lady of American Geography" (Paper presented at the fifty-seventh annual meeting of the Association of American Geographers, East Lansing, Michigan, 30 August 1961).

Berkeley Geography, 1923-33

William W. Speth

In the annals of American geography, the decade following 1923 witnessed the rejuvenation of the Department of Geography at the University of California. Under the leadership of Carl Sauer, Berkeley geography emerged as a distinctive school of thought. The developing internal structure of the department—its curriculum, personnel, and research—is recorded, and an interpretation of Sauer's changing outlook on geography is presented.

The Michigan Years

Sauer's experience at the University of Michigan in the period from 1915 to 1923 was ironic prelude to his California orientation. These were years when his professional energies became enlisted by the practical interests of the day. The land utilization movement of the 1920s influenced the ideals of people who sought to rationalize the limits of major uses of the land and guide the future exploitation of the country's resources. Sauer assimilated these concerns, and the subject of the inventory and classification of uses being made of the land, and soils, appeared in his writings and teaching at Ann Arbor. The pragmatic motive, moreover, colored his conception of regional geography, in which, he proclaimed, "there are two leading questions to be answered: To what uses is the area in question being put; and: What are its possibilities? On these two questions the fundamental techniques of regional analysis rests."[1] Culminating this phase of his work in 1922, Sauer and the forester-conservationist P. S. Lovejoy initiated the Michigan Land Economic Survey. The survey was organized to accumulate the facts upon which to found a policy for the development of resources in Michigan's cutover lands. Sauer recalled that "the first thing

I really found to take hold of was the study of destructive land use in Michigan. Lovejoy said to me once that until I got hold of that I had impressed him as being all dressed up with no place to go."[2] By participating in the land utilization movement, Sauer figured in the rise of the "service intellectual" in America, the academic person who accepts government office in the service of society. When Sauer left Michigan, he did not forsake the service role, for which the American Geographical Society honored him in 1935, but this practical engagement did not dominate his work in California.[3]

Sauer's article "The Survey Method in Geography and its Objectives" is the capstone and symbol of the series of pragmatic articles that he began in 1917. Although the "Survey Method" was written before Sauer left Ann Arbor, it was published after he moved to Berkeley.[4] In this paper, continental influences already are evident, and his desire to unify the discipline by restrictive definition is made explicit.[5] The main methodological elements that identify Sauer's problem-directed geography are lodged in this statement. They are distilled here to provide a basis for comparison with his later position: (1) Sauer's Michigan geography contains confident censure of the reaction model of geography. As a science, geography can not subscribe a priori to the "argument from physical cause to human consequence," as found in the deterministic tradition of Ratzel (p. 18). Neither method of approach nor content of subject should rest on presumed geographic influence. (2) It is an anthropocentric geography of the contemporary scene, possessing a dualistic goal. Geographic field study seeks to represent both the natural area and the manner in which it is used by its human occupants. The selection of physical geographic materials, however, depends on their significance to man. (3) Time relation is virtually ruled out as belonging to history, and "areal relation of human groups" becomes the hallmark of geographic studies (p. 17). (4) The Michigan position is guided by possibilism: in the appropriation of area, man encounters opportunities and handicaps whose significance varies according to the occupying group. (5) Precise, numerical data are desired for a method that is quantitative, in a rudimentary sense. By means of intensive field study (survey), the manner in which an area is utilized can be measured and statistically shown on maps and in notes. (6) It is home geography, in which the "familiar scene" is recommended as an essentially untouched field of geography (p. 32). Appreciation of significant contrasts of foreign regions can follow only after experience with the problems of domestic areas. (7) Finally, Sauer's Michigan geography was oriented to shaping land use policy for the future. By measuring and recording the results of man's current use of an area, the geographer can judge its "outlook for the future" (p. 33).

The person who is familiar with Sauer's mature thought can appreciate the radical nature of the reorganization of his view of geography at Berkeley. He later recognized the changes in his outlook as an odyssey in which he wasted years finding his way as a young geographer: "Most of the things that I was taught professionally as a geographer, I had either to forget or unlearn at the cost of considerable effort and time."[6] Expectedly, some continuity in his position was maintained. He persisted in his adherence to antienvironmentalism, and, substantively, he continued to censure destructive use of the land and to subscribe to the thesis of man as a modifier of the original vegetation. However, his fundamental standpoint became recast dramatically. Within less than two years after leaving Ann Arbor, Sauer veered from regional economics (pragmatism) to landscape morphology (historicism).[7]

In the final phase of his Michigan tenure, Sauer grew dissatisfied with conditions there. Summer obligations had become increasingly oppressive for him. Between the university summer field camp and the Michigan Land Economic Survey, Sauer felt "tied down for an indefinite time into the future and [he] wanted to get out on [his] own and roam new areas." He wished, moreover, to establish an independent department of geography at Michigan, where geography was the subordinate unit of a joint Department of Geology and Geography. The attitude of his dean, however, obstructed this plan.[8] Sauer thus desired to "change the direction of [his] work," and he accepted the call in 1923 from the University of California. In the two years before leaving Michigan, he had declined offers from Clark, Minnesota, and Yale, and even an offer of a professorship in the Department of Economics at Michigan failed to hold him in the Midwest.[9] After completing fieldwork in the Pennyroyal region of Kentucky, he moved to California in August 1923.

California

Instruction in geography was introduced at Berkeley in 1898, when George Davidson was appointed professor of geography. Long associated with the U.S. Coast and Geodetic Survey on the Pacific coast, Davidson began teaching full time after he left government service at the age of seventy-two. He taught for seven years and, before his retirement in 1904, brought Ruliff S. Holway to the staff as assistant professor of physical geography. Holway remained active for nineteen years, training pupils and preparing the foundation for the growth of physical geography in California.[10] Burton M. Varney, instructor in meteorology, was on the regular staff with him. When Holway retired, Varney left the department for Clark University, where he earned the doctorate in 1925. Several assistants in geography, including Richard J. Russell, completed the staff in the last years before Sauer's arrival.

The curriculum developed under Holway mirrored the prevailing geographic opinion of the time. Davisian physiography and rationalist anthropogeography were manifest in course titles and descriptions. Holway, for instance, taught "Geographic Influences in Human Affairs," and Varney's climatology embraced climatic factors "especially in their relation to human activities." A sure accent on physical factors, with attention to human tropisms, distinguished geography at Berkeley before it became rejuvenated under Sauer.[11]

A small, changing roster of personnel characterized the department after 1923. During the formative years under Sauer, the regular staff did not exceed three persons in a given semester.[12] Nevertheless, Sauer was able to realize his belief that "a university should assemble men from different lands." The teaching responsibilities of the staff, with its progressive accretions and losses, are given in Table 1. (Tables 1 and 2 re complementary and should be read together.)

A native of California and candidate for the advanced degree in geology, Russell formed a tie between the two administrations. Holway believed that Russell had done "unusually good work" as a teaching fellow and recommended his reappointment as associate in geography "for the good of the department." Russell remained with Sauer for three years, earning his Ph.D. in 1925. This exposure turned him from geology to geography, in which he saw greater scholarly opportunity.[13]

John Leighly had assisted Sauer in the Michigan Land Economic Survey and the Kentucky Geological Survey and accompanied him to Berkeley with an associateship. Sauer was impressed by Leighly's abilities and requested approval to bring out another man from Ann Arbor. Sauer wrote Holway:

> We have here a graduate student, John Leighly, who is the most promising student I have ever had and possesses as fine intellectual equipment as I have ever known. He is without doubt one of the most brilliant men in the university. He has had several years of service as teaching assistant in physiography and is a born cartographer. He has also assisted in general geography. He reads German and French with real fluency and his intellectual curiosity is insatiable. I consider him the sort of man one finds only once in a

blue moon. It is not certain that I could induce [him] to come with me, but I should certainly be glad to try.... He could work into the field of Cartography and Physical Geography ultimately and help in getting my work established.[14] Sauer, Russell, and Leighly thus composed the first faculty group in the revitalized department.

In the third year, Leighly went abroad under a fellowship from the American-Scandinavian Foundation to gather materials for his dissertation on towns. It was Russell's last regular year. The Berkleley tie was strong, however, for Russell returned there from his base at Louisiana State University three times to teach in the interwar period. Leighly's absence coincided with the appointment of Oskar Schmieder, whom Sauer invited to Berkeley from a post at the Universidad Nacional, Córdoba, Argentina. Schmieder's appointment as temporary lecturer in Geography turned into a permanent position at the rank of associate professor for the next four years. However, he accepted a call in 1930 from the University of Kiel to become professor of geography and director of the Geographical Institute. "In the five years he spent at Berkeley," Sauer reported, "Schmieder became established as the leading student of Latin-American geographic problems in the country. He was a vigorous teacher and his buoyant personality is missed."[15]

Schmieder's final year in California (1929-30) overlapped with Russell's first visiting appointment. John Leighly had achieved the Ph.D. in 1927 and was absent on leave in the Baltic countries as a fellow of the Social Science Research Council. Wolfgang Panzer was appointed lecturer in geography for one year; he was *Dozent* at the University of Berlin, where Albrecht Penck had retired in 1926. (In the summer of 1928, Penck had lectured in Sauer's department.)

During the academic year 1930-31, Edna Scofield accepted an associateship in geography for the first semester. She earned her master's degree at Berkeley in 1930, but went to Kiel for her advanced degree under Schmieder. Gottfried Pfeifer served as lecturer in geography for the second semester of this year. He had studied with Leo Waibel and Wilhelm Credner, both pupils of Alfred Hettner, and held a Laura Spelman Rockefeller Fellowship for 1928-30. During his fellowship, he accompanied Sauer on his "famous first big trip" to Mexico. Sauer was on sabbatical leave for the calendar year 1930 and, in the following year, received a Guggenheim fellowship. Sauer had been teaching economic geography, preferring to "wait with a proposal [to add a man in this field] until a suitable person should turn up." Sauer believed that Pfeifer, a man with "an enviable intellectual background, a fine mind, poise, and imagination" could "give intellectual dignity to a field that is in pretty bad shape academically."[16] With Pfeifer's installation, Sauer relinquished economic geography, a commitment he had accepted in moving to California. The youthful geographer taught an additional year, before returning to Germany in 1932. Pfeifer left reluctantly, being unable to secure a permit from immigration authorities to remain indefinitely in the U.S.

His departure enabled Sauer to add to the staff John Kesseli (1895-1980), a man of Swiss background. Kesseli was attracted to physical geography and had studied with Otto Schlüter and the geologist Johannes Walther. He was a "mature graduate student," whom Sauer wished to "try out on an Associateship." "He is," Sauer observed, "extraordinarily well grounded, has an incisive mind and good intellectual judgment. . . . He is the first of our students since Leighly and Russell whom I should consider with happy expectation as a member of the staff."[17] With the addition of Kesseli, the formative decade closed on the matter of personnel. They were years of transitory staffing, with Sauer and Leighly as mainstays.

Unhampered by the presence of an "old guard," Sauer swept away most of the inherited structure and established a new program of geographic education. New requirements for the major were formulated, and course titles or descriptions were replaced. Occasionally old titles were retained, as "Geography of North America" and "Geography of California," but their descriptions were rewritten and the unwanted terms "relations" and "influences" were expunged. Course announcements reveal a swing to the human side of geography, as expressed in terms such as "culture," at first set off with quotation marks, "human site value," and "modification [of natural regions] by human effort." (See Table 2.) A marked shift of emphasis was underway.

Yet, schools of thought in the scholarly world do not arise from the structure of an undergraduate curriculum. Undergraduate courses may be used for graduate training, but at Berkeley the seminar was the broad avenue of graduate apprenticeship. It served faculty ends as well, since seminar topics were drawn from the research activity of the staff. As a result, the seminar subjects reveal the trend and scope of Berkeley scholarship (Table 3). All the themes of Sauer's published writings and most of those of his colleagues were used as seminar topics. Faculty research and seminar themes covered the range of geography, which was parcelled into disciplinary history and the regional, cultural, and physical aspects of the field.[18] The published research that reposes in the departmental series in geography consists of twenty-eight monographs and represents the main body of Berkeley geographic thought in the nascent period.[19]

226

Insofar as faculty inquiry and graduate seminar coalesced, the former provided content and direction for the latter. Sauer intended the seminar for exploring the "borders of the known" and for preparing the student for "later sustained inquiry, specialized knowledge, and independent conclusion." The six candidates who were awarded the Ph.D. during the first phase of Berkeley geography were steeped in the seminr experience, but not exclusively in the geography department. The general trend at Berkeley, part of the broader impulse toward integration of the social sciences in the interwar period, was to "relax the departmental lines, among students really of University grade." Accordingly, the tyros commonly enrolled for graduate work with A. L. Kroeber and Robert Lowie in anthropology.[20] Warren Thornthwaite, Fred Kniffen, Peveril Meigs, and Donald Brand selected anthropology as their minor subject. Kniffen, for example, logged three seminars with Sauer, six with Schmieder, and one with Kroeber, in addition to two independent research studies with Kroeber and one with Sauer. Geology had subordinate appeal in the collective experience of this first small wave of graduates, and only Leighly, who studied also under Sten De Geer in Sweden, and Samuel Dicken claimed geology as their minor field.[21]

In the Berkeley setting, field study assumed a heightened significance; it was requisite complement to the seminar. Sauer himself embodied this value, spending at least four or five weeks each year in the field and archive. The long intersession at Christmas and the months of May and June were ideally suited to field investigation under desert conditons. By 1929, after extensive work in Lower California, the Colorado Delta, and eastern Sonora, Sauer formalized a program of geographic studies in northwest Mexico, "probably the biggest field of investigation that remains in North American geography" (Table 4). In a retrospect on field observation, Sauer explained that

the principal training of the geographer should come, wherever possible, by doing field work. . . . The class of forms, be they of land, vegetation, or culture, is optional; the important thing is to get this awareness of form started up, to recognize kind and variation, position and extent, presence and absence, function and derivation; in short, to cultivate the sense of morphology.[22]

Varied field experiences, in the company of Sauer and independently, marked the training of the advanced student at Berkeley. Local observation in the San Francisco Bay region, where Sauer "raised interesting questions, about land forms particularly," were facilitated by

Sauer's Saturday field course (Geography 101). On undergraduate field trips, however, "he taught very little, although he encouraged discussion and expressed his opinions freely. For him they were opportunities for students to see and for him to judge their perceptiveness."[23] The first group of doctoral candidates worked at length in the field. In conjunction with their dissertations, Leighly studied in Sweden; Kniffen, Meigs, and Brand probed northern Mexico; and Thornthwaite and Dicken worked in Kentucky.

The Berkeley apprenticeship thus rested on experience of the seminar and field observation, including field study under Sauer's direction. It was augmented by teaching undergraduate classes, as teaching fellows or associates, and by writing. Leighly, Kniffen, and Meigs published their dissertations, in whole or in part, in the department's monograph series, and Meigs and Brand coauthored with Sauer several studies. In addition, Leighly, Thornthwaite, Kniffen, and Brand published eleven articles among them before receiving their doctorates.

The thesis topics selected by students reflect Sauer's dominant influence (Table 5). Even at the junior level of graduate training, Sauer's morphologic preferences are evident in thesis titles, such as "The Integration of Geographic Forms in the Salinas Valley" and "Aboriginal Economic Geography of the Hopi." At the advanced level, one sees the nature and scope of Berkeley geographic thought in the theses on urban morphology, regional (historical) geography, geomorphology, and prehistoric geography. Among the doctoral dissertations, the five researches in human geography were informed by the anthropological notion of culture.[24]

By the end of the first decade, the basic personality of Berkeley geography was established. All aspects of the department bore the stamp of Sauer's authority. Under his leadership, not only a social identity but a conceptual pattern was developed that was synthesized from the several schools of German geography and from Boasian anthropology. The crisis of the Depression prompted a general taking of stock, and Sauer's letters began to reflect the gloom of the era. A major curtailment of university expenses was expected, possibly entailing reduction of teaching fellows as well as salary cuts. In a letter to Thornthwaite, Sauer lamented that the department was "traveling under a loose sail."[25]

The financial emergency, however, did not alter the general institutional profile. From its inception, it had been a department with "slender facilities," spare staffing, and a growing reputation for being tough. Its reputation did not encourage prospective graduate students. However, if they did their work well, they could anticipate "more favorable treatment" than the advance warning indicated. In correspondence with administrators, Sauer pointed out that his department attempted "to cover the range of geography . . . with a smaller personnel, more meagre support, and a more inadequate plant than is true at any American institution of rank."[26] He muted his critical tone by acknowledging the generous support of the university press and the Board of Research in financing publications, field expeditions, and manuscript acquisition.[27] With these ostensibly inadequate means, the Berkeley group established geography as a "field of inquiry rather than simply as a teaching discipline." In 1929, Sauer disclosed his vision that the department had "certain advantages of location and experience toward the development of a distinctive geographic school." Within ten years, the Berkeley intellectual tradition had gained sufficient prominence that observers recognized in it the properties of a school of thought.[28]

Sauer's View of Geography

Sauer's inquiries in field and archive were wide-ranging and often pursued concurrently. In the formative period, his major studies fall into five groups, roughly chronological: objectives and methods of geography, regional synthesis, geomorphology, archaeogeography (Sauer's own term), and historical geography. (His critique of the ecologic devastation entrained by profit economies came later.) Sauer considered his three methodologic utterances—the "Morphology," "Recent Developments in Cultural Geography," and "Cultural Geography"—as "successive orientations," in which he clarified his own views.[29]

"The Morphology of Landscape" was Sauer's blueprint for a new ediface. True, he recanted some of the views that he set forth in it. He had advocated, for instance, replacing genetic geomorphology with a descriptive and classificatory study of surface forms, but he returned eventually to the genetic view. To imply that Sauer discarded the "Morphology" would be to mistake some of the parts for the whole. Sauer's philosophy involved movement and growth, but one can scarcely conclude that he erased his previous outlook when he revised his strategy for geography.[30] Continuity is evident within the change.

What features persist and unify the three successive versions of Sauer's disciplinary world view? The recurring ideas in this compounding of methodology, metaphysics, and theory are: (1) trenchant criticism of environmentalism as the definition of geographic science; (2) advancement of the principle of utilization vis-à-vis possibilism—environmental significance rests on the appraisal of the environment as expressed in the cultural use of area, and, as a corollary, environmental limits, especially the limits of subsistence, are set increasingly by man himself as an agent of surface change; (3) espousal of the traditional meaning of geography as areal knowledge, that is, as regional geography; (4) reliance upon a phenomenological science, inductive and presupposing only a structured reality; (5) unswerving belief in geography as a science of observation, in which immediate observations are recorded mainly cartographically; (6) adherence to the historical method, which gives a developmental orientation to the subject; (7) conviction that there is no dualism of landscape in regional geography, since attention is directed to natural and cultural *forms*; (8) use of the notion of "culture area," wherein distinctive phenomena of material culture comprise the geographic version of the concept; (9) appraisal of man as engine of surficial modification, viewed bilaterally in terms of the impress of his works upon an area and the manner in which he husbands his natural resources; and (10) belief in the fictive device that the geographic area is a "corporeal thing," possessing forms and structure and understood in terms of origin, growth, and function. (As presented above, these ideas appear to have a uniformity and equivalence that in fact do not obtain. In each essay, the individual elements are found with variable stress, elaboration, and context, but their continuity cannot be gainsaid.) Under this view, Sauer's disciplinary outlook was recast fundamentally in the "Morphology" and elaborated in "Recent Developments" and in "Cultural Geography." In these programmatic writings, he gradually delineated time as the most important dimension of geography.

Apart from the stabilized tenets abstracted above, certain aspects of Sauer's position changed or strengthened. The argument of Otto Schlüter, who favored observation based on inductive assumption and limitation of the subject matter in geography, augmented Sauer's morphological approach after 1927. Stimulated by contact with Robert Lowie, Sauer incorporated the names and works of Eduard Hahn and Friedrich Ratzel, who emerged as symbolic "objects" in his thinking. Their exemplary achievements were kept before the eyes of Sauer's disciples, and, in time, their lives were recommended for study as an important "induction into geography."[31] In the "Morphology," Hahn and Ratzel are not mentioned, although Ratzel was criticized earlier as an apostle of environmentalism. Appraisal of Ratzel remained unchanged two years later, but Hahn appeared as early contributor to an understanding of the economic landscape. By 1931, Ratzel's anthropogeography was reinterpreted in cultural terms (diffusion), and Hahn was designated pioneer of an economic geography that was welded to culture history and expressed in the landscape.

Sauer labored to accommodate political and economic studies to the unitary orientation of landscape geography. He was skeptical of their potential as normally pursued, and he redefined and redirected these fields. He accepted Hahn's work on economic areas, in particular, as pointing the way to needed revision in economic geography. Political geography was the "wayward child of the geographic family," lacking in scientific objectivity. Too often it had been used as a "shield for political beliefs."[32] The urban study of great capitals by Vaughan Cornish, another though lesser symbol in Sauer's thought, was advanced, in the company of other works, as exemplar for political geography.

In these early years, Sauer believed that the "human" and the "cultural" approaches to geography divided the field. He discarded the terms *human geography* and *anthropogeography*, because they embraced subjects "concerned with the environmental conditioning of human actions," and, in "Recent Developments," he infused his remodelled definition of geography with culture theory. Disdaining the view of geography as the relationship (adaptation) of humans to their environment, he adopted the "more elastic term of cultural geography," in which the object of study was not man but "material culture in areal massiveness."[33] By giving priority to man's *works* as materials of observation, Sauer stripped his geography of the anthropocentric assumption. Accordingly, one of Sauer's most far-reaching achievements in the formative period was his application of the fluid term *culture* to the field of geography and, by extension, his amalgamation of anthropology with geography.

What crucial emphasis distinguishes Sauer's stance in the "Survey Method" from that in his early methodological papers at Berkeley? The complex morphological idea, adumbrated in 1924, was of course amplified in 1925, but in the "Survey Method," Sauer displayed a circumspect attitude toward history. He believed geography might "gain by the example of historical research," yet the historical approach demanded "unusual acumen and integrity." Time relation, the leading attribute of history in the earlier paper, was, nevertheless, confidently joined to geography in "The Morphology of Landscape." "We cannot," Sauer reasoned, "form an idea of landscape except in terms of its time relations as well as of its space relations. It is in continuous process of development or of dissolution and replacement." Still, the time factor is not stressed by any organizational device; it remains embedded in the general argument.[34]

Two years later in "Recent Developments," Sauer presented an explicit program for historical geography. By identifying the purpose of historical geography á la Ellen Semple and Harlan Barrows as explanation of history (geographic history) rather than as characterization of area, Sauer freed himself to pursue the subject after the continental model. The theme of historical geography was the "sequences of cultural landscapes," an idea that Derwent Whittlesey soon adapted as "sequent occupance." More a vision than an actuality in the late 1920s, Sauer asserted that "geography in all its branches has become genetic and therefore historical." Study of the "landscapes of the historic past" was distinguishable in principle neither from regional geography nor from cultural geography. Under the unitary view of the subject matter of the discipline, historical, regional, and cultural geography were synonymous.[35] They could, moreover, be conveniently expressed as "culture history," the geographic version of which signified the changing cultural landscape.[36]

By the close of the nascent period, history was no longer a challenging example; it had become integral to the whole of Sauer's geography. He restated the nature of this union in the short essay on "Cultural Geography." Here, his cultural morphology is "developmental, specifically historical in so far as the material permits, and it therefore seeks to determine the successions of culture that have taken place in an area." But Sauer already had identified his positon as "historical geography" in 1929. Although he did not designate it as a position paper in his letter to J. Russell Smith (see note 29), "Historical Geography and the Western Frontier" was programmatic also. In this paper, Sauer called for evaluation of the "amount and character of transformations induced by culture" in the reconstruction of landscapes occupied by man. His focus is clearly on the "transforming hand of man"[37] By underscoring the transformation of the landscape instead of the landscape itself, Sauer inverted the emphasis on the temporal and the formal factors. Despite the synonymy of morphology and metamorphosis, the formal aspect had dominated his "Morphology." The genetic aspect shared the stage in "Recent Developments" and in "Cultural Geography." However, it claimed the stage in 1929 in "Historical Geography and the Western Frontier," and subsequently in his well-known article "Forward to Historical Geography." Within four years after leaving Michigan, Sauer reinvented historical geography in terms of a changing cultural morphology.

Interpretation

The origin of Berkeley geography lies in the creative dynamism of Carl Sauer's values. Sauer desired certain professional ends and exerted himself to attain them. He abandoned the set of ties and much of the thought associated with the Michigan situation and went in search of another that suited him. In the process, he crafted a new philosophy of geography that was expressed in a novel program of research, and he instituted a new department.

Sauer's metaphysics is suffused with the idealism of the Romantic movement, which protested the naturalism of the Enlightenment and which derived much of its vigor from German thinkers. Naturalism and historicist idealism are conflicting world views, fundamental structures of logic and value that give scholarly life alternative meanings. Their fates may be conceived as an overarching dialectic in western intellectual history. In the development of western geographic thought, Sauer perpetuated this conflict, controverting naturalistic anthropogeography as definition of the geographic field and propounding the traditional chorological view. Moreover, he applied the idealist Boasian concept of culture to geography, giving shape and substance to a cultural morphology that is German, genetic, and Goethean.[38]

At the forefront of the Romantic reaction, Goethe developed and christened as morphology the study of life forms in process of constant change and transformation. Not content with simply opposing Newtonian science, the Romantics advanced a science of their own making. With Goethe's science of morphology, knowledge became shaped by a new ideal. The transition from the generic Linnean view to the modern genetic view of organic nature was completed. The world of science thus received from this towering thinker a morphologic point of view that was introduced into geography by Carl Ritter. By means of this monentous transference and its subsequent extension as chorographic science, German geography was transformed. American geography was changed perceptibly by the morphological model after Sauer made it the basis of his early work at Berkeley.

The foundation of Sauer's metatheory rests on Goethe's conception of morphological change. His influence on Sauer was both primary and secondary. Sauer knew Goethe's work and cited it in the "Morphology," and Goethe's thought was preserved by other writers whom Sauer read. Sauer's view of geography repeats several patterns in Goethe's thought: science is phenomenological. "One need not," Goethe believed, "seek for something beyond the phenomena; they themselves are the [knowledge]." He thus preferred a science of actuality to one of abstraction. Goethe was "born to see, appointed to look." With these words Ernst Cassirer alerts us to Goethe's principle of *Anschauung*. To Goethe, intuitive contemplation—a dialogue between reflection and visual experience—allows comprehension of the interworking of forces and forms. The object of observation, furthermore, is continuous growth itself rather than the product of growth. Morphology is metamorphosis; morphological change entails process, growth, and development. Now, Sauer's geography is phenomenological and opposed to a priori schemes; it is grounded somewhat mystically in observation; and it depends upon the developmental mode of explanation.[39]

Goethe, moreover, conceived of historical change as analogous to organic growth. He viewed all life and its environment as a structured whole whose parts were mutually interdependent. The fact that Germany has been the hearth of organic social theory from the beginning of the nineteenth century to the present rests heavily on Goethe's formulations. Goethe inclined to a monistic view of nature. The idea of unity, however, is inseparable from that of polarity, or opposites; e.g., light and darkness, subject and object, and matter and mind. If the monistic principle is applied to the landscape, man and nature comprise the poles of an interdependent duality rather than the paired elements of a clear-cut dualism. Again, Sauer reflects Goethe. Sauer's geography is guided by the metaphor of organicism, with its minimal assumption of structured reality that is subject to change. His geographic morphology avoids the dualism of "natural" and "cultural" by stressing the concept of forms: in this sense, all geography is physical geography. Whether in the writings of Goethe or Sauer, these ideas are intimately associated. One notion often implies another, or is expressed in terms of another, as when Goethe enjoins the student to make growth itself the purpose of observation.[40]

I have used the idea of affinities between the thought of Sauer and Goethe as a working hypothesis, which, I believe, has been fruitful. That Sauer's geographic morphology was preformed by nineteenth-century German historical thinking is confirmed. There are too many likenesses between the phenomena to deny the derivation of key presuppositions and, of course, actual ties are known from Sauer's documentation. That Sauer depended specifically on Goethe's morphology is less firmly established. The thesis requires amplification, but I doubt that it can be refuted.

Sauer's view of geography guided the organized activities of the Berkeley group. The lean look of the personnel and facilities in the department did not detract from its purpose. Scholarly inquiry and the inculcation of historicist values were dual aspects of a comprehensive and balanced enterprise. Sauer's unflagging curiosity, imagination, and industry turned the direction of American geography in the second quarter of the present century. The formative years anticipated this achievement.

TABLE 1

FACULTY AND COURSES, 1923-33

Course Number	23-24	24-25	25-26	26-27	27-28	28-29	29-30	30-31	31-32	32-33
1	COS JBL	RJR JBL	RJR	OS JBL	OS JBL	OS JBL	OS COS	JBL ES	JBL GP	JEK
2	COS JBL	COS JBL	COS	COS JBL	COS JBL	COS JBL	RJR	COS	COS	COS
3	RJR	RJR	RJR	JBL	JBL	JBL	WP	ES	JBL	JBL
4	RJR	RJR	RJR	JBL	JBL	JBL	*	JBL	JBL	JEK
101	COS	COS	COS	COS	COS	COS	*	COS	*	COS
102	RJR	-	-	OS	OS	OS	WP	JBL	GP	JEK
105	JBL	JBL	*	JBL	JBL	JBL	WP	JBL	JBL	JBL
113	JBL	JBL	OS	JBL	JBL	JBL	WP	JBL	JBL	JBL
121	COS	COS	COS	COS	COS	COS	COS	COS	COS	COS
122			OS	OS	OS	OS	OS	*	*	COS
123			OS	OS	OS	OS	WP	GP	JBL	JBL
131	RJR	RJR	RJR	JBL	JBL	JBL	*	ES	*	*
141	COS	COS	COS	COS	COS	COS	RJR	GP	GP	JEK
142									GP	*
151	COS	COS	COS	COS	COS	COS	WP	COS	GP	JBL
200		COS	COS	COS	COS	COS	*	COS	COS	JBL
201			OS	OS	OS	OS	?	JBL	COS	*
203				OS	OS	OS	OS	GP	GP	*
205							COS RJR	COS	JBL	JBL

Source: University of California Bulletin, *Announcement of Courses, 1923–24 to 1932–33.*

Symbols:
COS = Carl O. Sauer   WP = Wolfgang Panzer   - = course deleted
JBL = John B. Leighly   ES = Edna Scofield   * = course not given
RJR = Richard J. Russell   GP = Gottfried Pfeifer   ? = no data
OS = Oskar Schmieder   JEK = John E. Kesseli

TABLE 2

UNDERGRADUATE COURSE DESCRIPTIONS

1. Introduction to Geography: Elements.* Areal forms and their structure as expressed in major landscapes of the earth. Climate in particular is stressed as the major differentiating and connecting factor in physical area. Selection of type area affords opportunity for varied map studies.
2. Introduction to Geography: Natural and Cultural Regions.* Regional geography: natural divisions of the world and their utilization under different cultural systems. Systematic regional map studies.
3. Elementary Meteorology. Atmospheric changes that determine weather conditions; development of weather observations into climatologic data.
4. Map Reading and Map Interpretation.* Representation of geographic data by means of maps. Interpretation of projections, scales, symbols. Interpretation of land forms and culture from topographic maps; planimetration, measurements of cultural data on maps.

---

101. Field Geography.** Field study of a unit area with systematic mapping of the elements that constitute the natural region and of the forms of its utilization.
102. Field Study of Land Forms. A series of Saturday excursions, including one or more week-end trips to selected localities. Both physical and cultural land forms will receive recognition.
105. Cartography.** The course is concerned with the methods of making maps. Map projections, conversion of scale, graphic problems of representing geographic data, principle of isotaxic mapping of geographic values; field cartography, including sketch mapping and geographic applications of traverse methods.
113. Climatology. A survey of the principal classifications of climates of the world, of regional characteristics of climate and relation to vegetation and human activities.
121. Geography of North America.** First course in regional continental geography. Natural regions of North America: their occupational condition and historical evolution. Cultural interpretation of maps and exercises in mapping geographic distributions.
122. Geography of South America.
123. Geography of Europe.
131. Geography of California. Natural regions classified and contrasted; distribution of population and activities.
141. Economic Geography: Primary Production. Areal distribution of production of raw materials of world commerce. Physical, historical, and other bases of production in explanation of localization of producing area. Exercises in statistical analysis by means of graphs and map correlations.
142. Economic Geography: Industrial Centers. An examination of major industrial areas to determine (a) the bases for the localization of industry and (b) forms and structure characteristic of the industrial area.
151. Principles of Geography.** Reports and conferences on the objectives, subdivisions, and methods of geography, with special reference to different schools of geographic thought as expressed in recent literature. The course is intended to outline the critical problems of the subject, in which research topics are to be sought by those who expect to enter advanced studies.

---

200. Seminar in History of Geography. 203. Seminar in Cultural Geography.
201. Seminar in Regional Geography. 205. Seminar in Physical Geography.

Source: Descriptions are taken mainly from the *Announcement of Courses* for 1928-29; hence, this list is composite. Symbols: One asterisk after a course title denotes required as preparation for the major, two indicate normally included in the major program.

TABLE 3

SEMINARS, 1923–33

Year	Title, Topic, and Instructor
1923–24	No seminar given.
1924–25	200. Seminar in History of Geography. Geography among the ancients, and the developments in cosmography and cartography during the period of great discoveries (Sauer).
1925–26	200. Seminar in History of Geography. The history of geographic thought in the nineteenth century (Sauer).
	201. Seminar in Regional Geography. Geographic morphology; studies in extra-tropical South America (Schmieder).
1926–27	200. Seminar in History of Geography. Explorations of the Pacific coast and islands (Sauer).
	201. Seminar in Regional Geography. French and German areal studies (Schmieder).
	203. Seminar in Cultural Geography. Geographic methods in population studies (Schmieder).
1927–28	200. Seminar in History of Geography. Scientific explorations in North America (Sauer).
	201. Seminar in Regional Geography. French and German areal studies, with special reference to morphologic problems (Schmieder).
	203. Seminar in Cultural Geography. Primitive cultural areas, in particular South America (Schmieder).
1928–29	200. Seminar in History of Geography. 19th century analysis of land forms and soil areas (Sauer).
	201. Seminar in Regional Geography. Current and recent studies in tropical America (Schmieder).
	203. Seminar in Cultural Geography. *Siedlung* studies as related to the general field of historical geography (Schmieder).
1929–30	201. Seminar in Regional Geography. Neither topic nor instructor announced.
	203. Seminar in Cultural Geography. Historical geography of Middle America (Schmieder).
	205. Seminar in Physical Geography. Geomorphology of the Pacific margins (Sauer); climatic distribution of land forms (Russell).
1930–31	200. Seminar in Physical Geography (Sauer). No topic announced.
	201. Seminar in Urban Geography (Leighly). No topic announced.
	203. Seminar in Cultural Geography. Historical Geography of Middle America (Pfeifer).
1931–32	201. Seminar in Regional Geography. Mexico and Central America (Sauer).
	203. Seminar in Cultural Geography. The culture area concept as expressed in economic regions (Pfeifer).
	205. Seminar in Physical Geography. Mechanics and forms of aqueous erosion and aggradation (Leighly).
1932–33	200. Emergence of scientific geography in the 19th century (Leighly).
	203. Seminar in Cultural Geography. Early settlement and field conditions of Europe; primitive agricultural types for the world (Sauer).

Source: University of California Bulletin, *Announcement of Courses*, 1923–24 to 1932–33.

TABLE 4

OBJECTIVES OF GEOGRAPHIC FIELD STUDY, 1929

The geographic study of a region involves the following analysis:

1. Genetic description of land forms (surface, drainage, and soil), Geomorphology
(a) Determination and origin of the major structural lines
(b) Sculpture of relief
    (1) Modelling of slopes by relation of denudation to tectonic mobility
    (2) Incision of erosion features
(c) Effects of climate on weathering and removal
    (1) Effects of former climatic conditions
    (2) Present climatic expressions

2. Cultural modifications and expressions of the area, Culture morphology
  (a) Man's exploitation of surface (land utilization)
    (1) Type of areal economy
       'improved' vs. 'unimproved' land
       intensiveness of use
          size of producing unit
       destructiveness of use
       composition of subsistence area
    (2) Stages or successions of land utilization
  (b) Grouping of population
    (1) Dispersed population
    (2) Massed populations
       forms and sizes of settlements
       town patterns
       habitation types
    (3) Bases of support
  (c) Lines of communication
  (d) Limits of cultural unity

The human geography of [northwest Mexico] proceeds of necessity by historical reconstruction, in which documentary data, archaeologic data, and site appraisal are combined to establish or reestablish the character of the cultural succession. For example, there may be an important prehistoric stage as in Casas Grandes, characterized by major and minor settlements.... A similar reconstruction may be made for the early Spanish period when the missions were established and shifts in location and occupation of the natives took place. In third place comes the later colonial period in which the native population is dominated by mines and haciendas. Finally, comes the modern scene which can be evaluated properly only if the shifts of the past are known.

These separate themes lead to the regional synthesis by which the individuality of a region and its relation to other areas is determined. Quantitative determination is accomplished by the mapping of these several classes of data, so that ideally the development of a unit region is shown by a series of specialized maps.

Source: Leuschner to Campbell, 18 May 1929, University Archivist, Bancroft Library, Berkeley, California.

TABLE 5

GRADUATE THESES, 1923–33

1924 Rigdon, Vera Esta
"The Geography of the Carquinez Strait"

1927 *Leighly, John Barger
"A Study in Urban Morphology: The Towns of Mälardalen in Sweden"

Searls, May Lavinia
"The Geography of the Wooden, Gordon, Capelle Area of Napa County, California"

1928 King, Margaret Goddard
"The Growth of San Francisco as Illustrated by Shifts in Densities of Population"

Suhl, Alvena Marie
"Historical Geography of San Diego"

Wickson, Gladys Clare
"The Integration of Geographic Forms in the Salinas Valley"

1930 *Kniffen, Fred Bowerman
"The Delta Country of the Colorado"

Scofield, Edna Lois
"The Southeastern Lowland of Vancouver Island"

*Thornthwaite, Charles Warren
"Louisville, Kentucky: A Study in Urban Geography"

1931 Carthew, Arthur Williams
"The Lower Basin of the Santa Ana River"

*Dicken, Samuel Newton
"The Big Barrens: A Morphologic Study in the Kentucky Karst"

Post, Lauren Chester
"The Spokane Valley: A Study in Regional Geography"

1933 *Brand, Donald Dilworth
"The Historical Geography of Northwestern Chihuahua"

*Meigs, Peveril, III
"The Dominican Missions of Lower California: A Chapter in Historical Geography"

Munson, Esther Miriam
"Aboriginal Economic Geography of the Hopi"

Sources: "M. A. Degrees in Geography Granted by the University of California, Berkeley" (mimeographed) and "A List of Ph.D. Degrees in Geography Granted by the Univeristy of California, Berkeley, 1963" (mimeographed); University of California, Graduate Division, *Programmes of the Final Public Examination for the Degree of Doctor of Philosophy* (bound with doctor's theses).

Note: The asterisk before a name denotes a Ph.D. dissertation. Rigdon and Searls were not in residence in Sauer's department, being candidates for the master's degree from Holway's time. Other graduate students were present, however, between 1923 and 1933, including Herman Friis, Hugh Raup, Joseph Spencer, John Kesseli, Leslie Hewes, Anna Boschen, Russell Carlson, and Richard Nida.

Notes

1. C. O. Sauer, "The Problem of Land Classification," *Annals,* Association of American Geographers (hereinafter *"Annals")* 21 (1921): 3-16, ref. p. 3; J. B. Leighly, "Carl Otwin Sauer, 1889-1975," *Annals* 66 (1976): 337-48, ref. p. 338 (this memorial should be consulted for Sauer's complete bibliography); A. Z. Guttenberg, "The Land Utilization Movement of the 1920s," *Agricultural History* 50 (1976): 477-90.
2. N. J. Schmaltz, "Michigan's Land Economic Survey," *Agricultural History* 52 (1978): 229-46; Sauer to Hartshorne, 22 June 1946, Sauer Papers, Bancroft Library, Berkeley, California (hereinafter "SP"; quoted by permission, the Bancroft Library).
3. R. S. Kirkendall, *Social Scientists and Farm Politics in the Age of Roosevelt* (Columbia: University of Missouri Press, 1966); "Honorary Corresponding Members," *Geographical Review* 25 (1935): 486-87.
4. C. O. Sauer, "The Survey Method in Geography and Its Objectives," *Annals* 14 (1924): 17-33.
5. The act of offering restrictive definitions in a scholarly field reflects the trend toward professionalization, the process whereby a tradition becomes a discipline. In Sauer's experience, this process was intensified, for he combined the problem of definition with the polemic against the extension of naturalism into the realm of the social sciences. He rejected the view that geography was the study of man's relationship (adaptation) to his natural surroundings, preferring the chorologic delimitation. In the Michigan period, Sauer's blast at environmental determinism proceeded independently of the anthropological critique that Franz Boas launched, around the turn of the century at Columbia University. That is, its origin lay in the polemical literature of German geography. Eventually his attack became bolstered by the argument of American anthropologists. Whereas Sauer received environment as a deficient definition of geography, Boas coped with it as the sole determinant of culture. Sauer replaced environment with landscape as the proper content of geography, and Boas reduced it to but one item in the class of factors that determine culture. On professionalization in American anthropology, see G. W. Stocking, *Race, Culture, and Evolution: Essays in the History of Anthropology* (New York: The Free Press, 1968), pp. 303-5. Edward Shils provides an erudite analysis of the history of sociology that is relevant to the development of geography; see his "Tradition, Ecology, and Institution in the History of Sociology," *Daedalus* 99 (1970): 760-825. For an analysis of the Boasian solution of the problem of man-nature interaction, see W. Speth, "The Anthropogeographic Theory of Franz Baos," *Anthropos* 73 (1978): 1-31.
6. Sauer to Hartshorne, 22 June 1946, SP; Sauer to Herskovits, 15 September 1945, SP.
7. Landscape morphology is a substantive variant of the morphological science that Johann Wolfgang von Goethe refined and applied to living forms. In turn, Goethe's morphology is nested in the broader intellectual structure of German historical thought, or"historicism." Sauer's philosophy of geography is so deeply rooted in German historicism that it is futile to seek to grasp it fully without concomitant understanding of this phase of western intellectual

experience. The meaning of historicism remains elusive despite repeated attempts at clarification by philosophers and historians. Clearly, however, it is a manifestation of the classic idealist lineage that spawned Romanticism and the *Geisteswissenschaften*. Historicism unfolded dialectically as an individualizing movement in reaction against the generalizing impulses of the Enlightenment; it emerged as an ideology-critique. Most authorities agree that it is an outlook distinguished by the genetic method in the study of man, and that it is frontally opposed to naturalism. Historicism takes human action as value-laden, contextually informed, and unique in its development; its interpretation demands empathetic grasp of the meaning and intentionality of human behavior. A by-product of the Enlightenment, naturalism is an abstracting mode of looking at the world that subsumes historical individualities under a unified general law and, oftentimes, numeric formula. The word naturalism is cognate with the notions of "materialism," "rationalism," and "positivism." Indeed, these terms become linked, and students speak of "evolutionary (naturalistic) positivism." The commonly advanced oppositions "history vs. science" and "idiographic vs. nomothetic" tend to obscure the richness of cognitive and affective content that inheres in the mutually aggressive world views of historicism and naturalism. Under the view presented here, there are only two traditions in geography, and they polarize the discipline. For an elaboration of the nature of these traditions see T. Parsons, *The Structure of Social Action* (New York: McGraw-Hill, 1937) pp. 473–87, and G. H. von Wright, *Explanation and Understanding* (Ithaca: Cornell University Press, 1971), pp. 1–33.

8. Sauer to Jones, 9 November 1951, SP; Sauer to H. H. Barrows, 31 January 1921, SP; Holway to D. P. Barrows, 2 March 1920, University Archives, Bancroft Library, Berkeley, California (hereinafter "UA"; quoted by permission, University Archivist, University of California Archives, The Bancroft Library).

9. Sauer to Nisbet, 11 May 1962, SP; Sauer to Parsons [1960], SP.

10. G. S. Dunbar, "George Davidson, 1825–1911: Early West Coast Geographer and Historian of Discovery" (Paper read at the annual meeting of the Society for the History of Discoveries, Charleston, S. C., 5 November 1976), pp. 1–11; C. O. Sauer, "Memorial of Ruliff S. Holway," *Annals* 19 (1929): 64–65.

11. G. Pfeifer, *Regional Geography in the United States since the War: A Review of Trends in Theory and Method* (New York: American Geographical Society, 1938), trans. J. Leighly, pp. 1–37 (mimeographed); *University of California Bulletin, Announcement of Courses,* 1920–21, pp. 99–102.

12. The record of summer session activity, a distinctly subordinate feature of the department, includes the following faculty: Wellington Jones (1927); Albrecht Penck (1928); D. H. Davis (1929); Wolfgang Panzer, Carl Sauer, and Richard Russell (1930); John Leighly and K. C. McMurry (1931); Raoul Blanchard and Gottfried Pfeifer (1932); and Preston James and Russell Carlson (1933). F. Kramer, ed., "The Itinerant Geographer," mimeographed (Berkeley: Department of Geography, University of California, Berkeley, 1959).

13. Holway to D. P. Barrows, 12 April 1923, UA; F. B. Kniffen, "Richard Joel Russell, 1895–1971," *Annals* 63 (1973): 241–49; Sauer to von Wissmann, 23 January 1936, SP.

14. Sauer to Holway, 12 March 1923, SP.

15. *Biennial Report of the President of the University 1928–1929 and 1929–1930* (Berkeley: University of California Press, 1930), p. 55; O. Schmieder, *Lebenserinnerungen und Tagebuchblätter eines Geographen* (Kiel: Verlag Ferdinand Hirt, 1972).

16. Pfeifer to Speth, 15 February 1977; Sauer to Campbell, 5 December 1929, SP.

17. Sauer to Deutsch, 26 February 1932, UA; J. J. Parsons, *et al.,* "John Ernest Kesseli: An Appreciation," *The California Geographer* 3(1962): 64–67.

18. Sauer made tradition influential in his department by constant recourse to the monuments of geography's past. The ideas of early geographers, mainly German, frequently set research tasks for Berkeley geographers. For instance, Sauer's field investigations in the "geomorphology of the Far West" were undertaken to "try out the relative merits" of the position of W. M. Davis and of Walther Penck. Inevitably the first graduate course introduced ("History of Geography prior to the Nineteenth Century," 1923–24) was retrospective in nature and taught by Sauer. The early entry and persistence of history of geography at Berkeley, including attention to exploration, explains the extrordinary interest of the Berkeley group in the background of the discipline. Besides the master himself and Leighly, perhaps Clarence Glacken and David Lowenthal are best known in this regard. Sauer to Smith, 2 February 1939, SP.

19. *University of California Publications in Geography* (Berkeley: University of California Press, 1925–33), vol. 2, no. 2 to vol. 6, no. 4.

20. The relations between the departments of anthropology and geography were mutual and cordial. Ralph Beals, who in one capacity or another was in or about the anthropology department from 1922 to 1935, remembers that the "traffic in students, so far as formal seminars are concerned, was rather one way. Few if any anthropology students took seminars in geography, partly because they lacked adequate undergraduate training in geography and [because] the geographers were rather stricter in the requirements for admission to seminars and less hospitable to students from other departments than were the anthropologists." Sauer, moreover, sat on almost every Ph.D. examining committee in anthropology during the twenties and early thirties and therefore had "some effect" on anthropology students. Various sources indicate that Sauer was more receptive to budding anthropologists interested in historical ethnology and prehistory than to those whose interests were social, along lines of kinship. Beals to Speth, 22 February 1977.

21. C. O. Sauer, "The Seminar as Exploration," *Historical Geography Newsletter,* 6 (1976): 31–34, ref. pp. 31 and 34 (this article was written originally in 1948); G. W. Stocking, *Race, Culture, and Evolution: Essays in the History of Anthropology* (New York: The Free Press, 1968), p. 304; University of California, "Programmes of the Final Public Examination for the Degree of the Doctor of Philosophy," Graduate Division, Berkeley (these documents are bound with the dissertations and provide biographical chronologies, thesis abstracts, lists of graduate studies, and publications, if any, at the time of the doctoral examination).

22. C. O. Sauer, "The Education of a Geographer," *Annals* 46 (1956): 287–99, reprinted in J. Leighly, ed., *Land and Life: A Selection from the Writings of Carl Ortwin Sauer* (Berkeley and Los Angeles: University of California Press, 1963), pp. 389–404, ref. p. 400; Leuschner to Campbell, 18 May 1929, UA.

23. Meigs to Speth, 16 December 1976; D. Stanislawski, "Carl Ortwin Sauer, 1889–1975," *Journal of Geography* 74 (1975): 548–54, ref. p. 550.

24. The urban investigations of Leighly and Thornthwaite probably rest upon Sauer's early and repeated mention of the works of Vaughan Cornish and W. Geisler on city geography. The latter's study of the German city was avowedly a " 'contribution to the morphology of the cultural landscape.' " Thus, urban geography, which did not enter the curriculum on a continuing basis until well after World War II, enjoyed some popularity at Berkeley in the early years. C. O. Sauer, *The Morphology of Landscape*, Publications in Geography, vol. 2, no. 2 (Berkeley: University of California, 1925), p. 46; idem, "Recent Developments in Cultural Geography," in *Recent Developments in the Social Sciences*, ed. E. C. Hayes (New York: Lippincott, 1927), pp. 194 and 208..

25. W. Speth, "Historicist Anthropogeography: Environment and Culture in American Anthropological Thought from 1890–1950" (Ph.D. diss., University of Oregon, 1972), pp. 203–39; Sauer to Deutsch, 17 February 1932, SP; Sauer to Thornthwaite, 23 August 1932, SP.

26. Sauer to Blanchard, 3 June 1932, SP; Sauer to Lipman, 14 March 1932, SP; Sauer to Sproul, 8 April 1933, UA.

27. With his studies of Pueblo culture in Sonora, Sauer ceased to rely on the departmental series in geography, and a new outlet for his monographic researches was established. With the cooperation of A. L. Kroeber and Herbert Bolton, Berkeley historian, Sauer founded in 1932 *Ibero-Americana*. This new series was to range broadly over all aspects of Latin American cultures, and comprise in the main contributions to culture history. The original editorial board was made up of its cofounders, but Sauer was its "chief mover and remained on the board until his retirement." L. Constance to Speth, 10 July 1978.

28. Sauer to Treanor,13 September 1932, SP; Sauer to Campbell, 5 December 1929, UA; R. E. Dickinson, "Landscape and Society," *Scottish Geographical Magazine* 55 (1939): 1–15, ref. p. 13; G. Pfeifer, *Regional Geography in the United States*, p. 19.

29. Sauer to Smith, 2 February 1939, SP; W. Speth, "Carl Ortwin Sauer on Destructive Exploitation," *Biological Conservation* (1977): 145–60; Sauer to Hartshorne, 22 June 1946, SP.

30. Leighly, "Carl Ortwin Sauer, 1889-1975," *Annals* 66 (1976): 337–48 (for a contradictory view of the *Morphology*, see p. 340); Sauer, *The Morphology of Landscape*, pp. 19–53; idem, "Recent Developments in Cultural Geography," in *Recent Developments in the Social Sciences*, ed. E. C. Hayes (New York: Lippincott,1927), pp. 154–212; idem, "Geography, Cultural," in *Encyclopaedia of the Social Sciences*, ed. E. Seligman (New York: Macmillan, 1931), 6: 621–24.

31. C. O. Sauer, "Foreword to Historical Geography," *Annals* 31 (1941): 1–24, reprinted in J. Leighly, ed., *Land and Life*, pp. 351–79, ref. pp. 355–56.

32. C. O. Sauer, *"Recent Developments,"* p. 207.

33. Sauer to Whittlesey, 25 September 1929, Whittlesey Papers, Harvard University Archives, Cambridge, Massachusetts.

34. Sauer, *"The Survey Method,"* ref. pp. 17 and 19; idem, *The Morphology of Landscape*, p. 36.

35. Sauer, "Recent Developments in Cultural Geography," pp. 200, 204, and 211;

D. Whittlesey, "Sequent Occupance," *Annals* 19 (1929): 162–65.

36. At this time, "culture history" was a commonplace among the Berkeley anthropologists. Kroeber's *Anthropology* (1923) made easy use of the term, and Lowie was teaching a course on the subject. Also, Kroeber was urging the establishment of a "super-department of 'Anthropology, Geography, and Culture History,' " a proposal that was stillborn. A result of his contacts with Berkeley ethnologists and the move to integrate social science research and instruction at the University of California, culture history appeared in Sauer's thinking toward the middle of the formative period. In time, Sauer enlarged his acquaintance with continental culture historians. Not only Ratzel and Hahn, but eventually Leo Frobenius, Eduard Seler, Robert Heine-Geldern, and the "*Anthropos* group" shaped Sauer's thought. Kroeber to Sproul, 16 February 1932, SP; and Sauer to Speth, 30 June 1971 and 3 March 1972.

37. Sauer, "Geography, Cultural," p. 624; idem, "Historical Geography and the Western Frontier," in *The Trans-Mississippi West*, ed. J. F. Willard and C. B. Goodykoontz (Boulder: University of Colorado Press, 1930), pp. 227-89, reprinted in J. Leighly, ed., *Land and Life*, pp. 45–46.

38. W. Wagar, *World Views: A Study in Comparative History* (Hinsdale, Ill.: Dryden Press, 1977); C. Kluckhohn and O. Prufer, "Influences During the Formative Years," in *The Anthropology of Franz Boas*, ed. W. Goldschmidt (San Francisco: American Anthropological Association and Howard Chandler,1959) pp. 4-28; F. Boas, *Race, Language and Culture*, 2d ed. (New York: The Free Press, 1955), pp. 639–47 (this article was published originally in 1887).

39. Sauer, *The Morphology of Landscape*, p. 31; E. Cassirer, *Rousseau, Kant, Goethe: Two Essays*, trans. J. Gutmann et al. (Princeton: Princeton University Press, 1945), pp. 61–98, ref. p. 81; E. Wilkinson and L. Willoughby, *Goethe: Poet and Thinker* (New York: Barnes and Noble, 1962). pp. 167–84 and 214–28.

40. T. Parsons, *The Structure of Social Action* (New York: McGraw-Hill, 1937), p. 481; W. Hartner, "Goethe and the Natural Sciences," in *Goethe: A Collection of Critical Essays,* ed. V. Lang. (Englewood Cliffs, N.J.: Prentice-Hall, 1968), 145–160, ref. p. 152.

Geographia Generalis and the Earliest Development of American Academic Geography

William Warntz

Introduction

In considering the origin of academic Geography in America, one might select, depending upon breadth of purpose, either of two widely separated periods as the time of beginnings. Other essays in this collection strongly suggest that, conventionally, scholars have chosen the later of the two periods as the pertinent one for their concerns. That is to say, they appear to subscribe to the limiting notion that the meaningful introduction of geography into the curriculum of American colleges and universities occurred shortly after the middle of the nineteenth century as an imnport from Europe. In this they follow, of course, *American Geography, Inventory and Prospect* (1954), prepared by many committees at the behest of the Association of American Geographers and published in celebration of the fiftieth anniversary of the founding of that association. There, among the authorized combined establishment statements on the achievements of American geography, we find their conceit that "At the level of university scholarship, the study of the earth (geography) by Americans was imported piecemeal from various sources (European) between 1860 and 1925, but not always from exponents who were most representative or influential in their homelands."[1]

Earlier, in the introduction to his formidable work, *The Nature of Geography* (1939), the redoubtable Richard Hartshorne had stressed the same points and had chastised his colleagues mildly for their lack of sufficient attention to such matters. In his consideration of the "Historical Background of American Geography," he noted that:

Geographers are wont to boast of their subject as a very old one, extending, even as an organized science, far back to antiquity. But often when geographers in this country discuss the nature of their subject, whether in symposia or in published articles, one has the impression that geography was founded by a group of American scholars at the beginning of the twentieth century. Likewise many such discussions in the past have had only slight relation to similar discussions by European geographers, in spite of the well known fact that geography has had a greater development in the universities of Germany alone than in those of this country.

Hartshorne acknowledged that

it would of course be absurd to suggest that Amrican geographers were entirely unfamiliar with the concept of geography developed in Europe. Arnold Guyot of Princeton [from Switzerland], the first professor of geography in an American university [1854], was a follower of [the German] Carl Ritter, but he had no successors.[2]

Guyot actually did have followers in America in a well-developed network of teachers' institutes, seminars, courses, textbooks, and workbooks. However, it is not particularly pertinent to this occasion to debate this matter.

Concerning the immediately following years, Hartshorne suggests that it was Ellen C. Semple, with her presentation of Ratzel's concepts from Germany of anthropogeography, who set the course of human geography in this country for a quarter of a century. Also during the same period, William Morris Davis of Harvard University and Albrecht Penck of the University of Berlin established mutual relations between geography in this country and in Germany.

However, in 1961 John K. Wright noted casually but perceptively that "geography of some sort had been taught in American colleges and universities since the midseventeenth century." But, insisted Wright, "it was probably not until Arnold Henry Guyot (1807–1884) was appointed professor of geology and physical geography at Princeton in 1854 that it was taught to any substantial degree in a modern spirit and more or less independently." It was Wright's contention, furthermore, that probably the first person in the United States to hold a professorship devoted, nominally at least, to geography unlinked with any other subject was Daniel Coit Gilman, who served from 1863 to 1872 as professor of physical and political geography in the Sheffield Scientific School of Yale.[3]

There can, of course, be no denying the significance of the conventional recognition of such a mid-nineteenth century "origin" for American academic geography as suggested by those sometime established leaders in the discipline. Such a conception is useful and doubtless important in the attempt to understand the nature of modern geography (however substantially it now may differ in its nature from that of merely twenty-five years ago) as a cumulative development and synthesis in Hegelian terms of continuous interactions of theses and antitheses. The interested reader may refer as well to my own slender volume, *Geography Now and Then* (1964), in which the topic is considered with the century 1854 to 1954, shown in fact, as a *second* cycle of academic geography in America.[4]

More importantly, however, in that modest and informal work there is the examination and analysis of original materials discovered by the author principally in the archives of nine universities or colleges in the United States of pre–revolutionary War foundations.[5] That exercise convinced the author of the existence of an earlier origin and period, a *first* cycle of academic geography in America, extending for each college in a similar fashion approximately from the time of its individual foundation to the second or third decade of the nineteenth century.

Following that, there was for each college, without exception, a sharp, distinct, and dramatic break in the continuity of its geographical offerings. So pronounced and complete was the disruption (although the onset times varied slightly among the colleges) that the ensuing hiatus apparently has obscured to succeeding generations of geographers the existence and significance of the first cycle. For example in 1951, a modern geographer, Ralph H. Brown, commented upon the essay by Jared Sparks (class of 1815 at Harvard) written in 1813 for the Aurius Ramus society, a Harvard College debating group. In his essay, "Geography," Sparks (then an upperclassman, but later president of Harvard) offered a vigorous defense of (special) geography and emphasized it as particularly appropriate for that college's curriculum. Professor Brown maintained that "the essay was composed during a period of spirited intellectual interest" in the subject of geography, but "long before collegiate standing was assured it."[6]

Of course, the latter part of that statement can not be considered as correct. At Harvard (as in all the colleges with colonial origins) geography had long had collegiate standing, though the subject destined to lose it very soon there (and elsewhere) despite a very favorable report on the need for and the value of the geographic discipline by the Harvard College Geography Committee of 1804, on which the college's president, John Thornton Kirkland, served. Thus, many of the other comments of Brown become meaningless when it is recognized that Sparks wrote *not* sixty years *before* the introduction of geography into the Harvard curriculum, but rather at the *end* of over a century and a half of continuous instruction in geography at that college!

As I assembled the archival data, it became increasingly clear to me that it was not simply "geography of some sort" that had been taught in American colleges and universities since the mid-seventeenth century. It was by no means mere episodic, sporadic, disconnected, and irrelevant congeries that constituted the various colleges' offerings. Rather, consistent patterns of relationships revealed themselves in geography's disciplinary linkages everywhere to other disciplines, in the sequences of textbooks used, and perhaps most importantly in the general connections to the literature, science, and philosophy of the European Enlightenment.

It is an intention of this essay to examine the nature of that geography and its role during the "first" American academic origin of geography, with particular attention to the *Geographia Generalis Varenii*, the work which spearheaded America's first cycle of academic geography. First, however, consider the general context.

The Enlightenment, the Colonial Colleges, and the Constitution

The notion of "The Enlightenment," itself, is an abstract, systematized, cosmopolitan concept. Deriving from it, says W. O. Clough, is the

great body of words and phrases used frequently in the colonial period in the heat of revolutionary oratory and pamphleteering: natural law, the law of nature, natural rights, man in the state of nature, the law of nations, reason and nature, Nature's God, self-evident (i.e., natural) truths, the rights of man, the right of resistance, the will of the people, the authority of the people, a government of laws not men, public office as a trust, the consent of the governed, covenant and compact and contract theories of government, constitutional rights, no taxation without representation, no taxation without consent, the election of representatives of the people, magistrates as servants of the people, the liberties of the people, freedom of the press, objections to standing armies, and, in sum, the end and aim of government as the preservation of these rights. Not a single one of these terms is American in origin. Not a single phrase is without its long history, often running back far into the life of ancient Greece and Rome.[7]

These and other concepts came into the American stream of history through books, the inheritance of colonial Englishmen of the great books and ideas of their own past.

248

American political wisdom was the distillation of this long inheritance, originating in classical times, emerging again in the Renaissance, blended opportunely with a sturdy British tradition of common law, strengthened by the studies of continental scholars, and arriving as a whole in America as a common heritage. "American leaders were fortunate in this heritage, wise in selection from it, fortunate again in the climate of eighteenth-century liberalism and in the freedoms of a new world; and were thus able to forge from their opportunity a whole new, revolutionary and dynamic synthesis of their own."[8] One might add, also, that the ultimately distinctively "American" contribution was the firm belief that an ideal general form of government derived from this could be codified, written down, and applied successfully, thus transcending British empiricism.

In viewing this experience as an intellectual one for the "Founding Fathers" and their contemporaries, Clough shares the attitudes of such distinguished historians as Becker and Curti as reinforced most recently by Frances Fitzgerald, whose powerful, persuasive, and fascinating *America Revised* at once explains American independence and the Constitution as the result of conscious, deliberate, directed, and concerted acts of intellectuals, and as well accounts for the strong and pervasive antiintellectualism so characteristic of American life in most of its subsequent periods including, especially, the present.[9]

A contrary view, of course, has been offered by Daniel Boorstin, who asserted, in speaking of the colonial experience leading to independence no less than later periods, that

> it is peculiarly inappropriate, and can even be misleading to try to sum up American thinking— much less American culture—through great philosophic systems or the literary and philosophic words of great men. Rather, an American tendency to fuse the 'high' and the 'low' cultures which have been traditionally polarized in Western Europe, and an ineptitude at systematic philosophy and at monumental works of belles-lettres, have been striking features of our culture.[10]

In this, Boorstin reflected the attitudes of Perry Miller and others who found, for example, the Puritans' intense and continuing search of the Scriptures not so much deriving from a desire to discover principles for guidance, but rather to find vindications and justifications of their evolving forms.

Regardless of the position on this most monumental of issues, historians seem to be in substantially greater agreement regarding the independence movement and, most of all, the Constitution itself as a product of minds trained and educated in the colonial colleges. And, although the varieties of religious sectarianism involved in the foundings of the colleges, the dispersed populations through the colonies, and the substantial differences among the colonies in their relations to the English establishment (and church) combined to produce certain very distinctive differences among them in life-styles and manner, the significant thing is that their curricula, as distinct from their institutional framework, were remarkably similar. American colonial colleges stayed with the curriculum which the tutors had learned from their tutors, and which ultimately could be traced back to the English universities and their medieval forebears. What distinguished the American college was not its corpus of knowledge, but how, when, where, and to whom that knowledge was communicated.[11]

As indicative of the common literary and political sources that were then widely studied, discussed, and debated, Clough lists some fifty selections arranged in four categories: the classical heritage; the English tradition to 1700; the continental stream; and the emerging pattern, 1700–1790. To this list I would add, as well, the scientific works of Bacon, Descartes, Varenius, Hooke, Boyle, Newton, and other natural philosophers, and importantly the *Philosophical Transactions of The Royal Society* and the *Histoire de l'Academie Royale* as shown in the correspondence and writings of the "Founding Fathers."

The natural philosophers represented the new mathematical and empirical sciences. The weight of argument of Descartes and Newton and the reasoning of Locke represented the idea of general principles and systems that were seen to be no less applicable to human affairs than to the physical world.

"Study governments as you do astronomy by facts, observations, and experiments," wrote John Adams.[12] Such was the expression of the new thesis. A Newtonian mathematics and a successful science had predicated an orderly universe, discoverable by reason and experience. "Why, then, should not man and his political and social institutions be submitted to the same stimulating examination?" suggests Clough.[13] The rationalists insisted that governments were but human phenomena, to be regulated by humans for their own security and improvement. Governments were agents of individuals, designed to preserve the rights of the individual in an orderly society, and their authority was delegated by those who instituted them. Human rights were not gifts of king or government, but inalienable, as a long tradition had argued, and the present was the laboratory of experiment. America gave a new vitality to these theories and even subsumed them in a large conception of systems relating them.

The temper of the century was in part empirical. On the one hand were the lessons of self-reliance: the translation of peasant, indentured servant, and serf to free landholder, artisan, and merchant; the freedom from court, military, legal, and ecclesiastical controls; the very air and room of a vast continent. On the other, however, was the whole body of eighteenth-century literature, science, and philosophy and general principles.

It is in this framework both of attention to general principles and of the recognition of special characteristics that we understand the role in the colonial college curriculum of the *Geographia Generalis* (and its successors), with its emphasis on and development of general geography and its recognition of special geography and the complementary works for this purpose. In *Geography Now and Then* I have given the evidence for the widespread use of the *Geographia Generalis* and the remarkably similar detailed sequences of texts in geography, and the exercises everywhere performed in the American colleges in general and special aspects of the discipline, so I shall not do so here. However, it should be stressed that we must always remember that the subject occupied a prominent position in the curricula of the colonial colleges. Astronomy and geography as mixed mathematics were found in the curriculum under the professor of (pure) mathematics and natural philosophy (mixed mathematics). Prior to the establishment of American constitutional government, such human geography as was offered was included in this framework by treatises derived from the experience and obsevation of men who had described individual regions. Major attention in geography, however, centered on general physical geography, with exercises also on properly equipped terrestrial and celestial globes as the principal feature of overlapping combined work in geography and astronomy.

Geography and astronomy in all of their ramifications as natural philosophy represented the formidable framework of the unified science of the day, which to the eighteenth-century American mind exhibited a rational structure of "natural law." Natural law was acknowledged to be common to all disciplines, and formed the basis of the ideology of the War for Independence, culminating as it did in the convention held in the summer of 1787 in Philadelphia for the purpose of drafting the Constitution.

If nothing else, the Constitution was a product of the colonial colleges of the day and the concept of natural law played the revolutionary rôle. Madison, a College of New Jersey (Princeton) alumnus who played the principal part in the forming of the Constitution, reveals this in his own writings recounting his extensive research preparation. In the *Federalist Papers* prepared by Madison, Jay, and Hamilton, we find the expression of the conscious effort made to produce a Constitution that not only provided the means to regulate society but also reflected the nature—i.e., the "constitution"—of that society itself, in contrast to a mere league,confederation, or treaty. In addition, an impression gained from examining the preserved debates on the *Federalist Papers* is that the founding fathers held firm ideas concerning the United States, with its interrelated social and physical phenomena as a space-occupying system in terms of natural law coupled with the special geography of states' rights as natural rights.

A majority of the fifty-five delegates to the constitutional convention were lawyers. To them, the success of positive law lay in its formulation to agree with the natural law which is above and beyond all human regulation. "With genuine scientific enthusiasm," Woodrow Wilson wrote in 1908, albeit without approval, "the founding fathers followed the leads of Montesquieu under whose hand politics turned into mechanics. The imitation of the checks and balances of the solar system was a conscious one yielding a balancing of powers among president, congress, and the courts, and in the congress between big and little states."[14]

The physical science of that day was largely systematized in mechanics. We see now that the subtlety, sophistication, and level of abstraction of that time in political science seemed far to outrival it. Even though the various forms of physical energy and their conversions were yet to be fully described, analogous social energies such as reason, feeling, and authority and their rich interplay were specifically spelled out in judicial, legislative, and executive branches.

The Constitution was a consciously planned and deliberately written application of all available knowlege to the design of political machinery for relating citizens en masse in a natural law framework. The Bill of Rights was quickly added because debaters at once demanded recognition also of the lively theater where citizens act not in great groups but as individuals. It represented the adopting of precepts which had grown slowly and unplanned in the centuries of development of English common law.

The Bill of Rights made good the campaign promises and patriotic propaganda of the Declaration of Independence. Together, this document and the philosophy of natural rights which guided it complement the Constitution and its origins in the appreciation of natural law. We may liken the body of the Constitution to principles of a rigorous "field theory" while the Bill of Rights not too fantastically might be said to incorporate corresponding "quantum conditions." In politics as well as physics, the contrast between mass regularity and individual spontaneity is subtle and paradoxical. The social atom or corpuscle engages in action which would be disruptive or impossible for the multitude. But physicists did not present this succinctly in their science until our own times!

If for a time social and political thought led in the patterning of human affairs, more and more now do we seem to find it necessary to resort to political and social expediencies to cope with the disquieting consequences of the technological outpourings of a physical science that has forged far into the lead.

As a part of a well-organized and influential curriculum, the academic geograpy of the colonial colleges placed proper emphases on its general and special parts, that is to say, an appreciation of the roles and relations of natual law and natural rights. In the period following the successful establishment of constitutional government, the pendulum swung to a pronounced position of emphasis on natural rights. The nineteenth century opened in sight of a promised land. People thought they were on the threshold of a golden age illuminated and organized by science, and warmed by humanism and fraternity. The "manifest destiny" of the new United States, turning in on its own political affairs, lay in occupying new territory. Academic geography turned in on itself, becoming preoccupied with the particular special geography alone of the new nation, which culminated in the subsequent dismissal of the subject from the college curriculum and the hiatus noted above.

George H. Daniels has remarked that the deluge of facts generally assailing "Baconian" science in the early years of the nineteenth century in America required and, in the successful sciences, led to newer, better, and higher levels of generalization.[15] The "geographical details" of the new nation, one can infer, were of paramount interest to the people and of vital importance to the government, but since there were no appropriate organizing concepts of relations beyond existing nominal categories in special geography, it was "academic geography" as a new subject in the lower schools that emerged to transmit this mass of random, undirected, undigested geographical detail to the youth of the citizenry. Descriptions of this along with connections to patriotism, bias, and prejudice are to be found also in *Geography Now and Then* and certain of the works I cite there. However, let us now consider the *Geographia Generalis.*

The Development of the "Geographia Generalis Varenii"

In 1650, the Elzevir Press of Amsterdam published the *Geographia Generalis* by Bernhardus Varenius, M.D., a German-born refugee scholar who had been educated at Leyden University and was still living and working in the Netherlands. This 784-page duodecimo book in Latin (unchanged 1664 and 1671 editions also) is cited frequently now as the first truly modern comprehensive scientific statement of geography (concepts *and* data) as an intellectual discipline, presaging "The Enlightenment" to come in geography as in other disciplines. Such current recognition, however, seems to derive not from ongoing evaluation and critical discussions of the work, but rather from the transmittal in sloganlike fashion from generation to generation of the nineteenth-century encomium of this work by Alexander von Humboldt in his *Kosmos*. His tribute was not without error, however, in its statements of sequence of editions.

No published modern English translation from the original Latin of the 1650 *Geographia Generalis* exists, nor has the work been discussed critically in light of the methods, techniques, and demands of current scholarship with respect to the sources of its contents; their substantial development through subsequent Latin editions by Isaac Newton and his disciple, James Jurin, at Cambridge University; and the social and cultural milieu of the presentations, and the direct and indirect impacts on academic and scientific life in Europe and North America in succeeding years of these early works and their derivatives.

My current research involves the translation into English of the original 1650 work and also of the revisions and additions made in subsequent editions, including especially those edited and substantially revised by Isaac Newton and published in Latin at Cambridge, England, in 1672 and 1681. Newton added many important tables and especially thirty-three diagrams or schemes particularly of geometrical application to geographical phenomena when he adapted and revised this work for his students at Trinity College, Cambridge. It was Newton's responsibility, as defined in the terms of his appointment, to lecture, tutor, and assign readings in mathematics and natural philosophy when he succeeded in 1669 to the Lucasian Professorship (as second incumbent) at Cambridge University. He was charged, as a part of his duties detailed in the statutes pertaining to the Lucasian Professorship, specifically with responsibility for instruction in geography as a part of natural philosophy. It was in connection with these responsibilities and opportunities as Lucasian Professor that Isaac Newton twice revised the *Geographia Generalis.* Also being considered is the Cambridge edition of 1712 by Dr. James Jurin, intellectually and literally a student of Newton, who incorporated in an appendix many more changes based upon Newton's contributions to science in the intervening years. This work was done in the direct line of Newton and his associates with the strong support and determination of Richard Bentley, the dynamic, influential, and extraordinarily contro-versial master of Trinity College, Cambridge, who upon gaining control of the university press wished to use this work, among others,as at once a political and an intellectual weapon against his adversaries in the university. Jurin was materially assisted in this also by Roger Cotes, who shortly thereafter distinguished himself by his significant substantive revisions of Newton's *Principia* (1687) in 1713.

The Jurin edition of the *Geographia Generalis* represents the definitive statement of Isaac Newton on geography at Cambridge then, as it draws from Newton's *Principia* and also from Newton's (and many others') contributions to the *Philosophical Transactions* of the Royal Society and elsewhere. Other editions to be considered are those from Jena, Germany (1693), and Naples, Italy (1715), both in Latin. These seem to be merely reprintings of the second Newton edition and the Jurin edition respectively, although this matter, of course, must be investigated in detail. Derivative volumes to be regarded include Richard Blomes's *Cosmography and Geography*—an often inaccurate, confused, and, in parts, worthless work based on Varenius and Sanson (London: 1682), with unchanged editions following in 1683 and 1693—and the more respectable Dugdale's *A Compleate System of General Geography* (London: 1733).

The Dugdale work was advertised as revised and corrected with large additions by Peter Shaw, M.D. Three more editions appeared, with the last of these (i.e., the fourth edition) in 1765. In many of its sections, of course, it has its own introduced strengths and weaknesses.

The editions of Varenius, Newton, and Jurin were studied in their turn in the earliest of the American colonial colleges but it is, of course, a Dugdale and Shaw edition that was referred to frequently as the Varenius to be read in the American colleges just prior to the American Revolution. It can not, however, in itself, be regarded as a fair indication of the actual sequences and development of ideas in the presentations of Varenius and Newton. Further modifications occur in a number of subsequent European works which appear to be translations from the English works of Blome or of Dugdale and Shaw. Examples include volumes published in Dutch (Haarlem: 1750), definitely a translation from early Dugdale and Shaw; and in French (Paris: 1755), also from Dugdale and Shaw. Other editions of interest include those in German (e.g., Gottingen: 1755) and in Russian (Moscow: 1718) translated from the "Cambridge Latin edition," or at least sponsored, by Peter the Great (i.e., Czar Peter I of Russia), himself. In 1932 a Japanese translation of selected extracts appeared. In the author's present research there are under consideration the six basic Latin editions, and nineteen related versions in English or other European languages. The effort will continue to trace all related works. It will require diligence especially since virtually every standard reference encyclopedia, for example, cites editions which have never existed and omits some that do. As noted, von Humboldt in his *Kosmos* clearly was in error in his accounting of extant editions. This is one important original source of error. The other original source of error seems to lie in a footnote added by Hutton, et al., in the later abridgements of the very early *Philosophical Transactions* of the Royal Society, 1809. There is a tangle.

The *Geographia Generalis* focused, as the title suggests, on general (or universal) geography. General geography was one of the two major divisions of the work, the other being "special" geography, which Varenius defined, outlined, and subdivided but did not deal with. General geography was subdivided into three parts: the absolute part (which dealt with the form, dimensions, and position of the earth; the distribution of lands, water, mountains, woods, deserts; hydrography and the atmosphere); the relative part (which dealt with the appearance of the earth and accidents that happen to it from celestial causes: i.e., latitude, climatic zones, longitude, etc.); and the comparative part (which contained an explication of those properties which arise from comparing different parts of the earth together). Varenius defined geography as "that part of mixed [i.e., applied] mathematics which explains the state of the earth and of its parts, depending on quantity, viz., its figure, place, magnitude and motion, with the celestial appearances."[16]

Varenius dealt with the rotundity, dimension, movements, and climatic divisions of the earth. Here the works of Copernicus, Kepler, Galileo, and especially Descartes were applied for the first time to a major geographical treatise. Varenius described various methods of map projection. He noted that the study of air, its composition and physical properties, and the laws of motion should form the basis of meteorology. The sun was the source of heat, and he drew correlations between movements of air and the "movements" of the sun. He also discussed precipitation, and elaborated upon regional climatic variations as well as the traditional classical zones.

In the section on hydrography, Varenius made statements concerning the origins of rivers and seas, and variations in levels of seas and oceans. He divided ocean movements into two types (currents and tides), gave reasons for their existence, and noted a current flowing out of the Gulf of

Mexico, though he did not realize the climatic importance of this Gulf Stream.

The section in the *Geographia Generalis* on physical features included Varenius's theory of the origin of mountains, coastal and fluvial shoreline deposition, and morphology. He also announced his belief in erosion by the sea, but not by running water.

Varenius did not deal with details of special geography of the world in the *Geographia Generalis*. (However, he announced in the *Geographia Generalis* his intentions to do this as a future work. He perhaps would have done so had he not died at the age of twenty-eight in 1650). But he set out in the *Geographis Generalis* the following categories for presentations in that branch of geography: celestial properties (the appearance of the heavens and climate); terrestrial properties (those which are observed on the face of every country, viz. position, boundaries, shape and size, mountains, rivers, woods and deserts, fertility, minerals and animals); and human properties (i.e., the description of inhabitants, food and drink, their appearances, arts, commerce, culture, language, government, religion, cities and famous places, and famous men and women).

Moreover, as J. N. L. Baker has shown,[17] the outline for special geography set forth but not elaborated in the *Geographia Generalis* was very nearly exactly the one filled in by Varenius in his detailed *Descriptio Regni Japoniae et Siam* published in Amsterdam in 1649, the year before his general geography. Varenius realized then, as we do now, the great value, indeed the ofttimes crucial importance, of detailed descriptions of particular places. His interest in and concern for the merchants in the important trade center of Amsterdam attests to that. Yet Varenius chose not to include special geography in his general geography textbook, for that is exactly what he intended it to be, saying that much of special geography can not be proved by mathematical laws or derived deductively, but must rest on experience. Varenius himself depended upon the traders who visited Amsterdam for much of his knowledge of special geography.

Clearly, general laws and that which could be demonstrated from them or described with reference to them were of paramount concern to Varenius in this work intended for university students. While not denying the necessity of recognizing special geography in the completeness of the whole subject, Varenius apparently felt that general geography was most suitable for study at higher levels, and that it had not been receiving proper consideration.

The terms *general* and *special* as applied to geography were not original with Varenius. They had been used, for example, by Bartholomew

Keckermann in his *Systema Compendiosum: totius mathematices, hoc est, Geometriae, Opticae, Astronomiae, et Geographiae*, published in Hanover in 1617 after Keckermann's death. Varenius is known to have made use of this work, the principal contents of which had been given as a series of lectures at Danzig in 1603. Varenius also used Keckermann's *Brevis Commentatio Nautica*, also published in 1617. Keckermann had written a third book, *Geographia seu Brevissima Geographiam Manductio*, of less significance. Golnitzius had stated in 1643 that geography is to be explained externally and internally, but Varenius rejected these specific terms, so suggestive of the modern concepts of "site" and "position," as improper and ill chosen.

That ancient Aristotelean-Platonic debate concerning the relationship of the general to the special—the universal to the particular—was, of course, a focus of attention in the seventeenth-and eighteenth-century search for system in the various fields of learning, and it was in this very sense that the *Geographia Generalis* (and the subsequent editions which transformed it slowly, carefully, and cautiously from a Cartesian work to a thoroughly Newtonian one) made its impact and important contribution to British and North American learning. Of particular importance is the caution and concern shown by Newton himself, however, in this connection as, for example, his hesitation with regard to the dismissal of Descartes's vortices. The reasons have been made explicit in the work of D. T. Whiteside concerning Newton's mathematics.[18]

It is, as noted earlier, the Jurin edition that is to be regarded as the definitive Cambridge-Newton edition. And it is the Dugdale-Shaw editions commencing in 1733 that display the full flower of Newtonian science in geography, drawing heavily as they do upon the spate of relevant publications in science at that time. (The Dugdale and Shaw work was no relic preserving the contents of an "outdated" text although it did retain the outline. Rather, it attempted to be a modern geography text and it succeeded. And that very fact requires the historian of science to go to the 1650 and susequent editions to trace the development of ideas.)

An examination of the original sources for certain data and concepts employed by the various authors and revisers of the *Geographia Generalis* reveals a remarkable range from the scientific works of classical Greece, through the writings of medieval scholars, to the substantial works of the contemporaries of Varenius, Newton, and Jurin in Holland and England. In the 1650 edition about 300 classical and contemporary authorities were cited. By the time of the Cambridge Latin edition of 1712, the total had reached nearly 400 and in the 1733 English language derived edition about 450, these eighteenth-century additions deriving solely from contemporary work in geography.

Varenius's treatment of general geography was comprehensive, detailed, and insightful. His ideas were in advance of the general presentation of geography in the mid-seventeenth century. It must always be remembered, however, that the work was intended simply as a textbook for beginning university students and not as an advanced treatise for scholars, and that the mathematics, although strongly endorsed and stressed, were at an intermediate level. However, in Europe, England, and America the work was also read with approval by men of affairs outside the universities.

As noted above, the original edition by Varenius is significant in the very important respect that it embodied and exemplified the philosophy and the physics of Descartes. This work, along with other thoroughly Cartesian works, proved initially attractive to the Cambridge Platonists in their continuing search for an accommodation of religion and natural philosophy, and the introduction of the *Geographia Generalis* into Cambridge University in the 1660s was as part of the Cambridge Platonist movement. The place of the work itself, at least as its author perceived it, in the general intellectual scheme of things in the Europe of the day can be assayed from Varenius's statements in his "Epistola Dedicatoria" to those establishment members in the Netherlands whose support and patronage he sought.

In these prefatory remarks, for example, Varenius discusses and critizes four schemes on human ecology. He takes great pains to argue for and demonstate the "unity of nature." In essence, Varenius joined in the attempt to overthrow the scholastics' statement of the Aristotelean cosmology, with its conception of different orders of being and perfection and the essential assertion that everything in the heavens was perfect. These conceptions were, of course, being attacked on a multitude of fronts in science and art, and with an increasing boldness. It is worth examining the *Geographia Generalis* as a work of the rising scepticism joining reason and empiricism.

Varenius also points out that those who have hitherto written on geography

have treated almost exclusively of Special Geography, and at tedious length. They have described very little which concerns General Geography, ignoring or completely omitting many necessary aspects of the subject. The result is that our young men while learning more and more Special Geography are largely ignorant of the foundations of the study, and thus Geography scarcely vindicates her claims to be called a Science.

I saw this state of affairs, and to remedy what was amiss, I began to bend my thought towards supplying the deficiency by composing a General Geography. I did not desist from my labors until I had completed the task. According to such powers as God has granted me, cultivated by years spent in Mathematics, my object was to render service to the World of Letters and to the studies of youth or at least to leave no doupt of my good-will to do so.[19]

It is this same concern for the general and the special that underpinned the attention to and the cultivation of *Geographia Generalis* in seventeenth-and eighteenth-century Cambridge and, as it happened, Oxford University, and most importantly, in the terms of reference of this volume on the origins of American academic geography, in the American colonial colleges. It is foolish, of course, to attribute too much importance to this book, a single minor one, in the overall scheme of things. Yet the *Geographia Generalis* was in so very many ways typical of the new knowledge, the organization of thought, and the philosophical attitudes that constituted the intellectual framework for not only the academic origins of geography and the organization of the colleges, but especially the political origins of the new American republic. It is only in such a context, or a more recondite rival one, that the origins of academic geography in the United States should be assessed. The persistent interplay of "general" and "special," and the attendant swings between isolationism and internationalism have seemed to dominate the life of the nation itself, and with it the organization of the academic discipline of geography within its colleges. It remains a vital concern today.

The following table summarizes these ideas, and provides a framework against which geography and its several American revivals through time might be judged.

Acknowledgements

Acknowledgement is made, with gratitude, of the continuing support of the Social Sciences and Humanities Research Council of Canada in the investigation of various ramifications of the "Development of the *Geographia Generalis Varenii.*" The author wishes also to express his deep appreciation to the fellows and members of Clare Hall college, University of Cambridge, for the opportunities they provide him to continue his research in this and other matters.

TABLE 1

SOME ASPECTS OF THE ORIGIN AND CYCLES OF
AMERICAN ACADEMIC GEOGRAPHY

Period	National Attitudes	Status of Academic Geography
I. Colonial—culminating in the Revolutionary War and the establishment of contitutional government (c. 1790)	Internationalism	General geography in prominent position in college curriculum. Education for leadership. Systematic geography featuring the "Use of the Globes" in framework of natural law.
II. Rounding of the republic to the Civil War	Isolationism	Geography dismissed from the colleges as emphasis shifted to encyclopedic special regional description in the subject for the schools. Individuality and uniqueness of areas stressed as natural rights philosophy gained upper hand.
III. Civil War to World War I	Internationalism	General geography again offered in colleges. Natural law emphasized through teleology and then evolution. Environmental determinism organized discipline but failed to admit importance of growing "sociological intensity."

TABLE 1
(continued)

Period	National Attitudes	Status of Academic Geography
IV. World War I to World War II	Isolationism	Special geography leading to alleged "regional sytheses." Microgeography, as reaction to excesses of environmental determinism, unfortunately involved loss of broad outlook and methods to handle significant aspects of human geography. Subject grew on basis of regionally organized public colleges, but declined very seriously in outstanding private colleges important in the education of the nation's leaders as no suitable analysis of sociological intensity emerged to organize descriptions.
V. Post World War II (c. 1955)	Internationalism	Sociological intensity defined and analyzed. The conceptual revolution in geography. Systems, models of interactions, flows, mathematical-logical formulations, spatial-predictive capacities combine to regain for geography some prominence in academia and a recovery of lost prestige.

[Periods I and II constituted the first cycle and periods III and IV the second cycle of academic geography in the United States. Period V entails a most remarkable "new departure" in the conception of geography. Will this also prove to be cyclical in nature?]

Notes

1. P. E. James and C. F. Jones, eds., *American Geography: Inventory and Prospect* (Syracuse, N.Y.: Syracuse University Press for The Association of American Geographers, 1954), p. 23.
2. Richard Hartshorne, *The Nature of Geography, Annals of the Association of American Geographers* (Lancaster, Pa.: The Association of American Geographers, 1939), pp. 22–23.
3. John K. Wright, "Daniel Coit Gilman, Geographer and Historian," *Geographical Review* 51 (1961): 381–99. See especially p. 383, including note 1.
4. William Warntz, *Geography Now and Then* (New York: American Geographical Society, 1964).
5. The colleges with pre—revolutionary War origins are: Harvard, 1636; William and Mary, 1693; Yale, 1701; Pennsylvania (College of Philadelphia), 1740; Princeton (College of New Jersey), 1746; Columbia (King's College), 1754; Brown (College of Rhode Island), 1764; Dartmouth, 1769; Rutgers (Queen's College), 1776.
6. Ralph H. Brown, "A Plea for Geography, 1813 Style," *Annals of the Association of American Geographers* (1951): 233.
7. W. O. Clough, *Intellectual Origins of American National Thought* 2d rev. ed. (New York: Corinth Books, 1955), pp. 3–4.
8. Ibid.
9. Frances Fitzgerald, *America Revised* (Boston: Atlantic-Little, Brown, 1979).
10. Daniel J. Boorstin, *The Americans: Colonial Experience* (New York: Vintage Books, 1958), p. 393.
11. Ibid., p. 184.
12. Quoted by Clough, *Intellectual Origins*, p. 13.
13. Ibid.
14. Woodrow Wilson, "Constitutional Government in the United States," in *The Papers of Woodrow Wilson*, ed. Arthur S. Link (Princeton: Princeton University Press, 1974), 18:106.
15. George H. Daniels, *American Science in the Age of Jackson* (New York: Columbia University Press, 1968), p. 102.
16. Varenius, Bernhardus, *Geographia Generalis* (Amsterdam: Elsevir Press, 1650), p. 1 (my translation).
17. J. N. L. Baker, "The Geography of Bernhard Varenius," *Transactions and Papers of the British Institute of Geographers*, Publ. no. 21 (1955):53–55.
18. D. T. Whiteside, *The Mathematical Papers of Isaac Newton*, Vols. 1–7 (Cambridge: University Press, Cambridge, 1967–). (The final volume is in preparation.) This monumental work goes far beyond the mathematical papers of Newton, and provides the most penetrating insights available into the scientific and the general mathematical thoughts and modes of the seventeenth and early eighteenth centuries.
19. Varenius, *Geographia Generalis*, "Epistola Dedicatoria" (my translation).

Darwin's Influence on the Development of Geography in the United States, 1859–1914

David R. Stoddart

Introduction

The general outlines of the impact of Darwinian thinking on geography are now so well known that the fact is often overlooked that there are almost no detailed studies of the manner in which this influence was transmitted, and the ways in which individual geographers became aware of and reacted to the intellectual revolution which Darwin's work required. That geographers saw in Darwin's work the concepts of progressive change, of organization, and environmental influence, but not that of chance, is widely accepted (Stoddart 1966), but how these ideas were accepted, and by whom, has been only superficially explored. In this essay I discuss the impact of Darwinian views on academic geography in the United States in the half-century following the publication of *The Origin of Species*. I wish to explore the questions already outlined, but also to suggest reasons why answers to them have as yet scarcely been sought.

The first edition of *The Origin* was published in London on 24 November 1859. Almost two weeks earlier, on 11 November, Darwin had sent advance copies across the Atlantic: to Louis Agassiz and J. D. Dana, expecting opposition, and one, more hopefully to Asa Gray. Pirated editions appeared in New York in January 1860, and within months the book had provoked sharp controversy. Gray reviewed it in the *American Journal of Sciences and Arts* in March 1860, and Agassiz, "very much annoyed by it,"[1] replied in July.

The main lineaments of the book's reception in America have been described by Loewenberg (1933, 1935) and Smallwood (1941). Americans had the advantage of being able to read the book it its original language, and of having the argument forcefully presented and interpreted by Asa

265

Gray, whose *Darwiniana* (1876) collected many of his periodical essays. But there was also severe opposition, led but by no means typified by Agassiz, and for a time also the full impact of Darwin's views was muted by the preoccupations of the Civil War. In considering the reactions of geographers to this extended controversy, it will be convenient first to discuss those who were already senior and established in 1859; second, those in early adulthood at the time of publication; and third, those born later in the century for whom the experience of evolutionary thought was necessarily derivative.

The Immediate Reaction

The first group is a small one, and consists mainly of George Perkins Marsh (1801–82), Matthew Fontaine Maury (1806–73), and Arnold Guyot (1807–84). Of these, only Guyot occupied an academic position, as professor of geography and geology at Princeton from 1854. He was a deeply religious man, whose geographical philosophy (in, for example, *The Earth and Man*, 1850) mirrored that of Ritter (Libbey 1884; Dana 1886; Jones 1929). When *The Origin* appeared Guyot was occupied with delivering eulogies of Humboldt and Ritter to the American Geographical Society: his admiration for the former was qualified, for the latter unrestrained—"Humboldt furnishes the means; Ritter marks the goal" in understanding the earth (Guyot 1860, p. 63). Not surprisingly, in his fifty-third year, Guyot had nothing to learn from *The Origin*: he wrote to Asa Gray on 20 April 1860 insisting on the importance of "the Creator's plan,"[2] and even in the year of his death was still attempting to reconcile his own versions of science and religion, in his *Creation, or the Biblical Cosmogony in the Light of Modern Science* (1884). As Dryer (1920, p. 7) much later pointed out, it was Guyot's "tragic fate" never to know that his philosophy had been destroyed in 1859.

Maury, also a religious man, proved equally impervious. His inaugural address at the University of the South on 30 November 1860 was pure teleology: physical geography, "based on the Biblical doctrine 'that the earth was made for man,'" is of all subjects "the most Christianising." He was particularly dismissive of those who declined to accept the Bible as an authority in this field: "the fault is not with the witness of His records, but with the worm who essays to interpret evidence which he does not understand" (Maury 1860, in Corbin 1888, pp. 176, 178; see also Williams 1963).

Of the three, George Perkins Marsh was the only unreligious man. A lapsed Calvinist, he was disgusted by the "miserable" sectarianism of the

David R. Stoddart

churches, and in 1877 lamented that he had "given nine-tenths of my long years to sin, one tenth to remorse, nothing to repentance."[3] He was also the only one to make explicit use of Darwin's work, though the three citations in his *Man and Nature* (1864)—to earthworms, orchids, and plants in heath and woodland—are all trivial. There is nothing in his philosophy of physical geography as late as 1869 to suggest direct Darwinian influence (Lowenthal 1960).

The Younger Men

In a sense this initial reaction by geographers is not surprising. The 1860s and early 1870s were years of religious opposition as well as scientific scepticism, and the tide did not begin to turn until the death of Louis Agassiz in 1873. Othniel C. Marsh had been building up fossil evidence from the West for vertebrate evolution through the 1860s; Clarence Dutton accepted an evolutionary interpretation of fossil Mollusca in 1871; and James Dwight Dana, whose long discussion of "Science and the Bible" (1856–57) just predated *The Origin* (which he avoided reading for years on the grounds of illhealth), finally admitted evolution into the second edition of his *Manual of Geology* in 1874.[4]

In this reversal, one of the catalysts was Daniel Coit Gilman (1831–1908), professor of physical and political geography at Yale from 1863 to 1872, president of the University of California 1872–75, and subsequently president of the Johns Hopkins University. Although primarily a university administrator (Flexner 1946), Gilman lectured on biblical as well as other aspects of geography (Wright 1961). He had known Ritter in the latter's declining years, and as a student at Harvard had even lived in Arnold Guyot's house. Yet he kept an open mind, and it was he who was responsible for inviting Thomas Henry Huxley to give the inaugural lecture at the opening of the Johns Hopkins University in Baltimore on 12 September 1876. Huxley, who spoke "On University education,"[5] also lectured widely on evolution and confirmed at Yale Marsh's interpretation of the history of the horse. His lecture was a triumph,[6] and it is strange that Wright (1961), in his evaluation of Gilman, fails to see the significance of this event, not so much in what was said but more in the fact that Gilman, with his background, was able to invite so redoubtable an agnostic and evolutionist as Huxley to speak at all at such an event.

While creating an academic atmosphere in which Darwinian views could be discussed, however, Gilman's own administrative duties prevented him from doing so within geography itself. Thomas Chrowder

267

Chamberlin (1843–1928) occupied a similar position, first as president of the University of Wisconsin, then as head of the Department of Geology at the University of Chicago from 1892 to 1919, but thoughout his life he continued to publish scientific work. Chamberlin had taken Darwin as an "intellectual exemplar" while still a student (Pyne 1978, p. 414), and while it is often said that he resisted Davis's concept of the cycle of erosion, there is no doubt that evolutionary ideas permeated his theoretical work. While accepting evolution in scientific explanation, however, he could not, as an Arminian Christian, divorce his science from questions of morality and ethics (Winnik 1970, pp. 451–52). Perhaps in consequence he did not develop the single-minded enthusiasm for evolutionary interpretations of some of his contemporaries, but just as at Johns Hopkins Gilman created the open-minded intellectual environment in which men such as Frederick Jackson Turner developed their ideas, so too with Chamberlin at Chicago. Here he encouraged the emergence of geography as an integral discipline, first with Rollin D. Salisbury (1858—1922) as professor of geographic geology, and after 1903 with a separate Department of Geography.

Many of Gilman's and Chamberlin's contemporaries in the earth sciences were mainly practical men, better known as field scientists than as philosophers. They included Cleveland Abbe (1838–1916), Clarence E. Dutton (1841-1912), and N. S. Shaler (1841–1906). All were young men in 1859. They were geologists or physiographers rather than geographers, and it is not difficult to read into their historical interpretations of landforms the format of evolution. Shaler, whose work converged with that of George Perkins Marsh, demurred as a religious man over some of the apparent social implications of Darwinism (Shaler 1879), but his geographical writing was impressionistic and lacking in rigor, and this was recognized even by his peers. Of this group the two most distinguished, for very different reasons, were G. K. Gilbert (1843–1918) and John Wesley Powell (1834—1902). Perhaps alone, Gilbert combined rationalist beliefs[7] with what amounted to "indifference" to Darwin (Pyne 1978, p. 414; Baker and Pyne 1978), and he stands apart from the prevailing modes of explanation of the second half of the nineteenth century.

John Wesley Powell's science is antithetical to Gilbert's in many respects, but while he is generally known as geologist and physiographer a major part of his intellectual effort was devoted to the fields of anthropology and sociology, especially after his appointment as first director of the bureau of American Ethnology in 1879. At the end of 1876 he delivered at the American Geographical Society a "discourse on the philosophy of the North American Indians" (Powell 1878), and for a decade thereafter he wrote constantly on the implications of evolution for the human rather than the physical sciences. In this he was deeply influenced by Lewis Morgan, and also by his colleague, the Geological Survey's paleobotanist and founder of American sociology, Lester Ward.

Powell closely followed Huxley in his view of causality as a concept central to both the scientific method and the framework of evolution. In 1882, when Darwin died, Powell spoke at the National Museum of Natural History on "Darwin's contribution to philosophy" (Powell 1882), and made the connection explicit:

> Facts have genetic relations.... [The] highest function of scientific philosophy is to discover the order of succession of phenomena—how phenomena follow phenomena in endless procession, how every fact has had its antecedent facts, and every fact must have its consequent fact. This part of science is called *evolution*, and by this expression scientific men mean ... that the causes of all of the phenomena of the universe that we wish to explain in a system of philosophy run back into the infinite past; that the consequences of all of the phenomena which we may now observe in the universe will run on into the infinite future. This is evolution [Powell 1882, pp. 64–65].

But, like Kropotkin later, he declined to extend this simplistic framework to human beings:

> The laws of biotic evolution do not apply to mankind. There are men in the world so overwhelmed with the grandeur and truth of biotic evolution that they actually believe that man is but a two-legged beast whose progress in the world is governed by the same laws as the progress of the serpent or the wolf; and so science is put to shame.... That which makes man more than beast is culture. Culture is evolution [Powell 1890, pp. 4–5].

He emphasised altruism and cooperation in human societies, and bluntly stated that "morality repeals the law of the survival of the fittest in the struggle for existence" (Powell 1884, p. 48).

It was an argument he frequently repeated (Powell 1883, 1888), most formally in his *Truth and Error* (1898, pp. 200–201), the first and only volume of a treatise on knowledge dedicated to Lester Ward.[8] Yet it was an argument apparently unheeded, at least by geographers. Ellen Semple in her *Influences of Geographic Environment* quotes Powell but once, and then on a matter of fact, not philosophy. The propositions Powell was elaborating in the 1880s had to be painfully rediscovered by geographers in the 1920s and 1930s. Why was this so? Partly because his physiographic colleagues, with the exception of W J McGee, were not concerned. Partly because Powell was speaking directly to the newly organized fields of anthropology and sociology in North America, whose courses rapidly diverged from the earth sciences. But partly, and most simply, because there were at that time no geographers to talk to: except as a learned society the subject had yet to establish a corporate identity in North America.[9]

The New Geographers

The generation trained in the university departments established by Gilman and Chamberlin supplied the first generation of professional geographers in the United States. They had all been born fifteen to twenty-five years after the publication of *The Origin of Species*: by the time they came to maturity the impact of the book had been made and largely accepted, and both Darwin and Huxley were dead. The group included men who were to dominate the subject during the whole of their working lives, up to World War II, partly at least because the rapid expansion of departments of geography in the universities during the 1920s and 1930s created positions for them. They included W. W. Atwood, Sr. (1872–1949); O. E. Baker (1883–1950); H. H. Barrows (1877–1960); Isaiah Bowman (1878–1950); N. M. Fenneman (1865–1945); V. C. Finch (1883–1959); Ellsworth Huntington (1876–1947); D. W. Johnson (1878–1944); Wellington Jones (1886–1957); and J. Russell Smith (1874–1966).[10] In contrast to their predecessors, many were remarkable for the simplistic fervor of their "Darwinian" views, and several (such as Smith and Brigham) found no difficulty in reconciling religious conviction with such a social philosophy.[11]

Huxley himself had foreseen that this would happen. In his celebration of the "coming of age" of *The Origin of Species*, published in the year of Darwin's death, he noted that it was the "fate of new truths to begin as heresies and to end as superstitions," and he forecast that in another twenty years a new generation "will be in danger of accepting the main doctrines of the 'Origin of Species', with as little reflection ... as so many of our contemporaries, twenty years ago rejected them" (Huxley 1882, p. 312). By 1888, he noted, terms such as the "struggle for existence" and "natural selection" had become "household words and everyday conceptions" (Huxley 1888, p. 180), and had in consequence largely lost their technical connotation. And it was in this period, too, as we have seen with Powell, that such ideas penetrated into many aspects of social, economic, and political life, largely through the proselytizing writings of Herbert

Spencer, W. G. Sumner, and Lester Ward (Hofstadter 1955; Russett 1976), and thus became increasingly remote from their original context in the natural sciences.

That geographers continued to concern themselves primarily with the surface of the earth rather than with social and economic matters largely explains why these new interpretations affected them less than they did sociologists and political scientists. But they cannot have been unaware of the intellectual excitement surrounding them: Spencer's visit to the United States in 1882 made Darwinism respectable in the human sciences, just as had Huxley's for the natural six years before.

The Darwinian Paradigm

In this analysis I have made no mention of two figures who, through their uncompromising positions, may be said to typify and codify the impact of Darwin on geography in the United States. They are, of course, William Morris Davis (1850-1935) and Ellen Churchill Semple (1863-1932). As an adolescent and young man when *The Origin* was published, Davis made the most comprehensive and explicit admission of his intellectual debt. In 1900 he wrote that "the time is ripe for the introduction of these [evolutionary] ideas. The spirit of evolution has been breathed by the students of the generation now mature all through their growing years, and its application in all lines of study is demanded" (Davis 1909, p. 86). In the same paper, by powerful metaphor, he demonstrated how an evolutionary interpretation could organize the understanding of landforms in both time and space:

> in a word it lengthens our own life, so that we may, in imagination, picture the life of a geographical area as clearly as we now witness the life of a quick-growing plant, and thus as readily conceive and as little confuse the orderly development of the many parts of a landform, its divides, cliffs, slopes, and water courses, as we now distinguish the cotyledons, stems, buds, leaves, flowers, and fruit of a rapidly maturing annual that produces all these forms in appropriate order and position in the brief course of a single summer [Davis 1900, p. 169].

As early as 1884 Davis (1885) had used explicit biological terminology (birth, youth, adolescence, maturity, infantile features, struggle) in outlining what he then called a "cycle of life," and he later spoke of a process of "inorganic natural selection" being responsible for the drainage

271

adjustments in scarplands (Davis 1895, 1899). His own personal position, as demonstrated in "The faith of Reverent Science" (1934; Chorley, Beckinsale, and Dunn 1973, pp. 759-91) was rationalist, profoundly anticlerical, and quite incredulous of the early religious opposition to Darwin.

The metaphor of deterministic development in the individual plant is a curious one, given the random basis of variation implicit in Darwin's theory (Stoddart 1966, p. 695). There were two reasons for its use. First, as Davis stated at the end of his life, he was profoundly more impressed with the mystery of growth from egg or seed to adult than he was with the cumulated effect of small-scale changes over many generations (Davis 1934). And second, it accorded more readily with his philosophy of explanation through causality. The point is an important one, for Davis extended his explanatory views into a general framework for geography based on this principle:

> any statement is of geographical quality if it contains a reasonable relation between some inorganic element of the earth on which we live, acting as a control, and some element of the existence or growth or behavior or distribution of the earth's organic inhabitants, serving as a response.... There is, indeed, in this idea of a causal or explanatory relationship the most definite, if not the only, unifying principle that I can find in geography [Davis 1906, p. 72].

Without this causal relationship—which almost inevitably was expressed in deterministic terms—the studies properly belonged to other subjects. And as late as 1920 Dryer was to refer to "physiographic control and organic response" as "the most notable geographic phrase that has appeared in the English language in the 20th century" (1920, p. 8).

It is, of course, through this position, already undermined by the Harvard pragmatists, that Leighly (1955) explained the intellectual failure of physical geography within American geography, and Herbst (1961) saw the main reason for the demoralization of geography as an intellectual discipline after 1914. Yet misintepretation was built into the Darwinian revolution itself. For Huxley, through misinterpretation of the terms of the debate, chance was no more than ignorance of cause, and he insisted on "the absolute validity, in all times and under all circumstances, of the law of causation" (1888, pp. 199-200). His *Physiography* (1877) was structured around causality, which for him seemed less a methodological device than a description of reality (Stoddart 1976). In this at least he parallelled Maury's fundamentalism (in Corbin 1888, pp. 179-80), though for different reasons, and we have seen that Powell's position was no less extreme than Huxley's. Darwin himself merely compounded the difficulty with the profound ambiguity of his remark that "there is no more design ... than in the course which the wind blows" (Barlow 1958, p. 87).

There is no need to carry this analysis further, or to examine the later determinism of Semple, Barrows, and Huntington. The point has been established that those geographers who were most explicitly "Darwinian" in their views were mainly born twenty years after *The Origin* was published, and derived their ideas not from any reading of Darwin himself but from a confused and popularized amalgam of simplified notions in the way that Huxley feared would happen. Those most exposed to the new ideas in 1859 were least receptive to them. The breakthrough came with the spread of the new universities, and especially of the creation of a new atmosphere free from doctrinaire constraint, which in geography owed much to Gilman and to Chamberlin. That the ideas which came to dominate geography at the beginning of the twentieth century in the work of Semple and Huntington represented a cruder image of the Darwinian revolution was partly an accident of timing, partly a response (as Billington [1971, pp. 95-108] recognized of Turner) to more general currents of thought in both Europe and America.

Notes

1. Asa Gray to J. D. Hooker, 5 January 1869, quoted by F. Darwin (1887), 2:268.
2. A. H. Guyot to Asa Gray, 20 April 1860, quoted by Dupree (1959), p. 279.
3. George Perkins Marsh to F. P. Nash, quoted by Lowenthal (1958), p. 326.
4. Darwin sent Dana a copy of *The Origin* two weeks before publication with the "hope that you will read my book straight through" and would "spare time to read it with care" (C. Darwin to J. D. Dana, 11 November 1859; quoted by Sanford 1965, p. 535). As late as February 1863 Dana was writing to Darwin that he had still not read *The Origin*, on the bizarre and implausible grounds that "my head has all it can now do in my college duties" (quoted by Gilman 1899, p. 313). Given that Dana published his *Manual of Geology* in 1862 (812 pages) and a dozen papers on zoological systematics and geology in 1863, it is difficult to avoid the conclusion that he purposely *avoided* reading Darwin's book: he was, after all, a devoutly religious man all his life. In spite of not having read the book, he nevertheless specified his objections to evolutionary ideas in the *Manual of Geology*, and the letter to Darwin of 5 February 1863, quoted above, goes on to repeat his arguments. It is perhaps not surprising that Darwin replied somewhat stiffly: with respect to the doubts on evolution in the *Manual*, he wrote that "perhaps it would have been better if, when you had condemned all such views, you had stated that you had not been able yet to read it [i. e., *The Origin*]. But pray do not suppose that I think for one instant that, with your strong and slowly

acquired convictions and immense knowledge, you could have been converted. The utmost that I could have hoped would have been that you might possibly have been here or there staggered" (quoted by Gilman 1899, p. 315). Curiously, like Darwin, Dana spent the last thirty-six years of his life—beginning with a nervous breakdown in (of all years) 1859—in constant exhaustion and illness, and the two men used to commiserate with each other over their respective symptoms (Gilman 1899, pp. 311-14). It is tempting to see in Dana's ill health psychosomatic causes of the kind often advanced in explanation of Darwin's.

5. Published in *American Addresses* in 1877 and reprinted in *Science and Education* in 1893. See Huxley (1877b).
6. See the account given by L. Huxley (1900), 1: 467.
7. Davis (1927) treats Gilbert's religious views (or lack of them) at some length.
8. *Truth and Error* was to be followed by *Good and Evil* and *Pleasure and Pain*, but only part of the second appeared in the periodical literature. See the account by McGee (1903), p. 125.
9. The society was of course the American Geographical Society, whose *Journal*, by coincidence, commenced publication in 1859. I have found virtually no reference to *The Origin* or to Darwin in its pages, or those of the *Bulletin*, up to 1900. In his presidential address on the progress of physical geography, Judge Daly admitted that "Darwinism" was a "marked feature" of recent developments, and used such terms as struggle for existence, natural selection, and survival of the fittest; but he went on to complain that it ignored "a spiritual nature in man," and his heroes were Ritter, Varenius, and Mary Somerville rather than Huxley (Daly 1890, pp. 8-9).
10. There is little direct evidence of the acquaintance of most of these geographers with Darwin's own works. Curiously, Mark Jefferson (1863-1949) recorded that he was repelled by *The Origin of Species* and read little of it, in contrast to his excitement over Darwin's *Journal of Researches* (1839). In this case the impact of evolution was made by his reading in 1885-86 of John Fiske's *Excursions of an Evolutionist*, published in 1884. We owe these details to Martin's excellent biography (1968, p. 21).
11. Thus Smith, arguing the case for the new subject of economic geography, stated that: "The theory of evolution has paved the way for modern geography, which has had to await the development, spread, and general acceptance of the revolutionizing truths commonly associated with the name of Darwin" (Smith 1907, p. 472). Similar statements were frequent at this period.

References Cited

This list includes source references only, and not the many works to which only incidental text reference is made.

Baker, V. R., and Pyne, S. 1978. "G. K. Gilbert and Modern Geomorphology." *American Journal of Science* 278: 97-123.

274

Barlow, N., ed. 1958. *The Autobiography of Charles Darwin 1809-1882.* London: Collins.

Billington, R. A. 1971. *The Genesis of the Frontier Thesis: A Study in Historical Creativity.* San Marino: The Huntington Library.

Corbin, D. F. M. 1888. *A Life of Matthew Fontaine Maury, U.S.N. and C.S.N.* London: Sampson Low, Marston, Searle, and Rivington.

Daly, C. P. 1890. "Annual Address: On the Progress of Physical Geography." *Bulletin of the American Geographical Society* 22:1-55.

Dana, J. D. 1856-57. "Science and the Bible." *Bibliotheca Sacra* 13 (1856): 80-129, 631-56; 14 (1857): 388-413, 461-524.

———. 1886. "Arnold and Guyot." *American Journal of Science,* 3d ser., 31: 358-70.

Darwin, F., ed. 1887. *The Life and Letters of Charles Darwin, Including an Autobiographical Chapter,* 3 vols. London: John Murray.

Davis, W. M. 1885. "Geographic Classification, Illustrated by a Study of Plains, Plateaus and their Derivatives." *In Proceedings of the American Association for the Advancement of Science (33rd Meeting, Philadelphia. 1884*), pp. 428-32. Salem: The Association.

———. 1895. "The Development of Certain English Rivers." *Geographical Journal* 5: 127-46.

———. 1899. "The Drainage of Cuestas." *Proceeding of the Geologists' Association* 16: 75-93.

———. 1900. "The Physical Geography of the Lands." *Popular Science Monthly* 57: 157-70. Reprinted in D. W. Johnson, ed., *Geographical Essays* (Boston: Ginn and Co., 1909), pp. 70-86.

———. 1906. "An Inductive Study of the Content of Geography." *Bulletin of the American Geographical Society* 38: 67-84. Reprinted in D. W. Johnson, ed., *Geographicl Essays* (Boston: Ginn and co., 1909), pp. 3-22.

———. 1934. "The Faith of Reverent Science." *Scientific monthly* 38: 395-421. Reprinted in R. J. Chorley, R.P. Beckinsale, and A.J. Dunn, The History of the Study of Landforms or the Development of Geomorphology, vol. 2 *The Life and Work of William Morris Davis,* (London: Methuen, 1973), pp. 759-91.

Dryer, C. R. 1920. "Genetic Geography: The Development of the Geographic Sense and Concept." *Annals of the Association of American Geographers* 10: 3-16.

———. 1924. "A Century of Geographic Education in the United States." *Annals of the Association of American Geographers* 14: 117-49.

Dupree, A. H. 1959. *Asa Gray 1810-1888.* Cambridge, Mass.: Belknap Press.

Flexner, A. 1946. *Daniel Coit Gilman: Creator of the American Type of University.* New York: Harcourt Brace.

Gilman, D. C. 1899. *The Life of James Dwight Dana: Scientific Explorer, Mineralogist, Geologist, Zoologist, Professor in Yale University.* New York: Harper and Brothers Publishers.

Guyot, A. H. 1850. *The Earth and Man: Lectures on Comparative Physical Geography in Its Relation to the History of Mankind.* Translated by C. C. Felton. London: Richard Bentley.

———. 1860. "Carl Ritter: An Address to the Society." *Journal of the American Geographical Society* 2: 25-63.

Herbst, J. 1961. "Social Darwinism and the History of American Geography," *Proceedings of the American Philosophical Society 105:* 538-44.

Huxley, L., ed. 1900. *Life and Letters of Thomas Henry Huxley.* 2 vols. London: Macmillan.

Huxley, T. H. 1877a. *Physiography: An Introduction to the Study of Nature.* London: Macmillan.

———. 1877b. "On University Education." *In American Addresses, with a Lecture on the Study of Biology*, pp. 97-127. London: Macmillan. Reprinted in *Science and Education: Essays* (London: Macmillan, 1893), pp. 235-61.

———. 1882. "The Coming of Age of 'The Origin of Species'." *Proceedings of the Royal Society of London* 9: 361-68. Reprinted in *Science and Culture and Other Essays* (London: Macmillan, 1882), pp. 310-24.

———. 1888. "On the Reception of the 'Origin of Species'." In *The Life and Letters of Charles Darwin*, edited by F. Darwin, 2: 179-204.

Jones, L. C. 1929. "Arnold Guyot et Princeton." *Reoueil de Travaux publiés par la Faculté des Lettres, L'Université de Neuchâtel* 14: 1-125.

Leighly, J. 1955. "What Has Happened to Physical Geography?" Annals of *the Association of American Geographers* 45: 309-18.

Libbey, W. 1884. "The Life and Scientific Work of Arnold Guyot." *Journal of the American Geographical Society* 16: 194-221.

Loewenberg, B. J. 1933. "Darwinism Comes to America, 1859-1900." *American Historical Review* 38: 687-701.

———. 1935. "The Controversy over Evolution in New England, 1859-1873. "*New England Quarterly* 8: 323-57.

Lowenthal, D. 1958. *George Perkins Marsh: Versatile Vermonter.* New York: Columbia University Press.

———. 1960. "George Perkins Marsh on the Nature and Purpose of Geography." *Geographical Journal* 126: 413-17.

Marsh, G. P. 1864. *Man and Nature; or, Physical Geography as Modified by Human Action.* New York: Charles Scribner.

Martin, G. J. 1968. *Mark Jefferson, geographer,* Ypsilanti: Eastern Michigan University Press.

Maury, M. F. 1860. "Address on the Study of Physical Geography." In *A Life of Matthew Fontaine Maury, U.S.N. and C.S.N.,* by C. F. M. Corbin, pp. 176-180. London: Sampson Low, Marston, Searle, and Rivington.

McGee, W. J. 1903. "Powell as an Anthropologist." *Proceedings of the Washington Academy of Sciences* 5: 118-26.

Pfiefer, E. J. 1974. "United States." In *The Comparative Reception of Darwinism*, edited by T. F. Glick, pp. 168-206. Austin: University of Texas Press.

Powell, J. W. 1878. "A Discourse on the Philosophy of the North American Indians." *Journal of the American Geographical Society* 8: 251-68.

_____. 1882. "Darwin's Contribution to Philosophy." *Proceedings of the Biological Society of Washington* 1: 69-70

_____. 1883. "Human Evolution." *Transactions of the Anthropological Society of Washington* 2: 176-208.

_____. 1884. "The Three Methods of Evolution." *Bulletin of the Philosophical Society of Washington* 6: xxvii-lii.

_____. 1888a. "From Barbarism to Civilization." *American Anthropologist* 1: 97-123.

_____. 1888b. "Competition as a Factor in Human Evolution." *American Anthropologist* 1: 297-323.

_____. 1890. "Evolution of Music from Dance to Symphony. *Proceedings of the American Association for the Advancement of Science (38th Meeting, Toronto, 1889),* pp. 1-21. Salem: The Association.

_____. 1898. *Truth and Error, or the Science of Intellection.* London: Kegan Paul, Trench, Trübner and Co.

Pyne, S. J. 1978. "Methodologies for Geology: G. K. Gilbert and T. C. Chamberlin." *Isis* 69: 413-24.

Russett, C. E. 1976. *Darwin in America: The Intellectual Response 1865-1912.* San Francisco: W. H. Freeman.

Sanford, W. F., Jr. 1965. "Dana and Darwinism." *Journal of the History of Ideas* 26: 531-46.

Semple, E. C. 1911. *Influences of Geographic Environment on the Basis of Ratzel's System of Anthropo-geography.* New York: Henry Holt.

Shaler, N. S. 1879. "The Use of Numbers in Society." *Atlantic Monthly* 44: 321-33.

Smallwood, W. M. 1941. "How Darwinism Came to the United States." *Scientific Monthly* 52: 342-49.

Smith, J. R. 1907. "Economic Geography and Its Relation to Economic Theory and Higher Education." *Bulletin of the American Geographical Society* 39: 472-81.

Stoddart, D. R. 1966. "Darwin's Impact on Geography." *Annals of the Association of American Geographers* 56: 683-98.

———— 1975. "'That Victorian Science': Huxley's *Physiography* and Its Impact on Geography." *Transactions of the Institute of British Geographers* 66: 17-40.

Williams, F. L. 1963. *Matthew Fontaine Maury: Scientist of the Sea*. New Brunswick: Rutgers University Press.

Winnik, H. C. 1970. "Science and Morality in Thomas C. Chamberlin." *Journal of the History of Ideas* 31: 441-56.

Wright, J. K. 1961. "Daniel Coit Gilman: Geographer and Historian." *Geographical Review* 51: 381-99. Reprinted in *Human Nature in Geography, Fourteen Essays, 1925-1965* (Cambridge, Mass.: Harvard University Press, 1966), pp. 168-87.

Ontography and Davisian Physiography

Geoffrey J. Martin

Following the conceptualization of his "geographical cycle," first mentioned in 1884, Davis synthesized the work of Powell, Gilbert, Dutton, and the U. S. Geological Survey and attempted to bring system to the study of landforms. To the mass of data hitherto collected, Davis brought order and provided a terminology, numeracy, advocacy, and analysis. To the whole he gave the name *physiography*, a term borrowed from T. H. Huxley's *Physiography* (1878).[1] The detail of the intellectual structure which Davis created stands revealed in his biography.[2] Yet it was in the departure from this widely accepted physiography that twentieth-century U.S. geography received an initial and enduring inspiration. Physiography continued to find practitioners who, during Davis's lifetime, included more notably Douglas W. Johnson, Armin K. Lobeck, Nevin M. Fenneman, Lawrence Martin, Raphael Pumpelly, Erwin Raisz, T. Wayland Vaughan, and Jay B. Woodworth.

Davis proposed as geographic the relationship between some "inorganic element of the earth ... acting as a control ... and some element of the existence or growth or behavior or distribution of the earth's organic inhabitants, serving as a response."[3] This organic part of geography Davis referred to as ontography. The word *ontography* was apparently minted by Davis in 1902, though ontogeny (the history or science of the development of the individual being) and ontology (the science or study of being) preceded Davis's ontography. Davis's theme outlived the term he minted. He urged the study of organic response to a physical environment and thus stimulated disciplinary evolution. This Davisian approach, which perhaps created the first paradigm in U.S. geography, constituted a departure from his own physiography. A new synthesis for American geography had been initiated. J. Russell Smith has observed:

No one had more to do with the un-Davising of geography than did Davis himself. He went up and down the land between 1899 and

279

1903 delivering addresses before various scientific groups, laying out the point that geography was a relationship between the earth and the organisms that lived upon it. He is almost the father of the idea of relationship. The others had been geologists and interested in talking about the earth, describing the earth, telling how it got cut and chiseled and blown and washed into certain shapes.[4]

In "Systematic Geography," a paper Davis presented before the American Philosophical Society, he suggested:

Let it then be here agreed that the whole content of geography is the study of the relation of the earth and its inhabitants. ... It is the relationship between the physical environment and the environed organism, between physiography and ontography (to coin a word) that constitutes the essential principles of geography today. Mature, fully developed geography therefore involves the study of physiography and ontography in their mutual relations.[5]

He published on the need for and significance of ontographic study, but it was with his own students that he labored most vigorously. Those who studied under Davis and accepted to a larger or smaller extent his urging for ontography included Robet LeMoyne Barrett, Isaiah Bowman, Albert Perry Brigham, Alfred H. Brooks, Robert M. Brown, Collier Cobb, Sumner Cushing, Richard E. Dodge, Herbert E. Gregory, William M. Gregory, Ellsworth Huntington, Mark S. W. Jefferson, Curtis F. Marbut, Lawrence Martin, Vilhjalmur Stefannson, Ralph S. Tarr, Walter S. Tower, and Robert DeC. Ward.

In the courses Davis offered at Harvard, physiography was dominant, but he firmly insisted on the place of ontography. He persistently urged his students to take up the ontographic work. Three of his most eminent students,[6] Mark Jefferson (1863-1949), Ellsworth Huntington (1876-1947), and Isaiah Bowman (1878-1950), were to help develop the movement, each in his own way, for Davis had not designed ontography in any detail. Jefferson developed anthropography, Huntington developed the causal notion that led to a variety of physiological climatology, and Bowman developed regional geography.

To his student Mark Jefferson, whom he helped place in 1901 at the Michigan State Normal College (now Eastern Michigan University), Davis sent many a postcard urging more ontographic work. Jefferson studied the distribution of people on the earth in relation to Davisian physiography, which he termed anthropography: Jefferson's anthropography did not traffic in controls, influences, or determinisms. It was a splendid model of the proposed Davisian ontography and was typified by such papers as[7] "The Distribution of People in South America" (1907), "Where Men Live in North America" (1909), "The Anthropography of North America" (1911), "The Growth of American Cities"(1913), "Regional Characters in the Growth of American Cities" (1914), "Utah, the Oasis at the Foot of the Wasatch" (1915).

Jefferson's work in anthropography was augmented by the work (abstracted in the *Annals of the Association of American Geographers*) of several geographers including Marcel Aurousseau, "The Geographic Study of Population Groups" (1922); Clarence E. Batschelet's work for the U.S. Census Bureau; Frank M. Chapman, "The Distribution of Life in Colombia" (1913); and Frederick V. Emerson, "The Geographic Distribution of Slavery in Missouri" (1907), "Life Along the Graded Missouri" (1908), and "Population in Missouri as Related to Physiographic Provinces" (1910).

Ellsworth Huntington's first page of notes (on deposit at the Yale University library), taken as a student at Harvard on 9 February 1903 in Davis's course "Geology 6" say that ontography must supplement physiography in a total schema constituting the discipline. When Raphael Pumpelly undertook a "preliminary examination of the Trans-Caspian region"[8] in 1903, he took his former student of 1869-70, Davis, with him for the physio-geographical part of the preliminary reconnaissance. Davis selected Huntington as his assistant. Huntington's diaries of this trip contain numerous references to ontography: "to make a complete ontographic study of this region. You see we want to study not only the country and climate but the relation which these have had to life of every form."[9] He wrote numerous essays at this time with the help and approval of Davis; one such unpublished article was entitled "Bread-making: an Ontographic Example." Davis approved the direction of Huntington's work and arranged for the wealthy Robert Lemoyne Barrett to take Huntington to Inner Asia, 1905-6.[10] As a result of this expedition, Huntington wrote *The Pulse of Asia* (1907) while resident in Cambridge and while in frequent consultation with Davis. Huntington dedicated his book to Davis, "first of modern geographers." Huntington more so than any other of Davis's disciples pursued Davisian ontography, revealing something of this in a little-known article, "William Morris Davis, Geographer" published in *The Bulletin of the Geographical Society of Philadelphia* (1912).[11] In 1920, Huntington's *Principles of Human Geography* was published. It was the first human geography college text written by an American to be published in the United States. Davis wrote to Huntington "that the object of the book as a whole is excellent," but became quite bitter over Huntington's statement that "for practical purposes it makes relatively little difference how a plain or mountain originates."[12] Davis reasoned that ontography could not be developed apart from a logical and well reasoned physiography, that ontography could not stand apart and isolated from physiography.

> Personally, I do not believe that in the fuller geography ontography and especially its human phases will play the dominant part. Just in so far as one of two related factors is subordinated, and the other is made dominant, the relation between (and that is the essence of the fuller geography) becomes vague and undisciplinary.... [13]

Huntington's earliest work concerning influence, control, or determination by the physical environment was taken up by studies (abstracted in the *Annals of the Association of American Geographers*) such as Poultney Bigelow, "Influence of Climate on Human Features" (1914); Alfred H. Brooks, "The Influence of Geography on the Exploration and Settlement of Alaska" (1905), "Geographic Control in the Development of the Alaska Coal Fields" (1910), and "The Geography of Alaska in Its Relation to Man" (1915); Frank Carney, "Springs as a Geographic Control in Humid Climates" (1907), and "Geographical Influences in the Development of Ohio" (1908); Charles J. Kullmer, "Storm Frequency and Civilization," and "The Shift of the Storm Track" (1911); and works by Sumner W. Cushing, J. Walter Fewkes, Roderick Peattie, and Ray H. Whitbeck.

Ellen C. Semple trod the causal path independent of Huntington. She received her inspiration directly from Germany and more particularly from Friedrich Ratzel. When the Roorbach questionnaire was completed in 1914, twenty-two out of twenty-nine geographers opted to list "the exact determination of the influence of geographic environment" as the most important task confronting geographers.[14] But by the latter part of that same year, Brigham, at least has begun to recognize the difficulties inherent in the causal scheme. Brigham wrote of his own A.A.G. presidential address to Bowman: "You can put it down as 'Problems of Geographic Influence.' It's a tough nut. I don't know how much a fellow can crack it. Crack at it—I guess."[15]

Isaiah Bowman, having graduated from Harvard with a B.S degree in 1905, was placed by Davis in the Department of Geology and Geography at Yale University, where he remained until 1915. In 1906 Davis wrote to Bowman:

> You have an extraordinarily good chance, and I expect to see you make fine use of it. The chief thing I wish to emphasize is that you

should develop geography proper, physiography and ontography properly combined, and not simply physiography (as I have done too much).[16]

At Yale Bowman offered courses in regional geography which were among the first in the United States; he claimed that his regional course on Latin America was probably the first such in the country. During his ten years as a geographer at Yale, he made trips to South America in 1907, 1911, and 1913; the three expeditions meant a total of two thousand miles by mule through the Central Andes, eighteen months in the field, a camp at 4° F. below zero, and the discovery of human habitation in Peru at 17,100′. During these ten years he published twenty articles and four books. Bowman's response to Davis's admonition to "develop geography proper" is to be noted in the early papers (abstracted in the *Annals* of the association) he read before the Association of American Geographers: "Hogarth's 'The Nearest East' in Regional Geography" (1905); "The Deserts of Peru and Chile in South American History" (1906); "Geographic Relations in Chile and Bolivia" (1907); "Trade Routes in the Economic Geography of Bolivia" (1908); "The Regional Geography of Long Island" (1909); "The Geographical Results of the Yale Peruvian Expedition" (1911); "Lake Titicaca and the Rivers of Tiahuanaco" (1912); and "Results of an Expedition to the Central Andes" (1913). These papers were copied, read by other geographers lecturing in colleges and universities, and occasionally used as classroom texts. Bowman's 1905 paper is one of the earliest expressions of regional geography extant in North America.

Most notable of his regional work resultant to his South American travel and research are *The Andes of Southern Peru* (1916) and *Desert Trails of Atacama* (1924). The first of these books resulted from a two-hundred-mile transect from the Urubamba to Camana on the desert coast of Peru. This route along the seventy-third meridian was accurately mapped for the first time on the scale of 1:125,000, and eight regional diagrams were constructed to cover the same route. They bear "somewhat the same relation to the facts of human geography that a block diagram does to physiography."[17] These were apparently the first regional diagrams ever published. And original contributions were made on physiographic subjects including the origin of coastal terraces, dune formation, and the bergschrund hypothesis. *Desert Trails of Atacama* represented one of the earliest regional geography books written in the United States (probably the first was Bowman's improbably titled *Forest Physiography: Physiography of the United States and Principles of Soils in Relation to Forestry* [1911].

Bowman's work concerning the region was developed by studies such as Oliver E. Baker, "Agricultural Regions of the United States" (1916); Fred J. Breeze, "Southern Indiana: A Regional Study" (1919); Charles R. Dryer, "Natural Economic Regions" (1914); W. L. G. Joerg, "The Subdivisions of North America Into Natural Regions" (1913); Wellington D. Jones, "Geographic Regions and Their Sub-divisions as Illustrated by China" (1919); J. Russell Smith, "The Division of North America into Economic Regions" (1921), and "The Regional Map of North America" (1922); and Walter S. Tower, "The Importance of Studies in Regional Geography" (1905).

While these disciples of Davis were developing ontography, Emory R. Johnson, an economist at the Wharton School of Finance and Commerce at the University of Pennsylvania, began to offer economic geography in 1896.[18] J. Russell Smith, one of Johnson's students, aided him with a cost-benefit study of proposed routes of the Panama Canal in 1899-1901. Reflecting on his days at the Wharton School, J. Russell Smith later wrote:

There was in the college in the year 1900, a professor of geology or two and they had a course in physical geography which was practically straight physiography with a dozen or so students. In the Wharton School of Finance and Commerce on the other side of the square, they wanted geography not as a part of the training of specialists but as a part of students going into economics or business. There wasn't time for a preparatory course in physiography and geology, and meteorology, there was time for about one course or possibly, two.

I think the first book to meet that demand was Industrial and Commercial Geography by J. Russell Smith, published by Henry Holt & Co. in 1913. As an example of the two points of view, a good many men in economics getting hold of that book said, "Why, I can teach that book," and they did. A man in the University of Illinois taught it for 3 or 4 years and he had 600 students. That raised the ire of the Department of Geology, where they had a nice course in geology, physiography and a few other things. Geography, says they, should be taught in the Department of Geography, so they took it away from the economics man who had the 600 students and gave it to a nice, hard rock specialist over in the Department of Geology and Geography and in a short time he had ... 30 students.[19]

J. Paul Goode, a student of Davis, completed his doctorate in economics under Emory R. Johnson in 1901 at Pennsylvania. (His dissertation was entitled "The Influence of Physiographic Factors Upon the Occupations and Economic Development in the United States.") He continued to teach economic geography classes at Pennsylvania which included "Economic Geography of America," "Economic Geography of Europe," "Geomorphy with Economic Application," "Climatology with Applications in Economic Geography," "Political Geography," and "Geodesy and Cartography." In 1903 Goode received a call to Chicago from Rollin D. Salisbury. It was Goode who formulated the courses and course designs for the initial departmental offering at Chicago. This little-known fact is revealed in a letter Goode wrote to Bowman:

> Very few people know that it was my outline and argument that was presented at the University of Chicago on the formation of the Department of Geography in 1903. Every course that has been offered since, with one or two exceptions in the case of work outlined by Mr. Barrows, was outlined by me.[20]

At three consecutive meetings of the Association of American Geographers Goode read "Commercial Geography for Secondary Schools" (1905), "The Geographical Perspective in the Course of Study" (1906), and "A College Course in Ontography" (1907). In abstracting the latter paper Goode wrote:

> Outlines of a course in the principles of geography, with the purpose of emphasizing the inter-relationship of life and its physical environment. Essentially an elementary course in plant, animal and human ecology.[21]

That may well have been the first time the term *human ecology* was adopted in the history of U.S. geography. Significantly, Goode substitutes the notion of earth-organism reciprocity for the one-way environmental causality of Davis. Shortly thereafter Park, Burgess, and McKenzie (also of Chicago) exploited this theme in sociological studies. and in 1922 Barrows, in his now oft-quoted A.A.G. presidential address, "Geography as Human Ecology," took the term and theme to a wider audience of geographers.

Walter S. Tower replaced Goode at the University of Pennsylvania. He proceeded to offer initially the same set of courses as Goode, adding "Climate and Civilization" in 1906; then accepted a call to the Chicago Geography Department in 1911, following trial periods in two summer school sessions and publication in 1910 of a keen analysis of ontography.[22]

285

Though physiography was offered in many geography departments and probably a majority of geology departments until the early twenties, nonphysiographic courses proliferated. By 1902 Lincoln Hutchison at the University of California offered "Introduction to Economic Geography," "Geography of International Commerce," and "Commercial Resources of the Spanish-American Countries." In 1908 Lawrence Martin began offering "Regional Geography" at the University of Wisconsin, to be followed by "Economic Geography" (Whitbeck, 1909) and "Agricultural Geography" (Finch, 1911). Also in 1908 Edward Lehnerts at the University of Minnesota offered "Industrial Geography" and "Problems in Industrial Geography." By 1909 the University of Nebraska was offering "Industrial Geography" (Condra), "Regional Geography" (Bengtson), and "Field Geography" (a separate course for ladies was offered by Mrs. Condra); "Commercial Geography" was added in 1910 (Bengtson) and "Agricultural Industries" in 1912 (Condra and Bengtson). By 1915 Sauer was offering "Commercial Geography" and "General Geography" at the University of Michigan, to which he soon added "Strategic Geography," "Geography of North America," and "Field Course in Regional Geography." At the University of Missouri Thomas offered "Advanced Commercial Geography" in 1917; regional courses of North America, Europe, and Asia were introduced in 1918.

Davis had left Harvard in 1912, and although he remained authoritative and to an extent authoritarian in the established physiographic orthodoxy, eclecticism characterized the ontographic departure. Change in content and method of study within the United States was facilitated by the sophistication of European geography and more particularly the geographical events of 1911, 1912, and 1919.

In 1911 Davis led the Liverpool-Rome Geographical Pilgrimage. Davis took Mark Jefferson with him on this extended undertaking, which commenced in southern Ireland on 1 August and ended at Lugano, Italy, on 5 October. Thirty-two members of the excursion, representing fourteen countries, participated in what was essentially a traveling seminar. Davis remained in Europe that year lecturing in Germany, and preparing the European contingent for the American Geographical Society Transcontinental Exursion of the following summer. That excursion lasted eight weeks, and extended some thirteen thousand miles around the United States. All the while the more developed human geography of the forty-three European geographers was being rendered. Each evening discussion would follow the meal, and from this amalgam invaluable exchange occurred—the very sort of competitive discussion which hones untidy viewpoints and enlarges the structure of the paradigm. The European point of view enriched the American posture to an extraordinary extent.

> A very lively discussion it was that ended in Dr. Niermeyer telling Davis that he was no geographer but a geomorphologist.... Davis gave a talk last night on the physical features of the [Yellowstone] Park and then another on "method of geographic description." As usual he spoke only of physical geography. He is too fair to deny this when accused of it and admits that he is really a physical geographer, but when Dr. Niermeyer of Utrecht rose and called attention to the point, everyone got excited and seemed to feel that Niermeyer was out of order.[23]

And again in 1919 on the occasion of the Paris Peace Conference, the American geographers I. Bowman, A. H. Brooks, L. Dominian, M. Jefferson, and L. Martin and the physiographers D. W. Johnson and A. K. Lobeck were brought into close association with French geographical thinking. In the diaries maintained by Bowman and Jefferson at the time of the peace conference, it is revealed that the American geographers had frequent meals and discussions with, more particularly, Jean Brunhes, de Margerie, de Martonne, Albert Demangeon, Pierre Denis, Lucien Gallois, and Charles Rabot.

When Bowman was in Paris, Davis wrote to him:

> While you are abroad, will you not inquire as far as possible into the various societies of commercial geography? ... I have an idea that three such societies ought to be started in the U.S. One in New York, one in Chicago, one in San Francisco (or Seattle?). As to the one in New York, my difficulty is, as to its relations with the A.G.S. Is there room for both? I have written briefly on this point to J. R. Smith, and will talk it over in our committee meeting.... their publications also would be strictly along the economic lines, but even these lines ought in my opinion to have a physiographic basis.[24]

Davis, nearly seventy years old, was still finding enthusiasm for the amalgam of ontography and physiography. But as the twenties wore on Davis became deeply involved—almost obsessed—with *The Coral Reef Problem* (American Geographical Society, Special Publication, no. 9 [New York: American Geographical Society, 1928]), and then returned to a more elaborate geomorphology in which he exercised his knowledge of the Far West. Meanwhile a new disciplinary posture was advanced in Carl

Sauer's "Geography as Regional Economics" and *The Morphology of Landscape*.[25] The latter, a personal manifesto, offered the spectacle of an alternative to the Davisian cause—effect physiography and ontography. Although there remained a place for eclectics and eclecticism, the ambit of the discipline was removing itself from the immediate domain of Davisian physiography and concomitant ontography. Yet these physiographic and ontographic constructs remained a large, formative, and vital contribution to American geography in the making.

Notes

1. Thomas H. Huxley, *Physiography: An Introduction to the Study of Nature* (London: Macmillan, 1877).
2. Richard J. Chorley, Robert P. Beckinsale, and Antony J. Dunn, *The History of the Study of Landforms or the Development of Geomorphology, vol. 2 The Life and Work of William Morris Davis,* (London: Methuen, 1973), pp. xxii and 874.
3. William Morris Davis, "An Inductive Study of the Content of Geography," *Bulletin of the American Geographical Society* 38 (1906): 67-84.
4. Smith to Geoffrey J. Martin, June 1962.
5. William Morris Davis, "Systematic Geography," *Proceedings of the American Philosophical Society* (1902): 235-59.
6. Geoffrey J. Martin, *Mark Jefferson: Geographer* (Ypsilanti: Eastern Michigan University Press, 1968); idem, *Ellsworth Huntington: His Life and Thought* (Hamden, Conn.: Archon Books, 1973); idem, *The Life and Thought of Isaiah Bowman* (Hamden, Conn.: Archon Books, 1980).
7. The following references may be found in the abstracts of programs listed in the *Annals of the Association of American Geographers.*
8. Raphael Pumpelly, ed., *Explorations in Turkestan with an Account of the Basin of Eastern Persia and Sistan* (Washington, D.C.: Carnegie Institution, 1905), p. 3.
9. Diary of Ellsworth Huntington, 1903B, p. 7, Yale University manuscript and archive collection.
10. Geoffrey J. Martin, "Robert LeMoyne Barrett, 1871-1969: Last of the Founding Members of the Association of American Geographers," *The Professional Geographer* 24, no. 1 (Feburary 1972): 29-31.
11. Ellsworth Huntington, "William Morris Davis, Geographer," *The Bulletin of the Geographical Society of Philadelphia* 10, no. 4. (October 1912): 224-34.
12. Davis to Huntington, 9 July 1921, Yale Archives.
13. Davis to Huntington, 22 August 1921, Yale Archives, quoted in Martin, *Ellsworth Huntington,* pp. 136-37.
14. G. B. Roorbach, "The Trend of Modern Geography: A Symposium," *Bulletin of the American Geographical Society* 46, no. 2 (November 1914): 801-17.
15. Brigham to Bowman, 13 November 1914, Archives of the Association of American Geographers.

16. Davis to Bowman, 18 March 1906, G. J. Martin Archives.
17. Isaiah Bowman, *The Andes of Southern Peru* (New York: Henry Holt & Co., 1916), p. 51.
18. P. E. James and Geoffrey Martin, *The Association of American Geographers: The First Seventy Five Years, 1904-1979* (Washington, D.C.: Association of American Geographers, 1979), pp. 17-20.
19. Smith to Geoffrey J. Martin, June 1962.
20. Goode to Bowman, 24 October 1918, G. J. Martin Archives.
21. J. Paul Goode, "A College Course in Ontography," *Annals of the Association of American Geographers* 1 (1911): 111.
22. W. S. Tower, "Scientific Geography: The Relation of its Content to its Subdivisions," *Bulletin of the American Geographical Society* 42 (1910): 801-25.
23. Martin, *Mark Jefferson*, p. 140.
24. Davis to Bowman, 17 September 1919, G. J. Martin Archives.
25. Carl Sauer, "Geography as Regional Economics," *Annals of the Association of American Geographers* 11 (1921): 130-31; idem, *"The Morphology of Landscape,"* in Berkeley, University of California Publications in Geography, vol. 2, no.2, (Berkeley: University of California, 1925), pp. 19-54.

Textbook Chronicles: Disciplinary History and the Growth of Geographic Knowledge

Henry Aay

[The] transformation of the tombstones of the passionate dead into a set of hurdles for the living to leap on their way to [a] profession.

John Updike *A Month of Sundays*

Among the several genres of history of academic geography (for example, biographical, philosophical, thematic/topical, institutional/educational), disciplinary history represents perhaps the largest and most ambitious historical undertaking. Disciplinary history seeks to generalize and integrate into a single account the changing diversity of individual scholarly effort, of findings and concepts, of philosophical orientations and institutional settings that characterizes the field of geography at large, geography in a particular country, one of geography's subdisciplines, or a specific research program. In geography, disciplinary history most often has been organized around personalities, philosophical themes, and research trends; institutional and societal frameworks have been less common. While all divisions of works in the history of geography also deal with the question of conceptual and academic change, it is the particular task of disciplinary history to shed light on the larger scale structure of growth and change in geography. It is the purpose of this essay to examine this high-profile division of works in the history of geography, and seek to discover how the growth of geographic knowledge has been explored and presented in a number of large-scale English-language disciplinary histories.

Textbook Chronicles

The literature of the disciplinary history of geography is dominated by textbook surveys; moreover, these surveys also project to the geography profession at large the most visible and public profile for the history of geography. As textbooks, such histories exemplify the external motivations for producing studies in the history of a discipline: educational purposes pattern historiography in important ways. One main purpose is that history must possess contemporary usefulness. As such, disciplinary history as found in textbook chronicles aims to furnish students with a more complete understanding of the present state of affairs of their field. This pedagogic concern often lends itself to a "presentist" or "Whig" historiography that studies the past only with direct reference to the present.[1]

Presentism serves as a principle for organizing and streamlining history. It permits the writer to cut through the complexity and individuality of historical situations to present a chronicle of progressive events that converges smoothly with the present. It leads us to hunt for founders, precursors, anticipations, and analogues.[2] Presentist disciplinary history simplifies the process of historical change by abstracting the work and accomplishments of scholars from their contemporary milieux, and by regarding great people and great ideas as the primary agencies of change. Furthermore, with a goal of contemporary usefulness, little purpose is served by probing into the process and deeper structure of conceptual change; the *finished* products of past academic praxis—achievements, findings, theories, and techniques—are sufficient in and of themselves to understand the contributions of the past to the present.

A presentist perspective, in affirming the present state of affairs to be desirable or undesirable, pushes those people and ideas that have contributed very little to the here-and-now into the background. As a discipline develops and incorporates new viewpoints into its cognitive structure, its history requires extensive revision and rewriting. New philosophical and methodological points of view initiate, if not a search for new founders and antecedents, then a reappraisal of the contributions of the past to the present.[3] In many textbook chronicles there is an explicit or implicit view of the nature of the discipline that is highly determinative for the broad outline, if not the fine texture, of that discipline's past. These presentist philosophical assumptions serve both as selection criteria for what to include in textbook chronicles, and as standards for arbitrating issues in the study of the field's past.

Because the behavioral and social sciences are marked by ongoing debate about their nature and aims, they are particularly vulnerable to the vices of presentism. George W. Stocking, Jr., supplies such a lucid summary of the reasons for and consequences of presentism in these fields that I will quote from his work at some length:

> When there is no simple framework which unites all the workers in a field, but rather competing points of view or competing schools, *historiography simply extends the arena of competition among them.* At its most neutral, the result is the sterile tracing of theoretical lineages which is served up in "history of theory" courses in many behavioral science departments. As the degree of partisan involvement and historiographical effort increases, the author may attempt to legitimize a present point of view by claiming for it a putative "founder" of the discipline. Or he may sweep broadly across the history of a discipline, brushing out whigs and tories in the nooks and crannies of every century. Inevitably the sins of history written "for the sake of the present" insinuate themselves: anachronism, distortion, misleading analogy, neglect of context, oversimplification of process [italics mine].[4]

The functional nature of textbook chronicles may also be seen perhaps as a stage in the evolution of the historiography of science, from which the history of the physical sciences and medicine have passed into the more refined historiographical paradigms currently employed in the history of science, but from which the history of the social and behavioral sciences have not fully extricated themselves. Although this evolutionary sequence should not in any way be regarded as inevitable, the history of most sciences has passed through a stage of descriptive chronology. The behavioral and social sciences today stand at the same point in their historiographical development as the physical sciences some forty years ago. More recently established, unsure of their epistemological foundations, they have only lately discovered and systematically explored their pasts. The historiography of their disciplinary history reveals the same characteristics as earlier in-house histories of the physical sciences: a preoccupation with great people, great insights, and great dates;[5] an inclination toward a stocktaking of accomplishments; a reliance on secondary sources; an emphasis on biography and bibliography; an approach that is descriptive and expository rather than analytical; and a progressive, incremental view of scientific change.[6]

Textbook Chronicles in Geography[7]

The leading scholarly challenge for disciplinary histories in the field of geography is to compose and integrate the content of their sources into a coherent and continuous narrative. It is not to carry out original research into the finer texture and smaller scale of geography's past by sifting through and interpreting primary sources. Yet in its own terms this task of colligation is highly original and primary research: to form disparate sources into a unified and compreshensive sequence of development.

The chief obstacle in this task of synthesis is that a second major category of works in the history of geography is in short supply. This category consists of definitive pieces of limited scope which, by carefully sifting through all the pertinent primary sources, present dynamic accounts of the *development* of unitary or grouped ideas, of the careers of individuals as well as communities of scholars, and of subfields, institutions, techniques, and theories. Because such works are scarce, they are not the sources upon which textbook chronicles have been erected. Rather, the impedimental challenge facing those disposed to write geography's disciplinary history is to compose into a history sources that are not in themselves studies in the history of geography but time-specific research achievements, general topical overviews, and methodological pronouncements.

Without studies in this second category, it is not surprising that some disciplinary histories are not chronicles but in fact general overviews illustrated with examples from the past. Thomas Freeman's *A Hundred Years of Geography*, for example, presents its readers with an ahistorical, static tableau of geography and its principal branches, illustrated with historical examples. It is also not surprising that descriptive chronology—the chronological listing of accomplishments—is one of the historiographical trademarks of synthetic histories of geography. Given the nature of the sources, their writers are consigned more to a chronological catalogue than a development process.

The lack of smaller scale, circumscribed studies in the history of geography may also help to explain why textbook chronicles are more often than not wedded to continuity and an incremental view of the growth of knowledge. To connect together these essentially static secondary sources, an externally imposed and artificial process of cumulative addition, of a steadily expanding disciplinary core, is substituted for the largely unknown character of the development process. Because both the large-and small-scale structure of development of geographic knowledge are terrae incognitae, such a mechanistic and unidimensional process lies readily at hand. The development process that historically integrates the discrete achievements, ideas, and knowledge of the past, however, ought not to be imposed or assumed; it must emerge from careful historical analysis just as much as our understanding of the singular ideas, careers, accomplishments, and concepts of the past.

Within the fields of history and philosophy of science there have been advanced several models of scientific change, in the light of which the structure and process of growth within a discipline, subdiscipline, or research program may be studied. Thomas Kuhn's model of alternating "normal" science and intellectual revolutions; Stephen Toulmin's model of the evolutionary transformation of academic enterprises by means of intellectual innovation and the selection of concepts; and M. J. Mulkay, G. N. Gilbert, and S. Woolgar's model for studying the appearance, development, and decline of research areas exemplify theories of scientific change that may profitably be used as guidelines for the study of geography's disciplinary history.[8] While Kuhn's ideas and terminology have found their way into the geographical literature, they have been applied more to the contemporary action-structure of the discipline than to its history, and more as an interpretive framework than a tight research design. A significant exception is William Speth's study of the history of American anthropogeographic thought.[9]

Besides theories of scientific change, social history of science, sociology of science, and Marxist historiography of science also supply indispensable signposts for joining the content of geographic scholarship to its socioeconomic, technological, and cultural context—a task that is especially important for understanding the structure and process of large-scale disciplinary change.[10]

The lack of scholarly attention accorded the development process in disciplinary histories and/or the imposition of an oversimplified process provides a ready opportunity for this history to be streamlined by prescriptive philosophies of geography. The influence of the writer's views on the nature of geography is one of the leading historiographic constituents of geography's textbook chronicles. The discrete careers and accomplishments of geographers must be joined into a continuous narrative; combining an incremental view of disciplinary growth with a normative philosophical viewpoint makes such a synthesis possible. The first provides a mechanism for the growth of geographic knowledge, and the second serves as a principle of selection and interpretation.

Nevertheless, that large-scale studies in the history of geography act as stalking horses for philosophical outlooks is not only because there has been little systematic research in the *process* of development of geographic knowledge. A more telling reason is that several of these accounts are marked by a philosophical presentism. Unifying and interpreting the history of geography by means of a present-day paradigm links it to instrumental purposes, firstly by entering and adjudicating the ongoing debate between competing schools of thought and, secondly, by schooling readers in the essentiality of this paradigm through affirming its historical necessity and tracing its historical antecedents.

In its most energetic form this philosophical presentism streamlines the entire account, as, for example, in Dickinson's *The Makers of Modern Geography*. The regional viewpoint is for Dickinson a principle of selection for what and who to include in his account, a principle for interpreting and arbitrating issues in the history of geography, and a standard by which the present (the historical present of the 1930s and 1940s) is ratified by the past and projected into the future. Moreover, Dickinson's generational model of the growth of geographic knowledge serves to demonstrate the continuity and progressive refinement of this one geographic tradition.

In its weaker forms this philosophical presentism exerts influence especially on the more recent history of geography. In this case, there is the recognition of a diversity of viewpoints in the past, or that the historical antecendents under consideration belong to only one school of geography, among others. Yet the history is made to flow toward the favored paradigm and culminates in its broad acceptance in the most recent period.

In *All Possible Worlds*, James's concept of "occupied space" streamlines, engulfs, and ostensibly unifies the diversity of geography's past. In present-day geography, the various historical ways of studying "occupied space" are synthesized by James into a "super-paradigm," and post-World War II geography is launched into a last and permanent phase of its history, an operational period in which plurality of viewpoints is sanctioned and in which disciplinary viewpoints are thoroughly inconsequential.[11] The historical antecendents of theoretical-predictive geography traced in *Breakthroughs in Geography* are regarded by Warntz and Wolff as converging, consolidating, and culminating in the post-World War II period, providing a discipline-wide cognitive identity for geography.[12] Although presentist purposes are less strident in Dickinson and Howarth's *The Making of Geography* than in Dickinson's *The Makers of Modern Geography*, it is clear from the overall plan of organization that Dickinson and Howarth wished to employ their history to demonstrate the historical necessity of adopting their regional viewpoint.[13]

In each of these accounts, the vicissitudes in the growth of academic geography are portrayed as finally coming to rest on firm ground in the contemporary period. It is this period of certitude that provides the rationale for chronicling the fluctuating life of geographic scholarly lineage (*Breakthrough in Geography*). These contemporary periods, however, are more a desired than an actual state of affairs.

That historiography has enlarged the forum of competition among rival schools of thought is also evident from the highlighting of philosophical concerns in several textbook chronicles. On the one hand, it would seem unexceptional that they would accent the philosophical disposition of the discipline at particular times and places because such large-scale synthetic accounts can only present broad currents and general tendencies of thought. On the other hand, in the portrayal of the life and works of individual scholars there is an inclination to particularize their views on the nature of geography at the expense of other contributions. *A Question of Place*, in defining geographical thought in terms of the nature of geography, takes this direction to the extreme,[14] but it is also notably present in Dickinson's *The Makers of Modern Geography*.[15]

In this elevation of philosophical thought in histories of geography, there lurk several historiographical postulates both in reference to contending schools of thought and to the history of geography in general. First, the past is able to speak more authoritatively to the present when fitted with methodological and philosophical content. Such content is regarded as intrinsically more normative than a discussion of more substantive states of affairs. In this way we can see that a philosophical presentism and a general philosophical disposition work hand in hand in the history of geography.

Second, there appears to be a presumption that what is historically most enduring in the history of geography is methodological controversy and declaration. While the past's empirical findings and substantive concepts and techniques pale with time, the historical significance of this philosophical mother lode persists. It is readily apparent that such a view of the essential content of the past also serves the present especially well.

Last, and closely related to the above, the promotion of philosophical contributions endorses a stereotyped image of the growth of geographic knowledge. Geographic praxis is regarded as flowing in a rather direct way from individual methodological writings. Such contributions are seen as the levers that set the direction for the substantive texture of the development of knowledge. While not in any dismissing the remarkable influence of several philosophical pieces on the course of geographic thought, many others are to be regarded as repetative and incidental elements in cognitive systems (which also include theoretic and substantive components) more than as formative elements that blaze the geographic trail.

Disciplinary histories are predominantly internal, in-house accounts, not social histories. The connecting links between the content of geographic scholarship and its socioeconomic, technological, and cultural context are not systematically explored in reconstructing and, more importantly, explaining geography's past. The preprofessional history of geography cannot as easily escape the larger history of science and civilization, but the academic history of geography, if it concerns itself with the external environment of geographical knowledge at all, generally does so only in the most circumferential manner. The histories of academic geography put forward are in-house accounts that chronicle achievements and concepts largely in biographical settings. It is mainly through the biographies of the principal actors that external conditions are introduced into the history of geography as, for example, in *The Makers of Modern Geography* and *All Possible Worlds.* Such external conditions, however, consist chiefly of intellectual debts, largely incurred during formal education, that are owed by geographers of the past to their mentors, teachers, and colleagues. Such individualized intellectual influences are still predominantly in-house concerns.

That the extrascientific milieu has not assumed a more important place in these textbook chronicles is due to a variety of factors. Certainly, building bridges between the content and context of geography's past is historiographically far more demanding than chronologically cataloguing scientific achievements. It requires both a knowledge of the conceptual, methodological, and empirical content of past geography and a knowledge of the social, political, economic, and religious factors impinging on that content. A greater commitment to process and explanation would, quite uncoerced, introduce an external perspective into disciplinary histories and, indeed, into the history of geography in general. Another possible reason why disciplinary histories are principally internal accounts is the widespread attachment to the idea that science and scholarship are (or should be) autonomous, quarantined enterprises. This has perhaps led us to picture geography's past as one of proceeding, quite independently, from intellectual triumph to intellectual triumph. That our supposedly autonomous professional past has been deeply influenced and compromised by commerce, colonialism, and politics is not something we would want to highlight.

That large-scale histories of geography are stamped with philosophical presentism, oversimplification of development, and inattention to context points up their dualistic character. At one level, disciplinary histories may be read as resource texts for the history of geography, providing hitherto unavailable biographical sketches of many of geography's leading practictioners. They are written to furnish the student with a reportorial survey that features biographical and bibliographical highlights as well as minutiae. Yet at another level, and this often is the level promoted, their authors wish to go beyond a factual survey to construct, usually on the basis of a hermeneutic standard, an integrated and continuous narrative. Superimposed upon the historical survey, the larger aim is not well supported unless new content is added and old material is reorganized. In this way it can be seen that a historiography adapted to the survey character of a text is illsuited to its larger aims.

Textbook chronicles are not likely to upgrade their historiography independently. As long as the large-scale history of geography is in service to geography in general and is unsupported by critical articles, monographs, and book-length accounts that have explained the development of ideas, subfields, techniques, and discoveries, and as long as the history of geography in general does not become an autonomous subdiscipline defined by common aims and methods and a body of specialists, receptive to what the encompassing fields of history of science and intellectual history have to offer, disciplinary history will continue to display the historiographic characteristics that we have noted. These include: a stocktaking of accomplishments, an emphasis on biography, an incremental view of scientific change, a neglect of context, and a disregard for process.

All districts within the history of geography as a specialized field—biographical, institutional, thematic, and disciplinary history—require not only more cultivation but also greater critical attention to historiography. In this essay disciplinary history has been singled out for discussion and appraisal. More than other divisions of study in the history of geography, disciplinary history is still heavily weighed down by a functional association with and dependence upon geographic education and the philosophy of geography. These functional links have marked this genre of history of geography with a prescriptive orientation and with a clear preoccupation with philosophical content, historical antecedents, and magisterial scholars and their achievements.

The history of geography is today still struggling to secure a cognitive and professional identity. Although the body of specialized studies is expanding, the demand to provide only an in-house service for the profession at large remains difficult to resist. This is especially true for disciplinary history. Attention to the structure of growth of geographic knowledge and regard for its extrascientific milieu will help historiographically to reform disciplinary histories of the kind that have been appraised. The appearance of more small-scale and definitive studies in the history of geography will provde a needed foundation of sources to investigate the extensive patterns in geography's past. Robert Young's counsel for the history of the behavioral sciences is perhaps also well taken for geography: "there should be no more general survey for some time to come: we have reached the stage where we know enough not to write them until we know a great deal more."[16]

Notes

1. The classic statement of "presentism" in history in general is Herbert Butterfield, *The Whig Interpretation of History* (London: G. Bell and Sons, 1931).
2. George W. Stocking, "On the Limits of 'Presentism' and 'Historicism' in the Historiography of the Behavioral Sciences," *Journal of the History of the Behavioral Sciences* 1 (1965): 214.
3. A noteworthy example of this is found in P. G. Hall's review of the second edition (republished) of Bunbury's *A History of Ancient Geography*. Hall censures Bunbury for not including the antecedents to the regional domain in Geography that emerged thirty years after Bunbury wrote this work: "Of these developments hardly a premonition appears in Bunbury's pages." Clearly Hall wished to have the history of geography rewritten to accord with the then-present prevailing philosophy of geography. P. G. Hall, review of *A History of Ancient Geography*, 2d. ed., republished, 1959, by E. H. Bunbury, in *British Journal for the Philosophy of Science* 12 (1962): 344; cited in Joseph Agssi, *Towards an Historiography of Science*, ('S-Gravenhage: Mouton, 1963), *History and Theory* beiheft p. 3, note 13.
4. Stocking, "On the Limits," p. 215. For other discussions of presentism in the history of science, consult D. S. L. Cardwell, "Reflections on Some Problems in the History of Science," *Manchester Literary and Philosophical Society* 106 (1963-64): 108-23; Julien Jaynes, "the Routes of Science," *American Scientist* 54 (1966): 94-102. In the field of psychology particularly, historiographical issues have been the subject of spirited and acrimonious debate. Consult, for example, Walter B. Weimer, "The History of Psychology and Its Retrieval from Historiography, "*Science Studies* 4 (1974): 235-58, 367-96.
5. Robert M. Young, "Scholarship and the History of the Behavioral Sciences," *History of Science* 5 (1966): 35.
6. Ibid., po. 15-19, 32-37 passim; *International Encyclopedia of the Social Sciences*, 1968 ed., s.v. "Science: The History of Science," by Thomas s. Kuhn, pp. 74-75; idem, "The Relations Between History and the History of Science," *Daedalus* 100 (1971): 289-90; A. Rupert Hall, "Can the History of Science be History?" *British Journal for the History of Science* 4 (1968-69): 207-12.
7. This section is bsed on a detailed historiographical appraisal of the major English-language disciplinary histories found in chapter 4 (pp. 146-244) of Henry aay, "conceptual Change and the Growth of Geographic Knowledge: A Critical Appraisal of the Historiography of Geography" (Ph.D. diss., Clark University, 1978). The following works were included in this appraisal: Robert E. Dicksinson, *The makers of Modern Geography* (New York: Praeger, 1969); Preston e. James, *All Possible Worlds: A History of Geographical Ideas* (New York: Odyssey Press, Bobbs-Merrill, 1972); Thomas w. Freeman, *A Hundred Years of Geography* (Chicago: Aldine, 1961); Eric Fischer, Robert D. Campbell, and Eldon S. Miller, *A Question of Place* (Arlington, Va: R. W. Beatty, 1967); Robert E. Dicksinson and O. J. R. Howrth, *The Making of Geography* (Oxford: Clarendon Press, 1933); Robert Fuson, *A Geography of Geography* (Dubuque, Iowa: Wm. C. Brown

Co., 1969); William Warntz and Peter Wolff, *Breakthroughs in Geography* (New York: New American Library, 1971).

8. Thomas S. Kuhn, *The Structure of Scientific Revolutions, International Encyclopedia of Unified Science*, vol. 2, no. 2, 2d ed. en. 1. (Chicago: University of Chicago Press, 1970). Idem, "Logic of Discovery or Psychology of Research?" in *Criticism and the Growth of Knowledge*, I. Lakatos and A. Musgrave ed. (Cambridge: Cambridge University Press, 1970), pp. 1-23; idem, "Reflections on My Critics," in *Criticism and the Growth of Knowledge*, pp. 231-78; idem, "Second Thoughts on Paradigms," in *The Structure of Scientific Theories*, ed. F. Suppe (Urbana: University of Illinois Press, 1974), pp. 459-82. Stephen Toulmin, *Human Understanding* (Princeton: Princeton University Press, 1972) vol 1, *General Introduction, and the Collective Use and Understanding of Concepts*: M. J. Mulkay, G. N. Gilbert, and S. Woolgar, "Problem Areas and Research Networks in Science," *Sociology* 9 (1975): 187-203. For a recent critique of and alternative to historic theories of scientific progress, see Larry Laudan, *Progress and its Problems* (Berkeley: University of California Press, 1977).

9. William Wayne Speth, "Historical Anthropogeography: environment and culture in American Anthropological Thought from 1890 to 1950" (Ph.d. diss., University of Oregon, 1972).

10. Access to the large and growing literature in each of these three fields may be gained by consulting, for social history of science, I. Bernard Cohen, "The Many Faces of the History of Science," in *The Future of History*, ed. Charles F. Delzell (Nashville: Vanderbilt University Press, 1977), pp. 69-83; for socieology of science, Robert K. Merton, *Social Theory and Social Structure* (New York: The Free Press, 1957), and Robert K. Merton, *The Sociology of Science, Theoretical and Empirical Investigations*, ed. Norman W. Stover (Chicago: University of Chicago Press, 1973); for Marzist historiography of science; Mikulas Teich and Robert M. Young, eds., *Changing Perspectives in the History of Science* (London: Heineman, 1973)—jwithin this volume, in particular, Robert M. Young, "The Historiographic and Ideological Contexts of the Nineteenth Century Debate on Man's Place in Nature," pp. 344-438.

11. James, *All Possible Worlds*, chapter 15, "The Concept of Occupied Space," pp. 457-70. This chapter should be read, not as a component part, but as an introduction to the book. It represents James's historiographic motto.

12. See, for example, Warntz and Wolff, *Breakthroughs in Geography*, p. 10.

13. Consult, in particular, Dickinson and Howarth, *The making of Geography*, chapters 19 and 20.

14. Fischer, et al., *A Question of Place*, pp. 2, 5, 6, and 82.

15. Murray McCaskill, review of *The Makers of Modern Geography*, by Robert E. Dickinson, in *The Australian Geographer* 11 (1969-71): 641.

16. Young, "Scholarship and the History," p. 18.

Paradigms, Revolutions, Schools of Thought, and Anarchy: Reflections on the Recent History of Anglo-American Human Geography

R.J. Johnston

Introduction

Thomas Kuhn's ideas about the development of a science have provided a model which has been favored by geographers attempting to describe changes in their discipline since the Second World War. Thus the concept of a paradigm, a dominant mode of research ("normal science"), has been widely accepted and used. Not all "contemporary historians" of the discipline are convinced of the model's value, however; this paper attempts an evaluation of changes in Anglo-American human geography since 1945 using Kuhn's framework as the context.

The Paradigm Model

A paradigm, according to Kuhn (1962, 1970), is the framework within which scientific activity proceeds. It indicates: (1) the accepted facts; (2) the puzzles which remain to be solved; and (3) the procedures to be used in seeking solutions. A scientist uses the tools defined within the paradigm to solve certain puzzles, and thereby to provide further facts on which the next round of puzzle solving will be based. The procedures and the currently accepted body of knowledge are enshrined in the textbooks through which scientists are socialized into the discipline.

Some attempts at solving puzzles will either fail to produce results or come up with answers that are at variance with the accepted facts. These findings are frequently set aside, as isolated anomalies which cannot be accounted for. Eventually, the volume of such anomalies may become considerable and their perceived salience is such as to throw doubt on the whole paradigm. This encourages some scientists to seek an alternative paradigm, one which will successfully integrate both the accepted facts and the anomalies of the preceding one; a new set of puzzle-solving procedures will probably be needed. Presentation of the new paradigm will demonstrate its superiority to those working with its predecessor, who recognize the improvement offered and are converted to the new. A revolution in scientific practice thus occurs, the textbooks are replaced, and a new paradigm settles in for a period of scholarly dominance.

This model was introduced to geographers by Haggett and Chorley (1967), who argued that by the mid-1960s the paradigm then dominant in Anglo-American geography was unable to cope with the questions geographers were asking and the data they were seeking to analyze. They proposed an alterntive, "scientific" paradigm, one that was already well on the way to acceptance in North America. Indeed, two years earlier Burton (1963) had used Kuhnian terminology to suggest that a paradigm shift, a theoretical and quantitative revolution, had recently occurred: quantification and theorizing had become part, he claimed, of the "conventional wisdom."

Others to use the Kuhnian model include Harvey (1973), seeking to generate a further revolution, and Taylor (1976), who identified seven postwar revolutions; Webber (1977) has recently talked of an "entropy-maximizing paradigm." But not all commentators have been so certain: Chisholm (1975), for example, prefers an evolutionary interpretation, although he accepts that there has been a technical revolution. Both Bird (1978) and Stoddart (1977) have been stringent critics: "Paradigm as 'the one and only' is dead" (Bird 1978, p. 134); "the concept sheds no light on the processes of scientific change, and readily becomes caricature" (Stoddart 1977, p. 1).

Anglo-American Human Geography since 1945

In order to evaluate the paradigm model in the context of these contradictory opinions, a brief review of the main changes in the content of human geography since 1945 is needed. Only a cartoonlike survey is presented; a fuller account is available elsewhere (Johnston 1979).

It is common for those employing Kuhn's model to recognize three major paradigms in human geography during the period 1870–1950. These are exploration, environmental determinism, and regionalism (James 1972, Herbert and Johnston 1978); the last was dominant at the beginning of the period under review. Commentators suggest that it has been succeeded by a sequence of three further paradigms—spatial science,behaviorism, and radical/structural (Johnston 1977, Herbert and Johnston 1978).

The revolution which introduced the first of this second set of paradigms had multiple origins in the United States.Four major contributing "schools" can be identified: (1) the Iowan, led by McCarty and, to a lesser extent, Schaefer, who produced two revolutionary "treatises" (Schaefer 1953, McCarty 1954) arguing for the adoption of the scientific method and procedures associated with the Vienna school of logical positivists; (2) the Wisconsin, led by Robinson, which concentrated on the technical problems of map comparisin; (3) the social physics school, led by Stewart and Warntz (1958), which proposed a macrogeographical approach; and (4) the Washington school, under Garrison, whose burgeoning literature focussed on the description of spatial patterns in the context of ideals (models) constructed on assumptions regarding rational economic behavior (see Garrison 1969). (Note that Northwestern University was linked to both the Washington and the Iowan schools during their formative years.)

The examples set by these four groups were enthusiastically taken up by many others. Most attention was given to quantification, to the use of statistics in the description of patterns and the testing of hypotheses. (The use of mathematics for deriving models was largely shunned.) There was some debate, but quantification was apparently rapidly accepted within the discipline, hence the revolution identified by Burton and by Taylor. The epistemological underpinnings were largely ignored (the only real debate was initiated by Lukermann; see Johnston 1979, chapter 3), and their first detailed presentation in the literature (Harvey 1969) came well after general acceptance of the new paradigm.

The major change of the 1950s and early 1960s was in techniques, therefore, and many of the "revolutionaries" were at pains to emphasize the continuity of ultimate objectives (e.g., Berry 1964). Over time human geographers became attracted to the idea that their major contribution to the social sciences lay in a focus on "the spatial variable"; as Pooler (1977) points out, nearly all the stimulus for this view came from outside the geographical discipline. Again, there was the lack of any clear programmatic statement (though see Nystuen 1968). Spatial science developed by stealth. It involved acceptance of a general disciplinary orientation—study of the operation of the distance variable in a variety of contexts—but substantively the subject fragmented into a series of quasi-independent branches (urban, agricultural, transport etc.). These shared methods but worked apart in terms of substantive content,despite some attempts to provide a unifying focus (e.g., Haggett 1965).

Although widely acclaimed, the spatial science approach was not universally adopted. Some argued that its separate focus was untenable; their conclusions seemed to deny the existence of human geography (e.g., Sack 1974, May 1970).Others ignored it, despite pleas for their cooperation (e.g., National Academy of Sciences-National Research Council 1965);regional (Paterson 1974), cultural (Mikesell 1967), and historical geographers continued to plough their own furrows, although some at least of the latter were attracted to quantification and theorizing (Baker 1972).

During the mid-1960s, a major criticism of the models used in spatial science was launched (e.g., Wolpert 1964 and Pred 1967), involving attacks on its assumptions of economically perfect rational behavior. A positive approach was proposed to replace the normative one, and was based on observation and analysis of actual decision making. Much of the methodology followed that already established, however, and the "behavioral geography" that was launched came to occupy niches within the general corpus of spatial science rather than to present a strident alternative to it.

Another "behavioral revolution" promised to be much more far-reaching. The logical positivist position was criticized (largely from the historical/cultural rump),both for ignoring the anomalies which its puzzle solving had produced, and for failing to establish exact criteria for the verification of its hypotheses (Guelke 1971, 1974). The alternative offered emphasized the characterisics of humans as thinking beings, using hermeneutic approaches such as phenomenology and idealism to investigate the subjectively defined perceived worlds that humans live in and make decisions about. Much of the literature was of a negative character, however, being more concerned with attacking spatial science than with developing an alternative philosophy and methodology, and relatively little substantive work has been reported (see Ley and Samuels 1978).

Yet another revolution has been in the offing since about 1968; what to call it is not clear, for the term *structural/radical* introduced earlier really applies to only half of it, and two competing would-be paradigms can be identified. During the 1960s, human geographers joined in the growing concern about inequalities within society, about environmental despoilation, and about the continuing economic problems of capitalist systems. Initially, their reaction was to call for diagnosis and preventative medicine (e.g., Zelinsky 1970) within the current mode of production; geography and public policy became a catch phrase and the image of geographers as applied social scientists actively influential in the corridors of power was nurtured,alongside welfare-focussed, humanitarian attempts to reshape the discipline's subject matter (Smith 1977).

This so-called "liberal" search for solutions to societal problems came under attack in the 1970s by those who perceived that it offerd no real hope for improvement (Peet 1977). Structuralist arguments were forwarded, particularly the Marxist one that questions of distribution could not be separated from those of production. Led initially by Harvey (1973), who attacked the liberal influence-seekers in his paper "What Kind of Geography for What Kind of Public Policy?" (1974), a major debate was initiated. New forms of research methodology were tried and an overtly political stance was introduced to the discipline's literature.

All of these changes and attempts to alter the focus of geographical research and teaching can be associated with parallel changes in the environmental matrix of scholarship during the three decades. The adoption of a logical positivist/spatial science, for example, followed the dominance of science and technology in the Second World War, which continued into the Cold War and the space race. "Hard" science was reputable in the 1950s and 1960s and economists and social psychologists had won respect for social science too; the growth of town and regional planning was providing an outlet for geographical research and manpower. By the mid-1960s, however, the dominance of science and of big organization was increasingly being questioned, even resented. The technological developments were seen to be accentuating rather than reducing inequalities, to be failing to solve the problems of poverty and racism, and to be contributing to the destructive exploitation of the environment. Concern for the plight of the individual in society, especially the underprivileged individual, was reflected in the growth of welfare-oriented studies, and investigation of the role of such studies in capitalist societies led to the radical questioning of both the role of social science within capitalism and the prospects for capitalism itself.

The Paradigm Model Evaluated

Superficially, the above outline suggests the relevance of the paradigm model to changes in human geography since 1945. The dominance of one approach—spatial science— is clear in the research literature, and there is evidence of it proceeding as a "normal science," sharpening its tools, testing and revising its theories, and expanding its range of substantive interests (compare Haggett 1965 with Haggett, Cliff, and Frey 1977). Recognition of some anomalies led to certain changes, as with the incorporation of the behaviorist mode of analysis in the mid-1960s,* but

---

*"Behaviorist" psychology is the study of "unambiguously observable, and preferably measurable, behaviour" (Hunter 1977, p. 57).

as the volume of anomalies increased so did the calls for a revolution. Two were made. The first, also behavioral but with a strong humanistic flavor, an apparently reductionist philosophy, and a nonreplicable methodology, had its roots in the then fairly widely discredited historical, cultural, and regional geographies. It did not succeed in overthrowing the spatial science paradigm, but neither was it defeated; instead, it became established as a revolutionary enclave within the geographical corpus, winning a few converts over time. The other attempted coup began within spatial science, but broke from it on ideological grounds; again, it has neither succeeded nor failed, and large-scale sniping continues.

Has there ever been paradigm dominance during recent decades, therefore? Have human geographers ever displayed a clear disciplinary consensus? Have there been any real revolutions? Before spatial science there was no homogeneity of outlook within the regional paradigm, as illustrated by the differences between Hartshorne and Sauer (Guelke 1977), and an examination of the journal literature in the 1970s will similarly indicate much eclecticism, continuing the interests outlined in the previous section. Several potential paradigms (not necessarily competing but possibly complementary; Gregory 1978; Hay 1979) are being advocated to human geographers at the present time, some of them capable of division into identifiable subparadigms. And so is Kuhn's model valid, even as a general descriptive device?

Kuhn Revisited

Geographers appear to have given too little attention either to the intense debate that Kuhn's model has engendered among historians of science, or to his own revisions of it. Indeed, Suppe has claimed that "Kuhn's views have undergone a sharply declining influence on contemporary philosophy of science" (1977,p. 647). The full breadth and depth of the debate on paradigms cannot be reviewed here, but certain strands are relevant.

One important strand, which links to that of the previous section, concerns the degree of consensus within a science. Is the considerable agreement suggested by the concepts of a paradigm and normal science likely within a large body of scholars, especially when they are dealing with very complex problems, some of which are related to their own life-style? A major element in this discussion of consensus concerns scale. Two scales seem appropriate here. The first deals with definitions of disciplinary ends and means, with what Kuhn (1977) calls the disciplinary matrix—the world view which defines procedures. Within this matrix is a series of applications, relating to different topics. Each has its own exemplars, or stereotypes, which indicate how a particular class of puzzles is to be attacked. Training in a science thus involves acquiring an arsenal of exemplars relating to its range of applications. Once trained in the broad field, and socialized into its disciplinary matrix, the individual scientist then joins one or more of its specialist groups, each of which has its own exemplars and research leaders.

This division into research groups based on exemplars accommodates Mulkay's (1975) ideas regarding the existence of branches within a discipline. Within the same matrix, several different types of work may be proceeding almost independently. One branch may eventually break away as the trend of its work leads it to abandon the disciplinary matrix and to establish a new one. The outcome is a "quiet revolution" as a consequence of eclecticism. Only when the new group decides to challenge for disciplinary supremacy—by seeking to dominate curricula and grant-giving bodies, for example—will the revolution become apparent; if hegemony is not sought, debate may be slight, especially if the "dissidents" are allowed access to resources.

Using the above reformulation of the Kuhnian model, it can be argued that "quiet revolutions" have occurred in human geography. Thus regionalism had its disciplinary matrix, codified by Hartshorne, and within it different branches were established with their own foci and examplars; some, like Sauer's, were more successful, in terms of adherents at least, than were others, such as Whittlesey's. And then the quantitative revolution began, as another branch; the general goals outlined in the disciplinary matrix were accepted, but a new set of exemplars offered a very different means to the (Hartshornian) end. The new branch attracted supporters, through a combination of charismatic leadership and apparent social and academic relevance. Its publications came to dominate the research literature, after initial jousts with conservative editorial policies, and it reached apparent supremacy as the dominant branch.

As the hegemony of this new branch grew, and its leaders attained eminence within the discipline as a whole, so it became reoriented into spatial science. Its disciplinary matrix contained both a methodology (implicit until codified by Harvey [1969]) and an arsenal of technical procedures. Within it, new branches were established, applying the matrix in various ways and to various subject matters; each branch (whether urban geography or even its subdivisions, such as central place analysis and social area analysis) had its own leaders, exemplars, and members.

Certain of those branches in turn fostered new "quiet revolutions." One was the behaviorist trend (Wolpert, Pred, etc.), which proposed no major deviations from the current matrix—it deflected its orientation somewhat but remained a part of it. The other was the radical/structural branch, which was fostered within the matrix in the late 1960s, but broke away and challenged it in the 1970s.

One aspect of human geography since the 1960s has not been accounted for, however—the "second behavioral, or hermeneutic, revolution", with its strong humanist orientation (Ley and Samuels 1978). This did not arise as a branch of the spatial science matrix. Rather, it emerged out of the embers of the regionalism matrix, from branches which had not died and whose members, plus a new generation of disciples, sought to reestablish their dominance, by attacking those who had sought to replace them. Even the reformulated paradigm model cannot readily account for this revival.

Success or Failure in "Quiet Revolutions"

Why was the spatial science revolution a conspicuous success? Why did the hermeneutic attack fail to gain a major following? And is the structural/radical revolution likely to proceed to disciplinary hegemony? To answer such questions it is necessary to turn again to environmental constraints, in particular those which oversee the operations of an academic discipline.

The earlier discussion suggested that human geographers have reacted to societal changes in their attempts to realign their disciplinary matrix. Such changes provide a necessary but not a sufficient condition for a disciplinary realignment; associated with them must be a set of sympathetic internal conditions. Several commentators have argued that new paradigms are usually initiated by younger workers (Stegmuller 1976, Lemaine, et al. 1976), who react to the demands of their constraining environments. To have much impact, however, they generally require the catalyst of one or more leaders within the disciplinary establishment; without such leadership, they lack access to resources and the patronage which is so necessary for appointment into the establishment (Johnston 1979 chapter 1). Even with it, they may find access to the discipline's literature barred, and be forced to launch their own series.

There are several criteria to be met before an iconoclastic leader and his or her followers can establish a branch within a discipline. They include (van den Daele and Weingart 1976): an autonomous system of evaluation and reputation; an autonomous communication system; acknowledgement of puzzle-solving ability; a formal organization complete with accepted training programmes; and research resources. These are much more readily obtained during periods of expansion, when research institutes are growing and resources are plentiful. Such a period was the late 1950s–early 1960s, which allowed spatial scientists to reproduce in large numbers and to achieve a quantitative dominance with in the discipline which now extends to the heart of its establishment. Since then, resources have been relatively scarce. The structuralists have not wanted for either leaders or potential disciples, but relatively few have penetrated the permanent tenure categories of the disciplinary hierarchy, in part because of the lack of positions and in part because of a lack of sympathy within the orthodox (i.e., spatial science) establishment. When a revolution is brewing and is attracting support, and there is a seller's market for academic posts, then that revolution must be coopted, it seems; when it is unable to get external support, and jobs are in a buyer's market, then it can be repressed. Meanwhile, alongside the structuralists are the behaviorists, who have also been unable to make much headway. To some extent this is for the same reasons. In addition, however, the behavioral group has lacked iconoclastic leaders; with a few exceptions, the leaders have been individual scholars who have not attracted large followings of research students and who, apparently, have not sought to dominate the resource allocation procedure (see Harris 1978).

A Generational Model?

The import of the preceding paragraphs is that Kuhn's paradigm model should be replaced, for human geography at least, by a generational model (Johnston 1978). According to this, the external environment may occasionally create the conditions favorable to a redirection of scholarly effort. One or more established members of the discipline react to these conditions by creating new exemplars, within the established disciplinary matrix, and seek the resources which will support research programmes based on their ideas. If they are successful, then their followers may form one or more branches within the discipline, which come either to dominate the disciplinary matrix or, by quiet revolution, to replace it.

The development of spatial science within human geography occurred at a time when all of the criteria for success were met; iconoclasts were available to compete for the large volume of resources that could be employed to meet the demands of a planning-oriented, science-and-technology-based, mixed society, and they convinced sponsors of the value of geographical work. The result was a new generation of geographers, much larger than those preceding it, who rapidly achieved numerical and political dominance within the disciplinary hierarchy. Since then, the structuralists and behaviorists have fared relatively poorly; the lack of opportunities to enter the hierarchy has protected the growing hegemony of the spatial scientists, and has limited the potential for further revolutions, quiet or otherwise. (In the long term, this may ossify human geography, as the would-be quiet revolutionaries establish their own hostile camps elsewhere.)

Whereas Kuhn's model postulates a conversion process taking place as one paradigm replaces another, this generational model allows most scientists to continue working in the matrix within which they were academically socialized. Conversion may occur, and is necessary to catalyze most revolutions, but it is relatively rare; human geographers may migrate from one branch to another within a disciplinary matrix, but few of them make the major change that a revolution requires. Thus, according to this model, a revolution occurs within a discipline when a new generation of scientists, complete with its own philosophy and methodology, achieves numerical dominance.

Two queries are immediately raised: how does one account for the "historical/cultural school" of the late 1960s and early 1970s; and what happens to the preceding generation after an apparent revolution, if they are not converted? Both of these arise because the generational model (and also the paradigm model) focus almost exclusively on the discipline's research literature. Is this literature representative of the membership of the discipline as a whole? Many academics rarely if ever publish in the journals containing their discipline's refereed research reports.

Important in this context is the academic career cycle. For most academics their publication rate declines with age, for a variety of reasons, some of which are related to a bureaucratic channeling of their time and energy (which may be cause or effect). As "normal science" continues, so they become increasingly isolated from it, and revolutions, even noisy ones, may well pass them by unnoticed. But the great majority continue to teach—especially to undergraduates—using the disciplinary matrix and exemplars of their youth. Thus the range of courses offered by a university geography department is likely to be much wider than is suggested by a list of its staff's recent publications.

In the preface to his book *A Hundred Years of Geography*, T. W. Freeman (1961) points out that he was tempted to use the subtitle "no new idea under the sun." This reflects the above argument regarding the continued teaching of what are, to the current generation of researchers, outmoded disciplinary matrices, either by the original iconoclasts or by their disciples. Thus in a period of rapid change, many branches of different paradigms remain alive; occasionally they may be taken up by energetic workers, and used as the basis for attacks on the current orthodoxy (the present behavioral trend?); which are resurrected may be the result of a chance encounter between a good teacher and a student who is a potential iconoclast. This does not mean, of course, that new ideas are not brought in, but argues only that novelty is not the sine qua non of reorientation within a discipline.

Finally, it is not only the continuity of teaching activity, relative to research, which can lead to new branches being established, with or without paradigmatic ambitions. All the published results of previous research survive and are available to be exhumed by new generations of workers. A branch, then, may never die but only fall dormant: its revival results from a chance discovery, at a time when it is apparently relevant to an attack on a currently popular disciplinary matrix.

So Have There Been Paradigms?

No: for human geography at least, Kuhn's model would seem to have been a red herring. At all times during the last thirty years, several schools of thought have been thriving within Anglo-American human geography, often coexisting quite happily in a cosy oligopoly, rather than challenging for hegemony. Occasionally one of these schools has achieved an apparent numerical dominance, particularly within the research literature, as a relatively large generation of activists, stimulated to a particular and novel approach, publishes its work. But there remain many unconverted, waiting for the reaction, when at least some of the new students fail to be convinced by the current bandwagon; others lost their faith, and proclaim yet further alternative heresies. The overall impression, especially at the teaching level, may be one of anarchy (Johnston 1976); if the discipline continues to grow, so it might branch yet further, presenting both outsiders and potential students with a chaos of conflicting images of "geography is what geographers do."

Kuhn's model was developed in the context of the natural sciences, which are characterized by the least two features not common to human geography: (1) clear evidence that a hypothesis has been falsified, so that a certain theory must be discarded; and (2) the organization of research as a team effort. Much geographical work is exploratory, and is conducted by individuals who operate independently. Indeed, many, although influenced by what they read, are in no sense socialized into a particular matrix or set of examplars which might be associated with a "research school" and its leader. The charisma of certain individuals and their published works may occasionally produce the prophet and disciple situation. Much more usual, however, is a situation of fickle allegiances. If there are paradigms in human geography, then there is at least one—at any particular time—for each geographer, whether actively researching or not. General agreement on certain issues there may be, but widespread consensus is rare. Particular lines may appear to be popular at certain times, but always the underlying tendency is toward anarchy. The human factor among human geographers, and the variety of approaches to their subject matter, ensures a segmented disciplinary corpus.

References Cited

Baker, A.R.H. 1972. "Rethinking Historical Geography." In *Progress in Historical Geography*, edited by A.R.H. Baker, pp. 11-28. Newton Abbot: David and Charles.

Berry, B.J.L. 1964. "Approaches to Regional Analysis: A Synthesis." *Annals, Association of American Geographers* 54: 2-11.

Bird, J.H. 1978. "Methodology and Philosophy." In *Progress in Human Geography*, edited by A.R.H. Baker, 2: 133-40.

Burton, I. 1963. "The Quantitive Revolution and Theoretical Geography." *The Canadian Geographer*, 7: 151-62.

Chisholm, M. 1975. *Human Geography: Evolution or Revolution?* Harmondsworth: Penguin Books.

Freeman, T.W. 1961. *A Hundred Years of Geography*. London: Gerald Duckworth.

Garrison, W.L. 1959. Spatial Structure of the Economy II. "*Annals, Association of American Geographers* 49: 471-82.

Gregory, D. 1978. *Ideology, Science and Human Geography*. London: Hutchinson.

Guelke, L. 1971. "Problems of Scientific Explanation in Geography." *The Canadian Geographer* 15: 38-53.

———. "An Idealist Alternative in Human Geography." *Annals, Association of American Geographers* 14: 193-202.

———. 1977. "Regional Geography." *The Professional Geographer* 29: 1-7.

Haggett, P. 1965. *Locational Analysis in Human Geography*. London: Edward Arnold.

———, and Chorley, R.J. 1967. Models, Paradigms, and the New Geography." In *Models in Geography*, edited by R.J. Chorley and P. Haggett, pp. 19-42. London: Methuen.

Haggett, P., Cliff, A. D., and Frey, A. 1977. *Locational Analysis in Human Geography*. London: Edward Arnold.

Harris, R.C. 1978. "The Historical Geography of North American Regions." *American Behavioural Scientist* 22: 115-30.

Harvey, D. 1969. *Explanation in Geography*. London: Edward Arnold.

———. 1973. *Social Justice and the City*. London: Edward Arnold.

———. 1974. "What Kind of Geography for What Kind of Public Policy?" *Transactions, Institute of British Geographers* 63: 18-24.

Hay, A.M. 1979. "Positivism in Human Geography: Response to Critics." In *Geography and the Urban Environment: Progress in Research and Applications*, edited by D.T. Herbert and R.J. Johnston, 2: 1-26.

Herbert, D.T., and Johnston, R.J. "Geography and the Urban Environment." In *Geography and the Urban Environment: Progress in Research and Application,* edited by D.T. Herbert and R.J. Johnston, 1: 1-29.

Hunter, I.M. L. 1977. "Behaviourism." In *The Fontana Dictionary of Modern Thought*, edited by A. Bullock and O. Stallybrass, p. 57. London: Fontana/Collins.

James, P.E. 1972. *All Possible Worlds: A History of Geographical Ideas*. Indianapolis: The Odyssey Press.

Johnston, R.J. 1976. "Anarchy, Conspiracy and Apathy: The Three 'Conditions' of Geography." *Area* 8: 1-3.

———. 1977. "Urban Geography; City Structure." *Progress in Human Geography* 1: 118-29.

———. 1978. "Paradigms and Revolutions or Evolutions: Observations on Human Geography since the Second World War." *Progress in Human Geography* 2: 189-206.

———. 1979. *Geography and Geographers: Anglo-American Human Geography since 1945*. London: Edward Arnold.

Kuhn, T.S. 1962. *The Structure of Scientific Revolutions*. Chicago: University of Chicago Press.

———. 1970. *The Structure of Scientific Revolutions* 2d ed. Chicago: University of Chicago Press.

———. 1977. "Second Thoughts on Paradigms." In *The Structure of Scientific Theories*, edited by F. Suppe, pp. 459-82, plus discussion on pp. 500-517. Urbana: University of Illinois Press.

Lemaine, G., et al 1976. "Introduction: Problems in the Emergence of New Disciplines." In *Perspectives on the Emergence of Scientific Disciplines*, edited by G. Lemaine, et al., pp. 1-73. The Hague: Mouton.

Ley, D., and Samuels, M.S. 1978. "Introduction: Contexts of Modern

Humanism in Geography." In *Humanistic Geography,* edited by D. Ley and M.S. Samuels, pp. 1-17. Chicago: Maaroufa Press.

McCarthy, H.H. 1954. "An Approach to a Theory of Economic Geography." *Economic Geography* 30: 95-101.

May, J.A. 1970. *Kant's Concept of Geography: And Its Relation to Recent Geographical Thought.* Department of Geography, University of Toronto, Research Publication 4. Toronto: University of Toronto.

Mikesell, M.W. 1967. "Geographical Perspectives in Anthropology. *Annals, Association of American Geographers* 57: 617-34.

Mulkay, J.J. 1975. "Three Models of Scientific Development." *Sociological Review* 23: 509-26.

National Academy of Sciences—National Research Council. 1965. *The Science of Geography.* Washington, D.C.: National Academy of Sciences-National Research Council.

Nystuen, J.D. 1863. "Identification of Some Fundamental Spatial Concepts. *Papers of the Michigan Academy of Science, Arts and Letters* 48: 373-84. Reprinted in B.J.L. Berry and D.F. Marble, eds., *Spatial Analysis* (Englewood Cliffs: Prentice-Hall, 1968), pp. 35-41.

Paterson, J.H. 1974. "Writing Regional Geography." In *Progress in Geography,* edited by C. Board, et al., 6: 1-26. London: Edward Arnolds.

Peet, J.R. 1977. The Development of Radical Geography in the United States." *Progress in Human Geography* 1: 240-63.

Pooler, J.A. 1977. "The Origins of the Spatial Tradition in Geography: An Interpretation." *Ontario Geography* 11: 56-83.

Pred, A. 1967. *Behavior and Location: Foundations for a Geographic and Dynamic Location Theory. Part I.* Lund: C. W. K. Gleerup.

Sack. R.D. 1974. "The Spatial Separatist Theme in Geography." *Economic Geography* 50: 1-19.

Schaefer, F.K. 1953. "Exceptionalism in Geography: A Methodological Examination." *Annals, Association of American Geographers* 43: 226-49.

Smith, D.M. 1977. *Human Geography: A Welfare Approach.* London: Edward Arnold.

Stegmuller, W. 1976. *The Structure and Dynamics of Theories.* New York: Springer-Verlag.

Stewart, J.Q., and Warntz, W. 1958. "Macrogeography and Social Science." *Geographical Review* 48: 167-84.

Stoddart, D.R. 1977. "The Paradigm Concept and the History of Geography." Abstract of a paper for the conference of the International Geographical Union Commission on the History of Geographic Thought, Edinburgh, 1977.

Suppe, F. 1977. "Afterword—1977. "In *The Structure of Scientific Theories*, edited by F. Suppe, pp. 617-730. Urbana: University of Illinois Press.

Taylor, P.J. 1976. "An Interpretation of the Quantification Debate in British Geography." *Transactions, Institute of British Geographers*, n.s. 1: 129-42.

Van den Daele, W., Weingart, P. 1976. "Resistance and Receptivity of Science to External Direction: The Emergence of New Disciplines under the Impact of Science Policy," in *Perspectives on the Emergence of Scientific Disciplines,* edited by G. Lemaine, et al., pp. 247-75. The Hague: Mouton.

Webber, M.J. 1977. "Pedagogy Again: What Is entropy?" *Annals, Association of American Geographers* 67: 254-66.

Wolpert, J. 1964. "The Decision Process in Spatial Context." *Annals, Association of American Geographers* 54: 337-558.

Zelinsky, W. 1970. "Beyond the Exponentials: The Role of Geography in the Great Transition." *Economic Geography* 46: 499-535.

Geographical Ideas in America, 1890-1914

Preston E. James

In this concluding statement I want to examine some of the sources of geographical ideas in America between 1890 and 1914, at a time when professional geography was being formed in this country.

Though there were some distinctively American sources, as with many scholarly disciplines that were organizing as professional fields at about this same time, geography drew heavily on German sources.[1] First is the basic idea of a university as a center of scholarship. The older European universities were centers for the teaching of religious beliefs or political doctrine to young people. But in 1809 the world's first free university was established in Berlin. The prime mover was Wilhelm von Humboldt, the brother of Alexander, and the necessary support came chiefly from the king of Prussia. Here, for the first time, faculties were selected for their scholarly contributions to some field of learning, and students were free to apply for admission without reference to political or religious beliefs.

As the nineteenth century unfolded, the idea of the university as a center of scholarship spread to other German universities and to universities in other European countries. The idea of such a university was brought to the United States many decades later: Johns Hopkins University in 1876, Clark University in 1888, and the University of Chicago in 1891. The idea was quickly adopted by the older American universities. But before any learned profession can come into existence there are four prerequisites that must be met. First, there must be some minimum number of qualified specialists in the field, located close enough together so that communication among them is rapid. We may say that a "critical mass" of qualified specialists must be formed. Second, there must be university departments staffed by qualified scholars ready to offer advanced training in the objectives and methods of the field. Third, there must be opportunities for employment for those who have met the qualifications for membership in the profession—presumably by earning the Ph.D. degree. Incidentally the word *Doktor* in German identifies a person who is qualified to teach. And fourth, there must be a professional society and professional periodicals to promote competitive discussion of ideas concerning objectives and methods.[2] In the United States the first university department of geography offering the doctorate was established at the University of Chicago in 1903; and in 1904 the Association of American Geographers was founded.

Of course people were teaching and writing about geography in the United States long before 1903. Important contributions to geography had been made by Benjamin Franklin (1706-90) and by Thomas Jefferson (1743-1826). Matthew Fontaine Maury (1806-73) had published a major study of the world's oceans in 1855.[3] And there was that amazing figure— George Perkins Marsh (1801-82)—the Vermont lawyer who, in 1843, had been elected to Congress. But when Marsh was not reelected, he was promptly appointed as minister to Turkey in 1849, and as minister plenipotentiary to the Kingdom of Italy in 1861, a post which he held until his death in 1882. Marsh traveled widely in the Mediterranean countries, amplifying the observations he had started many years before in Vermont concerning the causes and result of soil erosion. In 1864 he published the preliminary results of his studies in *Man and Nature, or Physical Geography as Modified by Human Action* (reprint ed., ed. David Lowenthal, Cambridge, Mass.: Harvard University Press, 1965). In 1874 he published *The Earth as Modified by Human Action* (New York: Charles Scribner).

Marsh's illuminating studies of the causes of soil erosion remained to gather dust on library shelves, while large areas of the United States were being destroyed by the very processes he had described and predicted. Why? The answer is that when Marsh wrote his books there was no professional field to provide a forum for discussion. Only when the problems of soil erosion became critical during the thirties and forties were large numbers of geographers directly concerned to seek remedial action to protect the land from destruction by improper use. George Perkins Marsh's writings were rediscovered, and a report on a symposium brought together to discuss such problems was dedicated to him. A book containing the numerous papers on land destruction was published in 1955.[4]

But there is much more to this story of the neglect of earlier contributions, specifically contributions to the understanding of the causes and consequences of land destruction. Let's go back to 1799. In this year the great German geographer Alexander von Humboldt was beginning his exploration of the northern parts of South America. Humboldt had landed in Venezuela and was starting his examination of the northern Andes south of Caracas. Here he found an intriguing problem. Near the town of Valencia, in a basin set among the mountains some fifty miles southwest of Caracas, was the Lake of Valencia. During the settlement of that part of the country the lake level had dropped. At one time the water of the lake was discharged into a tributary of the Orinoco; but for many decades there had been no dischage and the level of the lake had continued to fall. The former lake bottom had been put to intensive use for farming. But in 1799 the lake waters were rising and would soon start emptying again into the Orinoco.[5] What caused these changes in water level? Humboldt recognized the relationship between rainfall and runoff and the vegetation cover of the slopes. When the vegetation was undisturbed, the water ran off slowly and drainage continued even during dry periods. But when the vegetation cover was destroyed, the runoff during a rain was torrential and destructive, and then during subsequent dry periods the streams would dry up completely. On the slopes of the Valencia Basin the workers, employed as tenant farmers on large estates, were permitted to clear the mountain slopes to plant their own subsistence crops—mostly maize. Shortly before Humboldt's arrival in Venezuela in 1799, the wars of independence had started and most of the tenants had been removed from their farms to fill the ranks of the army. The vegetation was growing back on the cleared slopes, and since the runoff was again retarded, the level of the lake was rising. For a time the lake again had its outlet to the Orinoco; but after the wars of independence were ended, the slopes were reoccupied by farms and again the level of the Lake of Valencia dropped.

Now let us introduce another actor in this little geographical drama. In 1879 the four separate surveys of the western territories were combined as the United States Geological Survey. Clarence King was its first director; but after a year he resigned and was succeeded by John Wesley Powell (1834-1902). In 1879 the Bureau of Ethnology was established in Washington and Powell was named as its director. Between 1880 and 1894, when he resigned from the survey, Powell was one of the most influential scientists in the government service.[6]

Powell was essentially a self-made scholar who possessed almost no academic credentials. He learned about geology, landforms, vegetation, and the human use of the land through the influence of a tutor at his home in Ohio. As a boy he accompanied his tutor in field surveys of resources. In the course of his reading and his field experiences he picked up an amazing amount of practical knowledge. From 1865 until 1879 he was engaged in a survey of the arid lands of the western territories, and of the Indian inhabitants of these lands.

Powell saw clearly the importance of the vegetation cover on the mountain slopes in the preservation of the mountains from disastrous erosion, and in the maintenance of a supply of irrigation water for the farmers in the intermont basins. He drew up a plan for the protection of the resources of this area. He recognized that a survey dividing the land into rectangles would inevitably leave many landowners without access to water, so he recommended resurveying the lands to place whole river systems under one political jurisdiction. He also urged the Congress to control the flow of new pioneer settlers—mostly from the humid East and wholly unprepared to deal with the problems of semiarid lands. He tried to close the still unoccupied lands of the western territories to new settlement until a detailed survey of the land could be completed. Of course he ran head on into various special interest groups: the agents who wanted to sell land; the lumbering interests who wanted to cut off the forests on the mountain slopes; the cattle interests who wanted to clear the mountain forests to create new pastures; the mining interests who wanted no hindrance to their search for minerals. In the end he was defeated; and the country is paying the price, even today.

Powell arrived independently at his discovery of many of the relations and processes that Humboldt, Marsh, and others had discovered. There is no evidence to suggest that he had ever read Humboldt's discussion of the Lake of Valencia, or Marsh's analysis of the causes of soil erosion in the Mediterranean countries.

There was one single outstanding leader who formulated the first statement regarding the objectives and methods of geographical study, and who took the first steps necessary to establish geography as a learned profession. This was the geologist William Morris Davis (1850–1934) of Harvard University. Davis saw the new field as made up of explanatory descriptions of the physical features of the earth surface, acting as controls, and the organic responses to these controls. He called the two parts physiography and ontography. His own chief contributions were to the description and understanding of the physical setting. He never failed to urge his followers to develop the two sides of geography in a balanced way, but he left the balancing act to his disciples. The story of William Morris Davis is told in a masterful biography by R. J. Chorley, R. P. Beckinsale, and A. J. Dunn, published in 1973.[7]

The first major effort to build the ontographic side of geography on a firm basis came from an unexpected source. Ellen Churchill Semple (1863–1932) went from Louisville, Kentucky, to Vassar to study history and languages.[8] She graduated from Vassar at the age of nineteen, with a record of excellence so great that she was selected class valedictorian. Returning to Louisville after graduation she tried teaching school for a time. Then she began to work toward a master's degree in history at

322

Vassar by undertaking a program of reading and writing a thesis, which she completed in 1891. She had heard of a German professor teaching at Leipzig whose lectures, she was told, made history come alive. Breaking all precedents, she went to Leipzig and applied for admission to advanced study with Friedrich Ratzel, then lecturing on anthropogeography. She was admitted—one woman in a class of some five hundred men—and she studied with Ratzel in 1891–92 and again in 1895.

Returning to the United States, she planned to undertake various studies in which she would apply Ratzel's ideas to American observations. Her first published paper on a geographical topic was "The Influence of the Appalachian Barrier upon Colonial History."[9] It was published in the newly launched *Journal of School Geography*. The editor was Richard E. Dodge, and on the editorial board were Davis himself and some of his close supporters. Through her publications, Semple became a part of the movement to establish a professional field of geography in America. Her first field study reported on the influence of isolation on settlements of Anglo-Saxons in the highlands of eastern Kentucky, who she reported were still speaking Elizabethan English.[10] Although, up to this time, she held no academic position, this article was said to have influenced a large number of young people to enter the field of geography.

Another source of German ideas in the development of professional geography in the United States was Alfred Hettner's first Ph.D. student at Heidelberg—Martha Krug-Genthe, who completed her Ph.D. in 1901 and accepted a teaching position at the Beacon School in Hartford, Connecticut, a position which she held until the school was closed in 1911. Then she returned to Germany.

It is worth noting that among the forty-eight original members of the Association of American Geographers in 1904 were two women: Ellen C. Semple and Martha Krug-Genthe. The latter was the only one who of the original members had earned a doctorate in geography.

All the followers of Davis, many of whom had trained as geologists, were accustomed to gather their basic information about problems in the field. Powell had no small part in making field study an essential part of the work of any scholar who called himself a geographer. But when the new field was launched in 1904 there were certain persons who were not primarily field-workers. This other source for members of the new professional field came to geography through economics rather than geology. And the economists, also, introduced ideas derived from German sources.

The American economist who occupies a position in economics similar to that enjoyed by Davis in geology would be Richard T. Ely (1854–1943). He was an economist who studied at the Universities of Halle,

Heidelberg, Geneva, and Berlin. Ely was very much concerned about mapping the facts that were relevant to the problems of particular places. Ely was a leader in the "new economics" as well as the founder of the subfield of land economics, and he was of great importance in training people in land economics during the early years of the century. Ely came back from Germany and went to work at Johns Hopkins University in 1881, where Frederick Jackson Turner (1861–1932) took courses from him.[11] Ely was spreading the idea of land economics—the application of economics to the study of the earth as the home of humanity.

At Johns Hopkins Ely was the teacher of Emory Johnson (1864–1950) who, after additional training at Munich and Berlin, went to the Wharton School of Finance and Commerce at the University of Pennsylvania, and established what amounted to a geography department.

Reference to the chapters by Rugg and Bushong will show that Johnson's dissertation is presently recognized as the first in America dealing with a grographical problem. The dissertation had to do with inland waterways—their relation to transportation—and Emory Johnson was certainly, in that sense, a geographer. His prime student was J. Russell Smith (1874–1966).[12] In 1899–1901 Emory Johnson and J. Russell Smith worked for the Isthmian Canal Commission, and Johnson remained a member of the commision until 1904. The two men were called upon to select a route and make an estimate of the amount of traffic that the canal would have to carry in 1915, when the waterway was supposed to be finished. Smith actually did a good part of the work on this. But what type of work? They did not go out with plane tables and alidades, and tramp across the isthmus and through the jungles. Most of the work done by Johnson and Smith was performed in an office and based on statistical data gathered by somebody else for other purposes and, of course, based on what maps were available to them. At any rate, they selected the route of the present Panama Canal and the work they did was of major practical importance. As soon as Smith finished the job in 1901, he went to study at Heidelberg following the usual practice of getting a touch of German geography. When Smith returned to the United States, he was made the chairman of a new department of geography established at the Wharton School. Although it was titled the Department of Commerce, it was a department in which geography was the main interest.

In 1904, when the Association of American Geographers was being founded, a committee was set up to pass on the qualifications of those who were proposed for membership.[13] William Morris Davis insisted on having only members who were qualified scholars and had made an original contribution to some branch of geography. Unfortunately, when

J. Russell Smith was first put up for membership he was rejected because he had never done any field work. The members of the advisory committee were the disciples of Davis, and they all believed in field work. Emory Johnson had not done any fieldwork, either, but he had written a book and was farther along in his career, so he was elected as an original member of the A.A.G. However, Johnson was constantly frustrated by Davis—directly or indirectly. A very eloquent arguer, Davis was never unkind in his arguments, but he could cut you down to size if you did not do what he thought was right. Davis impeded the types of things that Johnson wanted to see done and as a result Johnson resigned from the association in 1914. Many people found Davis too abrupt and too authoritarian in his methods, and they were alienated by his efforts to make the new professional society have a high intellectual standing. At any rate, Davis continued and Johnson left. J. Russell Smith, on the other hand, stayed to fight it out after being elected in 1905. Later he became president of the association.

What did the economists emphasize? What kind of training did they give at such institutions as the Wharton School where the training of geographers was in the hands of econonists? Firstly, emphasis was given to economic theory and the methods of theory building. Secondly, the use of statistical techniques was stressed. But economists did not do fieldwork. Thus evolved two important groups in the early years of the association: one devoted to field work and the other biased toward economic theory. Ideally, if these two groups could have gotten together in an open, friendly, competitive discussion, things would have gone very well. Unfortunately this could not be done and the result was that the economists, at that time, retired from the battle and the geologists continued to dominate the subject and the association.

In 1914 another phase began when Albert Perry Brigham (1855–1932) criticized Davis and his followers for their careless discussion of influences.[14] This is the beginning of the search for alternatives that characterized the 1920s.

Notes

1. Carl Diehl, *Americans and German Scholarship* (New Haven: Yale University Press, 1977).
2. Preston E. James, "The Process of Competitive Discussion," *The Professional Geographer* 28 (1976):1–7.
3. M. F. Maury, *The Physical Geography of the Sea* (New York: Harper Brothers, 1855).

Origins of Academic Geography

4. William L. Thomas, Jr., Ed., *Man's Role in Changing the Face of the Earth* (Chicago: University of Chicago Press, 1956).
5. Alexander von Humboldt, *Personal Narrative of Travels in the Equinoctial Regions of the New Continent During the Years 1799-1804*, trans. Helen Marie Williams (London: Longman, Hurst, Rees, Orme, and Brown, 1814-29).
6. W. Stegner, *Beyond the Hundredth Meridian: John Wesley Powell and the Second Opening of the West* (Boston: Houghton Mifflin, 1954).
7. R. J. Chorley, R. P. Beckinsale, and A. J. Dunn, *The Life of William Morris Davis*, The History of the Study of Landforms or the Development of Geomorphology, vol 2 (London: Methuen, 1973).
8. Judith C. Bronson, *"Ellen Semple: Contributions to the History of American Geography" (Ph.D. diss., St. Louis University, 1973).*
9. *Ellen C. Semple, "The Influence of the Appalachian Barrier upon Colonial History," Journal of School Geography (1897):33-41.*
10. *Ellen C. Semple, "The Anglo-Saxons of the Kentucky Mountains," Geographical Journal* 17 (1901):588-623, reprinted in the *Bulletin of the American Geographical Society* 42 (1910): 561-94.
11. Ray Allen Billington, *The Genesis of the Frontier Thesis: A Study in Historical Creativity* (San Marino: The Huntington Library, 1971), pp. 31-36.
12. Preston E. James, *All Possible Worlds* (Indianapolis: The Odyssey Press, 1972), pp. 382-84.
13. Preston E. James and Geoffrey J. Martin, *The Association of American Geographers: The First Seventy-Five Years 1904-1979* (Washington, D.C.: Association of American Geographers, 1978), p. 36.
14. Preston E. James, "Albert Perry Brigham," in *Geographers Biobibliographical Studies*, ed. T. W. Freeman and Philippe Pinchemel (London: Mansell, 1978), 2:13-19.

Appendix

Survey of Early Geography Teaching in State Universities and Land Grant Institutions

Brian W. Blouet and Teresa L. Stitcher

The following information was largely compiled from a circular sent to the archivists of institutions listed as members of the National Association of State Universities and Land Grant Colleges. Institutions that are not members of the association were not contacted. In a small number of cases the archivist asked the department of geography to respond. In those instances where no response was obtained, only the date of establishment of the institution and the department is included. These departmental foundation dates were taken from the *Guide to Graduate Departments of Geography in the United States and Canada 1979–1980*. The information published in the *Guide* was provided by the department concerned.

Code: a. = admitted
e. = established Geography Department (which is shortened to D.)
f. = founded
1st c. = first course in geography

University of Alabama	1829—f.
Tuscaloosa, Alabama	1831—students a.
	1837—1st c. "Modern Geography"
	1919— "Commercial Geography"
	1936—e. Geography D.
	Geography and geology are now combined under an earth science grouping which bridges the two fields.

Appendix

University of Alaska Fairbanks, Alaska	1915—f. 1924—geography subject established 1975—independent program associated with anthropology 1976—e. Geography D.
University of Arizona Tucson, Arizona	1885—f. 1961—e. Geography D.
Arizona State University Tempe, Arizona	1885—f 1923—e. Geography D.
University of Arkansas Fayetteville, Arkansas	1872—f. 1948—e. Geography D.
Auburn University Auburn, Alabama	1856—f. East Alabama Male College 1872—e. as land grant institution 1926/27—1st c. "Economic Geography" 1956—1st sequence of course work 1976— e. Geography D.
University of California—Berkeley Berkeley, California	1868—f. 1869—students a. 1870—Nonresident professor of geography and astronomy, George Davidson, was employed. 1898—e. Geography D. 1908—1st master's awarded
University of California—Davis Davis, California	1905—f. 1955—geography program combined with anthropology, economics, and sociology 1964—e. Geography D. 1965—master's program e.
University of California—Irvine Irvine, California	1964—f. 1965–66—e. Division of Social Sciences of which geography is a part
University of California Los Angeles, California	1881—f. Los Angeles Normal School 1895—e. Geography D. 1919—UCLA established 1922—four-year geography curriculum towards degree e.

328

University of California—Riverside Riverside, California	1954—f. 1954—geography part of the Social Sciences Division 1957—geography major e. 1963—e. Geography D. 1973—geography and geology combined into earth sciences for lower division offerings
University of California— Santa Barbara Santa Barbara, California	1891—f. 1975—e. Geography D.
Clemson University Clemson, South Carolina	1893—f. 1969—1st c. "Introduction into Geography" taught within History D. 1977—one course now taught, "Introductory Geography"
University of Colorado Boulder, Colorado	1876—f. 1927—e. Geography D.
Colorado State University Fort Collins, Colorado	1870—f. 1879—students a. 1879—1906— 1st cs. "Physical Geography," "Meteorology" 1906—69—cs. taught through business and agriculture A geographer is employed by the Economics D. to teach "Economic Geography" but there is no Geography D.
Cornell University Ithaca, New York	1865—f. 1868—students a. 1868-69—1st c. taught within School of Physical Geography 1868-69 catalogue—"In this school there are delivered, during the Winter Trimester courses by Professor Wilson on physical geography and climatology, with special reference to vegetable and animal life and the influence of physical causes

	upon the progress and character of civilization."
	1892–1912—Ralph S. Tarr taught in the D.
University of Delaware Newark, Delaware	1833—f. as Newark College 1836—Mathematics D. taught geography with the use of maps, globes, and charts. 1870— College reopened and geography was part of the agriculture course work, "Physical Geography" and "Meteorology". 1966— e. Geography D.
University of Florida Gainesville, Florida	1905—f. 1913–14—1st c. "Physical Geography" 1914–15— "Political Geography" 1948—e. Geography D.
Florida State University Tallahassee, Florida	1851—f. 1929—e. Geography D.
Fort Valley State College Fort Valley, Georgia	1895—f. as a high school 1939—four-year college 1940—1st c. "Economic Geography of the U.S." taught within the Social Sciences Division. 1949—land grant institution 1957—"Geography: World, Regional and Human" taught within the Social Sciences Division 1976— Agriculture D. taught "General Geology"
University of Georgia Athens, Georgia	1785—f. 1801—established as a university 1933—1st c. in Physical Science Junior Division, "Principles of Geography 1–2," "Climate and Land Forms"; Senior Division, "Regional Geography" "Geography of North America," "Geography of South America" 1946—e. Geography D.
University of Guam Agana, Guam	1952—f. 1977—e. Geography and Anthropology

(D. part of Social Sciences Division 1977)

University of Hawaii at Manoa Honolulu, Hawaii	1908—f. as College of Agriculture and Mechanical Arts with college-level classes 1920—e. as a university "Geology" and "Meteorology" were part of agricultural courses 1920—1st c. "Geography" and "Economic Geography" 1923—"Physical Geography" 1930–31—geography became part of arts and sciences 1930—1st master's in geography awarded
University of Idaho Moscow, Idaho	1889—f. 1892—students a. 1919–20—1st c. "Commercial Geography" by Geology D. 1921—"Geography of North and South America," "Europe, Asia, Africa and Australia" 1922—"Physiography" and "Commercial Geography" 1922–70—Geography was part of Geology D. 1970—e. Geography D.
University of Illinois at Chicago Circle Chicago, Illinois	1946—f. 1946—1st cs. "Elements of Geography," "Economic Geography," "General Geography" 1964—e. Geography D. 1974—Master's program e.
University of Illinois at Urbana-Champaign Urbana, Illinois	1867—f. 1867–68— 1st cs. "Meteorology" and "Physical Geography" 1934—e. Geography-Geology D. 1945—e. Geography D.
Indiana University Bloomington, Indiana	1820—f. 1946—e. Geography D.

University of Iowa	1847—f.
Iowa City, Iowa	1946—e. Geography D.
Iowa State University	1885—f.
Ames, Iowa	1898-99—1st c. "Physiography"
	1908-9—"Meteorology" and
	"Climatology"
	1923-24—"Industrial Geography"
	1977—e. Earth Sciences D. with
	geography courses included
University of Kansas	1866—f.
Lawrence, Kansas	1873—1st cs. "Commerce" and
	"Commercial Geography" by Economics
	D. and "Geography of Europe" by
	Geology D.
	1947—e. Geography D.
Kansas State University	1863—f.
Manhattan, Kansas	1873—1st c. "Geography"
	1965—e. Geography D.
Kent State University	1910—f.
Kent, Ohio	1914—e. Geography D.
University of Kentucky	1865—f.
Lexington, Kentucky	1st c. taught probably in the late
	1800s or early 1900s.
	1936-37—catalogue shows seven
	geography courses.
Kentucky State University	1944—e. Geography D.
Frankfort, Kentucky	1899—1st c.
Lincoln University	1866—f.
Jefferson City, Missouri	1903—1st c. Geography is an area
	but not a department.
Louisiana State University	1860—f.
Baton Rouge, Louisiana	1860-61—1st cs. "Geography" with
	Morse's text, and "Descriptive
	Geography" with Davies's text
University of Maine at Orono	1865—f. Maine State College of
Orono, Maine	Agriculture and the Mechanic Arts
	1868—students a.
	1871—1st c. "Physical Geography"
	1900s-1920s—Economic geology was a
	close ally of geography; in the thirties

through the sixties geography
was connected with geology, and from
the late sixties on it has been a part of
political science.

University of Maryland	1807—f.
College Park, Maryland	1941—e. Geography D.
University of Maryland,	
Eastern Shore	1886—f.
Princess Anne, Maryland	1938—1st c. "Economic Geography"
University of Massachusetts	1863—f. Massachusetts Agricultural
Amherst, Mass	College
	1931—Massachusetts State College
	1947—University of Massachussetts
	1955-56—1st c. "Principles of Physical Geography" in Geology D.
	1961—"Fundamentals of Geography" and "World Political Geography"
	1973—e. undergraduate degree program
Massachusetts Institute	No formal subject in geography
of Technology	has been offered at M.I.T.,
Cambridge, Massachusetts	but some aspects are included now and then in a few subjects with other primary subject covereage
Miami University	1809—f.
Oxford, Ohio	1824—students a.
	1826—1st c. "Modern Geography"
	1827—"Ancient Geography"
	1828—"Geography and Sacred History"
	1907—first reference to geography as a separate department within the School of Education
	1950—e. as a department within the Arts and Sciences College
University of Michigan	1817—f.
Ann Arbor, Michigan	1923—e. Geography D.
Michigan State University	1855—f.
East Lansing, Michigan	1875—seventy freshman completed Guyot's *Physical Geography* under Prof. A. J. Cook of zoology and entomology
	1921–22—"A study of the influences of

333

environment on the conditions and activities of man" was offered by the Zoology and Geology D.

1930–31—"Elements of Geography," "Geography of Europe," "Geography of North America," "Geography of Commercial Production" "Geography of Latin America," and "Physiography of North America"

1931—e. Geology and Geography D. Courses added were: "Elements of Human Geography," "Geography of Michigan," and "Routes and Centers of Trade."

1955—e. Geography D. within the Social Science Division with more courses offered.

University of Minnesota Minneapolis, Minnesota	1851—f. 1925—e. Geography D.
University of Missouri Columbia, Missouri	1839—f. 1840s and 1850s—Geography was taught primarily in "preparatory" and "primary" departments. 1st cs.—"Fish's Classical Topography and Chronology" and "Fish's Classical Geography" 1860—"Physical Geography" Later decades of the nineteenth century—"Geology and Palaeontology," "Hydrography," "Meteorology," "Natural History," "Ethnography," "Astronomy" 1950—e. Geography D.
University of Mississippi	1844—f. 1848—students a. 1956—e. Geography D.
Mississippi State University	1878—f. 1880—1st c. "Meteorology" 1936—e. Geography D.
University of Montana Missoula, Montana	1893—f. 1956—1st c. "Political Geography" within the Political Science D. 1956—e. Geography D.

Montana State University Bozeman, Montana	1893—f. Montana College of Agriculture and the Mechanic Arts 1893–96—"Meteorology" taught in Chemistry D. 1944—"Climatology" taught in Agronomy and Soils D. 1947—e. Geology-Geography D. 1960—e. Earth Sciences D.
University of Nebraska—Lincoln Lincoln, Nebraska	1869—f. 1871—students a. 1873—1st c. "Comparative Physical Geography" 1876—According to the 1876 biannual report of the Board of Regents, "Physical Geography is taught in daily recitations from Guyot's textbook." 1882—Houston's text replaces Guyot's. 1904—Clemments elected founder-member of the A.A.G. 1908—e. Geography D. G. E. Condra and Charles E. Bessey "recommend appointment of N. A. Bengtson as instructor in D. of Geography."
University of Nevada—Reno Reno, Nevada	1874—f. 1947–48—1st c. No regular program until after World War II, and it was then attached to the Geology D. and administered by the MacKay School of Mines 1951—e. Geography D.
University of New Hampshire Durham, New Hampshire	1866—f. New Hampshire College of Agriculture and Mechanic Arts 1923—e. as University of New Hampshire 1935–36—1st c. "Geography" 1936–37—"Geography of the World" 1943–44—geography had separate course listing from geology 1969—e. Geography D.
University of New Mexico Albuquerque, New Mexico	1892—f. 1892—1st cs. "Descriptive Geography" and "Physical Geography"

	1902—"Physiography"
	1914–42—part of the Geology D.
	1942-50—Geography is offered separately.
	1959–60—Division of Geography is mentioned but date of e. is unknown; sometime between 1960–65.
New Mexico State University Las Cruces, New Mexico	1888—f. Las Cruces College 1888—1st c. 1889–90—Intermediate D. offered "Geography—Swinton's Introductory" and the Academic D. offered "Geography—Barnes' Complete." Until 1948—only "Economic Geography" by the Business Administration D. 1948—e. Geography-Geology D.
State University of New York Albany, New York	1844—f. 1966—e. Geography D.
State University of New York Binghamton, New York	1946—f. as Triple Cities College 1946—Geography was taught with Geology. 1947—each field taught separately 1967—e. Geography D.
State University of New York Buffalo, New York	1846—f. 1938—1st c. "Introduction to Geography" and "Geography of North America" 1962—e. Geography D.
University of North Carolina Chapel Hill, North Carolina	1789—f. 1936—e. jointly with Geology D. 1962—e. Geography D.
North Carolina State University Raleigh, North Carolina	1887—f. North Carolina College of Agriculture and Mechanic Arts 1889—students a. 1895—1st c. "Meteorology" 1895-97—text was *Davis' Meteorology* 1899—"Physical Geography" 1901—"Mineralogy and Geology" 1903—"Elementary Geology" There is no Geography D.

North Dakota State University Fargo, North Dakota	1890—f. North Dakota Agricultural College 1899—1st c. "Astronomy," "Physical Geography," and "Meteorology" 1928—D. of Geology, Geography and Mineralogy 1957—Geography was a separate unit. 1960—subject matter in the Natural Sciences Division 1973—e. Geography D.
Ohio State University Columbus, Ohio	1870—f. 1871—1st c. "Physical Geography" by the Geology Mining and Metallurgy area 1922—e. D. of Economic and Social Geography 1924—e. Geography D.
University of Oklahoma Norman, Oklahoma	1890—f. 1892—students a. 1892—1st c. "Eclectic Physical Geography" by the preparatory d. 1893—"Descriptive Geography" and "Geography and Writing" 1899—"Geology 1/Advanced Geography" and "Geology 2/Physical Geography" 1921-22—e. Geography-Geology D. 1948—e. Geography D.
Oklahoma State University Stillwater, Oklahoma	1891—f. 1914—1st c. "Topographical Drawing" by Civil Engineering D. 1929—e. geography subdivision within Ds. of Economics and Sociology in the Divison of Commerce 1936—Commerce Division offered bachelor's degree in geography. 1941—e. Geography D. 1946—Geography D. part of College of Arts and Sciences 1949—Geography dropped ties with Commerce Division.

Appendix

University of Oregon	1876—f.
Eugene, Oregon	1920s—e. Geography D.

Oregon State University	1868—f.
Corvallis, Oregon	1908—1st cs. "Commercial Geography," "Local Industries" and "Economic Geography"
	1946—e. geography discipline
	1947—"Physical Geography"
	1952—e. Geography D. which offered work in physical geography and in resource geography; the School of Liberal Arts offered service courses in human geography.
	1968—Geography D. in College of Science offered doctoral degree in physical and resource geography, and College of Liberal Arts offered a minor in economic geography at the graduate level.

Pennsylvania State University University Park, Pennsylvania	1855—f.
	1859—1st c. "Physical Geography"
	1917—geography taught on a permanent basis
	1932—1st professionally trained geographer hired
	1940—e. Geography major
	1945—e. Geography Division
	1953—e. Geography D.

University of Pittsburgh	1787—f.
Pittsburgh, Pennsylvania	1943—e. Geography D.

University of Rhode Island	1892—f.
Kingston, Rhode Island	1960—e. Geography D.

Rutgers University	1766—f. as Queens College
New Brunswick, New Jersey	1825—f. as Rutgers University
	1846—received land grant status
	1919—1st c. "Physiography"

1935—"Physical Geography" by
Geology D.
1945—state university status
1946—"Physical and Economic
Geography"
1949—e. Geography D.

University of South Carolina Columbia, South Carolina	1801—f. as South Carolina College 1805—students a. 1830s—Geography was taught until then, when it became an admissions requirement. 1890—"Physiography" 1935—e. Geology, Mineralogy and Geography D. 1963—e. Geography D.
South Dakota State University Brookings, South Dakota	1884—f. 1884—Geography was offered in general science category. 1940s—"Regional Geography of Europe" offered during World War II 1949—e. Geography D.
Temple University Philadelphia, Pennsylvania	1884—f. 1961—e. Geography D.
University of Tennessee Knoxville, Tennessee	1794—f. 1844—1st c. "Ancient Geography" 1939—e. Geology-Geography D. 1967—e. Geography D.
Texas A & M University College Station, Texas	1871—f. 1876—students a. 1927—1st c. "Agricultural Geography of North America" 1936—1st graduate courses in geography 1944–45 and 1963–64—Geography D. existed 1965–68—e. Geography-Geology D. 1968–69—re-e. Geography D.

Appendix

University of Texas at Austin Austin, Texas	1881—f. 1940s—"Economic Geography" offered by Economics D. 1949—e. Geography D.; prior to this courses were offered by the Geological Sciences D.
University of Utah Salt Lake City, Utah	1850—f. 1947—e. Geography D.
Utah State University Logan, Utah	1888—f. Utah State Agricultural College 1928—1st c. "Geology and Geography of Utah" 1931—"College Geography" 1950—e. Geology-Geography D. 1954—Geography was dropped from the curriculum. 1957—Geography reintroduced in the History and Political Science D. 1965—e. History and Geography D.
University of Vermont Burlington, Vermont	1791—f. 1825—Jedediah Morse's *Geography* was one of four textbooks listed for freshman study. 1865—received land grant status 1966—e. Geography D.
University of Virginia Charlottesville, Virginia	1819—f. by Thomas Jefferson 1824—students a. 1920—1st c. "Economic Geography" offered by Economics D.; no other courses offered until 1946. 1946—e. Geography D. 1959—Geography and Geology Ds. consolidated into D. of Environmental Sciences. 1960s—Focus is now on meteorology, geodynamics, ecology, and environmental geology.

Virginia State College Petersburg, Virginia	1882—f. Virginia Normal and Collegiate Institute 1883—students a. 1883—1st c. "Physical Geography" taught in the Normal School 1886—"Descriptive" and "Physical Geography" taught by Academic College D.
College of the Virgin Islands Saint Thomas, Virgin Islands	1962—f. 1963—1st c. offered as elective in the Social Sciences Division.
University of Washington Seattle, Washington	1861—f. 1899-1900—1st c. "Physical Geography" 1908-9—"Geology and Geography of Washington" 1912-13—"Economic Geography of Washington" 1913-14—"Physiography of the U.S." offered by Geology D. until 1928-29, when the Geology D. was changed to Geology-Geography D. 1935-36—e. Geography D. separately
Washington State University Pullman, Washington	1890—f. No Geography D.; courses are offered through the Economics D.
West Virginia University Morgantown, West Virginia	1867—f. 1867-68—1st c.: Preparatory D., "Geography" "Physical Geography"; Literary D., "Ancient Geography and Roman Antiquities," "Ancient Geography and Greek Antiquities"; Scientific D., "Botany and Meteorology," "Mineralogy," and "Geology"; Agricultural D., "Physical Geography," "Meteorology Geology". All were required within these Ds. 1927-28—Geography appears for the first

time in a department heading: Geology,
Mineralogy and Geography.
1955—e. Geology-Geography D.

University of
Wisconsin—Madison
Madison, Wisconsin

1862—University catalogue lists
"Geography and Map Drawing"
and "Physical Geography"
1866–67—"Physical Geography" and
"Climatology"
1889—"Scientific Geography" taught in
summer session by William Morris Davis
1891—"Physical Geography" offered by
D. of Geology, Mineralogy and Petrology
by Rollin Salisbury
1893—Van Hise's geology course
included the physiography of the
United States
1896—"Economic Geography" offered by
the School of Economics, Political
Science and History
1904—Atmospheric science courses began
with "Climatology," "Meteorology," and
"General Climatology and the Climate of
the U.S."
1917—Geography courses and geology
courses are offered under separate
heading in the catalogue for the first time.
1921—e. Geology-Geography D.
1928—e. Geography D.

University of Wyoming
Laramie, Wyoming

1887—f.
1887—"Geology" and "Physical
Geography" taught by School of Mines
1955—Until this time geography was
taught by the School of Education.
1955-66—Geography is grouped with
sociology, anthropology, and economics
in the College of Arts and Sciences.
1966—e. Geography D.